CONJUGAL TRAJECTORIES

CONTEMPORARY PERSPECTIVES IN FAMILY RESEARCH

Series Editor: Sampson Lee Blair

Recent Volumes:

EDITORIAL BOARD

CONTEMPORARY PERSPECTIVES IN
FAMILY RESEARCH   VOLUME 22

CONJUGAL TRAJECTORIES: RELATIONSHIP BEGINNINGS, CHANGE, AND DISSOLUTIONS

EDITED BY

ANA JOSEFINA CUEVAS HERNÁNDEZ
University of Colima, Mexico

And

SAMPSON LEE BLAIR
The State University of New York, USA

United Kingdom – North America – Japan
India – Malaysia – China

Emerald Publishing Limited
Howard House, Wagon Lane, Bingley BD16 1WA, UK

First edition 2023

Reprints and permissions service
Contact: permissions@emeraldinsight.com

British Library Cataloguing in Publication Data
A catalogue record for this book is available from the British Library

ISBN: 978-1-80455-395-4 (Print)
ISBN: 978-1-80455-394-7 (Online)
ISBN: 978-1-80455-396-1 (Epub)

ISSN: 1530-3535 (Series)

Printed and bound by CPI Group (UK) Ltd, Croydon, CR0 4YY

ISOQAR certified
Management System,
awarded to Emerald
for adherence to
Environmental
standard
ISO 14001:2004.

Certificate Number 1985
ISO 14001

INVESTOR IN PEOPLE

CONTENTS

ABOUT THE AUTHORS

Olukemi K. Amodu is a Professor of Genetics/Molecular Biology and Public Health at the Institute of Child Health, University of Ibadan, Nigeria. She is engaged in building platforms for developing capacity in biotechnology, leveraging on her core expertise in molecular genetics with a focus on bringing together clinical and biomedical scientists for public health research. Her research interests also include Public Health impact research, bringing health services closer to the population by providing innovative strategies for increasing vaccination demand for working mothers in Ibadan metropolis Nigeria.

Kay Bradford is a Professor at Utah State University. His research focuses on relationship education for youth, adult singles, couples, and fathers. His funded projects include interventions in community and high-risk contexts.

Micaela A. Chavarin will receive her B.A. in Psychology from Whittier College in spring of 2023. She is currently working under the advisement of Dr Christina L. Scott as a Research Assistant and Teaching Assistant for Research Methods. She looks forward to obtaining her Master's and PhD in Psychology in order to pursue a career in veteran's affairs.

Javiera Cienfuegos-Illanes is an Associate Professor at Universidad Academia de Humanismo Cristiano (Chile) and obtained her PhD in Sociology at Freie Universität Berlin. Her main research areas include family diversity, transnational migration, and social emotions, which converge on the phenomenon of transnational families, an issue which has worked intensively since 2007. Her dissertation was awarded the triannual prize Friedrich Katz by the Latin American Institute of the Free University of Berlin. In addition, this work has been published as a book by RIL Publishing House. Between 2019 and 2021, she was a Visiting Scholar at the Latin American Institute in the Freie Universität Berlin, conducting research on family processes and labor trajectories of high-skilled migrants, including the countries of Germany and Chile. Her work is available in three different languages: book chapters and double-blind peer-reviewed articles. Recently, she has been editor and co-editor of three books, Special Issues. Her last editorial project is the *Handbook of Transnational Families* (2022, Springer), co-edited with Rosa Brandhorst and Deborah Bryceson. She lectured sociology of migration and emotions, qualitative and mixed social research methods. Furthermore, she promotes family diversity through an academic and community visual project called "Familia Glocal" the main objective is to render visible, rescuing quotidian experiences and issues the variety of forms of "doing family."

Mira Čudina – *Nationality*: Croatian. *Education*: elementary and high school finished in Zagreb, Croatia. Graduated Psychology, Filozofski fakultet, University of Zagreb, Ph.D. in Psychology, Filozofski fakultet, University of Zagreb. *Employment*: Teachers' College, University of Zagreb, Croatia; part-time employment at Croatian Studies and Catholic University, Zagreb, Croatia. *Teaching interests and Experience*: The main interest: applying research in various fields of Psychology to offer students modern knowledge of teaching/learning processes and methods (courses in Developmental and Teaching Psychology, Emotions, Motivation, Teaching Gifted children, and Psychology of reading), for undergraduate and graduate students. *Membership in Organizations*: Croatian Psychological Organization. *Participation in professional meetings*: Actively participated in more than 25 domestic and six international meetings. *Publications*: Published six books as co-author, five books as the only author, and more than 40 research papers in Croatian and English language.

Ana Josefina Cuevas Hernández is a Professor in the Faculty of Literature and Mass Media at the University of Colima. She earned her PhD in Sociology at Essex University. Her research interests include family diversity, gender and emotions and their intersections with intimacy, identity, and sociocultural change. Currently, she is researching on Intimacy and conjugal trajectories from an intergenerational perspective. She was a Visiting Scholar at the Centre for Family Research at the University of Cambridge and has taught family courses in Mexican, Colombian and Brazilian universities. She is the Journal Editor of GenEroos.

Shichao Du is a Ph.D. candidate in the Sociology Department at the State University of New York, Albany. His research interests fall in families, social networks, health, and culture. His dissertation examines parental intervention in their children's marital decisions in China as well as the marital consequences of such intervention. His work appears in *The China Quarterly*, *Marriage & Family Review*, and *IEEE Journal of Biomedical and Health Information*.

Karen Benjamin Guzzo is a Professor of Sociology at the University of North Carolina at Chapel Hill and serves as the Director of the Carolina Population Center. She is a Family Sociologist and Demographer whose work considers trends, patterns, and variation in childbearing and union formation/stability using survey data. Dr Guzzo is an expert on trends and differentials in US fertility preferences and fertility behaviors, such as delayed childbearing and childlessness, fertility intentions, nonmarital fertility, and childbearing across partnerships. Her work takes a reproductive career approach, which grounds childbearing and family behaviors both in the larger life course and in relation to individuals' past and future childbearing and family goals and behaviors. Dr Guzzo's research has been federally funded and appeared in top family and demography journals, including *Demography, Journal of Mariage and Family, Population and Development Review*, and *Journal of Family Issues*.

Brian J. Higginbotham is a Professor and Extension Specialist in the Department of Human Development and Family Studies at Utah State University. He has a Master's degree in Marriage and Family Therapy and a Ph.D. in Human Development and Family Studies from Auburn University.

Aaron Hoy, Ph.D., is an Assistant Professor of Sociology at Minnesota State University, Mankato. His research and teaching interests include families, sexualities, sex/gender, and qualitative methods. In particular, his research examines how lesbian, gay, bisexual, and transgender (LGBT) people experience and make sense of marriage and divorce following the legalization of same-sex marriage. His research has been published or is forthcoming in a range of sociology and interdisciplinary journals, including the *Journal of Family Issues, Sociology Compass*, and *Journal of Homosexuality*. He is also the Editor of *The Social Science of Same-Sex Marriage: LGBT People and Their Relationships in the Era of Marriage Equality* (Routledge, 2022). He completed his Ph.D. in Sociology at Syracuse University in 2018.

Bui Thu Huong attained her Doctoral degree in La Trobe University, Melbourne Australia in 2015. She is now working as a Senior Lecturer in the Department of Sociology and Development Studies, Academy of Journalism and Communication. She is interested and has experiences teaching and researching into issues relating to gender, health and communication. She used to work for a UNFPA-sponsored population and development advocacy project in the Academy of Journalism and Communication as an administrative assistant. In this position, she had the best opportunity to learn a lot about population-development, gender issues, reproductive and sexual health, communication and so on through the project's research activities and material development. It was here that her interest in these issues was initially kindled. She did not only embrace them in her own project at Master and Doctoral levels but also she continues to pursue these interests through her teaching responsibilities at the moment, specifically seven modules, *Introductory Sociology, Research Methods, Research Design, Introduction to Counseling, Advocacy of Social Issues, Cultural Sociology* and *Culture and Globalisation*. In addition, she has played an active role in numerous other inquiries undertaken by the Department. They include, among others, *Exploring Students' Needs of Education of Sexuality, Representation of Homosexuality in Newspapers, Gender Messages in Job Advertisement, Gender-based Violence, Sex ratio at birth in Vietnam, Women's Economic Contribution through their Unpaid Work and National Study on Health and Family in Vietnam.*

Olena Kopystynska is an Assistant Professor at Southern Utah University. She received her Ph.D. in Family Studies and Human Development from the University of Arizona and completed her post-doctoral training at Utah State University. Her research interests focus on examining the role of interparental conflict in relation to parenting and the quality of coparental relationships across different family structures (e.g., married parents, cohabiting parents, and stepfamilies).

Antoinette M. Landor is an Associate Professor and Millsap Professor of Diversity and Multicultural Studies in the Department of Human Development and Family Science at the University of Missouri. Her research focuses on the impact of colorism and racism on individual, relational, and family health and functioning. She also examines how sociocultural factors influence the sexual and romantic relationship behaviors of adolescents and young adults.

Nguyen Huu Minh is a High Senior Researcher of the Institute for Family and Gender Studies (IFGS), Vietnam Academy of Social Sciences (VASS) and is a Professor of Sociology, Vietnam Graduate Academy of Social Sciences (GASS). Currently, he is the President of Vietnam Sociological Association (VSA, 2017–2022 term). He received his Ph.D in Sociology in 1998 from the University of Washington, Seattle, USA. He is a Former Director of the IFGS (2005–2017), Former Vice-Director of the Institute of Sociology (1999–2005). In addition to teach for graduate program in GASS he has given lectures for graduate program in Sociology and Social Work in Ho Chi Minh National Academy of Politics; University of Social Sciences and Humanities at Ho Chi Minh city; Journalism Academy, Thu Dau Mot University, and some other Universities. He has been a PI or Co-PI of many international and national research projects. His publications include many books, articles in Vietnamese and some monographs, book chapters, articles in English on Urban studies; Marriage studies; Family relations studies; Gender Equality and Empowerment of women in Vietnam. Some of his publications (author or co-author) can be listed as: *Migration and urbanization in Vietnam: Patterns, trends and differentials; Intra-family relationships of the Vietnamese families: Key findings from indepth-analysis of the Vietnam Family Survey; Estimating the costs of domestic violence against women in Viet Nam; Vietnamese marriage patterns in the Red River Delta: Tradition and change; Vietnamese family in the context of industrialization, modernization and integration from comparative approaches; Marriage in contemporary Vietnamese society; Research methods in Sociology; Gender equality in the ethnic minority areas in Vietnam; etc.* He is interested in doing research on marriage and family relations, gender relation, elderly people.

Sarah N. Mitchell is an Assistant Professor in the Department of Human Development, Family Science, and Counseling at the University of Nevada, Reno. Her research focuses on the experiences of minoritized individuals (e.g., LGBTQ+ and those with minoritized gender and racial/ethnic identities) – especially the impact of intersecting minoritized identities – within the context of family.

Natalia Carballo Murillo is Costa Rican (1985). She has a bachelor's degree in History from the University of Costa Rica. She obtained his master's degree in Territorial and Population Studies, specializing in Demography, at the Autonomous University of Barcelona, Spain, with the thesis: "Evolution of fertility patterns, Costa Rica, 1970–2000". In 2021 she obtained his doctorate in Demography from the National University of Córdoba, Argentina, with the thesis entitled: "Dynamics of the transformations of Costa Rican households.

1985–2015". She is an associate professor at the University of Costa Rica, Pacific Campus, where she teaches courses on Costa Rican history, Latin America, and research methodologies. She is a researcher on families, households, and women's issues. Some research projects in which she has participated are: "Women heads of household in the province of Puntarenas, 1973–2011" (2012), "Demographic transition and family composition in Puntarenas, 1927–2011" (2013–2015), and "Social reproduction of Costa Rican households from 1980–2015" (2016–2017). She is a member of the Latin American Population Association (ALAP).

Some of his recent publications are:

Carballo, Natalia (2018). "Mejor alfabetizadas, en mejores trabajos, solteras y en sus cuarentas: Mujeres jefas de hogar en Costa Rica". En: Construyendo identidades y analizando desigualdades: Familias y trayectorias de vida como objeto de análisis en Europa y América. Siglos XVI-XXI. Coordinadores: Francisco Chacón, Albert Esteve y Ricardo Cicerchia. España, Centre d'Estudis Demografics.

Carballo, Natalia (2020). "Viudez y soltería en la costa pacífica de Costa Rica, siglos XX-XXI". En: Vivir en soledad: viudedad, soltería y abandono en el mundo rural (España y América Latina, siglos XVI-XXI). Francisco García González (ed.). Madrid: Iberoamericana Editorial Vervuert.

Carballo, Natalia (2020). "Un aporte al estudio del voto femenino en Costa Rica". En: Revista de Ciencias Sociales, número 167, volumen (I). Dirección electrónica: https://revistas.ucr.ac.cr/index.php/sociales/article/view/42973

Carballo, Natalia (2022). "Una propuesta conceptual-teórica para entender las medidas en materia de población en Costa Rica. Segunda mitad del siglo XX". En: Revista de Ciencias Sociales, número 172, volumen (II). Dirección electrónica: https://revistas.ucr.ac.cr/index.php/sociales/article/view/49944/49983

Josip Obradović - Nationality: Croatian. *Education*: elementary and high school finished in Zagreb Croatia. Graduated Psychology and Philosophy at the Filozofski fakultet University of Zagreb. Obtained Ph.D. In Sociology, Filozofski fakultet The University of Zagreb. *Employment*: Departement od sociology the Filozofski fakultet University of Zagreb. Part-time employment at Institut Pilar Zagreb. Croatian studies at the University of Zagreb. Presently at Croatian Catholic University Zagreb Croatia. *Fellowship*: Ford Foundation Fellow: Institute for Social Research, University of Michigan, Ann Arbor, Michigan, and Institute of Industrial Relations, University of California, Berkeley. *Visiting professor*: New York University New York USA, two times at the University of Georgia Athens Georgia USA, University of Calgary Calgary, Canada, and Fulbright Professor at Colorado College, Colorado Springs, USA.

Visiting scholar: Aston University, Birmingham, Great Britain, Charles University, Prague, Czech Republic, Lorand Eotvos University Budapest, Hungary, University of Pittsburgh, Pennsylvania, USA, University of Warwick, Coventry Great Britain. *Teaching Interest and Experience*: Teaching 20 different courses in Psychology and Sociology for undergraduate and graduate students in Croatian and English language at Croatian and North American universities

Invited lectures: Given talks at about 30 universities In European, North and South American countries. *Membership in organizations*: American sociological organization, Croatian psychological organization, and National Council of Family Relations. *Participation in professional meetings*. Actively participated in more than 50 domestic and international meetings. *Publications*: As coauthor or coeditor published 14 books and more than 100 research papers in Croatian and English language.

Chigozirim Ogubuike is a Doctoral Student at the Institute of Child Health, University of Ibadan Nigeria. She is a result-oriented public health professional with experiences in both quantitative and qualitative research. She is passionate about Innovation and strategic solutions, she is culturally and socially sensitive, technologically savvy and can adapt to multiple and changing demands. Her research interests are in Child and Adolescent Health, Sexual and Reproductive Health, Family Research, Contemporary Issues, Public Health Research, Gender Variations, and Women Health. She is a young researcher and open for fellowship opportunities, research funding and further trainings.

Mofeyisara Oluwatoyin Omobowale is a Senior Research Fellow at the Social and Behavioural Health Unit, Institute of Child Health, College of Medicine, University of Ibadan, Nigeria. She obtained a PhD in Anthropology from the University of Ibadan, Nigeria in 2014. She is a Fellow of the American Council of Learned Societies-African Humanities Programme (2012 and 2016), Cadbury Fellowship (Department of Anthropology and African, Birmingham University) 2014, Carnegie of New York, 2016 and a Short-Term Scholar, at Brown International Advanced Research Institute (BIARI), Brown University, USA, 2013. She was an Investigator on Bill and Malinda Gates Foundation Grand Challenge funded project (2019–2021) – Immunization Strategies for Working Mothers (SHEVACCS). She blends anthropological knowledge, theories and methods in teaching and researching public health issues to impact society's well-being positively.

David G. Schramm known as "Dr Dave" on campus and across the country, Dave Schramm is an Associate Professor and Family Life Extension Specialist at Utah State University in the Department of Human Development and Family Studies. After graduating with his Ph.D. from Auburn University, he worked as a Professor at the University of Missouri for nine years. Shortly after arriving at USU in 2016, he was appointed by Governor Herbert to serve on Utah's Commission on Marriage and he now serves as a Faculty Director of the Commission. He appears regularly on television and shares tips and videos on social media and YouTube to help individuals, parents, and couples thrive in their life journeys. In 2022, he launched a podcast called Stronger Marriage Connection. His research interests center on couple and family relationships, including marriage and divorce education, parenting education, and positivity and personal well-being. He enjoys translating research findings into principles, practices, and programming to help individuals and couples flourish. From British Columbia to Beijing, China, and from St. Louis to San Diego, Dr Dave has given over 500 presentations, classes, and workshops to a variety of audiences, including the United Nations and a TEDx talk in Florida. He married his high school sweetheart Jamie, they have four children, he just might have a slight addiction to peanut M&Ms, and the Schramm fam lives in North Logan, Utah.

Christina L. Scott, Ph.D., is an Associate Professor of Psychology with Whittier College in Los Angeles and earned her Ph.D. in Social Psychology at Kansas State University. Her program of research has spanned a range of topics focusing on women's personal and sexual empowerment, including friends with benefits relationships and women's sexual arousal. Currently, she is investigating perceptions of single mothers by choice and changing attitudes about motherhood. She has taught university courses in Shanghai, China and as a faculty member with Semester at Sea. She will be teaching at the University of Tokyo and Kyoritsu Women's University in Tokyo, Japan in 2023 as a Fulbright Scholar.

J. Bart Stykes is an Associate Professor of Sociology at Sam Houston State University, where he teaches Introduction to Sociology alongside courses on family sociology, research methods, and social statistics. His research examines (1) the links between the transition to parenthood, union formation/dissolution, and parental well-being, (2) children's experiences in the family (e.g., family structure, complexity, and instability) and well-being, and (3) men's experiences as fathers in families. Many of his contributions to existing research also consider data quality and survey measurement issues as well as the production and reproduction of gender inequity in families. Dr Stykes research has been published in family, demographic, and health journals including the *Journal of Marriage and Family, Demography, Demographic Research, Society and Mental Health, and Maternal and Child Health Journal.* He has also secured funding to support primary data collection to better understand the role conflict that student-parents experience and its implications for academic success.

Joshua J. Turner is a Postdoctoral Fellow at Utah State University. He received his Ph.D. in Human Development and Family Sciences from Mississippi State University. His research interests include relationship education, remarriage and stepfamily issues, and health and aging.

Siri Wilder received her B.A. from Whittier College in 2017 and her M.S. from the University of Texas at Dallas in 2022, where she is currently completing her Doctorate in Psychology. Her research interests include relational processes underlying committed and casual sex relationships and young adults' attitudes toward sexuality. She was the inaugural recipient of the UT Dallas IRB HIVE award, recognizing positive contributions to human subjects research, and in 2022 received the UT Dallas President's Teaching Excellence Award for Teaching Assistants. In addition to her research and teaching, she has enjoyed working on diversity, equity, and inclusion initiatives in several committee roles.

Katharine H. Zeiders is an Associate Professor in the Norton School of Family Ecology at the University of Arizona. Her research explores the physiological and psychological effects of stressors on adolescent and young adult development.

FOREWORD

Conjugal life is a process, rather than a steady state, which couples achieve once they establish a relationship. The trajectories they develop throughout the life cycle are closely linked to political, economic, cultural, and demographic processes that shape their decisions, arrangements, and the roles couples and families serve in society. By studying marriage and cohabitation decision-making, the process of mate acquaintance, the criteria for mate selection, the age difference between the mates and the changing family structures among some other topics, we are able to understand how society and culture shape individual decisions as well as how individuals challenge the norms and make space for cultural change.

Over recent decades, the study of how couples form and what happens after they establish has received increasing attention from social and human disciplines. As with most fields of study the approaches vary and emphasize aspects considered relevant for the discipline in question. The interest in conjugal life from different perspectives and fields of study has frequently connected this discussion to marriage and its social forms, problems, status, rights and role. Much of this interest has been paid to analyze the quality of the conjugal bond, the conflicts and harmony in marital life, the conjugality and capital, the changes in the calendar of marriage and cohabitation, long-distance conjugality, conjugal rights, and the connections of conjugality to love, consanguinity, fertility, sexuality, paternity, polygamy, monogamy, children's behaviour, and so on. These wide range of discussions come from both qualitative and quantitative approaches and allow us to see the dynamism of the conjugal trajectories.

Conjugal trajectories can be understood as the sexual-affective and domestic stories that married and cohabitant couples produce in order to stay together. The trajectory demands the acceptance of explicit and implicit agreements that are the reflection of wider social rules and norms that impact on their sexuality, displays of affection, rights and duties, and economy.

Conjugal trajectories are composed by four elements (Cuevas, 2019): the presence of at least one partner throughout the life cycle; the existence of a legal, symbolic or consensual relationship through which the marriage or union was formalized; the coexistence as a couple under the same or separate roofs and the recognition of these arrangements by the immediate family and social circles; and the presence or absence of children born out of that relationships or from previous marriages or unions.

Research on the formation of couples has changed and increased over the last several decades, improving and deepening our knowledge on the topic. Research literature from around the globe reflects that an increasing number of couples choose cohabitation over marriage, delaying marriage and getting divorced or separating in greater numbers than ever before. The changes have both a structural and cultural origin and show that given the extent of the phenomena that marital life is undergoing, people everyday feel more vulnerable and exposed to the pressures of having their private life under scrutiny in social networks, failing to achieve a balanced and happy relationship.

The chapters in this book present a coherent approach to the understanding of conjugal trajectories from different contemporary social problems. They represent the work of authors from different countries, disciplines and methodological perspectives who have approached it from both novel and classical objects of study to provide empirical research that contributes important results to the understanding of this knowledge. In this respect, the book contributes to the understanding of the evolving nature of marriage and cohabitation and does so from a contemporary perspective. The different chapters approach us to a variety of discussions of great relevance that shed light on complex arenas of marital life from the individual, group and intergenerational perspective of different cultures and social groups that, to a greater or lesser extent, show the impact of modernity on the intimacy of these individuals. A common finding made by several authors of the book is the increasing relevance of the partners' qualities and communication skills as crucial factors for the conjugal life; a valuation that played a key role for the election of partner for Africans, North Americans, Europeans and Latin Americans alike. This is a reflection of the deep and unequal impact modernity has had across the world, mainly among educated and highly schooled populations. Another important contribution to the knowledge of conjugal life is the discussion of the stability and length of the conjugal bond amidst the growth in life expectancy at birth, the creation and application of divorce laws, the access to education of women, and the rise of cohabitation in all socioeconomic and age groups. The evidence found by several authors in different countries point out that conjugal relationships are more intense and unstable than ever before and that individuals face both the possibility of having several partners throughout their life but also the opportunity to live with the same couple for many decades.

The discussion on conjugal trajectories this book offers can be organized in three main discussions. The first of them groups the works that consider that intimacy, subjectivity, and happiness play a crucial role in marital satisfaction and quality. In *An Exploratory Study of the Influence of Marital Attitudes and Skin Tone Perception on the Romantic Relationship Quality Among African American and Latinx Young Adults*, Sarah N. Mitchell, Antoinette M. Landor and Katharine H. Zeiders discuss, from a quantitative approach, the ways in which attitudes about marriage (i.e., desire, importance, and expectation) relate to young adults' current relationship quality (i.e., satisfaction, intimacy, and commitment). They used the Marital Horizon Theory as a lens to understand young adults' marital attitudes and relationship quality. Their research showed that for young adults, marital attitudes are associated with relationship quality. They aimed to shed light on how this association plays out for young adults of color, a research topic understudied. Additionally, they found that the influence of skin tone perception plays an important role in the relationship between marital attitudes and relationship quality. They studied these associations through a group of African American and Latinx young adults attending college. Their results indicated that marital expectations were positively associated with relationship quality in that young adults who expected to marry one day, reported greater relationship satisfaction, commitment, and intimacy in their current relationships. Additionally, skin tone perception moderated the association between marital attitudes and relationship quality in two ways (i.e., between expectations and satisfaction and between importance and intimacy). Collectively, their findings suggest that differing levels of marital attitudes and skin tone perception contribute to young adults' perceptions of relationship quality.

In *Breaking Up Is Hard to Do: Investigating Breakup Distress and Sexual Regret in Undergraduates' Casual and Committed Sexual Relationships*, Siri Wilder, Christina L. Scott and Micaela A. Chavarin explore how the rupture with the partner amongst teenagers was perceived and felt. The did so from a survey that considered a variety of demographic characteristics and several questions of their sexual history and divided the analysis in two groups, namely the distress caused by the breakup and the sexual regrets. In both groups, they explored the sex differences, the relationship differences, and the interaction when having casual sex and being in a romantic relationship. Their results show that there were statistically significant effects found for breakup distress as a function of sex and type of relationship and that women and men, as expected, behaved according to sex and gender roles and were deeply affected by their ideas on romantic love in the breakup. Whether casual or committed, teenagers had a wide range of emotional reactions to the end of their sexual relationships. However, the authors found that still remains to be seen whether these responses are significantly different across both types of relationships. They also found that there were statistically significant main effects found for breakup distress as a function of sex and the type of relationship.

In *Romantic, Confessional and Post-Romantic: The Timeline of Conjugality at a Distance Between Mexico and the United States*, Javiera Cienfuegos-Illanes discusses the construction of transnational marital bonds over time through a dual approach and a qualitative perspective. The author first, based on multi-site fieldwork carried out in 2011 and 2012 in two regions of Mexico and one of the United States, analyzes how transnational heterosexual couples with young children deal with being separated and construct their conjugality. This discussion considers two dimensions: intimacy and domestic organization. The second part of the chapter discusses the same results of the study after a decade, based on contact with the same participants and an exploration of their trajectories of intimacy and family organization. The author uses the notion of life cycle and family trajectory arriving at paths in the definition of intimacy that discuss the romantic component initially identified and add the confessional and post-romantic components as part of the experience of geographical distance for prolonged periods of migration, in addition to aging processes.

In *Age-Homogamy and Age-Heterogamy in Three Generations of Heterosexual Women and Men in Mexico*, Ana Josefina Cuevas Hernández uses the date gathered in 81 semi-structured interviews carried on with heterosexual men and women from two Mexican cities. The author divides the discussion in three sections, namely the age-gap and age-discrepancy in the three generations of study;

the role of schooling and social class in the significance of the age-gap and age-discrepancy relationships; and the gender inequality in couple relationships. Her work aims to contribute from a qualitative and sociological standpoint to this field of knowledge that has been understudied. The discussion focused on the meaning interviewers gave to the age difference from their subjectivity and intimacy to see how their ideas on the age difference were perceived. Her findings show a vigorous and strong trend of marriages and unions between older men and younger women where great gender inequalities persisted. This took place amidst signs of cultural change in the younger generations and highly educated men and women from middle classes who perceived the age difference negatively. This, rather than being a contradiction, reveals how schooling and social origin affect the resignification of the age difference, and moreover, suggests that the power relations in the couple were more equitable.

In *Predictors of Marital Quality: What Makes a Happy Marriage in Croatia?*, Josip Obradović and Mira Čudina explore the marital quality in Croatian marriage using the Socio-ecological model. The authors aim to contribute to this field of knowledge that has also been understudied in most non-western societies, where specific historical and cultural issues model conjugal life. Their work explores, from a quantitative perspective, the subjective and qualitative aspects of the couple's perceptions on their marital life. By doing so, they aim to contribute to the explanation of the quality of the marital relationship. Their results show great similarity to the studies carried out in other social contexts and point out that marital harmony and distress in Croatia were very important predictors of the marital quality and pretty similar to the results observed in the United States and some Western countries. Thus, it seems that the values of satisfaction, individuality, companionship and mutual help – all a reflection of intimacy and late modernity – are predictors of the quality of conjugal life irrespective of socio-cultural context. However, traditionalism, marital partners' personalities, and engagement in child care are elements of great value in the socio-cultural context in Croatia.

A second group of works analyze the conjugal trajectories through marriage formation. In *Marriage Formation in Vietnam: Characteristics and Changes*, Nguyen Huu Minh and Bui Thu Huong use data from the Vietnam Family Survey and Vietnam Marriage Survey to examine the changing patterns of marriage formation in Vietnam. Due to many of the changing socio-economic and legal factors, they find that traditional expectations concerning marriage have given way to a more individualist form, such that those seeking to get marriage focus primarily upon their desire for individual happiness. Although concerns about family obligations still remain, the various decision-making processes concerning mate selection and marriage are no longer controlled predominantly by parents. Instead, the independent preferences of contemporary young adults are slowly, but steadily, serving to change the patterns of marriage in Vietnam.

The distinctions between traditional forms of marriage, which often are controlled by parents, and more progressive forms, wherein individuals have greater choice in the selection of a partner, are also examined by Shichao Du in *Education, Marriage Cohorts, and Different Pathways to Marriage in East Asian Societies*. Using data from the East Asian Social Survey, this chapter examines the role of education and change over time in the marriage trajectories of young adults in China, Japan, South Korea, and Taiwan. Educational attainment (more years of schooling) is associated with fewer arranged marriages, and more self-initiated marriages. Over time, arranged marriages are shown to be on the decline, while individual choice is revealed as the evolving form in the selection of a partner. These patterns are discussed within the framework of developmentalism.

Natalia Carballo Murillo explores the nature of reproductive strategies across family generations in *Life Trajectories and Reproductive Strategies of Costa Rican Households: An Intergenerational Perspective*. Using qualitative interviews across multiple generations, she finds that both conjugal trajectories and reproductive strategies steadily changed. Contextual factors from the larger society, such as economic stress, are shown to bring about change in familial attitudes, gender roles, and fertility strategies. Older generations are shown to be more traditional and conservative in these regards, while younger generations are shown to feel compelled to adjust and adapt more readily. Given the complexity of Costa Rican families, such changes are not necessarily easy to accomplish, as the influence of familial ties across generations can be quite substantial.

In *What Difference Does Marriage Make? Life Course Trajectories and the Transition to Marriage for Gay Men and Lesbians*, Aaron Hoy examines the varied paths to marriage among gay and lesbian individuals. Using a series of semi-structured interviews, he finds that the various routes taken en route to marriage had lasting and meaningful impacts upon the transition into marriage. A distinction is found between the "short and direct" route to marriage, and the "long and winding" trajectory, with the former route often involving large and elaborate wedding ceremonies, while the latter commonly involved relatively small, and even unplanned, ceremonies. The emotional meanings and experiences of these two trajectories were quite different, and reveal much about the complex and nuanced nature of marriage transitions for gays and lesbians.

The third group of chapters explores the conjugal trajectories through marriage stability and family structures. In *Identifying Predictors of First Versus Subsequent Divorce Among Divorcing Parents*, Joshua J. Turner, Olena Kopystynska, Kay Bradford, Brian J. Higginbotham and David G. Schramm examine the various factors that promote vulnerabilities among remarried couples. Using data from a large sample of divorcing parents who participated in a state-mandated, online divorce education course, the authors found that individuals going through their first divorce were more likely to identify growing apart and infidelity as reasons for seeking a divorce. Among those going through a subsequent divorce, though, problems such as alcohol and drug abuse, disagreements concerning childrearing, financial problems, and a combination of emotional, verbal, and physical abuse, as the primary factors which prompted their decision to seek a divorce. Their research not only contributes to our conceptual and theoretical understanding of divorce, but also yielded implications for practitioners.

Using data from the National Survey of Family Growth, J. Bart Stykes and Karen Benjamin Guzzo examine the linkages between unintended childbearing and union dissolution. In *Unintended Higher-Order Births and Union Stability: Variation by Union Characteristics*, the authors find that unintended childbearing, cohabitation, and stepfamily status are all linked with a greater risk of dissolution. The impact of unintended childbearing is much more complicated, though, as it is associated with a higher risk of dissolution for married couples, as compared to cohabiting couples. Their findings strongly suggest that it is selection, rather than causation, which explains the association between unintended childbearing and union instability among higher-order births.

In *Dynamism and Changes in the Abia Family Structure and Conjugal Relationship: The Influence of the Nigerian Civil War*, Chigozirim Ogubuike, Mofeyisara Oluwatoyin Omobowale, and Olukemi K. Amodu focus on intergenerational variations in conjugality in different types of Abia families, comparing their changes and conjugal relations from traditional times to contemporary times. Specifically, they cast a glance at the dynamism and changes in the family structure and conjugal relationships at different eras of the family life cycle through a qualitative approach aiming to know how Nigerian Civil War affected their family structures and conjugal relationships. Their findings reveal a great dynamism and changes in family structures, with a prevalence of polygyny prior to the civil war, the emergence of step-parent and single-parent families during the civil war, and monogamy being most prevalent, with increasing single-parent and step-parent families contemporaneously. The conjugal relationship shifted from having concubines (acceptable and practiced covertly) to having side chicks (practiced covertly). The Nigerian civil war had an impact on the dynamics and the family structures of Nigerian families during the civil war and the immediate post-civil war. The authors also found out that other factors such as religion, education, civilization, and migration, among others, also influenced the contemporary Abia family structure. In short, their findings provide a better understanding on family structure dynamics and the possible use of this information in solving issues regarding family and conjugal trajectories.

We extend our most sincere gratitude to the authors for the excellent work, and for contributing to this volume. Additional thanks go out to the reviewers, members of the editorial board of Contemporary Perspectives in Family Research, and to the always helpful staff at Emerald Publishing.

Ana Josefina Cuevas Hernández
Sampson Lee Blair

CHAPTER 1

AN EXPLORATORY STUDY OF THE INFLUENCE OF MARITAL ATTITUDES AND SKIN TONE PERCEPTION ON THE ROMANTIC RELATIONSHIP QUALITY AMONG AFRICAN AMERICAN AND LATINX YOUNG ADULTS

Sarah N. Mitchell, Antoinette M. Landor and Katharine H. Zeiders

ABSTRACT

Research has shown that for young adults, marital attitudes (e.g., desire, importance, and expectation) are associated with relationship quality. However, how this association plays out for young adults of color is less known. Additionally, the influence of skin tone perception on the relationship between marital attitudes and relationship quality remains understudied. To explore these associations, the authors examined African American and Latinx young adults (N = 57, M$_{age}$ = 20.71 years, SD = 1.28; 75.4% female) attending a Midwestern university. Exploratory results indicated that marital expectations were positively associated with relationship quality in that young adults who expected to marry one day, reported greater relationship satisfaction, commitment, and intimacy in their current relationships. Additionally, skin tone perception

Conjugal Trajectories: Relationship Beginnings, Change, and Dissolutions
Contemporary Perspectives in Family Research, Volume 22, 1–23
Copyright © 2023 by Emerald Publishing Limited
All rights of reproduction in any form reserved
ISSN: 1530-3535/doi:10.1108/S1530-353520230000022001

moderated the association between marital attitudes and relationship quality in two ways (i.e., between expectations and satisfaction and between importance and intimacy). Collectively, findings suggest that differing levels of marital attitudes and skin tone perception contributes to young adults' perceptions of relationship quality. Considering these psychological factors of attitudes, skin tone perception, and relationship quality, together with systemic racial/ethnic discrimination, the authors discuss future research and practice considerations.

Keywords: Racial/ethnic minoritized identity; marital attitudes; skin tone; romantic relationships; relationship quality; mate selection

Demographics relating to marriage have been changing over time, especially within the last two decades. Young adults are cohabiting at increasing rates, while also delaying marriage (Lundberg & Pollak, 2013; Martin, Astone, & Peters, 2014; Pew Research Center, 2019). Despite these changing relationship preferences, most young adults in the United States expect to (and are projected to) marry and have generally positive attitudes toward marriage (Cherlin, 2004; Crissey, 2005; Goldstein & Kenney, 2001; Landor & Halpern, 2016; Scott, Schelar, Manlove, & Cui, 2009). Scott et al. (2009) examined data from the National Longitudinal Study of Adolescent to Adult Health (Add Health) and found that although most respondents in their early 20s did not want to currently be married, 83% reported that they felt it was important or very important to be married someday, and 70% indicated that there was a good or certain chance of being married within 10 years.

Although demographic information and trends related to marriage and marital attitudes are informative, it is important for relationship scholars to understand how these constructs are associated with romantic relationship functioning. Generally, research has shown that having favorable marital attitudes is positively correlated with relationship quality (Amato & Rogers, 1999; S. L. Brown, 2004). However, whereas most young adults have favorable views regarding marriage, marital attitudes and relationship quality may differ for racially/ethnically minoritized individuals (Blackman, Clayton, Glenn, Malone-Colon, & Roberts, 2005; Broman, 2005; Crissey, 2005; McLoyd, Cauce, Takeuchi, & Wilson, 2000; Scott et al., 2009). The assumption that having favorable attitudes about marriage is protective for relationship quality may not always apply when race and ethnicity are considered. What does research indicate regarding the relationship quality of young adults of color? How are attitudes toward marriage related to the quality of one's relationship for racially/ethnically minoritized individuals? Moreover, the ways in which skin tone differences *within* racially/ethnically minoritized groups affects these associations are even less understood. The purpose of the present exploratory study is to examine the nuanced influences of marital attitudes on the romantic relationship quality of young adults of color, and potential role of skin tone on that association. We hope the findings can inspire both future research on the topic and culturally responsive practitioners who work with racially and ethnically diverse young adults.

RELATIONSHIP QUALITY IN RACIALLY/ETHNICALLY MINORITIZED INDIVIDUALS

There are conflicting data regarding the overall incidence of racial/ethnic differences when it comes to relationship quality. McLoyd et al. (2000) point out that although some studies find no differences between African American and White couples in behaviors associated with marital happiness (e.g., sexual satisfaction, destructive conflict), other studies show that reports of marital happiness and satisfaction do differ by race, perhaps due to additional pressures faced by those with a minoritized racial/ethnic identity (e.g., discrimination, social stigma, community stressors, material hardships, and wage disparities; see also Blackman et al., 2005; Broman, 2005; Doyle & Molix, 2014a, 2014b; Kogan et al., 2013; Lincoln, Taylor, & Jackson, 2008; Phillips & Sweeney, 2006). The "harms" of cohabitation have also been discussed in relation to Black and Brown individuals. These groups are more likely to form cohabiting unions as an alternative to marriage as opposed to a step on the way (see Bumpass & Lu, 2000; S. L. Brown, 2000; S. L. Brown, Van Hook, & Glick, 2008). And cohabiting relationships are more likely to be characterized by lower relationship quality (S. L. Brown, 2004, S. L. Brown, Manning, & Payne, 2017; Landale & Oropesa, 2007).

It is important to remember context in understanding this association, as it may not be as simple as one of these factors *causing* lower relationship satisfaction. For instance, among cohabiters, plans to marry resulted in higher levels of relationship happiness and lower levels of instability compared to cohabiters who did not have plans to marry (S. L. Brown, 2004; S. L. Brown & Booth, 1996; S. L. Brown et al., 2017; Stanley, Rhoades, & Markman, 2006). Cohabitation itself does not cause lower relationship satisfaction; there are often psychological and other relationship factors at play. When looking at discrimination and stigma's role in lower reports of relationship quality for people of color, Doyle and Molix (2014a) found that discrimination's impact on relationship satisfaction for Black and Hispanic individuals is largely mediated by self-acceptance. In that same year (2014b), they published another study on the relationship between racial stigma and relationship quality for Black individuals, and found that when stigma is made salient, Black individuals report lower relationship quality only if their relationship is new. If they have been partnered for a longer period of time, they report higher levels of relationship satisfaction in the face of discrimination awareness.

Other studies have also focused on identifying protective factors for the relationships of people of color. For example, Ellison, Burdette, and Bradford Wilcox (2010) found in their study on Black and Hispanic couples, that shared core religious beliefs and practicing religious activities within the home were associated with better relationship quality (see also Wilcox & Wolfinger, 2008). Competence-promoting parenting (e.g., warmth, monitoring, and modeling indicative reasoning) paired with few community stressors in childhood predicted positive relationship schemas for adolescents, in turn predicting romantic relationship health in Black young adults (Kogan et al., 2013). Additionally, cultural beliefs and practices like familism were shown to be associated with higher partner closeness and support (via lower attachment avoidance) for Latinx[1] couples (Campos, Perez, & Guardino, 2016). Put together, these studies point to the need to consider culture, systemic forces, and psychosocial processes in order to better understand the relationship quality of those with minoritized ethnic/racial identities.

MARITAL ATTITUDES AND THE IMPACT ON RELATIONSHIP QUALITY

Marital attitudes comprise a set of psychological beliefs that could be better understood in their association to relationship quality for young adults of color. Scott et al. (2009) found that although a majority of *Add Health* young adults aged 20–24 did not want to be married at the time of the survey, Black and White respondents were more likely to want to be married currently (30% each) than Hispanic (25%) and Asian respondents (20%). In terms of endorsing marriage as an important future goal, Asian respondents were most likely to feel so (88%). White and Hispanic young adults trailed slightly behind (84% and 83%, respectively); Black young adults were least likely to feel that getting married was important to them (78%). Additional research finds that Black and Hispanic youth and young adults, especially Black youth, have lower marriage expectations and less desire to marry than do Whites (Crissey, 2005; Gassanov, Nicholson, & Koch-Turner, 2008; Manning, Longmore, & Giordano, 2007).

If Black and Latinx individuals generally have less favorable attitudes toward marriage than White individuals, how are these attitudes related to their relationship quality? Generally, research has shown that pro-martial and anti-divorce attitudes are associated with higher relationship quality, but these studies utilize majority White samples (S. L. Brown, 2004), report on non-US populations (Erol, 2016), do not discuss whether or not they found differences by race/ethnicity (Amato & Rogers, 1999; Riggio & Weiser, 2008), or provide no information about the racial/ethnic make-up of their sample at all (Riggio & Fite, 2006). There remains a gap in the literature regarding the associations between marital attitudes and relationship quality for people of color. Given the evidence which supports differing marital expectations for racially/ethnically minoritized individuals as compared to White individuals, as well as the conflicting data regarding differences in their relationship quality and outcomes, the influence of racially/ethnically minoritized individuals' marital attitudes on their relationship quality should be further examined.

THE ROLE OF SKIN TONE AND COLORISM

Past research has documented that colorism is another aspect that may be related to the marital attitudes and relationship quality of racially/ethnically minoritized individuals (Banks, 2000; Bryant, 2001; Fears, 1998; Hill, 2000, 2002; Hunter, 1998; Kerr, 2005; Landor & Halpern, 2016; Montalvo, 2005). Not only does this mean that White individuals are most often privileged over individuals of color, but that even within distinct racial/ethnic groups, individuals with lighter skin are often treated and evaluated more positively than those with darker skin (Dixon & Telles, 2017; Hunter, 2007; Jha & Adelman, 2009; Landor et al., 2013; Landor & McNeil Smith, 2019; McNeil Smith & Landor, 2018). This preference can be traced back to the era of slavery, when enslaved individuals with lighter skin were chosen to work in the house; their appearance being closer in shade to the European descended slave owners (Hunter, 2002). European colonization of other darker complexioned societies like those of Latinx backgrounds also serves as a context in which colorism was practiced (Hunter, 2002), and perhaps even before these eras, societies have generally preferred lighter skin tones over darker skin tones (Frost, 1990).

This preference based on skin tone persists in modernity and is exhibited in many contexts. Individuals with lighter skin are more likely to have higher education, more wealth, better career advancement, more positive psychological functioning, and benefit especially when it comes to mate choice (Hughes & Hertel, 1990; Hunter, 2002; Keith & Herring, 1991; Landor & Barr, 2018; Thompson & Keith, 2001). For example, having a lighter skin tone is associated with higher probability of marriage, earlier marriage, and marriage to those with higher status, especially for women (Edwards, Carter-Tellison, & Herring, 2004; Hamilton, Goldsmith, & Darity, 2009; Landor, 2017). There are nuances, however, in understanding exactly how skin tone may impact outcomes. For example, Hamilton and colleagues (2009) found that Black women with lighter skin tones were more marriageable in areas where there were few Black men, but not in all areas (see also Monk, 2014).

Furthermore, when examining relationship and marital outcomes related to colorism, it is important to consider both the attitudes of potential mates and the perceptions of those with light or dark skin tones – this consideration further highlights variables that may impact that association beyond "lighter skin tone equaling preference or better outcomes." Studies suggest that it is likely an interaction of others' attitudes and one's own perceptions that at least partially explain outcomes related to benefits afforded individuals with lighter skin in some circumstances. Examples of the impacts of others' perceptions include Stepanova and Strube's (2012) study where they found that White respondents give more positive skin tone evaluations to African American males that had more European features (Stepanova & Strube, 2012). Additionally, within group colorism happens. For instance, Black men are more likely to notice women with lighter skin and darker women are thought to be less attractive (Hill, 2002: Hunter, 2008; Wilder, 2010).

Racially/ethnically minoritized individuals of varying skin tones may be aware of these preferences and colorism in terms of how they impact themselves and others (Golden, 2007; Monk, 2015; Uzogara & Jackson, 2016; Uzogara, Lee, Abdou, & Jackson, 2014; Wilder & Cain, 2011). For instance, darker skin individuals report being aware that they may not have the same opportunities for relationships and marriage (Golden, 2007; Wilder & Cain, 2011). Is it the perception of having darker skin or just being aware of skin tone related discrimination. Monk (2015), Uzogara and Jackson (2016), and Uzogara and colleagues (2014) all used the same nationally representative data set – the NSAL (National Survey of American Life) and found that skin tone was associated with perceptions of colorism when those outcome measures of discrimination explicitly referred to skin tone or shade. Some studies suggest that skin tone might not be related to reports of overall discrimination, especially when skin tone is not explicitly mentioned in outcome measures of discrimination (see Keith, Lincoln, Taylor, & Jackson, 2010 who also used the NSAL and Krieger, Sidney, & Coakley, 1998; Landor et al., 2013). This may indicate that, in some instances, being *aware* of skin tone stigma may signal poorer outcomes as opposed to one having a certain shade of skin per se. None the less, previously discussed research points out the real impact of skin tone discrimination due to others' – *and* an individual's – understanding of their skin tone.

Whether it be treatment from others or personal perceptions, skin tone can impact racially/ethnically minoritized young adults' attitudes toward marriage. Landor (2017) found that African American young men with darker skin were more likely to endorse positive marital attitudes than those with lighter skin (e.g., desire to marry, feeling that marriage is important, and expectation to marry). Conversely, women with medium skin tones were more likely to rate these attitudes more positively as compared women with lighter or medium skin tones. In some instances, gender acts as a moderator in the association between skin tone and attitudes; light skin tone preference and advantage seems to exist more so for women (Frisby, 2006; Strutton & Lumpkin, 1993), but may vary depending on context. Our understanding is limited, since few studies looking at marital attitudes consider skin tone. Furthermore, to date, no studies have examined how attitudes and skin tone impact relationship quality. If those with lighter skin tones are aware of the privileges afforded them and have access to larger mate pools, choice may interact with specific marital attitudes to influence one's satisfaction with their partners (see D'Angelo & Toma, 2017). It would be beneficial to know how both African American and Latinx young adults' skin tone is related to relational experiences.

CURRENT STUDY

With a limited understanding of how marital attitudes are related to the relationship quality of racially/ethnically minoritized young adults, a better understanding of this relationship is warranted, especially considering the impacts of skin tone and colorism on the relationship experiences of people of color. This would result in richer, more inclusive, marriage and family scholarship and better-informed family practitioners who aim to provide resources for individuals and couples who experience added challenges to relationship functioning. The purpose of this study was to explore the ways in which attitudes about marriage (i.e., desire, importance, and expectation) relate to young adults' current relationship quality (i.e., satisfaction, intimacy, and commitment). We used the Marital Horizon Theory as a lens through which to understand young adults' marital attitudes and relationship quality (Carroll et al., 2007, 2009). This theory posits that for young adults, marriage is on the "horizon." It is a foreseeable transition, but not one that will happen immediately. Attitudes like marital importance, desire, and readiness influence how close or attainable marriage is seen to be. Our hypotheses are informed by this theoretical framework, coupled with research indicating that young adults are delaying marriage while still expecting to marry someday (but not right now; see Pew Research Center, 2019; Scott et al., 2009). We hypothesized that overall endorsement of pro-marital attitudes would be positively correlated with relationship quality, in particular, marital importance and expectation more so than desire. Additionally, we examined the moderating effect of skin tone on this association, recognizing that one's perception of skin tone could impact the relationship between marital attitudes and relationship quality in various ways.

METHOD

Procedure

The data for the current study came from a larger study focused on health, relationships, and stress in college students in the Midwest (Davenport, Landor, Zeiders, Sarsar, & Flores, 2021). Young adults were eligible to participate if they were between the ages of 18 and 25 years old, enrolled at the university, and self-identified as Black/African American, Hispanic/Latinx, or Hispanic/Latinx and White. Eligible participants were asked to come into the lab, where research assistants gave study instructions. After consenting, participants completed Qualtrics questionnaires assessing demographic information, factors related to health behaviors and outcomes, as well as dating and marriage attitudes and behaviors. Once finished, research assistants gave participants $10 in compensation, and provided them with a resource sheet since some of the questions were sensitive in nature. The datasets generated and analyzed during the study are not publicly available as we did not obtain permission from participants to share their data in this manner.

Participants

The full sample consisted of 145 participants; however, we utilized a subsample of 57 participants (African American, $n = 35$ and Latinx, $n = 22$) who reported that they were either in dating and/or committed relationships at the time of data collection. These participants had an average age of 20.71 years ($SD = 1.28$) and were majority women (75.4%). Only one participant was engaged to be married, the others were dating "one person on a regular basis" or were in a "steady, committed relationship."

Measures

Dependent Variables
We measured *relationship quality* using subscales from the Perceived Relationship Quality Component (PRQC) inventory (Fletcher, Simpson, & Thomas, 2000). For the purposes of this study, we looked at relationship satisfaction, commitment,

and intimacy specifically. The satisfaction subscale included three items (e.g., "How satisfied are you with your relationship?"), the commitment subscale included three items (e.g., "How committed are you to your relationship?"), and intimacy subscale included 3 items (e.g., "How intimate is your relationship?"). Participants responded using a Likert scale ranging from $1 = not\ at\ all$ to $5 = extremely$. The items in each subscale were averaged.

Independent Variables

To assess participants' *marital attitudes*, we asked three ADD Health Measure questions about marital desire, importance, and expectation: "*I would like to be married now.*" (desire), "*Being married is a very important goal for me.*" (importance), and "*I will be married one day.*" (expectation). Participants responded to items using a Likert scale ranging from $1 = strongly\ disagree$ to $5 = strongly\ agree$ (Carroll et al., 2007). To measure *skin tone perception,* participants responded to a single item (i.e., "How would you best describe your skin tone?") Responses ranged from $1 = Light$ to $5 = Dark$. This single item has been used before in previous research to assess participant's own ideas about their skin tone, as opposed to how others may judge them (Landor et al., 2013).

Covariates. Religiosity is linked to racial/ethnic minoritized status. For example, Black and African American individuals are the most religious racial/ethnic group in the United States (Chatters, Taylor, Bullard, & Jackson, 2008) and report higher rates of religious participation compared to other racial/ethnic groups (R. K. Brown, Taylor, & Chatters, 2013; Jones et al., 2011). Latino/a and Hispanic individuals are also a highly religious racial/ethnic group in that 83% identify as religious (Funk & Martinez, 2014). In addition to race/ethnicity, young adults' marital attitudes and relationship quality is often tied to religiosity (Ellison et al., 2010). Ellison and colleagues found that for Black and Hispanic individuals, higher religiosity was related to the importance of marriage being rated higher and stricter views on divorce not being an option. Thus, we wanted to control for religiosity in our examination of the influence of skin tone perception on the relationship between marital attitudes and relationship quality. To assess religiosity, participants responded to two questions. Responses for the first question about religious importance – "In general, how important are religious or spiritual beliefs in your day-to-day life?" – ranged from $1 = very\ important$ to $4 = not\ at\ all\ important$ ($M = 2.86$; scores were reverse coded so that higher numbers indicated more religious importance). The second question asked, "How often in the past month did you do the following: Attend church services?" Responses ranged from $1 = never$ to $5 = daily$ ($M = 1.70$).

Analysis

First, Levene's tests for equality of variances and independent samples one-tailed t-tests were conducted to see if any of the dependent, independent, and covariate variable means differed by gender or race/ethnicity. Because of the sample size we utilized one-tailed tests for more statistical power (see Hays, 1994).

Finally, hierarchical linear regressions (HLR) were conducted using the statistical software SPSS to predict various aspects of relationship quality (i.e., satisfaction, commitment, and intimacy) by marital attitudes (i.e., desire, importance, and expectation) and whether skin tone perception acted as a moderator. This method was used in order to control for covariates while testing the effects of each individual independent variable, as well as any interaction effects. Continuous independent variables were mean-centered prior to analysis to reduce multicollinearity, and interaction terms were computed (Aiken & West, 1991). Religiosity measures were used as controls. Study control variables were entered at Model 1, main effect variables (i.e., skin tone, marital desire, importance, and expectation) were entered at Model 2, and two-way interaction terms (skin tone × marital desire, skin tone × marital importance, and skin tone x marital expectation) were entered at Model 3.

RESULTS

Means, SDs, and correlations among the study variables (including race and gender) are presented in Table 1. Independent samples *t*-tests indicated that only religious importance means differed significantly by gender in that women indicated higher religious importance than men. For race/ethnicity, African American individuals indicated higher religious importance and rated marital desire higher than Latinx individuals (see Table 2). In performing HLR, we first entered religiosity as a covariate. We did not control for gender since the only variable that correlated with and differed by gender was religious importance which was being controlled for. Other researchers have also indicated the lack of associations among gender and many variables of interest examined in this study (see Guyll, Cutrona, Burzette, & Russell, 2010; Kogan et al., 2013; Lincoln et al., 2008 for examples). Religious importance differed by race/ethnicity as well, but again, was being controlled for. Results found in Tables 3–5 show that marital expectation were positively associated with relationship satisfaction ($\beta = 0.28$, $p < 0.05$), relationship commitment ($\beta = 0.44$, $p < 0.05$), and relationship expectation ($\beta = 0.32$, $p < 0.05$) respectively, even when controlling for religiosity. This means that higher expectations to marry one day were associated with higher levels of relationship quality in all three categories. The main effects for marital desire and importance were not significant, indicating no relationship between marital desire nor marital importance and relationship quality for these young adults.

Post-hoc simple slopes analyses were performed for interactions terms using methods described in Aiken and West (1991). Specifically, we examined the association between marital attitudes and relationship quality at high (1 Standard Deviation [*SD*] above) and low (1 *SD* below) levels of the moderator. Two significant interactions were found. The first significant interaction indicated that among these young adults, marital expectations were positively associated with relationship satisfaction and varied by skin tone ($\beta = -0.32$, $p < 0.05$). Among participants with lighter skin tones, higher endorsement of marital expectations was associated with higher levels of satisfaction in their relationships

Table 1. Correlation Matrix, Means, and Standard Deviations for Study Variables ($N = 57$).

Variable	1	2	3	4	5	6	7	8	9	10	11	Range	M	SD
1. Race/Ethnicity	—													
2. Gender	−0.20	—												
3. Religious Importance	−0.45**	0.27*	—									1–4	2.86	1.13
4. Religious Attendance	0.11	0.14	0.41**	—								1–4	1.70	0.91
5. Skin tone	−0.06	−0.02	−0.05	0.05	—							1–5	2.61	1.00
6. Marital Desire	−0.22	0.18	0.54**	0.45**	−0.22	—						1–5	2.05	1.27
7. Marital Importance	−0.01	0.15	0.60**	0.32*	−0.04	0.46**	—					1–5	3.86	1.38
8. Marital Expectation	0.01	−0.02	0.41**	0.21	0.03	0.38**	0.75**	—				1–5	4.32	0.86
9. Relationship Quality: Satisfaction	0.20	0.11	0.20	0.47**	0.09	0.25	0.27*	0.38**	—			1–5	4.19	0.53
10. Relationship Quality: Commitment	−0.07	0.08	0.22	0.26	0.20	0.11	0.23	0.38**	0.56**	—		1–5	4.43	0.75
11. Relationship Quality: Intimacy	0.02	−0.03	0.18	0.33*	0.17	0.12	0.13	0.29*	0.57**	0.61**	—	1–5	4.42	0.56

Note: Range of scores displayed is possible range, not observed range. *$p < 0.05$. **$p < 0.01$.

Table 2. Means and Standard Deviations for Study Variables by Gender and Race/Ethnicity ($N = 57$).

Variable	Gender, M (SD)		Race/Ethnicity, M (SD)	
	Male	Female	African American	Latinx
Religious importance	2.35 (1.22)*	3.05 (1.06)*	3.23 (0.96)***	2.23 (1.11)***
Religious attendance	1.50 (0.65)	1.79 (0.98)	1.62 (0.89)	1.82 (0.96)
Skin tone	2.64 (1.01)	2.60 (1.01)	2.68 (1.10)	2.55 (0.86)
Marital desire	1.64 (1.01)	2.17 (1.34)	2.29 (1.43)*	1.73 (0.94)*
Marital importance	3.50 (1.45)	3.98 (1.37)	3.85 (1.37)	3.82 (1.44)
Marital expectation	4.36 (0.75)	4.32 (0.91)	4.30 (0.92)	4.32 (0.78)
Relationship quality: satisfaction	4.10 (0.70)	4.23 (0.48)	4.10 (0.50)	4.32 (0.57)
Relationship quality: commitment	4.35 (0.69)	4.49 (0.76)	4.47 (0.80)	4.36 (0.67)
Relationship quality: intimacy	4.45 (0.59)	4.42 (0.56)	4.40 (0.56)	4.42 (0.60)

Notes: One-tailed *t*-tests were done to compare group means.
Significant differences between groups in each variable indicated by *$p < 0.05$ or ***$p < 0.001$.

Table 3. Regression Assessing Relationship Satisfaction and Marital Attitudes for African American and Latinx Young Adults ($N = 57$).

Variable	Model 1			Model 2			Model 3		
	B	*SE B*	*T*	*B*	*SE B*	*t*	*B*	*SE B*	*t*
Religious importance	0.006	0.064	0.090	−0.031	0.076	−0.402	−0.072	0.075	−0.961
Religious attendance	0.268***	0.080	3.368	0.260**	0.081	3.198	0.293***	0.080	3.665
Skin tone				0.030	0.067	0.453	0.085	0.066	1.292
Marital desire				−0.003	0.065	−0.052	−.018	0.062	−0.287
Marital importance				−0.064	0.078	−0.815	0.000	0.079	−0.006
Marital expectation				0.279*	0.113	2.464	0.230*	0.111	2.077
Skin tone × Marital desire							−0.012	0.058	−0.213
Skin tone × Marital importance							0.038	0.072	0.536
Skin tone × Marital expectation							−0.322*	0.140	−2.304
Intercept	3.718***	0.188	19.764	3.832***	0.246	15.607	3.901***	0.240	16.279
F	6.891			3.817			3.926		
df	2			6			9		
R^2 (Cox & Snell)	0.206			0.319			0.434		
Sig.	0.002			0.003			0.001		

Note: All independent variables were centered at their means.
*$p < 0.05$ ** $p < 0.01$ ***$p < 0.001$.

Table 4. Regression Assessing Relationship Commitment and Marital Attitudes for African American and Latinx Young Adults ($N = 57$).

Variable	Model 1			Model 2			Model 3		
	B	$SE\ B$	t	B	$SE\ B$	t	B	$SE\ B$	t
Religious importance	0.091	0.096	0.951	0.090	0.112	0.803	0.082	0.121	0.681
Religious attendance	0.159	0.120	1.323	0.163	0.120	1.354	0.168	0.129	1.305
Skin tone				0.131	0.099	1.321	0.151	0.106	1.424
Marital desire				−0.070	0.096	−0.729	−0.072	0.100	−0.723
Marital importance				−0.130	0.116	−1.127	−0.114	0.128	−0.895
Marital expectation				0.439*	0.167	2.629	0.431*	0.178	2.416
Skin tone × Marital desire							.014	0.093	0.152
Skin tone × Marital importance							−0.010	0.115	−0.085
Skin tone × Marital expectation							−0.110	0.225	−0.489
Intercept	3.903***	0.284	13.747	3.889***	0.362	10.739	3.908***	0.386	10.130
F	2.175			2.604			1.708		
df	2			6			9		
R^2 (Cox & Snell)	0.076			0.242			0.251		
Sig.	0.124			0.029			0.114		

Note: All independent variables were centered at their means.

*$p < 0.05$ ** $p < 0.01$ *** $p < 0.001$.

Table 5. Regression Assessing Relationship Intimacy and Marital Attitudes for African American and Latinx Young Adults ($N = 57$).

Variable	Model 1			Model 2			Model 3		
	β	SE β	t	β	SE β	t	β	SE β	t
Religious importance	0.023	0.071	0.319	0.051	0.085	0.597	-0.003	0.086	-0.039
Religious attendance	0.184*	0.089	2.051	0.190*	0.091	2.088	0.214*	0.091	2.353
Skin tone				0.085	0.075	1.132	0.076	0.075	1.008
Marital desire				-0.038	0.073	-0.528	-0.049	0.071	-0.691
Marital importance				-0.146	0.088	-1.672	-0.089	0.090	-0.986
Marital expectation				0.319*	0.127	2.523	0.241	0.126	1.908
Skin tone × Marital desire							-0.076	0.066	-1.157
Skin tone × Marital importance							0.206*	0.082	2.517
Skin tone × Marital expectation							-0.131	0.159	-0.823
Intercept	4.032***	0.211	19.081	3.934***	0.274	14.332	4.039***	0.274	14.765
F		2.872			2.475			2.587	
df		2			6			9	
R^2 (Cox & Snell)		0.098			0.233			0.336	
Sig.		0.065			0.036			0.017	

Note: All independent variables were centered at their means.
*$p < 0.05$ **$p < 0.01$ ***$p < 0.001$.

(*slope t* = 5.16, *SE* = 0.10, *p* < 0.001). For those with darker skin tones, the association between marital expectation and relationship satisfaction was not significant (*slope t* = −0.54, *SE* = 0.15, *p* = 0.30). Conversely, for those with low marital expectation, young adults with lighter skin tones had lower relationship satisfaction as compared to individuals with darker skin tones (see Fig. 1).

Secondly, a significant interaction was found between marital importance, skin tone, and relationship intimacy. Marriage as an important goal had a different association with intimacy depending on skin tone (*β* = 0.21, *p* < 0.05). Among participants with lighter skin tones, higher endorsement of marital importance was associated with lower levels of intimacy in their relationships (*slope t* = −2.79, *SE* = 0.10, *p* < 0.05). For those with darker skin tones, the association between marital importance and relationship satisfaction was not significant (*slope t* = 0.81, *SE* = 0.14, *p* = 0.22). Individuals with darker skin tones had relatively higher intimacy in their relationships than those with lighter skin tones regardless of the level of marital importance (see Fig. 2).

DISCUSSION

In exploring the main effects of martial attitudes (i.e., desire, importance, and expectation) on relationship quality, we found that only marital expectation or the expectation to be married one day was positively associated with all three factors of young adults' current relationship quality (i.e., satisfaction, commitment, and intimacy). Desire and importance were unrelated. These results partially confirm our hypotheses about the overall impact of martial attitudes on relationship quality. Martial Horizon Theory (Carroll et al., 2007, 2009) posits that young

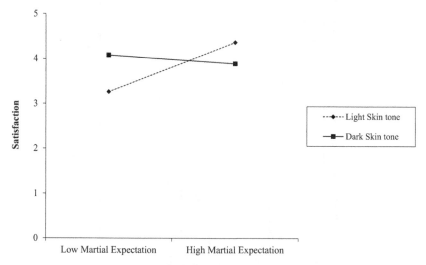

Fig. 1.   The Relationship Between Marital Expectation and Satisfaction by Skin Tone.

adults see marriage as something happening in the future. Considering current marriage trends and attitudes regarding the importance and expectation of marriage, we expected that the desire to be currently married would be less associated with relationship quality than would expectation and importance. According to our finding, only marital expectation was associated with relationship quality. Why would an explicit expectation to marry be more significant for these relationship variables than marital desire or marital importance? It could be that the desire to marry or having marriage as a goal is not as indicative of how one may be feeling about their current partners. These young adults who *know with certainty* that they *will be* married, perhaps feel more satisfied with, committed, and close to their partners than those who are a bit more uncertain of where their relationships are headed. Brown and Booth (1996) found that young and middle-aged cohabiting adults reported lower relationship quality than their married counterparts. However, these differences did not persist when the authors controlled for communication about marriage. When respondents were sure of their plans to marry their partners, both cohabitors and married individuals reported similar levels of relationship satisfaction. Again, asking about the level of certainty one feels about their relationship – the expectation that marriage will happen for them – perhaps is more telling of the quality of a relationship than other variables assessing desire or goals. The more certain someone is of the relationship, the better they feel about the relationship (see also Joel, MacDonald, & Page-Gould, 2017; Simpson, 1987).

We were unsure of how skin tone would moderate the relationship between martial attitudes and relationship quality, but two interesting interactions were found. The first indicated that skin tone perception interacted with marital expectation to predict current relationship satisfaction. Higher levels of marital expectation were associated with higher levels of satisfaction for individuals with lighter

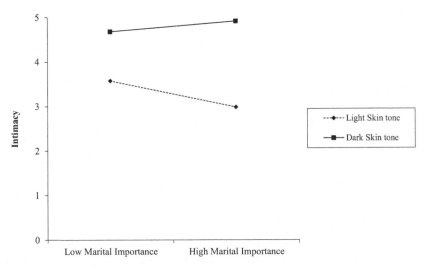

Fig. 2.   The Relationship Between Marital Importance and Intimacy by Skin Tone.

skin. This association did not exist for darker skin individuals. This could speak to the advantages and privileges that lighter skin individuals are aware of and given. Past research has shown that lighter skin individuals are often perceived as more attractive which affords these individuals more opportunities to meet eligible partners and enter into relationships with them (Bond & Cash, 1992; Robinson & Ward, 1995). If this greater likelihood of being in a relationship is usually matched with an increased expectation for marriage, those who know they are going to marry their partners may be more satisfied in their relationships than those who do not expect to marry their partners. Lighter skin young adults who believe they should be more desired, may not feel satisfied in relationships that they do not see resulting in marriage. Darker skin individuals, particularly women, may also be aware of this skin tone preference and feel that relationships may be less attainable for them, in turn reducing their expectations regarding their desirability (Landor, 2017; Landor & Halpern, 2016). Overall, if darker skin individuals have lower perceptions of themselves, they may be satisfied in relationships whether or not they expect to marry their partners. These perceptions of what young adult racial/ethnic minorities expect may mean that lighter skin individuals are more dissatisfied in relationships than darker skin individuals when they do not feel that they are going to marry the people they are in relationships with.

What may be happening with the interaction among marital importance, skin tone, and intimacy? Those with darker skin indicated that they had similar levels of intimacy regardless of marital importance. Again, if we consider the perceptions and expectations regarding marriage for racially/ethnically minoritized individuals, those with darker skin may feel that marriage is less attainable (Hamilton et al., 2009; Hunter, 2002, 2007) resulting in a very small pool of eligible partners (in terms of those who are desirable and desire a darker skin partner). Therefore, they may be more likely to feel closer to their partners, no matter their own marital preferences.

However, if lighter skin individuals feel they have more options, then that could result in a greater influence of their own marital attitudes on relationship quality. In fact, for lighter skin respondents, our findings suggest that when marriage is more of an important goal, they report less intimacy in their relationships. Endorsing marriage at a high rate and being more confident that marriage will likely happen may make those with larger dating pools feel less close with current partners. Research on "choice overload" indicates that often, the more choices we have, the more likely we are to be dissatisfied with the choice we make (especially if we feel that choice is reversable), whether deciding among different kinds of jams or potential mates (Chernev, Böckenholt, & Goodman, 2015; D'Angelo & Toma, 2017; Iyengar & Lepper, 2000; Scheibehenne, Greifeneder, & Todd, 2010). Lighter skin individuals who are aware of societal preferences, may also feel they have higher expectations of what they think they could and should get out of relationships; this is more likely to be higher than actual outcomes as compared to darker skin individuals. Moreover, this could translate to lower relationship closeness if one is thinking about what else might be out there, especially if marriage is an important goal (Cook, Cheshire, Rice, & Nakagawa, 2013; Ellis, Simpson, & Campbell, 2002; Kelly & Thibaut, 1978; Landor & Barr, 2018). If marriage is not a significant goal, then dating may be an acceptable relationship stage, relating to an increased likelihood of closeness and intimacy. Lighter skin racial/ethnic minorities may have more ability to judge and reflect on relationship quality based on their marital values. For darker skin young adults, marital attitudes may correlate less with relationship quality because of a perception of less choice or agency in mate choice (see Landor, 2017). There is high relationship quality despite marital attitudes.

Another issue to consider in differing marital preferences, expectations, behaviors, and outcomes among racial/ethnic groups are the historical and continued influence of racial discrimination faced by racially/ethnically minoritized individuals (Goldman, Westoff, & Hammerslough, 1984; Raley, Sweeney, & Wondra, 2015; Tucker & Taylor, 1989). Although marital rates are falling nationwide across groups, racially/ethnically minoritized individuals are more likely to be economically disadvantaged, a condition that is often cited as a barrier to marriage (Gibson-Davis, Edin, & McLanahan, 2005; Pew Research Center, 2017; Raley & Sweeney, 2007; Raley et al., 2015; Scott et al., 2009). Economic disparities are linked with other structural inequalities leading to smaller eligible mate pools, unequal treatment by the educational system, disproportionate incarceration, and deaths of ethnic/racial minorities. It is these structural inequalities that can contribute to perceptions that marriage may need to be delayed or may be unattainable (Raley & Sweeney, 2007; Tucker & Taylor, 1989). For African American young adults, in particular, harsh parenting, community crime, family instability, and discrimination were associated with distrustful views of relationships, and predicted future troubled romantic relationships and negative views of marriage (Simons, Simons, Lei, & Landor, 2012). Additionally, other factors may explain relationship disparities among racial/ethnic groups in the United States. For example, there is evidence for differing expectations regarding requirements for marriage (e.g., Black women may prefer to be sure of economic securities prior to marriage and as evidenced by their partners; see Bulcroft & Bulcroft, 1993). Given the sample was majority women, these differing expectations may be at work here.

Overall, our results indicate that psychosocial processes should be examined along with systemic forces to better understand these associations. Findings indicate protective and risk factors to relationship dynamics of young adults of color. These constructs certainly warrant further study in understanding the relationship among racially/ethnically minoritized young adults' marital attitudes, skin tone, and relationship quality in the larger societal and cultural contexts.

LIMITATIONS AND CONCLUSIONS

This study contributes to our understanding of how material attitudes, skin tone, and relationship quality relate to one another for racially/ethnically minoritized young adults, however, there remain important limitations worth noting. First, this study utilizes cross-sectional data. Without longitudinal study of the association between marital attitudes and relationship quality, directionality cannot be inferred. It could be that relationship quality influences a change in marital attitudes or another unknown variable influences both constructs. Second, this study included a small sample of young adults who reported being in a romantic relationship, including only one engaged person. Thus, we were unable to explore how these relationships differed based on level of commitment. It could be that among those who were in more committed relationships (e.g., engaged), marital desire, importance, and expectation would predict relationships quality. Third, African American and Latinx individuals have much diversity of skin tone, identity, culture, and experiences. Given the small samples size, we could not account for these differences in this study; the results and discussion are not meant to be generalizations about all members of these diverse groups, but to stimulate ideas around what could be influencing marital patterns and preferences. Additionally, we wanted to know about participants' own perceptions of their skin tone and cannot be sure that their perceptions match others' opinions. Still, we were able to speak to the participants own psychology processes (i.e., attitudes and skin tone perception) and the association with relationship quality. Next, our sampling strategy resulted in voluntary participation, as do most studies focused on human experiences. Participation was not required of all students at this university, and so those who felt comfortable doing a study centered around their racial/ethnic identities, health, and romantic experiences may be different from others who do did not respond to email recruitment efforts. Finally, our results are not generalizable to all young adults as the present study included college students. Research findings have indicated that college student samples differ from the general population. For example, college students exhibit more homogeneity, have higher cognitive skills, have less crystalized self-concepts and motivations, and less stable peer relationships (Henrich, Heine, & Norenzayan, 2010; Peterson, 2001; Peterson & Merunka, 2014). Factors such as motivations and peer relationship could have an influence on marital attitudes and relationship quality that is not yet understood. Research should examine whether the relationship between marital attitudes, skin tone, and relationship quality yield similar results among a non-college sample.

Despite the limitations, these results point to influence of marital expectations on relationship quality for young adults of color. In addition, findings highlight the importance of the awareness of colorism and beliefs regarding preferences for skin tone for young racial/ethnic minorities and their potential mates. Counselors and practitioners should have a better understanding of the interactions of these constructs when working with racially/ethnically minoritized individuals. Developers of relationship education programs may also be ignoring the unique relationship among marital attitudes, skin tone, and relationship quality, and should certainly take them into consideration when designing programs aimed members of this population.

NOTE

1. Latinx is a term used to describe individuals of Latin American descent. Latinx is a gender neutral and non-binary alternative to the terms Latino and Latina. Throughout the text, when discussing others' research, we describe race/ethnicity as those authors did

(e.g., using Hispanic, Latino/a, and/or Latinx); however, for the description of the current sample, we use the term Latinx.

ACKNOWLEDGMENTS

Work on this paper was supported, in part, by a University of Missouri Research Council Grant URC-15-073. We gratefully acknowledge graduate and undergraduate research assistants' involvement in the project, and the participating young adults. Correspondence concerning this article should be addressed to Sarah Mitchell.

REFERENCES

Aiken, L. S., West, S. G., & Reno, R. R. (1991). *Multiple regression: Testing and interpreting interactions.* Sage.

Amato, P. R., & Rogers, S. J. (1999). Do attitudes toward divorce affect marital quality? *Journal of Family Issues, 20,* 69–86.

Banks, T. L. (2000). Colorism: A darker shade of pale. *ULCA Law Review, 47,* 1705–1746.

Blackman, L., Clayton, O., Glenn, N., Malone-Colon, L., & Roberts, A. (2005). *The consequences of marriage for African Americans: A comprehensive literature review.* New York, NY: Institute for American Values.

Bond, S., & Cash, T. F. (1992). Black beauty: Skin color and body images among African-American college women. *Journal of Applied Social Psychology, 22,* 874–888.

Broman, C. L. (2005). Marital quality in Black and White marriages. *Journal of Family Issues, 26,* 431–441.

Brown, S. L. (2000). Union transitions among cohabitors: The significance of relationship assessments and expectations. *Journal of Marriage and Family, 62,* 833–846.

Brown, S. L. (2004). Moving from cohabitation to marriage: Effects on relationship quality. *Social Science Research, 33,* 1–19.

Brown, S. L., & Booth, A. (1996). Cohabitation versus marriage: A comparison of relationship quality. *Journal of Marriage and the Family,* 668–678.

Brown, S. L., Manning, W. D., & Payne, K. K. (2017). Relationship quality among cohabiting versus married couples. *Journal of Family Issues, 38,* 1730–1753.

Brown, R. K., Taylor, R. J., & Chatters, L. M. (2013). Religious non-involvement among African Americans, black Caribbeans and non-Hispanic whites: Findings from the national survey of American life. *Review of Religious Research, 55*(3), 435–457.

Brown, S. L., Van Hook, J., & Glick, J. E. (2008). Generational differences in cohabitation and marriage in the US. *Population Research and Policy Review, 27*(5), 531–550.

Bryant, E. V. (2001). Blue veins and Black bigotry: Colorism as moral evil in Charles Chesnutt's "A Matter of Principle".*American Literary Realism, 34,* 73–80.

Bulcroft, R. A., & Bulcroft, K. A. (1993). Race differences in attitudinal and motivational factors in the decision to marry. *Journal of Marriage and Family, 55,* 338–355.

Bumpass, L. L., & Lu, H. (2000). Trends in cohabitation and implications for children's family contexts in the United States. *Population Studies, 54,* 29–41.

Campos, B., Perez, O. F. R., & Guardino, C. (2016). Familism: A cultural value with implications for romantic relationship quality in US Latinos. *Journal of Social and Personal Relationships, 33*(1), 81–100.

Carroll, J. S., Badger, S. Willoughby, B., Nelson, L. J., Madsen, S. D., & Barry, C. (2009). Ready or not? Criteria for marriage readiness among emerging adults. *Journal of Adolescent Research, 24,* 349–375.

Carroll, J. S., Willoughby, B., Badger, S., Nelson, L. J., Barry, C., & Madsen, S. D. (2007). So close, yet so far away: The impact of varying marital horizons on emerging adulthood. *Journal of Adolescent Research, 22*, 219–247.

Chatters, L. M., Taylor, R. J., Bullard, K. M., & Jackson, J. S. (2008). Spirituality and subjective religiosity among African Americans, Caribbean Blacks, and Non-Hispanic Whites. *Journal for the Scientific Study of Religion, 47*(4), 725–737.

Cherlin, A. J. (2004). The deinstitutionalization of American marriage. *Journal of Marriage and Family, 66*, 848–861.

Chernev, A., Böckenholt, U., & Goodman, J. (2015). Choice overload: A conceptual review and meta-analysis. *Journal of Consumer Psychology, 25*, 333–358.

Cook, K. S., Cheshire, C., Rice, E. R., & Nakagawa, S. (2013). Social exchange theory. In *Handbook of Social Psychology* (pp. 61–88). Dordrecht: Springer.

Crissey, S. R. (2005). Race/ethnic differences in the marital expectations of adolescents: The role of romantic relationships. *Journal of Marriage and Family, 67*, 697–709.

D'Angelo, J. D., & Toma, C. L. (2017). There are plenty of fish in the sea: The effects of choice overload and reversibility on online daters' satisfaction with selected partners. *Media Psychology, 20*, 1–27.

Davenport, M. A., Landor, A. M., Zeiders, K. H., Sarsar, E. D., & Flores, M. (2021). Within - person associations between racial microaggressions and sleep among African American and Latinx young adults. *Journal of Sleep Research, 30*(4), e13226.

Dixon, A. R., & Telles, E. E. (2017). Skin color and colorism: Global research, concepts, and measurement. *Annual Review of Sociology, 43*, 405–424.

Doyle, D. M., & Molix, L. (2014a). How does stigma spoil relationships? Evidence that perceived discrimination harms romantic relationship quality through impaired self-image. *Journal of Applied Social Psychology, 44*(9), 600–610.

Doyle, D. M., & Molix, L. (2014b). Love on the margins: The effects of social stigma and relationship length on romantic relationship quality. *Social Psychological and Personality Science, 5*(1), 102–110.

Edwards, K., Carter-Tellison, K., & Herring, C. (2004). For richer, for poorer, whether dark or light: Skin tone, marital status, and spouse's earnings. In C. Herring, V. M. Keith, & H. D. Horton (Eds.), *Skin deep: How race and complexion matter in the "color-blind" era* (pp. 65–81). Urbana: University of Illinois Press.

Ellis, B. J., Simpson, J. A., & Campbell, L. (2002). Trait-specific dependence in romantic relationships. *Journal of Personality, 70*, 611–659.

Ellison, C. G., Burdette, A. M., & Bradford Wilcox, W. (2010). The couple that prays together: Race and ethnicity, religion, and relationship quality among working-age adults. *Journal of Marriage and Family, 72*, 963–975.

Erol, U. Ğ. U. R. (2016). Marital attitudes as a mediator on the relationship between respect toward partner and subjective happiness. *Journal of Family Counseling and Education, 1*(1), 25–30.

Fears, L. M. (1998). Colorism of black women in news editorial photos. *The Western Journal of Black Studies, 22*, 30.

Fletcher, G. J., Simpson, J. A., & Thomas, G. (2000). The measurement of perceived relationship quality components: A confirmatory factor analytic approach. *Personality and Social Psychology Bulletin, 26*, 340–354.

Frisby, C. M. (2006). "Shades of beauty": Examining the relationship of skin color to perceptions of physical attractiveness. *Facial Plastic Surgery, 22*, 175–179.

Frost, P. (1990). Fair women, dark men: The forgotten roots of colour prejudice. *History of European Ideas, 12*, 669–679.

Funk, C., & Martinez, J. (2014, May 7). *Fewer Hispanics are Catholic, so how can more Catholics be Hispanic*. Washington, DC: Pew Research Center.

Gassanov, M. A., Nicholson, L. M., & Koch-Turner, A. (2008). Expectations to marry among American youth: The effects of unwed fertility, economic activity, and cohabitation. *Youth & Society, 40*, 265–288.

Gibson-Davis, C. M., Edin, K., & McLanahan, S. (2005). High Hopes but even higher expectations: The retreat from marriage among low-income couples. *Journal of Marriage and Family, 67*, 1301–1312.

Golden, M. (2007). *Don't play in the sun: One woman's journey through the color complex.* New York, NY: Doubleday.

Goldman, N., Westoff, C. E., & Hammerslough, C. (1984). Demography of the marriage market in the United States. *Population Index, 50,* 5–26.

Goldstein, J., & Kenney, C. (2001). Marriage delayed or marriage forgone? New cohort forecasts of first marriage for U.S. women. *American Sociological Review,66,* 506–519.

Guyll, M., Cutrona, C., Burzette, R., & Russell, D. (2010). Hostility, relationship quality, and health among African American couples. *Journal of Consulting and Clinical Psychology, 78*(5), 646–654.

Hamilton, D., Goldsmith, A. H., & Darity, W., Jr. (2009). Shedding "light" on marriage: The influence of skin shade on marriage for black females. *Journal of Economic Behavior and Organization, 72,* 30–50.

Hays, W. L. (1994). *Statistics* (5th ed.). Fort Worth, TX: Harcourt Brace College Publishers.

Henrich, J., Heine, S. J., & Norenzayan, A. (2010). The weirdest people in the world? *Behavioral and Brain Sciences, 33,* 61–83.

Hill, M. E. (2000). Color differences in the socioeconomic status of African American men: Results of a longitudinal study. *Social Forces, 78,* 1437–1460.

Hill, M. E. (2002). Skin color and the perception of attractiveness among African Americans: Does gender make a difference? *Social Psychology Quarterly, 65,* 77–91.

Hughes, M., & Hertel, B. R. (1990). The significance of color remains: A study of life chances, mate selection, and ethnic consciousness among Black Americans. *Social Forces, 68,* 1105–1120.

Hunter, M. L. (1998). Colorstruck: Skin color stratification in the lives of African American women. *Sociological Inquiry, 68,* 517–535.

Hunter, M. L. (2002). "If You're Light You're Alright": Light skin color as social capital for women of color. *Gender & Society, 16,* 175–193.

Hunter, M. L. (2007). The persistent problem of colorism: Skin tone, status, and inequality. *Sociology Compass, 1,* 237–254.

Hunter, M. L. (2008). The cost of color: What we pay for being black and brown. In R. E. Hall (Ed.), *Racism in the 21st century: An empirical analysis of skin color* (pp. 63–76). New York: Springer.

Iyengar, S. S., & Lepper, M. R. (2000). When choice is demotivating: Can one desire too much of a good thing? *Journal of Personality and Social Psychology, 79,* 995–1006.

Jha, S., & Adelman, M. (2009). Looking for love in all the white places: A study of skin color preferences on Indian matrimonial and mate-seeking websites. *Studies in South Asian Film & Media, 1,* 65–83.

Joel, S., MacDonald, G., & Page-Gould, E. (2017). Wanting to stay and wanting to go: Unpacking the content and structure of relationship stay/leave decision processes. *Social Psychological and Personality Science, 9*(6), 631–644.

Jones, J. M., Peter, J. R. S., Fernandes, S. J., Herrenkohl, T. I., Kosterman, R., & Hawkins, J. D. (2011). Ethnic and gender variation in religious involvement: Patterns of expression in young adulthood. *Review of Religious Research, 53,* 207–225.

Keith, V. M., & Herring, C. (1991). Skin tone and stratification in the Black community. *American Journal of Sociology, 97,* 760–778.

Keith, V. M., Lincoln, K. D., Taylor, R. J., & Jackson, J. S. (2010). Discriminatory experiences and depressive symptoms among African American women: Do skin tone and mastery matter? *Sex Roles, 62,* 48–59.

Kelley, H. H., & Thibaut, J. W. (1978). *Interpersonal relations: A theory of interdependence.* New York, NY: Wiley.

Kerr, A. E. (2005). The paper bag principle: Of the myth and the motion of colorism. *Journal of American Folklore, 118,* 271–289.

Kogan, S. M., Lei, M. K., Grange, C. R., Simons, R. L., Brody, G. H., Gibbons, F. X., & Chen, Y. F. (2013). The contribution of community and family contexts to African American young adults' romantic relationship health: A prospective analysis. *Journal of Youth and Adolescence, 42*(6), 878–890.

Krieger, N., Sidney, S., & Coakley, E. (1998). Racial discrimination and skin color in the CARDIA study: Implications for public health research. *American Journal of Public Health, 88,* 1308–1313.

Landale, N. S., & Oropesa, R. S. (2007). Hispanic families: Stability and change. *Annu. Rev. Sociol., 33,* 381–405.

Landor, A. M. (2017). Beyond Black and White but still in color: Examining skin tone and marriage attitudes and outcomes among African American young adults. In L. L. Martin, H. D. Horton, C. Herring, V. M. Keith, & M. Thomas (Eds.), *Color struck: How race and complexion matter in the "color-blind" era* (pp. 37–53). Rotterdam: Sense Publishing.

Landor, A. M., & Barr, A. (2018). Politics of respectability, colorism, and the terms of social exchange in family research. *Journal of Family Theory & Review, 10*(2), 330–347.

Landor, A. M., & Halpern, C. T. (2016). The enduring significance of skin tone: Linking skin tone, attitudes toward marriage and cohabitation, and sexual behavior. *Journal of Youth and Adolescence, 45,* 986–1002.

Landor, A. M., & McNeil Smith, S. (2019). Skin-tone trauma: Historical and contemporary influences on the health and interpersonal outcomes of African Americans. *Perspectives on Psychological Science, 14*(5), 797–815.

Landor, A. M., Simons, L. G., Simons, R. L., Brody, G. H., Bryant, C. M., Gibbons, F. X., … Melby, J. N. (2013). Exploring the impact of skin tone on family dynamics and race-related outcomes. *Journal of Family Psychology, 27,* 817–826.

Lincoln, K. D., Taylor, R. J., & Jackson, J. S. (2008). Romantic relationships among unmarried African Americans and Caribbean Blacks: Findings from the National Survey of American Life. *Family Relations, 57*(2), 254–266.

Lundberg, S., & Pollak, R. A. (2013). Cohabitation and the uneven retreat from marriage in the United States, 1950–2010. In L. P. Boustan, C. Frydman, & R. A. Margo (Eds.), *Human capital in history: The American record* (pp. 241–272). Chicago: University of Chicago Press.

Manning, W. D., Longmore, M. A., & Giordano, P. C. (2007). The changing institution of marriage: Adolescents' expectations to cohabit and to marry. *Journal of Marriage and Family, 69,* 559–575.

Martin, S. P., Astone, N. M., & Peters, H. E. (2014). *Fewer marriages, more divergence: Marriage projections for Millennials to age 40.* The Urban Institute.

McLoyd, V. C., Cauce, A. M., Takeuchi, D., & Wilson, L. (2000). Marital processes and parental socialization in families of color: A decade review of research. *Journal of Marriage and Family, 62,* 1070–1093.

McNeil Smith, S., & Landor, A. M. (2018). Toward a better understanding of African American families: Development of the sociocultural family stress model. *Journal of Family Theory & Review, 10*(2), 434–450.

Monk, E. P., Jr. (2014). Skin tone stratification among Black Americans, 2001–2003. *Social Forces, 92*(4), 1313–1337.

Monk, E. P., Jr. (2015). The cost of color: Skin color, discrimination, and health among African Americans. *American Journal of Sociology, 121*(2), 396–444.

Montalvo, F. F. (2005). Surviving race: Skin color and the socialization and acculturation of Latinas. *Journal of Ethnic and Cultural Diversity in Social Work, 13,* 25–43.

Peterson, R. A. (2001). On the use of college students in social science research: Insights from a second-order meta-analysis. *Journal of Consumer Research, 28,* 450–461.

Peterson, R. A., & Merunka, D. R. (2014). Convenience samples of college students and research reproducibility. *Journal of Business Research, 67,* 1035–1041.

Pew Research Center. (2017, September). *As U.S. marriage rate hovers at 50%, education gap in marital status widens.* http://www.pewresearch.org/fact-tank/2017/09/14/as-u-s-marriage-rate-hovers-at-50-education-gap-in-marital-status-widens/

Pew Research Center. (2019, November). *Marriage and cohabitation in the U.S.* https://www.pewresearch.org/social-trends/2019/11/06/marriage-and-cohabitation-in-the-u-s/

Phillips, J. A., & Sweeney, M. M. (2006). Can differential exposure to risk factors explain recent racial and ethnic variation in marital disruption? *Social Science Research, 35,* 409–434.

Raley, R. K., & Sweeney, M. M. (2007). What explains race and ethnic variation in cohabitation, marriage, divorce, and nonmarital fertility? *California Center for Population Research, 2007,* 1–30. https://www.academia.edu/download/51077213/What_Explains_Race_and_Ethnic_Variation_20161227-16252-c3ag35.pdf

Raley, R. K., Sweeney, M. M., & Wondra, D. (2015). The growing racial and ethnic divide in U.S. marriage patterns. *The Future of Children, 25,* 89–109.

Riggio, H. R., & Fite, J. E. (2006). Attitudes toward divorce: Embeddedness and outcomes in personal relationships. *Journal of Applied Social Psychology ,36*, 2935–2962.

Riggio, H. R., & Weiser, D. A. (2008). Attitudes toward marriage: Embeddedness and outcomes in personal relationships. *Personal Relationships, 15*, 123–140.

Robinson, T. L., & Ward, J. V. (1995). African American adolescents and skin color. *Journal of Black Psychology, 21*, 256–274.

Scheibehenne, B., Greifeneder, R., & Todd, P. M. (2010). Can there ever be too many options? A meta-analytic review of choice overload. *Journal of Consumer Research, 37*, 409–425.

Scott, M. E., Schelar, E., Manlove, J., & Cui, C. (2009). Young adult attitudes about relationships and marriage: Times may have changed, but expectations remain high. *Child Trends, 30*, 1–8.

Simons, R. L., Simons, L. G., Lei, M. K., & Landor, A. M. (2012). Relational schemas, hostile romantic relationships, and beliefs about marriage among young African American adults. *Journal of Social and Personal Relationships, 29*, 77–101.

Simpson, J. A. (1987). The dissolution of romantic relationships: Factors involved in relationship stability and emotional distress. *Journal of Personality and Social Psychology, 53*, 683–692.

Stanley, S. M., Rhoades, G. K., & Markman, H. J. (2006). Sliding versus deciding: Inertia and the premarital cohabitation effect. *Family Relations, 55*, 499–509.

Stepanova, E. V., & Strube, M. J. (2012). The role of skin color and facial physiognomy in racial categorization: Moderation by implicit racial attitudes. *Journal of Experimental Social Psychology, 48*, 867–878.

Strutton, D., & Lumpkin, J. R. (1993). Stereotypes of Black in-group attractiveness in advertising: On possible psychological effects. *Psychological Reports, 73*, 507–511.

Thompson, M. S., & Keith, V. M. (2001). The blacker the berry: Gender, skin tone, self-esteem, and self-efficacy. *Gender & Society, 15*, 336–357.

Tucker, M. B., & Taylor, R. J. (1989). Demographic correlates of relationship status among Black Americans. *Journal of Marriage and the Family, 51*, 655–665.

Uzogara, E. E., & Jackson, J. S. (2016). Perceived skin tone discrimination across contexts: African American women's reports. *Race and Social Problems, 8*, 147–159.

Uzogara, E. E., Lee, H., Abdou, C. M., & Jackson, J. S. (2014). A comparison of skin tone discrimination among African American men: 1995 and 2003. *Psychology of Men and Masculinity, 15*, 201–212.

Wilcox, W. B., & Wolfinger, N. H. (2008). Living and loving "decent": Religion and relationship quality among urban parents. *Social Science Research, 37*(3), 828–843.

Wilder, J. (2010). Revisiting "color names and color notions": A contemporary examination of the language and attitudes of skin color among young Black women. *Journal of Black Studies, 41*, 184–206.

Wilder, J., & Cain, C. (2011). Teaching and learning color consciousness in Black families: Exploring family processes and women's experiences with colorism. *Journal of Family Issues, 32*, 577–604.

CHAPTER 2

BREAKING UP IS HARD TO DO: INVESTIGATING BREAKUP DISTRESS AND SEXUAL REGRET IN UNDERGRADUATES' CASUAL AND COMMITTED SEXUAL RELATIONSHIPS

Siri Wilder, Christina L. Scott and Micaela A. Chavarin

ABSTRACT

For many emerging adults, committed romantic relationships are perceived as offering the ideal context for sexual exploration and companionship. However, these relationships are often short-term and breakups between committed partners can be emotionally intense and create a significant amount of distress. While casual sex relationships appear to be an increasingly popular alternative, providing many of the same benefits of committed relationships without the emotional involvement, they are also consistently associated with sexual regret. Previous research indicates that both emotional reactions are reported at higher levels by women, but the extent to which breakup distress and sexual regret differ by relationship type remains unclear. The current study examined differences in breakup distress and sexual regret as a function of sex and type of sexual relationship (committed vs casual) among a sample of 230 undergraduate college students. As expected, women reported more breakup distress and sexual regret as compared to men, and men and women in committed

Conjugal Trajectories: Relationship Beginnings, Change, and Dissolutions
Contemporary Perspectives in Family Research, Volume 22, 25–40
Copyright © 2023 by Emerald Publishing Limited
All rights of reproduction in any form reserved
ISSN: 1530-3535/doi:10.1108/S1530-353520230000022002

relationships reported more breakup distress than those in casual relationships. Contrary to previous findings, there was no significant difference in sexual regret between committed and casual relationships, and this was consistent for both men and women. In addition, participants reported relatively low levels of both breakup distress and sexual regret overall. The results suggest that, in general, breakups may not pose a severe emotional threat to young adults, who seem to be confident in their sexual decision making regardless of relationship type.

Keywords: Breakups; casual sex; gender; sex partners; romantic relationships; sexual regret

By the time they reach emerging adulthood (18–24), 95% of individuals will have had at least one partnered sexual experience (Copen, Chandra, & Febo-Vazquez, 2016), most commonly in the context of a dating relationship (Reissing, Andruff, & Wentland, 2012). For many young adults, the transition to college coincides with the formation of their first adult sexual relationships (Schwartz, 2016). The majority of male and female college students report a preference for traditional dating relationships and identify many of the same benefits, including having someone to confide in and depend on, feeling loved, and having a healthy relationship (Bradshaw, Kahn, & Saville, 2010). However, with generational changes in the acceptance of premarital sex (Clarke, 2018) and exposure to television, film, advertising, and social media portrayals of "the college experience" (Hanks, 2019), a growing number of college students are turning to casual sex relationships to explore their sexual options (Zhang, Freeman, & McNeese, 2020). Although both committed and casual sexual relationships tend to be relatively unstable and short-term among emerging adults, there is limited research examining how emotional reactions to the termination of both types of relationships differ.

COMMITTED SEXUAL RELATIONSHIPS

When asked about what type of relationship they would like to be in, 70% of Snider's (2018) participants responded that they would prefer a romantic or dating relationship, and 68% of Kuperberg and Padgett's (2016) sample wished that they had more opportunities to find a long-term relationship partner on campus. Evidence suggests that emerging adults may be idealizing romantic relationships, in part, due to media portrayals. When asked about the influence of media on adolescent romantic relationships, both high school and college students noted that mainstream media emphasizes the importance of being in a romantic relationship and creates unrealistic expectations about living "happily ever after" (Vaterlaus, Tulane, Porter, & Beckert, 2018). Unmet expectations for romantic relationships, in turn, are related to relationship dissatisfaction (Vannier & O'Sullivan, 2018), and in fact the romantic relationships of emerging adults are often short-term and unstable. Vennum and Fincham (2011) found that, over the course of

14 weeks, 41% of their college student sample had broken up with their romantic partner. This finding was replicated almost exactly a few years later; among over one thousand college students who began the semester with a romantic partner, 42% ended the semester having ended their committed relationship (Vennum, Monk, Pasley, & Fincham, 2017).

Previous research suggests that, regardless of the circumstances, romantic relationship breakups are often highly emotionally impactful, leaving ex-partners with overwhelming feelings of betrayal, grief, and depression (Field, 2011). When infidelity is involved, these emotions can be amplified (Walsh, Millar, & Westfall, 2019). These breakups have even been implicated in the development of somatic symptoms and reduced immune function (Chandra & Parija, 2021; Field, 2017), substance abuse, and mental health problems (Chandra & Parija, 2021). Breakup distress has been conceptualized and measured as a form of grief, which has negative impacts on multiple life domains, including academic performance (Field, 2011). Notably, these effects appear to be stronger for women than men. On average, women report more breakup distress (Field, Diego, Pelaez, Deeds, & Delgado, 2009), and Simon and Barrett (2010) found that the association between a recent breakup and depression was stronger for women. They suggested that this may be due to the relative influence of romantic relationships on women's identities and self-worth, as well as persisting societal inequalities that render women more dependent on these relationships as compared to men (Simon & Barrett, 2010).

For current Generation Z college students (those born after 1996; Dimock, 2019), social media may complicate the already difficult breakup experience due to pressure to disclose the breakup publicly, combined with their continued observation of other people's happy relationships displayed online. Over 90% of 18- to 29-year-olds in a national survey of US adults reported that they "often" or "sometimes" saw posts about other people's romantic relationships while scrolling through social media, and nearly half reported that they had posted about their own relationships (Vogels & Anderson, 2020). For Generation Z college students, viewing these social media posts "aimed at displaying happy relationships to a wide audience" (Goldberg, Yeshua-Katz, & Marciano, 2022, p. 1844) will most likely coincide with managing the dissolution of their own relationship as played out via social media, including deleting online references to their ex-partner (Goldberg et al., 2022), changing their online relationship status, and announcing their breakup online (Haimson, Andalibi, De Choudhury, & Hayes, 2018).

CASUAL SEXUAL RELATIONSHIPS

To avoid the emotional stress and "messy break-up" in public postings on social media that often come with the end of a romantic relationship, many emerging adults are turning to casual sex relationships (Zhang et al., 2020). Casual sex relationships are generally defined by young adults based on what they *do not* involve, namely emotional attachment, commitment, and love (Banker, Kaestle, & Allen, 2010) – without having to give up the "college experience." In contrast to the distress experienced as a result of a romantic relationship breakup, emotional responses to casual sex relationships can be positive (seen as providing a self-esteem boost, companionship, and sexual learning experiences) or negative (causing hurt feelings, awkwardness, and disappointment), although some evidence suggests that positive reactions are more common (Fielder & Carey, 2010; Owen & Fincham, 2011; Rodrigue & Fernet, 2016). For many, casual sex relationships alleviate feelings of depression and loneliness (Owen, Fincham, & Moore, 2011), however for some they may contribute to these negative emotions (Grello, Welsh, & Harper, 2006). In addition, it appears that much of the negative reactions to casual sex relationships relate to situational factors, such as condom use (Owen & Fincham, 2011), or the fear of social stigma (McHugh, Pearlson, & Poet, 2012). The expected absence of a "relationship status" and intentional secrecy associated with casual sex relationships (Rodrigue & Fernet, 2016) allow ex-partners to avoid publicly addressing the end of their sexual relationship.

However, casual sex relationships come with their own risks. Sexual regret (defined as feelings of regret for having had sex; Kennair, Bendixen, & Buss, 2016) has appeared frequently in the literature as a potential outcome of casual sex, and is itself associated with anxiety, depression, and low self-esteem (McKeen, Anderson, & Mitchell, 2022; Napper, Montes, Kenney, & LaBrie, 2016). Sexual regret is especially prevalent among women (Eshbaugh & Gute, 2008; Kennair, Grøntvedt, & Bendixen, 2021), which may be related to the continued existence of the sexual double standard (Endendijk, van Baar, & Deković, 2020). In McKeen et al.'s (2022) exploration of emotional responses to hookup relationships, women reported significantly more negative reactions to hookups than men, including fear of negative social judgment. This fear does not appear to be unfounded; Marks, Young, and Zaikman (2019) found that, even among friends, women were evaluated more negatively as their number of sexual partners increases, whereas there was no such effect found for men.

THE CURRENT STUDY

Whether casual or committed, emerging adults have a wide range of emotional reactions to the end of their sexual relationships. However, it remains to be seen whether these responses are significantly different across both types of relationships. In addition, there has been little investigation regarding the prevalence and intensity of sexual regret following sexual activity within a romantic relationship. Oswalt, Cameron, and Koob (2005) found that almost three quarters of their student sample had experienced sexual regret at some point, but it is unclear whether previously observed sex differences in this emotion persist when comparing by type of sexual relationship (i.e., committed or casual). This lack of clarity is notable, given that it is likely that many emerging adults in Generation Z are choosing what types of sexual relationships to engage in based on their social and entertainment media observations, which may provide incomplete information and unrealistic expectations regarding the pros and cons of these relationships.

The primary aims of the current study are to examine differences in (1) breakup distress and (2) sexual regret, as a function of sex and type of sexual relationship. Our hypotheses are as follows:

HYPOTHESES FOR BREAKUP DISTRESS

H1. Consistent with Field et al.'s (2009) findings, women will report higher levels of breakup distress than men.

H2: Participants whose most recent relationship was committed will report higher levels of breakup distress than those whose most recent relationship was casual.

H3. No interaction effect is anticipated; both men and women will report higher levels of breakup distress in committed relationships as compared to casual sex relationships.

HYPOTHESES FOR SEXUAL REGRET

H4: Consistent with Bendixen, Asao, Wyckoff, Buss, and Kennair's (2017) findings, women will report higher levels of sexual regret than men.

H5: Participants who recently ended a casual sex relationship will report higher levels of sexual regret than those who recently ended a committed relationship.

H6. An interaction effect is hypothesized; women who were in casual sex relationships will report higher levels of sexual regret than women who were in committed relationships, while there will be no difference between the men in either type of relationship.

METHOD

Participants

Data collection concluded with a total of 230 participants who were undergraduates at a small liberal arts college on the West Coast of the United States.[1] Participants were drawn from a convenience sample in primarily lower-level psychology classes. Although all participants had the opportunity to participate for research credit, the sample was reduced to 193 after evaluating that respondents met the following criteria: (1) they had previously engaged in sexual activity, (2) they had previously experienced a breakup, (3) they reported their sex, and (4) they reported the nature of their last sexual relationship. The final sample included an even distribution of men and women (97 men and 96 women), the majority of whom identified as heterosexual (87%). The most commonly reported ethnicities were White (39.1%) and Hispanic (31.1%); additional sample demographic information can be found in Table 1. Participants ranged in age from

Table 1. Sample Demographic Information.

Sex	50.3% Male
	49.7% Female
Sexual Orientation	87% Heterosexual
	4.7% Homosexual
	8.3% Other
Ethnicity	39.1% White
	31.3% Hispanic
	15.1% Multiracial
	8.3% Asian/Pacific Islander
	5.2% Black
	0.5% Native American/Alaska Native
	0.5% Other
Age	95.9% 18–22
	4.1% 22–26
Year in School	21.3% Freshmen
	23.9% Sophomore
	29.3% Junior
	25.5% Senior
Age of First Oral Sex	Men: 16.3 (1.5), Women: 16.6 (1.9)
Age of First Penetrative Sex	Men: 16.8 (1.5), Women: 16.8 (3.0)
Total Number of Committed Relationships	Men: 2.5 (1.4), Women: 2.6 (1.8)
Total Number of Casual Sex Relationships	Men: 7.4 (8.1), Women: 3.7 (4.1)
Type of Last Relationship	67.7% Committed (60 Men, 65 Women)
	32.3% Casual (37 Men, 31 Women)

Note: values in parentheses denote the standard deviation, unless otherwise noted.

18 to 26 ($M = 19.9$, $SD = 1.5$), and more than half (67.7%) reported that their last relationship was romantic and committed in nature.

Procedure

The study was advertised in classrooms during class meetings, and interested students signed up for scheduled time slots in assigned spaces. Upon arriving for their scheduled time slot, students were asked to read a consent form that provided an overview of the study. Those who consented to participate in the study and signed the consent form were then provided the paper and pencil survey, which took approximately 20–25 minutes to complete. After completing the survey, students were provided with a debriefing form and were given research credit for their participation. The study was approved by the college's Institutional Review Board and participation was anonymous; consent forms were stored separately from the surveys and participants' names were never associated with their survey data.

Materials and Measures

The survey first asked participants to report on a variety of demographic characteristics (e.g., sex, sexual orientation, age), in addition to several questions about their sexual history (including their previous engagement in sexual behaviors and relationships). The rest of the survey comprised a series of measures that participants were asked to respond to with their most recently ended relationship in mind.

Breakup Distress

Participants were asked to respond to the 16-item Breakup Distress Scale (Cronbach's $\alpha = 0.94$; Field et al., 2009) regarding how they felt during the two weeks following the termination of their most recently ended sexual relationship. The scale assesses the extent of emotional distress felt following a relationship breakup; higher scores indicated greater distress. For the purposes of this study, all items were modified to specifically address the end of a sexual relationship (e.g., "I could not accept that the sexual relationship had ended," "Immediately following the end of the sexual relationship, I felt distressed about the way the relationship ended," "After the end of the sexual relationship, I went out of my way to avoid this person"). Total possible scores ranged from 6 to 96.

Sexual Regret

Participants responded to a modified 8-item version of the Emotional Sexual Regret subscale of the Sexual Regret Scale (Cronbach's $\alpha = 0.91$; Marelich, Wright, Ziegler, & Henry, 2016). Items included, "After the sexual relationship ended, I had regrets about having sex with that individual," "I felt confident in my decision to have sex with my partner" (reverse-scored), and "I was uncomfortable thinking about that sexual relationship." There was a total possible score range of 8–48; higher scores indicated more feelings of regret for engaging in the sexual relationship.

Data Analysis

A multivariate analysis of variance was performed using SPSS (version 28) to test the hypotheses. The dependent variables comprised breakup distress and sexual regret scores, and sex (female vs male) and the nature of the participant's most recently ended sexual relationship (committed vs casual) were entered as independent variables.

RESULTS

The sample reported a relatively modest level of breakup distress and sexual regret on average, and there was no significant correlation between the dependent variables (see Table 2). Cronbach's alphas were consistent for both scales.

Breakup Distress

There were statistically significant main effects found for breakup distress as a function of sex ($F(1, 177) = 15.80$, $p < 0.001$) and type of relationship ($F(1, 177) = 13.29$, $p < 0.001$); see Table 3. As expected, women reported more breakup distress on average (M = 38.82, SD = 1.58) as compared to men

Table 2.   Means, Standard Deviations, Cronbach's Alphas, and
Intercorrelations for the Dependent Variables.

	Mean (SD)	Range	Alpha reliability	Correlation
1 - Breakup distress	35.5 (15.0)	12–96	0.93	
2 - Sexual regret	21.4 (9.3)	8–48	0.83	0.22

Note: SD = standard deviation.

Table 3.   Multivariate Analysis of Variance Results for Breakup Distress.

Effect	Category	Mean (SD)	95% CI	Df	F	Sig.
Sex	Women	38.82 (1.58)	[35.70, 41.94]	1, 177	15.80	<0.001
	Men	30.08 (1.53)	[27.06, 33.10]			
Type of relationship	Committed relationship	38.46 (1.30)	[35.90, 41.02]	1, 177	13.29	<0.001
	Casual relationship	30.44 (1.78)	[26.94, 33.95]			
Sex × Type of relationship	Women × Committed relationship	42.44 (1.79)	[38.91, 45.96]	1, 177	0.13	0.720
	Men × Committed relationship	34.48 (1.88)	[30.77, 38.19]			
	Women × Casual relationship	35.21 (2.61)	[30.01, 40.36]			
	Men × Casual relationship	25.68 (2.41)	[20.92, 30.44]			

Note: SD = standard deviation; CI = confidence interval; df = degrees of freedom.

($M = 30.08$, $SD = 1.53$) (*H1*), and individuals who had been in a committed relationship reported more breakup distress on average ($M = 38.46$, $SD = 1.30$) than those who ended a casual relationship ($M = 30.44$, $SD = 1.78$) (*H2*). In support of *H3*, the interaction effect was not significant ($F(1, 177) = 0.13$, $p = 0.720$). Post hoc *t*-tests revealed that both men and women whose last relationship was committed reported greater breakup distress than those whose last relationship was casual (men: $t(93) = 2.76$, $p < 0.01$, women: $t(91) = 2.12$, $p < 0.05$). In addition, *t*-tests indicated that women whose last relationship was committed reported more breakup distress than men whose last relationship was committed ($t(120) = -3.44$, $p < 0.001$), and women whose last relationship was casual reported more breakup distress than men whose last relationship was casual ($t(64) = -2.83$, $p < 0.001$).

Sexual Regret

As expected, there was a statistically significant main effect for sex ($F(1, 177) = 12.25$, $p < 0.001$; see Table 4), such that women reported more sexual regret on average ($M = 23.67$, $SD = 1.02$) than men ($M = 18.71$, $SD = 0.99$) (*H4*). However, there was no main effect for type of relationship ($F(1, 177) = 1.15$, $p = 0.284$), suggesting that there was no significant difference in the level of sexual regret between individuals who had ended a committed relationship ($M = 21.95$, $SD = 0.84$) and those who had ended a casual relationship ($M = 20.43$, $SD = 1.15$). Thus, *H5* was not supported. *H6* was also not supported; the interaction effect

Table 4. Multivariate Analysis of Variance Results for Sexual Regret.

Effect	Category	Mean (SD)	95% CI	df	F	Sig.
Sex	Women	23.67 (1.02)	[21.66, 25.69]	1, 177	12.25	< 0.001
	Men	18.71 (.99)	[16.77, 20.66]			
Relationship type	Committed relationship	21.95 (.84)	[20.31, 23.60]	1, 177	1.15	0.284
	Casual relationship	20.43 (1.15)	[18.17, 22.69]			
Sex × Relationship type	Women × Committed relationship	23.69 (1.15)	[21.42, 25.97]	1, 177	1.10	0.296
	Men × Committed relationship	20.21 (1.21)	[17.82, 22.61]			
	Women × Casual relationship	23.66 (1.68)	[20.33, 26.98]			
	Men × Casual relationship	17.21 (1.56)	[14.14, 20.27]			

Note: SD = standard deviation; CI = confidence interval; df = degrees of freedom.

was not significant ($F(1, 177) = 1.10$, $p = 0.296$). Post-hoc t-tests revealed that there was no significant difference in the level of sexual regret reported by men who had ended a committed relationship as compared to men who had ended a casual relationship ($t(88) = 1.83$, $p = 0.071$), and the same was found for women ($t(92) = 0.009$, $p = 0.992$). Additional t-tests indicated that women reported more sexual regret than men across relationship type (committed relationships: $t(119) = -2.15$, $p < 0.05$, casual sex committed relationships: $t(42) = -2.62$, $p < 0.05$).

DISCUSSION

Bombarded with social media posts, films and television, peers, and the fear of missing out (Przybylski, Murayama, DeHaan, & Gladwell, 2013), college is often a time for emerging adults to engage in sexual experimentation (Schwartz, 2016). In general, college students' sexual relationships fall into two categories: committed romantic relationships and casual sex relationships. Evidence suggests that both types of relationships have their benefits and disadvantages. The purpose of the current study was to compare college students' post-breakup reactions (including breakup distress and sexual regret) by sex (male/female) and type of sexual relationship (committed/casual).

Breakup Distress

Sex Differences

Consistent with previous findings, women in the current sample reported more breakup distress, on average, as compared to men. In their meta-analysis examining mental health outcomes associated with romantic relationship breakups among young adults, Mirsu-Paun and Oliver (2017) suggested that women may be more susceptible to negative outcomes associated with the end of a romantic

relationship due to their internalization of societal messages regarding the importance of a woman's relationship status. However, these same social norms may
also restrict men: whereas women are allowed more freedom to express emotion
(including feelings of hurt and distress associated with committed relationship
dissolutions), men are traditionally expected to remain stoic (Mirsu-Paun &
Oliver, 2017; Towne, Ruggles, Crane, & Root, 2019). This may also contribute to
men's relatively lower ratings of emotional distress following the end of an intimate relationship. For Generation Z (the current generation of emerging adults),
the impact of this socialization may be even more complex due to the influence
of pervasive social media portrayals of "picture-perfect" romantic relationships –
which women are both more likely to view, and to report being negatively affected
by (Vogels & Anderson, 2020). Women are also more likely to share social media
posts about their intimate relationships online (Vogels & Anderson, 2020), which
may contribute to negative feelings following relationship dissolution related to
the publicity of their breakup online.

Relationship Differences
As expected, participants who had experienced the end of a committed relationship reported significantly more breakup distress as compared to those who
experienced the end of a casual sex relationship. Previous research suggests that
certain factors, such as higher relationship commitment (Fox & Tokunaga, 2015;
Rhoades, Kamp Dush, Atkins, Stanley, & Markman, 2011), feeling rejected by a
relationship partner and having a fear of being single (Field, 2020) may contribute to negative feelings following the end of a sexual relationship. Whereas casual
sex relationships are characterized by their lack of commitment (Wentland &
Reissing, 2014), romantic relationships typically involve defining the parameters
of the relationship, including partners discussing sexual exclusivity and their
expectations for the future of the relationship (Knopp, Rhoades, Stanley, &
Markman, 2020). In comparison, casual sex relationships are perceived as inher-
ently transient (and valued for that same reason; Rodrigue & Fernet, 2016) and
lack any expectation of being a "couple" (Wentland & Reissing, 2014). Although
negative feelings may arise at the end of a casual sex relationship, partners may
simply be less likely to define this dissolution as a "breakup" since a lasting relationship was not likely from the beginning.

Interaction Effect
As anticipated, there was not a significant interaction effect; both men and
women in committed relationships reported higher levels of break up distress
as compared with their same-sex peers in casual sex relationships. However, it
was noteworthy that the severity of breakup distress was considerably lower for
both sexes than expected. Respondents seem to have been able to avoid significant
cognitive and emotional distress following the end of the relationship; in general,
they disagreed that they had felt lonely, emotionally distressed, or preoccupied

with their ex-partner. This challenges the existing body of research (see a review by Field, 2017). It is possible that emerging adults may recognize the challenges to achieving a lasting romantic relationship during their undergraduate experience. This sense of pragmatism may be uniquely related to the experiences of American members of Generation Z, who are growing up in a society in which 22% of first marriages end within five years (Copen, Daniels, Vespa, & Mosher, 2012), marriage rates are at an all-time low (Curtin & Sutton, 2020), and less than a quarter of nationally surveyed adults believe that being married is essential to living a fulfilling life (Horowitz, Graf, & Livingston, 2019).

Sexual Regret

Sex Differences

Oswalt et al. (2005) found that over 70% of their college student sample regretted having sex at some point, and findings indicate that, among casual sex relationships, women are more prone to sexual regret as compared to men (Kennair, Wyckoff, Asao, Buss, & Bendixen, 2018). Consistent with previous research, women in the current sample reported higher levels of sexual regret than men. Previous research suggests that feelings of regret following casual sex encounters may be influenced by a variety of factors, including the quality of the sexual encounter (Fisher et al., 2012), the imagined negative consequences (Eshbaugh & Gute, 2008; Kennair et al., 2018), and fear of negative stigma (McKeen et al., 2022). All of these factors appear to be more consequential for women, who (1) report less satisfactory sexual encounters, on average (Petersen & Hyde, 2010), (2) bear more responsibility for many of the negative consequences of sex (Galperin et al., 2013; Napper et al., 2016), and (3) are more susceptible to negative social stigma associated with engagement in sexual relationships overall (Conley, Ziegler, & Moors, 2013), as compared to men. However, as with breakup distress, data from the current sample evidenced a lower amount of sexual regret overall among both women and men than anticipated. On average, participants reported slight to moderate disagreement when asked about negative responses to their sexual relationships, such as discomfort when reflecting on the relationship, avoidance of their sexual partner, and residual resentment.

Relationship Differences

Contrary to our hypothesis, there was no significant difference in the levels of sexual regret reported by participants who had ended committed and casual sexual relationships. Previous research suggests that more permissive attitudes toward casual sex, as well as greater intrinsic motivations for engaging in sexual activity in general (such as having sex because it is fun, pleasurable, or meaningful to one's identity), are related to positive sexual outcomes (Gravel, Pelletier, & Reissing, 2016; Vrangalova & Ong, 2014). In America, generational shifts in sexual permissiveness have been associated with greater acceptance of premarital sex as well as increasing prevalence of casual sexual partners (Twenge, Sherman, & Wells, 2015). Generation Z, in particular, has been identified as more open-minded

(Mohr & Mohr, 2017), sexually self-aware (Turner, 2015), and accepting of others (Francis & Hoefel, 2018). Many emerging adults view sexual behavior as a "natural step" into adulthood (Carpenter, 2002), and it appears that for Generation Z, the journey to adulthood, whether it be in a committed or casual sexual relationship, may be more comfortable than it was for previous generations.

Interaction Effect
The lack of an interaction effect suggests that there was no significant difference in the level of sexual regret between women (or men) in casual and committed relationships. While these results were not surprising among men, previous research would suggest that social norms governing women's sexuality might contribute to negative sexual outcomes. The current findings may reflect, in part, the psychosocial impact of progressive media representations on young adults. In recent years, female scriptwriters have made targeted efforts to showcase empowered female role models as television and movie leads (Dodge, 2020). Media portrayals of women, although still impoverished in comparison to those of men (Sink & Mastro, 2017), have started to fight back against the one-dimensional, stereotyped female characters that came before them (Nash & Grant, 2015). Modern television shows depicting young women have started to explore the nuanced experiences of sexual exploration in emerging adulthood by allowing female characters to experiment with and talk about sex casually and without emotional gravitas, which viewers perceive as normalizing female sexual empowerment (Stroozas, 2020). For Generation Z, a cohort immersed in pop culture and mass media, the influence of this societal messaging is likely significant. The current findings provide support for the existence of a generational shift in social norms associated with increasing openness and comfort with sexual identity exploration, such that students in the current sample were less likely to look back on their sexual behavior negatively and may even be more likely to see their past sexual relationships as opportunities to learn more about themselves and develop their sexual self-concept moving forward. Emerging adults in the current generation appear to be embracing the Generation Z motto of "radical inclusivity" when it comes to sexuality (Francis & Hoefel, 2018) – and it seems they are reaping the benefits.

Strengths and Limitations
This study had a variety of strengths, particularly related to the sample, which was equally distributed among men and women, ethnically diverse, and primarily within the 18–22 age range. In addition, we strengthened the reliability of participants' classification of their most recently ended relationship by providing them definitions for casual sex and committed relationships. However, the study was also subject to limitations. First, there were no limitations given as to how long ago a "break up" might have taken place. Some respondents may have been reporting on relationships that ended more recently than others, leading to a possible recall bias. Since participants were instructed to indicate how they

felt "within two weeks of the breakup," we were not able to compare their feelings immediately after the breakup versus at the time they were completing the survey. Data were also collected from participants in a more liberal portion of the country and therefore may not be generalizable to the wider population of undergraduates across all areas of the United States.

Conclusion and Future Directions

While many Generation Z undergraduates may view marriage as a long-term goal, the current findings suggest that they may be less emotionally impacted by the dissolution of their romantic relationships and/or their casual sex relationships than expected. Generation Z is projected to be the most educated, most diverse, and most socially progressive generation yet (Parker & Igielnik, 2020). They are accustomed to the instant gratification and limitless possibilities awarded by online dating apps, which many see as convenient avenues for entering casual sex relationships (Joyce, Lubbers, & Miller, 2022). Although women in the current sample reported stronger negative responses to the end of their sexual relationships as compared to men, overall they appeared to be more secure in their sexual choices than previous findings would suggest. Female respondents reported generally low levels of distress at the end of their sexual relationships and there was no significant difference in their level of sexual regret across romantic and casual sex relationships. Future research might find it beneficial to assess participants' emotional responses immediately following the termination of their sexual relationship, as compared the emotional perspective they may have 3–6 months later. In addition, exploring factors which may promote more "sex positive" attitudes in undergraduate men and women, including establishing healthy boundaries, communicating sexual expectations, and promoting mutual sexual gratification, would be valuable for all sexual partners.

NOTE

1. Data were collected prior to the COVID-19 pandemic.

REFERENCES

Banker, J. E., Kaestle, C. E., & Allen, K. R. (2010). Dating is hard work: A narrative approach to understanding sexual and romantic relationships in young adulthood. *Contemporary Family Therapy, 32*(2), 173–191.

Bendixen, M., Asao, K., Wyckoff, J. P., Buss, D. M., & Kennair, L. E. O. (2017). Sexual regret in US and Norway: Effects of culture and individual differences in religiosity and mating strategy. *Personality and Individual Differences, 116*, 246–251.

Bradshaw, C., Kahn, A. S., & Saville, B. K. (2010). To hook up or date: Which gender benefits? *Sex Roles, 62*(9), 661–669.

Carpenter, L. M. (2002). Gender and the meaning and experience of virginity loss in the contemporary United States. *Gender & Society, 16*(3), 345–365.

Chandra, A., & Parija, P. P. (2021). The Love – Breakup study: Defining love and exploring reasons for the breakup of romantic relationships. *Indian Journal of Health Sexuality and Culture, 7*(2), 41–48.

Clarke, G. R. (2018). Why have Americans changed their minds about premarital sex?*International Journal of Economics and Finance, 10*(3), 120–132.

Conley, T. D., Ziegler, A., & Moors, A. C. (2013). Backlash from the bedroom: Stigma mediates gender differences in acceptance of casual sex offers. *Psychology of Women Quarterly, 37*(3), 392–407.

Copen, C. E., Chandra, A., & Febo-Vazquez, I. (2016). Sexual behavior, sexual attraction, and sexual orientation among adults aged 18–44 in the United States: Results from the 2011–2013 National Survey of Family Growth. *National Health Statistics Reports, 31*, 1–14.

Copen, C. E., Daniels, K., Vespa, J., & Mosher, W. D. (2012). First marriages in the United States: Data from the 2006–2010 National Survey of Family Growth. *National Health Statistics Reports, 49*(1), 1–22.

Curtin, S. C., & Sutton, P. D. (2020). *Marriage rates in the United States, 1900–2018*. National Center for Health Statistics. https://www.cdc.gov/nchs/data/hestat/marriage_rate_2018/marriage_rate_2018.pdf

Dimock, M. (2019). Defining generations: Where millennials end and generation Z begins. *Pew Research Center, 17*(1), 1–7.

Dodge, S. (2020). *The renaissance era of television: Exploring pioneer screenwriters behind psychologically empowered female characters.* Doctoral dissertation, Antioch University. ProQuest Dissertations Publishing.

Endendijk, J. J., van Baar, A. L., & Deković, M. (2020). He is a stud, she is a slut! A meta-analysis on the continued existence of sexual double standards. *Personality and Social Psychology Review, 24*(2), 163–190.

Eshbaugh, E. M., & Gute, G. (2008). Hookups and sexual regret among college women. *The Journal of Social Psychology, 148*(1), 77–90.

Field, T. (2011). Romantic breakups, heartbreak and bereavement: Romantic breakups. *Psychology, 2*(4), 382–387.

Field, T. (2017). Romantic breakup distress, betrayal and heartbreak: A review. *International Journal of Behavioral Research and Psychology, 5*(2), 217–225.

Field, T. (2020). Romantic breakup distress in university students: A narrative review. *International Journal of Psychological Research and Reviews, 3*(30), 1–20.

Field, T., Diego, M., Pelaez, M., Deeds, O., & Delgado, J. (2009). Breakup distress in university students. *Adolescence, 44*(176), 705–727.

Fielder, R. L., & Carey, M. P. (2010). Predictors and consequences of sexual "hookups" among college students: A short-term prospective study. *Archives of Sexual Behavior, 39*(5), 1105–1119.

Fisher, M. L., Worth, K., Garcia, J. R., & Meredith, T. (2012). Feelings of regret following uncommitted sexual encounters in Canadian university students. *Culture, Health & Sexuality, 14*(1), 45–57.

Fox, J., & Tokunaga, R. S. (2015). Romantic partner monitoring after breakups: Attachment, dependence, distress, and post-dissolution online surveillance via social networking sites. *Cyberpsychology, Behavior, and Social Networking, 18*(9), 491–498.

Francis, T., & Hoefel, F. (2018). 'True Gen': Generation Z and its implications for companies. McKinsey & Company. http://www.drthomaswu.com/uicmpaccsmac/Gen%20Z.pdf

Galperin, A., Haselton, M. G., Frederick, D. A., Poore, J., Von Hippel, W., Buss, D. M., & Gonzaga, G. C. (2013). Sexual regret: Evidence for evolved sex differences. *Archives of Sexual Behavior, 42*(7), 1145–1161.

Goldberg, S., Yeshua-Katz, D., & Marciano, A. (2022). Online construction of romantic relationships on social media. *Journal of Social and Personal Relationships, 39*(6), 1839–1862.

Gravel, E. E., Pelletier, L. G., & Reissing, E. D. (2016). "Doing it" for the right reasons: Validation of a measurement of intrinsic motivation, extrinsic motivation, and amotivation for sexual relationships. *Personality and Individual Differences, 92*, 164–173.

Grello, C. M., Welsh, D. P., & Harper, M. S. (2006). No strings attached: The nature of casual sex in college students. *Journal of Sex Research, 43*(3), 255–267.

Haimson, O. L., Andalibi, N., De Choudhury, M., & Hayes, G. R. (2018). Relationship breakup disclosures and media ideologies on Facebook. *New Media & Society, 20*(5), 1931–1952.

Hanks, C. L. (2019). *Get Lit: An analysis of the framing of party schools in the US* [Master's thesis]. Virginia Tech. VTechWorks. http://hdl.handle.net/10919/90394

Horowitz, J., Graf, N., & Livingston, G. (2019). *Marriage and cohabitation in the US*. Pew Research Center. https://www.pewresearch.org/social-trends/wp-content/uploads/sites/3/2019/11/PSDT_11.06.19_marriage_cohabitation_FULL.final_.v2.pdf

Joyce, T. A., Lubbers, C. A., & Miller, K. J. (2022). Love is in the app: Gen Z use and perception of dating apps. *Quarterly Review of Business Disciplines, 9*(1), 33–48.

Kennair, L. E. O., Bendixen, M., & Buss, D. M. (2016). Sexual regret: Tests of competing explanations of sex differences. *Evolutionary Psychology, 14*(4), 1–9.

Kennair, L. E. O., Grøntvedt, T. V., & Bendixen, M. (2021). The function of casual sex action and inaction regret: A longitudinal investigation. *Evolutionary Psychology, 19*(1), 1–12.

Kennair, L. E. O., Wyckoff, J. P., Asao, K., Buss, D. M., & Bendixen, M. (2018). Why do women regret casual sex more than men do? *Personality and Individual Differences, 127*, 61–67.

Knopp, K., Rhoades, G. K., Stanley, S. M., & Markman, H. J. (2020). "Defining the relationship" in adolescent and young adult romantic relationships. *Journal of Social and Personal Relationships, 37*(7), 2078–2097.

Kuperberg, A., & Padgett, J. E. (2016). The role of culture in explaining college students' selection into hookups, dates, and long-term romantic relationships. *Journal of Social and Personal Relationships 33*(8), 1070–1096.

Marelich, W., Wright, M., Ziegler, S., & Henry, J. (2016). Development of a measure of sexual regrets: The sexual regret scale. In *Annual Meeting of the Society for Personality and Social Psychology* (pp. 28–30), San Diego, CA.

Marks, M. J., Young, T. M., & Zaikman, Y. (2019). The sexual double standard in the real world: Evaluations of sexually active friends and acquaintances. *Social Psychology, 50*(2), 67–79.

McHugh, M. C., Pearlson, B., & Poet, A. (2012). Who needs to understand hook up culture? *Sex Roles, 67*, 363–365.

McKeen, B. E., Anderson, R. C., & Mitchell, D. A. (2022). Was it good for you? Gender differences in motives and emotional outcomes following casual sex. *Sexuality & Culture, 26*, 1339–1359.

Mirsu-Paun, A., & Oliver, J. (2017). How much does love really hurt? A meta-analysis of the association between romantic relationship quality, breakups and mental health outcomes in adolescents and young adults. *Journal of Relationships Research, 8*, E5. doi:10.1017/jrr.2017.6

Mohr, K. A., & Mohr, E. S. (2017). Understanding Generation Z students to promote a contemporary learning environment. *Journal on Empowering Teaching Excellence, 1*(9), 84–94.

Napper, L. E., Montes, K. S., Kenney, S. R., & LaBrie, J. W. (2016). Assessing the personal negative impacts of hooking up experienced by college students: Gender differences and mental health. *The Journal of Sex Research, 53*(7), 766–775.

Nash, M., & Grant, R. (2015). Twenty-something *Girls* vs. Thirty-something *Sex and The City* women: Paving the way for "post? feminism". *Feminist Media Studies, 15*(6), 976–991.

Oswalt, S. B., Cameron, K. A., & Koob, J. J. (2005). Sexual regret in college students. *Archives of Sexual Behavior, 34*(6), 663–669.

Owen, J., & Fincham, F. D. (2011). Young adults' emotional reactions after hooking up encounters. *Archives of Sexual Behavior, 40*(2), 321–330.

Owen, J., Fincham, F. D., & Moore, J. (2011). Short-term prospective study of hooking up among college students. *Archives of Sexual Behavior, 40*(2), 331–341.

Parker, K., & Igielnik, R. (2020). *On the cusp of adulthood and facing an uncertain future: What we know about Gen Z so far*. Pew Research Center. https://www.pewresearch.org/social-trends/2020/05/14/on-the-cusp-of-adulthood-and-facing-an-uncertain-future-what-we-know-about-gen-z-so-far-2/

Petersen, J. L., & Hyde, J. S. (2010). A meta-analytic review of research on gender differences in sexuality, 1993–2007. *Psychological Bulletin, 136*(1), 21.

Przybylski, A. K., Murayama, K., DeHaan, C. R., & Gladwell, V. (2013). Motivational, emotional, and behavioral correlates of fear of missing out. *Computers in Human Behavior, 29*(4), 1841–1848.

Reissing, E. D., Andruff, H. L., & Wentland, J. J. (2012). Looking back: The experience of first sexual intercourse and current sexual adjustment in young heterosexual adults. *Journal of Sex Research, 49*(1), 27–35.

Rhoades, G. K., Kamp Dush, C. M., Atkins, D. C., Stanley, S. M., & Markman, H. J. (2011). Breaking up is hard to do: The impact of unmarried relationship dissolution on mental health and life satisfaction. *Journal of Family Psychology, 25*(3), 366–374.

Rodrigue, C., & Fernet, M. (2016). A metasynthesis of qualitative studies on casual sexual relationships and experiences. *The Canadian Journal of Human Sexuality, 25*(3), 225–242.

Schwartz, S. J. (2016). Turning point for a turning point: Advancing emerging adulthood theory and research. *Emerging Adulthood, 4*(5), 307–317.

Simon, R. W., & Barrett, A. E. (2010). Nonmarital romantic relationships and mental health in early adulthood: Does the association differ for women and men? *Journal of Health and Social Behavior, 51*(2), 168–182.

Sink, A., & Mastro, D. (2017). Depictions of gender on primetime television: A quantitative content analysis. *Mass Communication and Society, 20*(1), 3–22.

Snider, J. (2018). *Engagement in and desire for romantic and sexual relationships in college: Associations with mental health*. Bachelor's thesis, University of Michigan. Deep Blue Repositories. https://deepblue.lib.umich.edu/bitstream/handle/2027.42/147393/jasnider.pdf?sequence=1

Stroozas, S. V. (2020). "We Are Like Feminist Heroes Right Now": A study of female sexual empowerment communication for female-identifying viewers of broad city. *UWL Journal of Undergraduate Research*. https://www.uwlax.edu/globalassets/offices-services/urc/jur-online/pdf/2020/stroozas.samantha.cst2020.pdf

Towne, A., Ruggles, E., Crane, B., & Root, M. (2019). Does she want you to open the door? New realities for traditional gendered sexuality. *The Qualitative Report, 24*(10), 2486–2505.

Turner, A. (2015). Generation Z: Technology and social interest. *The Journal of Individual Psychology, 71*(2), 103–113.

Twenge, J. M., Sherman, R. A., & Wells, B. E. (2015). Changes in American adults' sexual behavior and attitudes, 1972–2012. *Archives of Sexual Behavior, 44*(8), 2273–2285.

Vannier, S. A., & O'Sullivan, L. F. (2018). Great expectations: Examining unmet romantic expectations and dating relationship outcomes using an investment model framework. *Journal of Social and Personal Relationships, 35*(8), 1045–1066.

Vaterlaus, J. M., Tulane, S., Porter, B. D., & Beckert, T. E. (2018). The perceived influence of media and technology on adolescent romantic relationships. *Journal of Adolescent Research, 33*(6), 651–671.

Vennum, A., & Fincham, F. D. (2011). Assessing decision making in young adult romantic relationships. *Psychological Assessment, 23*(3), 739–751.

Vennum, A., Monk, J. K., Pasley, B. K., & Fincham, F. D. (2017). Emerging adult relationship transitions as opportune times for tailored interventions. *Emerging Adulthood, 5*(4), 293–305.

Vogels, E. A., & Anderson, M. (2020). *Dating and relationships in the digital age*. Pew Research Center. https://www.pewresearch.org/internet/wp-content/uploads/sites/9/2020/05/PI_2020.05.08_dating-digital-age_REPORT.pdf

Vrangalova, Z., & Ong, A. D. (2014). Who benefits from casual sex? The moderating role of sociosexuality. *Social Psychological and Personality Science, 5*(8), 883–891.

Walsh, M., Millar, M., & Westfall, R. S. (2019). Sex differences in responses to emotional and sexual infidelity in dating relationships. *Journal of Individual Differences, 40*(2), 63.

Wentland, J. J., & Reissing, E. (2014). Casual sexual relationships: Identifying definitions for one night stands, booty calls, fuck buddies, and friends with benefits. *The Canadian Journal of Human Sexuality, 23*(3), 167–177.

Zhang, R., Freeman, G., & McNeese, N. J. (2020, October). Breakups on social media: Social behaviors and dilemmas. In *Conference Companion Publication of the 2020 on Computer Supported Cooperative Work and Social Computing*, October 17–21, 2020 (pp. 431–435).

CHAPTER 3

ROMANTIC, CONFESSIONAL AND POST-ROMANTIC: THE TIMELINE OF CONJUGALITY AT A DISTANCE BETWEEN MEXICO AND THE UNITED STATES*

Javiera Cienfuegos-Illanes

In memory of Enrique del Solar

ABSTRACT

This chapter reflects on the construction of transnational marital bonds over time. First, based on multi-site fieldwork carried out in 2011 and 2012 in two regions of Mexico and one of the United States, an extensive discussion on the transnational family and the construction of conjugality is presented from the point of view of two dimensions: intimacy and domestic organization in heterosexual couples with young children and conjugal unions recognized as successful. The second part discusses the same results of the study after a decade, based on contact with the same participants and an exploration of their trajectories of intimacy and family organization. The notion of life cycle and family trajectory is introduced into the discussion, arriving at paths in the definition of intimacy that discuss the romantic component initially identified and add the confessional and post-romantic components as part of the experience of

---

* Parts of this chapter comes from a previous reflection entitled "Swing conjugality: Mexican couples living at a distance" (2017, ECrann Publishers).

Conjugal Trajectories: Relationship Beginnings, Change, and Dissolutions
Contemporary Perspectives in Family Research, Volume 22, 41–58
Copyright © 2023 by Emerald Publishing Limited
All rights of reproduction in any form reserved
ISSN: 1530-3535/doi:10.1108/S1530-353520230000022003

geographical distance for prolonged periods of migration, in addition to aging processes.

Keywords: Transnational family; conjugality; Mexico–US migration; family trajectories; intimacy; romance

1. INTRODUCTION

Every day, thousands of people move from one region of the world to another, looking for better job opportunities or simply economic subsistence. However, in their daily lives, migrants find ways to maintain contact with their families, producing a sense of familyhood through interchanges and interdependencies, which involves the circulation of communications and care-remittances, gifts, pictures, recipes, and so on – known as a transnational family (Boccagni & Bonizzoni, 2015; Bryceson & Vuorela, 2002).

By the end of the twentieth century, the literature showed that transnational family bonds tend to be stereotyped as synonymous with family rupture. Migration tends to be interpreted, from the origin societies' point of view, as the cause of a vast amount of anomalies in the population (e.g., low school achievement, teenage pregnancy, or childhood depression). However, it is not frequently acknowledged that these problems, before being caused by migration, have been produced by an asymmetric distribution of resources, power, and structural inequalities (Therborn, 2015). Fewer still are able to view migration as a way to cope with domestic conflicts, like marital violence, child abuse, alcoholism, and unemployment in origin communities.

In addition, more recent studies have pointed out that, together with demographic dynamics such as ageing in host societies and increasing poverty and precarity in the communities of origin, transmigration processes started to include several diverse actors: from low-skilled and refugees (Brendixon & Näre, 2023) to skilled and high-skilled professionals (Cienfuegos-Illanes, 2023; Thomas-Brown, 2023); from clandestine male-breadwinner to youth opportunity seekers, as well as circulating children (Celero, 2023). In the same vein, the transnational family research agenda has turned to new issues, as is the case of fleeing (Chikwira & Madizva, 2023), Youth Agency (Ossei, Mazzucato, & Haagsman, 2023), and the circulation of highly-skilled transmigrants (Cienfuegos-Illanes & Ruf-Toledo, 2022).

Based on empirical research, this chapter will discuss the personal relationships (Holmes, 2014) in the experiences and strategies of "conjugality at a distance," considering the life stories of low-income Mexican couples who are separated due to the migration of one of the spouses to the United States. The discussion confronts two central hypotheses. On one side, the conviction that transnational families succeed in producing interpersonal intimacy and managing domestic organization and, on the other hand, that transnational bonds tend to break with romantic or traditional intimacy meanings and to produce strategic relationships based on, ultimately, economic benefits. Furthermore, a life cycle consideration is crucial to understanding how intimacy evolves, encompassing distance, time, and ageing; the aim is to highlight how a transnational conjugal bond works over time and the main factors that impact its stability and intimacy.

The chapter is divided into four parts. First, I briefly discuss the theoretical framework and the methodology of the study carried out between 2011 and 2012. Secondly, taking into account the results obtained from life stories and participant observation, a summary of "creative adjustments" within transnational couples will be presented. Components that produce stability in the long-distance relationship are stressed. Thirdly, I will suggest some challenges regarding the idea of a "stable couple" (or "stable family"). Finally, after a decade of these analyses, the chapter reflects on the idea of a "stable transnational family," considering the testimony of the same participants, contacted by phone and through social networks. Conclusions will turn to the hypothesis about conjugal bonds at a distance, referring to how intimacy and domestic necessities converged in a post-romantic version.

2. THEORETICAL BACKGROUND: FAMILY LIFE, INTIMACY AND CREATIVE ADJUSTMENTS

Family life includes two interconnected dimensions. On one hand, the organization of survival, domestic and care necessities are a crucial component. On the other hand, "togetherness" encompasses affective needs and the construction of intimacy. Normative ideas of the family contain a desirable structure of family relationships and marital bonds. Within the hegemonic version, the partnership appears synonymous with marriage. It is responsible for various functions of social reproduction, including the socialization of minor-aged children and providing each member with food, shelter, and clothing. Whether official or informal, the conventionalist idea of a stable relationship is connoted by the term marriage.

> Among other things, the marriage system defines a set of mutual obligations and rights, but asymmetric, between men and women. We also know that marriage, while bond between a man and a woman clad in social public recognition, is, at the same time, a device which is crucial for the establishment of partnerships between groups. (D'Aubeterre, 2000, p. 16, my translation)

The definition of the family not only produces distinct roles between spouses, but the distribution of these tasks also contains an unequal partnership agreement – the same for intergenerational bonds. For decades, feminist and gender studies have attempted to account for the asymmetric terms – patriarchal and ideological – in which this negotiation has historically been held. In the late sixties and seventies, they began to question the legitimacy of the unequal labor division between men and women in the social order in both the public and private domains. As a result, the model that the literature defined as the "breadwinner system" began to be questioned in Europe, the United States, and other regions of the globe, which incorporated issues like race, class, and colonialism. After that, the image of family promoted by the State and the industry would be seen as an ideology and way of imprisoning of women in everyday life (Beck-Gernsheim, 1998; Lagarde, 1990).

On the other hand, inherent in the idea of family is the connotation of home, a refuge from the sorrows of the modern subject, a space of personal development, of private life and intimacy (Beck & Beck-Gernsheim, 2001). For Zelizer (2009), the word intimacy has multiple meanings, considering a spectrum ranging from cold and thorough observation to passionate commitment. For this reason, the common factor in all forms of intimacy is that it implies specific knowledge (that only one person possesses) and particular attentions (that only one person provides), without being accessible to third parties.

In the 1990s, the discussion about family roles and intimacy became more complex due to changes in family structure and routines, among which were: the increase in divorces, the increase in children born out of wedlock and cohabiting couples, as well as the increasing incorporation of women into paid labor force. In addition, the issue of sexual division of labor added (heterosexual) family diversity as a concern:

> It is no longer clear whether to marry and live together, whether to have a child within or outside the family with the person with whom one lives or with the person you love, but lives with another, or to have a child before or after a career or in the middle. (Beck & Beck-Gernsheim, 2001, p. 33, my translation)

Authors have described this phenomenon as an uncoupling. Differentiation of life forms once relegated to the family and marriage "as a result will become increasingly difficult to establish a relationship between concept and reality" (Beck & Beck-Gernsheim, 2001, p. 35, my translation).

Taking the words of Giddens at that time (2000, p. 143), there are a variety of family forms in different societies around the world; in some areas, traditional systems have been slightly altered. Whereas in others a considerable range of complex transformations has become evident, partly due to cultural exchanges that occur with incredible variety and speed thanks to social media and technologies.

The traditional, patriarchial notion of "nuclear family" exists in the modern era, however, two main deviations from this conception of family are important in this sense. The second wave of feminism in the 1960s introduced one such deviation, that of the heterosexual nuclear family wherein both parents work, due to the increased incorporation of women into the labor force. This initial challenge to the idea of a nuclear family forced researchers to explore the concept from a broader view. In this context, there not only are the arrangements of deinstitutionalization involved, named by Beck-Gernsheim (2002) as the "post-familial family," but also the transnational family as a practice beyond the borders of the local household, the Nation-State, and the co-presence of its members.

Recognizing the more recent discussions about sex-gender heteronormative systems and feminism, my research, differently, has sought to explore the questions that this "third" group of family configurations, the second deviation from the traditional norm, raises. Transnational families are diverse in kinds of actors and routes, each more frequent worldwide. Therefore, their complexity makes it difficult to understand the variety of ways a transnational family bond could be constructed.

2.1. Creative Adjustments as a Lens for Interpreting Family Life

From the above, I advance the concept of "creative adjustment" (Cienfuegos, 2017) for analyzing family practices (Morgan, 2011), which considers the theoretical works of Margaret Archer (2003), Hans Joas (1996) and Raymond Williams (1977). Firstly, family configurations involve the personal thoughts and processes that individuals perform regarding contextual changes. These were named by Archer as "internal conversation," which refers to the production of a running commentary about what is happening in the everyday lives of the individuals. In other words, it is the regular exercise of the mental activity of considering themselves within their social contexts and vice-versa (Archer, 2003).

Secondly, it is the concept "structure of feelings," which Raymond Williams (1977) used to suggest a common set of perceptions and values shared by a specific generation, allows me to claim that there is an implicit normative order determining what is legitimately possible to express as an emotion. In addition, the term allows me to place the original (unexpected) expression of emotions as a way of instilling a struggle, which is personal and social at the same time:

> [a structure of feelings] is that we are concerned with meanings and values as they are actively lived and felt (...) We are talking about characteristic elements of impulse, restraint, and tone; specifically affective elements of consciousness and relationships: not feeling against thought, but thought as felt and feeling as thought: practical consciousness of a present kind, in a living and inter-relating continuity. We are then defining these elements as a 'structure': as a set, with specific internal relations, at once interlocking and in tension. (Williams, 1977, p. 132)

Finally, drawing on Hans Joas (1996), I argue that the emergence of particular adjustments can only be explained by means of a creative ability:

> I am saying that the conception of action which is so crucial to how sociology understands itself needs to be reconstructed in such a way that this conception is no longer confined to the alternative of a model of rational action versus normatively oriented action, but is able to incorporate the creative dimension of human action into its conceptual structure and thus also to take adequate account of the intellectual currents which hinge on this dimension. (Joas, 1996, p. 72)

When looking at the case of family at a distance, particularly conjugal bonds, the creativity of the individuals is particularly relevant since they have to deal with the geographical distance of their sentimental partners and relatives. This means that, on one hand, there are creative adjustments in the construction and maintenance of the family bonds. On the other hand, there are strategies of re-signification and negotiation about the contents of the marital relationship, which indicates a more considerable change.

In sum, in the context of transnational conjugality, a creative adjustment comprehends the *sayings* and *doings* that have been produced due to a reflexive process – i.e., internal conversations – carried out by the individuals with regard to their personal and social contexts. In those, actors combine social expectations regarding conjugality – i.e. sentimental structures – as well as their projects, values, and beliefs. Then, it is a socio-emotional equation that can have normative consequences (emotional struggle), as was observed in my empirical approach. Lastly, creative adjustments change along with the social dynamics that produced them, an issue I will refer to afterwards.

3. METHODOLOGY: A MULTI-SITED AND LIFE-COURSE PERSPECTIVE

Some essential points from the previous discussion inspired methodological decisions in my research and post-research reflections. Firstly, the experience of a transnational family varies according to the role that each person holds in the domestic system, considering the duties and status of family members (i.e., their gendered, generational, and social positions). Secondly, a family experience changes over time. Life cycles are marked or determined in personal trajectories from the change in the balance between intimacy, care, and domestic organization in family arrangements. In this sense, migration will always represent a shift in the life cycle that is not linear.

Between 2010 and 2013, I conducted a qualitative case study involving low-income heterosexual Mexican couples with children; one partner was working in the United States, male or female. The Study was carried out in three regions (Morelos, Tabasco, and Oregon) using two approaches: collecting life stories and observing the affected parties in their separate surroundings. First, participants were recruited through key informants – e.g., other researchers in the field, institutional networks and non-profit organizations in which I volunteered, community leaders, visiting familiar places such as restaurants, Hispanic churches, and missions, among others, and secondly, following the snowball method.

Stress was placed on how the conjugal bond is experienced at a distance, as related both by those who remained in Mexico and those who had left for the United States. The profiles that the Study specified were: "woman who stays" (Morelos, Mexico), "man who migrates" (Oregon, the United States), "woman who migrates" (Tabasco, Mexico), "man who stays" (Tabasco, Mexico) and "woman whose husband has been deported" (Oregon, the United States). The regions involved in the fieldwork represent canonic flows of the profiles defined theoretically. Unlike the transversal male-undocumented migration, Tabasco's migration of women to the packing Seafood Industry (in Louisiana and North Carolina) is relatively recent, seasonal and documented.

Participants were informed about the Study's objectives and scope and consented to the educational use of their testimonies and pictures. Their names were changed, as well as their relatives. In addition, some known places, like restaurants and tiny towns, were also anonymized. Individuals could access recorded conversations and have my phone number if they decided to stop participating. The transcription of 49 interviews was codified using qualitative software (Nvivo), which allowed detailed textual descriptions and issued interwoven analysis. In the end, three field diaries and eleven life stories were compiled, contributing to a rich source of research. As Márquez shows (1999, pp. 9–10), conjugal narratives are composed of interwoven or entangled single life stories:

The interweaving of life stories not only clearly shows the contradictory and conflicting versions of the same family story but also allows the reconstruction of the principles of centrality and power within the family. While each member tends to conceive of themselves as the protagonist of the narrated story, the encounter opens us to a reading that allows us to relativize and relocate these positions through understanding the disputed spaces within this story, which is always a family story.

Most of the persons involved in the Study were explicitly informed about the dissemination and publication of the research results: a Conference in 2012, my public dissertation in 2013, and in 2017, year of the book launch, respectively. Copies of my book are available at several Universities in Mexico: El Colegio de la Frontera Sur (ECOSUR), El Colegio de México (COLMEX), Universidad Nacional Autónoma de México (UNAM), and Universidad Autónoma de México (UAM Iztapalapa).

The second insight of this Study was provided in 2022, as a consequence of 10 years of maintaining sporadic contact with the research participants from 2011 to 2012, which allowed me to observe their bonds across time. In the face of these observed bonds, I return to seven broader life stories: two in Morelos, four in Oregon, and one in Tabasco. Differently, Facebook chats, WhatsApp messages and phone calls managed contacts. In this stage, the analysis put me in the center as a participant and observer over time.

4. INTERWOVEN LIFE STORIES

4.1. Living Apart Together in Low-Income Migration

In my first approach, the narratives of the participants and my field notes allowed me to identify some creative adjustments that couples perform in their daily lives. Empirically, adjustments are innovative in the stories of the couples and have shown a "before" and an "after" departure within conjugal trajectories.

Perhaps the first decision that couples make is to confirm their willingness to maintain regular contact, using technologies which they are not used to employing. In the majority of the cases, this adjustment includes a learning process. For those who migrated to the United States, this process has been quicker and wider in nature (including also the use of GPS, Facebook, e-mail, and smartphones), because technology is useful and necessary for finding a job and getting in touch with social networks in the United States.

The willingness to communicate, as well as the use of technologies, has been documented in previous studies (see, for instance, Bonizzoni, 2012; Cantó-Milà, Núñez, & Seebach, 2014; Chiyoko King-O'Riain, 2014; Constable, 2007; Wilding, 2006). All of these pointed out the crucial role that technologies play in the conformation of transnational family bonds, transnational virtual rituals and practices, as well as virtual intimacy. Certainly, the decrease in the cost of technologies is a very important element which makes it possible to maintain contact. Nevertheless, the argument must be contextualized: in my study, a decade ago, the most frequent technology used by participants and their relatives was mobile telephony (not Skype or chats, nor Facebook). This fact suggests that we should not forget that a digital gap in the world between rich and poor communities exists, despite the huge progress of technology. The gap becomes evident even when comparing the technological skills among migrants and non-migrants in transnational families. According to interviews, those who stayed in Mexico did not have computational knowledge or Internet access in their houses. Those who migrated, in contrast, acquired technological skills in order to become more integrated in host societies. Today, in 2022, this gap seems to be lesser but still persists, especially when I reached one family in Tabasco.

However, when looking at the couple's communication, not just its regularity in time, but also an improvement in the variety of issues that couples share, including emotions and personal worries, have been noted. These kinds of exchanges have produced a sense of proximity, reciprocal trust, and intimacy (Zelizer, 2009) in the relationship between the spouses. The frequency in communication also illustrates what Eva Illouz (2009) called "liminal rituals": special and exclusive moments that couples have constantly, providing an environment for the production of intimacy in the bond. Additionally, with respect to the content of communications, narratives in my study have shown that, due to the physical absence, the production of intimacy relies mainly on its expressive component, its main elements being shared emotions, confidence, and full information about the partner. This kind of intimacy was not only described by Illouz (2009), but also coincides with the definitions of Gabb and Silva (2011), Holmes (2011), Jamieson (1998, 2011), and Zelizer (2009).

In a similar direction, regarding the multiplication of currency agencies, sending and receiving remittances has become a regular practice. In the reviewed stories, this was assumed before transnational bonds started and reveals another adjustment that concerns the survival of the whole family: those who migrated embrace the duty of sending money and gifts, while those who remain in Mexico maintain domestic tasks and care responsibilities (i.e., reproductive work). The money regularly sent by migrants provides the family with subsistence. Also, part of the remittances is used for carrying out family projects, increasing the chances of upward social mobility, and the remittances are interpreted (in a more abstract sense) as support and companionship by the couple. This was particularly true in the case of seasonal migrant women from Tabasco to the United States. The uses of remittances (managed by those who remain in Mexico), consequently, might have diverse meanings, one of which is about balancing companionship.

Moreover, migrants also tend to take a role of emotional support for their partners in Mexico. This division of labor is novel, since the sex of the spouse is not the distinctive criteria; but rather, the fact that the spouse is in Mexico or has migrated. This result partially differs from the literature, which refers to the work overload for women, both if they are migrants or if they are undertaking the care duties for the family in the origin society (D'Aubeterre, 2000; Tuñón Pablos, 2007). The previous comments indicate an adjustment which concerns the roles of the spouses within the couple, which indeed become more flexible and even interchangeable between them. Studies about family organization have shown this pattern both for the case of women who stayed and men who migrated (e.g., D'Aubeterre, 2007; Marroni, 2000; Pribilsky, 2004), but this is especially evident in the case of male partners who stayed in Mexico; it is true that the vast majority of the men who stayed in Mexico received support from other women in the family (their mothers, mothers in law, or sisters) at the beginning of the transnational conjugality, but shortly after, they fully adopted the chores and caring labor, a process that brought an incremented valuation of their wives and women's roles in general. As Julio Rivera mentioned:

> The truth is that the woman suffers, it is the majority, 95 percent of women suffer, the woman is worth more than the man... I think it's machismo, because we don't know how to value them and sometimes we are sitting down, "I want this, I want this"; No! You have to do your part if you want it... (Julio Rivera, 47 years, male in Tabasco)

Derived from life stories, another adjustment emerges, which is the existence of an imaginary space (i.e., a representational space) that is pursued due the lack of information that the spouses have about the practical – concrete and quotidian – lives of their partners. Despite the fact that intimacy becomes more intense, there are some subjects that spouses do not communicate about, such as is the case with unemployment, illness, or accidents. In this space of hidden communication converges, on the one hand, the information and knowledge about the couple, but also, on the other hand, the negative stereotypes about both, those who left and those who stayed, this being a "place" full of emotions and anticipations (or internal conversations in the words of Archer).

Related to the production of a representational space, there is a sort of moral adjustment that consists in a shift about the idea of conjugality, emphasizing communication and trust, which were explicitly mentioned in all the interviews as fundamental elements in conjugality. This change has also been described in the work of Hirsch (2003, 2007) as the transition of one marriage based on respect and mutual fulfillment of gender responsibilities (*respeto*) to another based on intimacy or trust (*confianza*). In the profiles analyzed in my study there is a small distinction against Hirsch's claims; while the author described a generational shift, in the participants of the study it has been experienced internally – in the couple's trajectories – because of geographical distance; several couples experienced problems of domestic violence, infidelity, or the absence of quotidian communications before migration.

In addition to the importance of communication and trust in a conjugal bond, a flexible opinion about eventual unfaithfulness was detected. Infidelity issues concerned all the participants of the study, who discussed with their partners and have agreed on the decision of "telling the truth" in case that they (or their partners) find someone else. Just the fact that the couples talk about (un)faithfulness represents a change in Mexican popular culture, therefore, being open to the possibility of betrayal (and most of the time being able to forgive the partner) is a remarkable modification.

In the case of women who have a deported husband, adjustments to their stay in the United States have been noted (i.e., they do not go back to Mexico despite the fact that their husbands are there) for the reason that there are better opportunities for their children as well as for themselves in the United States. This illuminates a valuation of the idea of sacrificial motherhood over the value of obedience to the husband. Paradoxically, women's determinism, initially added stability to their conjugal bonds.

With regard to parenthood, those who migrated have developed closer relationships with their children, while decreasing their authority and control over them at the same time. The labor of discipline – social education – is transferred to the partner who stays, but in a deficient manner. Additionally, in the case of the women with deported husbands, it has been observed that the parental role in socialization is not more focused on one single (national) culture. For the children in the United States, socialization is wider in cultural terms, highlighting belonging to an hispanic culture, rather than to a Mexican or Anglophone one. This strategy also protects the children in case of deportation, which would mean transporting them to Mexico and confronting a new (but not so far from Hispanic) culture.

Last but not least, referring to the agreements that couples made, the fact of not respecting the (new) division of labor (mentioned in adjustment 2) causes several problems within the couple, even risking the continuity of the bond. It is here that economic elements, money, become more important, showing that intimacy and money are inseparable in family ties at a distance (Hochschild, 2000), and at the same time it is very difficult to generate a balance between them (Cienfuegos, 2017). Transnational divorce has recently been thematized (Fresnoza-Flot & De Hart, 2022).

5. (IN)STABILITY OF THE BOND

In consequence of the previous discussion, it appears that adjustments make the maintenance of transnational conjugality possible over time. Some of these arrangements started with the departure of the spouse, while others came afterwards. Both types formed a daily life "at a distance." Adjustments described above are summarized in Table 1.

Nevertheless, adjustments can change during the years of separation. So, what makes the bond stable? Something interesting about the adjustments presented is that not all of them would be thought of as factors that give continuity to the bond. Some are counterintuitive as intimacy- or bond-building factors, such as disagreements about the roles of spouses. Yet these factors contribute to the bond between partners. Good examples are the adjustments developed by women in the United States with deported husbands, or even relationships full of – both small and bigger – arguments, as has been seen in at least three couples from the sample.

Taking the previous discussion as a reference, as well as the cases in my study, I argue that conjugal stability through time is highly guaranteed due to three processes. Firstly, there are frequent communications about family organization as well as regarding personal subjects. The regularity mentioned before also suggests a shift in relation to the previous routines of the couples, in which daily conversation was not necessarily included.

Secondly, there are emotional reactions that spouses have as a result of their quotidian interaction. These are similar through time and produce a sense of

Table 1.   Adjustments: Explorations in How Conjugality at a
Distance Is Constructed.

1. Learning to maintain virtual contact and demonstrate the willingness to communicate regularly despite the distance.
2. Increase in frequency and content of communication, creation of *liminal rituals* (Illouz, 2009). Intimacy is created by the expansion of its symbolic-expressive component.
3. The distinguishing criterion in the family division of labor would no longer be the sex of the spouse, but rather their status as migrant or non-migrant.
4. There is flexibility about roles and responsibilities.
5. Generation of an "imagined space" in response to the lack of information about the life of the spouse.
6. Prominence of communication and trust as fundamental aspects of conjugality.
7. Talk about topics that are taboo in their societies of origin and "telling the truth" [*decirse las cosas*] in the case of problems like infidelity, unemployment, or sickness.
8. Flexibility concerning the value of faithfulness.
9. Contempt of male authority.
10. There is a loss of parental authority of the spouse who migrates, at the same time a weak transference of authority to the spouse who stays.
11. Socialization of children born in the United States in a wider Hispanic culture.
12. Breaking social expectations to re-signify relationship.

knowledge about the partner: what annoys, what produces happiness and hope, and even what kind of behavior could cause a conflict between the spouses. This sort of "emotional attitude" produces the anticipation from the actor (ego) to the reaction of his/her beloved (alter), which Luhmann described as the essence of intimate communication (Luhmann, 1998).

In my view, the "emotional attitude" is not necessarily (valued as) positive or constructive for the bond, but as a recurrent style in the way that they live out their relationships: for instance, Natalia (Morelos) knows that if she goes out dancing without her husband's permission, he – whom she describes as a very jealous person — will be quite angry. Also, Ariel (Tabasco) knows that if he cheats on Ana, he would lose his house. And Marisol (Morelos) is sure that if her youngest son asks Juan to come back for Christmas, Juan will say "yes" but afterwards he will find some reason for delaying the trip. Antonia (Oregon) suspects that her husband lied to her when he said that he quit drinking in Mexico. All these anticipations fit with Archer's concept of internal conversations.

Thirdly, the stability of a conjugal bond at a distance strongly depends on the negotiations that couples make regarding family organization and the life projects they want to achieve. Having economic and domestic agreements produces the idea of "carrying out a common project," "working as a team," or living in what Giddens called a "companionate love" (Giddens, 1992). In the reverse situation, non-compliance with responsibilities creates a gap in the reciprocal expectative (as well as in communication), generating a source of conflict within the couple.

Fourthly, it is relevant to note that the stability of the bond many times rests on unequal dynamics between the spouses. This result is evident in the case of those who stay in Mexico, absorbing full domestic and care labor, while earning money at the same time. For the men of Tabasco, this fact should be analyzed as flexibility in gender roles. Nevertheless, in the case of women who are in Morelos the same tendency could be described as continuity with historical gender inequalities. Consequently, we need to assess how much change and continuity within social order lies in the family adjustments mentioned until now. The idea of stability that I stress, looking at the life stories studied, does not assume stability is synonymous with a harmonious relationship. Two quotations suggest the uncertain future I found in 2012: one phone text from Jesús Suárez (Tabasco) the day I left Mexico; the other from Humberto, after 6 years in the United States.

> Javiera, good morning, I have good news: my wife did not go (to sign) the divorce papers and gave me another opportunity that I will not let pass, everything will be as it was before (Jesús, 38 years, staying in Tabasco)

> I'm going to tell you frankly what my idea of this place is: it's that we are passengers here and we are getting old. In any job, employers come and see you and say "no, this one is very old"; they want young people, people who are 20 or 25. So I say to many, "here comes one to work, meet up, and return with the family." (Humberto, 56 years, immigrant in Portland).

6. SOME CHALLENGES TO THE IDEAS OF FAMILY AND CONJUGALITY FROM THE TRANSNATIONAL "YOUNG" EXPERIENCE

Taking into account the analysis after my field work in 2012, I argue that four main challenges to the modern notion of family exist in the revised cases of conjugal distance. First, the maintenance of a non-physical intimacy was examined. Transnational intimacy is primarily virtual and symbolic in nature rather than physical, with communication and trust serving as fundamental elements. The existence of a symbolic-expressive component in the marital relationship combines parts of a romantic model of conjugality with a more current element about companionship and complicity (i.e., companionate love).

Secondly, with regard to household organization, the transnational family requires a relatively new division of labor, in which the decisive criterion is not the sex of the spouse, but rather whether they are living in Mexico or in the United States. In general terms, the spouse who migrates has little information about how his/her family is managing the household and distributing the work back home. Those who remain in Mexico do not know how their spouses are earning their living. Especially in the case of female migration, a more flexible gender division is emerging, as well as a renegotiation of responsibilities and duties. In many cases, non-compliance with these new responsibilities leads to an excessive workload for one spouse, and is thus a source of conjugal conflict, particularly when the husband/wife is abroad and is unable to send money home.

Thirdly, changes taking place with regard to the socialization that couples provide to their children are less evident. It has been observed that the exercise of parenthood continues, despite the distances involved, and that the affective component increases while the authority of the absent parent declines. The relationships become more emotional and original in ways of being in contact and generate routines. The work of socialization and discipline rests largely on the spouse who stays or, also, on other institutions, such as the school or the church. On the other hand, there is the case of "women with deported husbands" who choose their children's socialization in a culture that they named as "Hispanic." These two trends suggest that there are new dynamics of socialization in which the transmission of a "national culture" may have been a relevant criterion, but due to the migration routes it becomes less relevant, especially in the case of deported husbands.

The fourth challenge is about emotions and is divided into two parts. On the one hand, couples have to deal with the emotions and ambivalence produced by the lack of knowledge about much of the life led by the other spouse. With this in mind, one important transformation which is established as part of the communication routines is the expression of feelings, moods, and sentiments. Consequently, on the other hand, the conversations of the couples open up to new subjects, which are taboo in their origin society. The couple discussing taboo subjects is consistent with the reformulation of intimacy I described earlier. Also, the scenario would suggest a flexibility of the couple, to varying degrees, concerning cases of eventual infidelities, modifying the value of staunch faithfulness, but denying monogamy in any case.

Many of the solutions performed by individuals pointed out a transformation regarding the ways of being a family and what a stable family bond means empirically. Nevertheless, it should be noted that although the solutions partly questioned normative ideals about families, another part of the strategies adopted is consistent with this background. This is the main reason I have used the notions of "adjustments" and "challenges," because these showed that in the transnational family there exists as much change as continuity.

7. IT IS NOT ABOUT SPACE: INTIMACY MUTATIONS OVER TIME IN CONJUGAL RELATIONSHIPS

From her studies of couples consisting of professionals with double residence within the United Kingdom, Mary Holmes (2014) argues that there are new contents in contemporary experiences of family relationships, which deepen the conventional notion of intimacy, especially in the assumption of physical closeness as the basis of it. Indeed, this argument applies to the phenomenon of the transnational family that I have described. But at the same time there are differences.

On the one hand, in the case of academic couples, these seek to reconcile personal processes of individuation with life as a couple (Beck & Beck Gernsheim, 1998), which is possible due to the possession of certain capitals, mainly the economic and a cultural capital that is valued globally (Weiß, 2005). The costs of this option may include the expenses of maintaining two residences, emotional distance from partners, fears about infidelity, and the expense of travel. There are benefits, such as the intensive time that can be spent at work and the high quality of the time the couple has together when they are reunited. Costs for one can also be benefits for the other (Holmes, 2014, p. 7).

On the other hand, life as a couple for translocal or transnational families, with scarce resources and few years of formal education, turns out to be different, at the level of conciliation strategies as in the radicality of distance, going several years without seeing each other and with a certain "opacity" about the daily life of the other spouse. This makes the link more perishable and leads me to discuss the results of my research from a decade ago.

Another factor that nourishes these closing reflections is the change in the research agenda on transnational families. The results of recent research have shown a new plurality in the phenomenon of the transnational family, considering, among others, families of elderly or retired migrants (Bolzman, Kaeser, & Christe, 2017; Zontini, 2015), families that were transnationalized by exile or refuge (Ramírez, 2013; Sánchez & Roniger, 2010), and also several of those enunciated that are constituted due to skilled migration (Landolt & Da, 2005; Wall & Bolzmann, 2013, among others). When we look at the case of Latin American migration through the corridor to the United States, we have various empirical transnational families studies that focused primarily on relations between an emigrant parent or both parents from similar geographical origins, and their offspring who remained in the country of origin (Bolzman, 2023), as is the case of Pribilsky (2004), Dreby (2010), Yarris (2017), among many others. Most people who migrate do so in early adulthood, but family change as the family life cycle progresses. Then, members begin to age and family roles and solidarities mutate (D. Bryceson, 2023; D. F. Bryceson, 2019).

Based on the passage of time, ageing, and change in family solidarities and configurations, a third issue is the discussion between stories and life stories. In the end, the life stories, tracked during the years 2011 and 2012, were transformed into static photographs. The same has happened with the theoretical idea of the transnational family. If before it was said that the transnational family as a practice came to challenge the traditional notion of the modern and co-existing nuclear family, the focus on the life course of people comes to challenge the very idea of what the transnational family is. In fact, challenges about conjugality at-a-distance also emerged from my revision of the accounts after a decade of my fieldwork.

When contacting seven of my life-stories, I found the bonds changed, but persisting in a different manner. No longer consisting of a love relationship in six accounts (Marisol, Natalia, Jesús, José, Antonia and Eliana), but as a friendship and co-parenting bond (i.e., confesional intimacy) or as a functional, strategic, and post-romantic bond, more focused on personal interests while being aware of the interests of the loved one (Illouz, 2007).

A clear example is Eliana's husband in Mexico, who calls his children when he needs money. They do not speak anymore since he falsified documents in order to divorce her in 2015 and obtained the deed to the family house in Mexico. She made her life in the United States, with children and grandchildren, and now has bought her own house. She has never had a romantic partner apart from her ex-husband.

In a diverse sense, Marisol's ex-partner, in Chicago, became a good friend. He never abandoned his children and has paid to repair the family house several times, more than when they were sentimentally engaged. He listened to Marisol when she was suffering domestic violence from her new partner. They regularly interchange comments, "likes," and posts on each other's Facebook profiles. Marisol told me he covered medical costs when she needed an urgent surgery.

He cared about the alcoholism of two of the three children they have in common, and the fragile health of their daughter, who has diabetes and experienced two miscarriages and severe COVID-19.

In 2013, one of my stories, José, married a middle-age US-lady from Kansas in Portland. Until 2018, I am certain he interchanged some salutations with some of his seven children in Mexico. As can occur with technologies as Facebook, the messages seemed empty and the communications lacking in meaning. It is not clear to me whether he still is married, but three years ago he was. Ten years ago, José used to see movies and cook with his Mexican (ex)wife, la "güera," by phone.

We told each other, we both fell asleep on the phone, "did you already go to bed," "have you already snuggled in?," "yes, settle in here on my arm." That is, things like that, that you were full, you were filled with what you brought here (in the mind) and here (in the heart).

Children became adults, some of them are young fathers and mothers. Antonia Gómez, at 32, is the youngest grandmother I ever known. One of the newer grandmothers, Natalia González, in her mid-40s, wrote on her Facebook some months ago: "I asked God to give me a man who would love me for all of my life and he sent me my grandson." That post from 2022 signifies for me the closure of her ten years of waiting for Rogelio's return.

In Tabasco, women continue to migrate seasonally in search of opportunities for survival, as confirmed to me by a colleague who lives there. Due to lack of access to technology, I could not contact Jesús Suárez and his daughter further. In 2012, Jesús was confident in the new opportunity of his marriage, but he never returned to be with Rocío again. She returned, he fell ill with diabetes and his children moved to other locations in Mexico, as employees in the hotel sector. The twin brothers contacted each other to resolve the economic precariousness of the father, who possibly works less, as he has aged. Finally, one of the participants, Enrique del Solar, died in 2018 and never returned. I contacted his daughter in Mexico but never asked about the cause of death.

8. FINAL REMARKS ABOUT THE UNFINISHED LIFE STORIES

Family life is marked by a continuum of adjustments, especially when resources – social, work, educational – are precarious. After a decade of my fieldwork, the perspective on how the conjugal bond occurs at a distance has changed, especially with the follow-ups that I have conducted with several of the case studies, including issues such as return, aging, and survival. To a large extent, the latter is continually the foundation of distance.

In the cases of the couples and families that participated in this study, the adjustments that were mentioned managed to resignify in form and maintain the content of the conjugal life at a distance, while the spouses declared that they were living life projects in common, where communication and trust are fundamental. The stability of the bonds varied from case to case and several times the links showed organizational or emotional instability. The lives of these couples and their families were highly precarious and highly creative at the same time. Although the field work lasted about a year, the results are now viewed as a portrait of a stage in the life of transnational couples; young couples, with young children and the potential for participation in the unqualified labor market with tasks requiring resiliance and physical energy. All in all, it was a photograph of the link. After 10 years, these ties and actors have changed significantly; perhaps because of the same precariousness that makes these long-term life-cycle bets unsustainable.

Once romantic, intimacy in some cases became a friendship, mutating into confessional relationships. In other cases and with different intensities, it became a post-romantic intimacy, based on a prioritization of one's own desires and needs as an orientation of relationships still necessary, mainly by the possession of children in common. If at some point the idea of intimacy was founded on the romantic ideal, today it is in the most pragmatic sense.

REFERENCES

Archer, M. (2003). *Being human: The problem of agency*. Cambridge: Cambridge University Press.

Beck, U., & Beck-Gernsheim, E. (2001/1990). *El normal caos del amor. Las nuevas formas de la relación amorosa*. Barcelona: Paidós Ibérica.

Beck-Gernsheim, E. (1998). On the way to a post familial family. *Theory, Culture & Society, 15*, 53–70.

Beck-Gernsheim, E. (2002). *Reinventing the family*. Hoboken, NJ: Blackwell Publishers.

Beck, U., & Beck-Gernsheim, E. (1998). *El normal caos del amor*. Barcelona: El Roure.

Boccagni, P., & Bonizzoni, P. (2013). Care (and) circulation revisited: A conceptual map of diversity in transnational parenting. In L. Baldassar & L. Merla (Eds.), *Transnational families, migration and the circulation of care* (pp. 94–109). London: Routledge.

Bolzman, C. (2023). The elderly in transnational family configurations: Migration, inter-generational relations and care support in Switzerland. In J. Cienfuegos-Illanes, R. M. Brandhorst, & D. F. Bryceson (Eds.), *Handbook of transnational families around the world* (pp. 169–185). Cham: Springer.

Bolzman, C., Kaeser, L., & Christe, E. (2017). Transnational mobilities as a way of life among older migrants from Southern Europe. *Population, Space and Place, 23*(5), e2016.

Bonizzoni, P. (2012). Here or there? Shifting meanings and practices in mother-child relationships across time and space. *International Migration, 53*(6), 166–182.

Brendixon, S., & Näre, L. (2023). The migration-kinship nexus: Mobilising kinship during fragmented Afghan and Iraqi journeys to European Union countries. In J. Cienfuegos-Illanes, R. M. Brandhorst, & D. F. Bryceson (Eds.), *Handbook of transnational families around the world* (pp. 220–235). Cham: Springer

Bryceson, D. F. (2019). Transnational families negotiating migration and care life cycles across nation-state borders. *Journal of Ethnic and Migration Studies, 45*(16), 3042–3064.

Bryceson, D. (2023). Ageing: Generational change, reconfiguring family care for the elderly and repositioned family belonging. In J. Cienfuegos-Illanes, R. M. Brandhorst, & D. F. Bryceson (Eds.), *Handbook of transnational families around the world* (pp. 315–328). Cham: Springer.

Bryceson, D., & Vuorela, U. (Eds.). (2002). *The transnational family: New European frontiers and global networks*. Oxford: Berg.

Cantó-Milà, N., Núñez, F., & Seebach, S. (2014). *Send me a message and I'll call you back: The late modern webbing of everyday love life*. London: Routledge.

Celero, J. (2023). International marriage, migration and transnational family life in Asia: Japanese-Filipino families. In J. Cienfuegos-Illanes, R. M. Brandhorst, & D. F. Bryceson (Eds.), *Handbook of transnational families around the world* (pp. 131–145). Cham: Springer.

Chikwira, L., & Madizva, R. (2023). Transnational families and complex gender relations: Zimbabwean migrant women living in the United Kingdom. In J. Cienfuegos-Illanes, R. M. Brandhorst, & D. F. Bryceson (Eds.), *Handbook of transnational families around the world* (pp. 39–52). Cham: Springer

Chiyoko King-O'Riain, R. (2014). *Transconnective space, emotions and skype: The transnational emotional practices of mixed international couples in the Republic of Ireland*. London: Routledge.

Cienfuegos, J. (2017). *Conyugalidad a distancia. Resignificaciones en la intimidad y organización de familias transnacionales*. Santiago: Ril Editores.

Cienfuegos-Illanes, J. (2023). Transnational professional mothers and family care dilemmas in Santiago and Berlin. In J. Cienfuegos-Illanes, R. M. Brandhorst, & D. F. Bryceson (Eds.), *Handbook of transnational families around the world* (pp. 146–163). Cham: Springer.

Cienfuegos-Illanes, J., & Ruf-Toledo, I. (2022). Profesionales de nacionalidad venezolana en Chile: barreras, estrategias y trayectorias de su migración. *Estudios Públicos*, (165), 77–104.

Constable, N. (2007). Love at first site? Visual images and virtual encounters with bodies. In M. B. Padilla, J. S. Hirsch, M. Muñoz-Laboy, R. Sember, & R. G. Parker (Eds.), *Love and globalization. Transformations of intimacy in the contemporary world* (pp. 252–270). Nashville, TN: Vanderbilt University Press.

D'Aubeterre, M. E. (2000). *El pago de la novia: matrimonio, vida conyugal y prácticas transnacionales en San Miguel Acuexcomac, Puebla*. Michoacán: El Colegio de Michoacán.

D'Aubeterre, M. E. (2007). "Aquí respetamos a nuestros esposos". Migración masculina y trabajo femenino en una comunidad de origen Nahua del estado de Puebla. In M. Ariza & A. Portes (coords.), *El país transnacional. Migración mexicana y cambio social a través de la frontera* (pp. 513–544). México, DF: Instituto de Investigaciones Sociales, UNAM.

Dreby, J. (2010). *Divided by borders: Mexican migrants and their children*. Berkeley, CA: University of California Press.

Fresnoza-Flot, A., & De Hart, B. (2022). Divorce in transnational families: Norms, networks, and intersecting categories. *Population, Space and Place*, *28*, e2582.

Gabb, J., & Silva, E. (2011). Introduction to critical concepts: Families, intimacies and personal relationships. *Sociological Research Online*, *16*(4), 23. http://www.soresonline.org.uk/16/4/23.html

Giddens, A. (1992). *The transformation of intimacy: Sexuality, love and eroticism in modern societies*. Stanford, CA: Stanford University Press.

Giddens, A. (2000/1989). *Sociology*. Cambridge: Polity Press & Blackwell Publishers.

Hirsch, J. (2003). *A courtship after marriage: Sexuality and love in Mexican transnational families*. Berkeley, CA: University of California Press.

Hirsch, J. (2007). "Loves makes a family": Globalization, companionate marriage, and the modernization of gender inequality. In M. B. Padilla, J. S. Hirsch, M. Muñoz-Laboy, R. Sember, & R. G. Parker (Eds.), *Love and globalization: Transformations of intimacy in the contemporary world* (pp. 93–106). Nashville, TN: Vanderbilt University Press.

Hochschild, A. (2000). Global care chains and emotion surplus value. In W. Hutton & A. Giddens (Eds.), *On the edge: Living with global capitalism* (pp. 130–146). London: Jonathan Cape.

Holmes, M. (2011). Love lives at a distance: Distance relationships over the life course. *Sociological Research Online*, *11*(3). http://www.socresonline.org.uk/11/3/holmes.html

Holmes, M. (2014). *Distance relationships: Intimacy and emotions amongst academics and their partners in dual-locations*. Cham: Springer.

Illouz, E. (2007). *Intimidades Congeladas. Las emociones en el capitalismo*. Buenos Aires: Katz Editores.

Illouz, E. (2009/1992). *El consumo de la utopía romántica. El amor y las contradicciones culturales del capitalismo*. Buenos Aires: Katz Editores.

Jamieson, L. (1998). *Intimacy: Personal relationships in modern societies*. Cambridge: Polity Press.

Jamieson, L. (2011). Intimacy as a concept: Explaining social change in the context of globalisation or another form of etnocentrism? *Sociological Research Online*, *16*(4), 15. http://www.soresonline.org.uk/16/4/15.html

Joas, H. (1996). *The creativity of action*. Chicago, IL: The University of Chicago Press.

Lagarde, M. (1990). *Cautiverios de las mujeres: madresposas, monjas, putas, presas y locas*. Mexico, DF: Universidad Nacional Autónoma de México (UNAM).

Landolt, P., & Da, W. (2005). The spatially ruptured practices of migrant families: A comparison of immigrants from El Salvador and the People's Republic of China. *Current Sociology*, *53*(4), 625–653.

Luhmann, N. (1998/1982). *Love as passion. The codification of intimacy*. Standford, CA: Standford University Press.

Márquez, F. (1999). Relatos de vida entrecruzados: Trayectorias sociales de Familia. *Proposiciones, 29*, 1–11.

Marroni, M. G. (2000). "Él siempre me ha dejado con lo chiquitos y se ha llevado a los grandes...". Ajustes y desbarajustes familiares de la migración. In D. Barrera Bassols & C. Oehmichen Bazan (Eds.), *Migración y relaciones de Género en México* (pp. 87–118). Mexico, DF: UNAM-IIA/ GIMTRAP.

Morgan, D. (2011). *Rethinking family practices*. Cham: Springer.

Ossei, O. E., Mazzucato, V., & Haagsman, K. (2023). Sustaining Ghanaian transnational parent–child relationships through WhatsApp: A youth-centric perspective. In J. Cienfuegos-Illanes, R. M. Brandhorst, & D. F. Bryceson (Eds.), *Handbook of transnational families around the world* (pp. 97–111). Cham: Springer.

Pribilsky, J. (2004) "Aprendemos a convivir": Conjugal relations, coparenting, and family life among Ecuadorian transnational migrants in New York City and the Ecuadorian Andes. *Global Networks, 4*(3), 313–334.

Ramírez, C. (2013). "It's not how it was": The Chilean diaspora's changing landscape of belonging. *Ethnic and Racial Studies, 37*(14), 668–684.

Sánchez, M. A., & Roniger, L. (2010). El destierro paraguayo: aspectos transnacionales y generacionales. *Revista mexicana de ciencias políticas y sociales, 52*(208), 135–158.

Therborn, G. (2015). *Los campos de exterminio de la desigualdad*. Mexico, DF: Fondo de Cultura Económica.

Thomas-Brown, K. (2023). Jamaican female migration to the United States: Brain drain, left-behind families and 'barrel children'. In J. Cienfuegos-Illanes, R. M. Brandhorst, & D. F. Bryceson (Eds.), *Handbook of transnational families around the world* (pp. 53–66). Cham: Springer.

Tuñón Pablos, E. (2007). Mujeres mexicanas despulpadoras de jaiba en EU. *Amérique Latine Histoire et Mémoire. Les Cahiers ALHIM*, 14|2007. Retrieved from http://alhim.revues.org/index2312. html (Revised on March 19, 2022).

Wall, K., & Bolzman, C. (2013). Mapping the new plurality of transnational families: A life course perspective. In L. Baldassar & L. Merla (Eds.), *Transnational families, migration and the circulation of care: Understanding mobility and absence in family life* (pp. 77–93). London: Routledge.

Weiß, A. (2005). The transnationalization of social inequality: Conceptualizing social positions on a world scale. *Current Sociology, 53*(4), 707–728.

Wilding, R. (2006). Virtual intimacies? Families communicating across transantional contexts. *Global Networks, 6*(2), 125–142.

Williams, R. (1977). *Marxism and literature*. Oxford: Oxford University Press.

Yarris, K. (2017). *Care across generations: Solidarity and sacrifice in transnational families*. Standford, CA: Standford University Press.

Zelizer, V. (2009). *La negociación de la intimidad*. México, DF: Fondo de Cultura Económica.

Zontini, E. (2015). Growing old in a transnational social field: Belonging, mobility and identity among Italian migrants. *Ethnic and Racial Studies, 38*(2), 326–341.

CHAPTER 4

AGE-HOMOGAMY AND AGE-HETEROGAMY IN THREE GENERATIONS OF HETEROSEXUAL WOMEN AND MEN IN MEXICO*

Ana Josefina Cuevas Hernández

ABSTRACT

Age-difference in couple relationships in Mexico and Latin America has been a field of study predominantly approached by demographers and sociodemographers. In Western Europe and North America, the tendency is similar yet sociologists and anthropologists have contributed important knowledge to this discussion. The results of both groups of studies show that in most societies men marry and cohabitate with women younger than them and that in a rather small percentage women are older than men. The discussion on the reasons for which men prefer younger women or women prefer older men when marrying and cohabitating go from psychological to economic grounds. This study aims to contribute to the discussion on the reasons for which this pattern persists by study examining the narratives of 81 Mexican heterosexual men and women from three generations. This is done from a qualitative and sociological standpoint that approaches the age differences from the subjectivity and intimacy of the interviewees aiming to understand (i) the meanings of the age-gap and age discrepancy, (ii) the role of schooling and social class in the significance of the age-gap and age-discrepancy relationships, and (iii) the gender inequality

Conjugal Trajectories: Relationship Beginnings, Change, and Dissolutions
Contemporary Perspectives in Family Research, Volume 22, 59–80
Copyright © 2023 by Emerald Publishing Limited
ISSN: 1530-3535/doi:10.1108/S1530-353520230000022004

in age-gap relationships. The data show that amid a vigorous and strong trend of unions between older men and younger women where great gender inequalities may persist, there are signs of cultural change that show the discomfort and stigma of such differences. This, rather than being a contradiction, reveals how schooling and social origin affect the resignification of the difference, and moreover, suggests that the power relations in the couple are more equitable.

Keywords: Age-homogamy; age-heterogamy; heterosexual men; heterosexual women; intergenerational studies; Mexico

INTRODUCTION

Age difference at the time of marriage and union[1] in most western societies (Atkinson & Glass, 1985; Bozon, 1990; Cabré, Cortina, & Esteve, 2007; Casterline, Williams, & McDonald, 1986; Cowan, 1984; Kalmijn, 1998; Mazzeo, Martínez, Gil, & Lascano, 2015; Mier, 2009; Pyke & Adams, 2010; Solís, 2009, 2010, 2016; Vera, Berardo, & Berardo, 1985), tends to favor men, i.e., the man is older than the woman. In the social narratives and imaginaries, it is considered that such difference assures the relationship a greater psychological and economic stability. This idea has permeated scientific thinking and led several authors to test the quality of the relationship and the relations of power through the lenses of homogamy and heterogamy as the works of Vera et al. (1985), England and McClintock (2009), Pyke and Adams (2010), Solís (2016), and Quilodrán and Arrieta (2002) show. Van Poppel, Liefbroer, Vermunt, and Smeenk (2001, p. 2) point out from a socio-economic and cultural framework that "men's socio-economic resources, income, and social standing generally increased with age and therefore women had ample reason not to marry young men." This shows how popular wisdom reflects in scientific work.

Age gap relationships have been understudied in most societies despite in most of them the age difference favors men. In western Europe and the United States, there is a growing interest in this topic since early 1980 (see Atkinson & Glass, 1985; Bozon & Heran, 1989; Bozon, Rault, & Dutreuilhm, 2012; Cabré, 1993; Cortina, 2007; Kalmijn, 1994, 1998, 2010; Sura, 1990; Van Bavel, 2021; Van Poppel et al, 2001; Vera et al., 1985; Wheeler & Gunter, 1987). In the Latin American region (Cosse, 2008; Esteve & McCaa, 2007; Fernández, 2010, Mazzeo et al., 2015) and in Mexico in particular – where I will focus the analysis of age-gap relationship as – family demographers and sociologists and socio demographers (Gayet, 2002; Mier, 2009; Solís, 2016) started researching on this topic from mid 1990 onwards. These approaches, by their scope and nature, provide useful quantitative explanations.

The research of Casterline et al. (1986) on the age difference between spouses in 28 developing countries sheds a rich light on three aspects: the age gap pattern of preferences in each country around the ideal age at the time of pairing, the extreme difficulty to give a solid explanation of the meaning of the age at the time of the first marriage given the age gap differences between countries, and the lack of a clear pattern of the age at the time of pairing.

Cortina (2007) states that the positive age difference for men is one of the most common features in pairing; and perhaps such approach has been of little interest for demographics and sociodemographics precisely because it is commonality. Cabré et al. (2007) support this reasoning. On the other hand, Mier (2009) states that the age difference between spouses may vary greatly from one culture to the other which would be the result of the moral and cultural standards followed by each society, while Gayet (2002) argues that we know little about the changes in the social life of married and cohabiting life.

In the Latin American and Mexican scenario, age gap relationship research has focused on the socioeconomic origin of the couple at the moment of the union, the average age of men and women at the time of their first union, the gender differences in forming couples, the changes in the marital situation, and the fertility, among the main aspects. Some of these studies are from Parrado and Zenteno (2002), Solís (2009, 2010); Mier (2009); Mazzeo et al. (2015), and Rodríguez (2016). From this research, it is possible to cast a glance at it and to imagine how men's preferences for younger women – and women's preferences for older men – take form and the questions and different scenarios that can be postulated.

Among the most studied aspects of age-homogamous and age-heterogamous unions in Mexico have been educational and occupational homogamy (Esteve & McCaa, 2007; Solís, 2010; Solís, Pullum, & Bratter, 2007), spatial (Mier, 2009), and socio-economic (Solís, 2009, 2010). The literature at hand for the Latin America region shows a similar trend as educational, occupational, and social homogamy is what we know best (Cuevas, 2019; Esteve & McCaa, 2007; Solís et al., 2007).

The research made by Quilodrán (1993), Gayet, (2002), and Mier (2009) on age gap relationships in Mexico show that in almost half of the unions, there is a just over three-year difference for men, which suggests that the age gap widens in subsequent unions. Quilodrán and Arrieta's (2022) recent publication confirms that the difference between the two widens substantially in second unions in addition to making very interesting findings regarding the meaning of union for women, and how this new relationship allows them to overcome the fears and the problems of the previous relationship.

Cabré (1993, p. 3) argues that

the great majority of couples legally constituted correspond to predominant social models, uniting a man and a woman that, given their age, level of education, social origin, socio-economic characteristics, and other variables, constitute reciprocal options that may be considered, from a rational perspective, close to optimal.

Mier (2009) and Quilodrán and Arrieta (2022) state that the study of age difference between spouses has given rise to specific theoretical views that, based on empirical evidence, postulate that structural differences show that the age differences between both spouses increase in second and subsequent unions. In Mexico, there is a mean three-year difference in first unions (Gayet, 2002;

Mier, 2009). According to the INEGI 2020 statistics on marriage (2021, p. 2), in 2020 the average age difference in married couples in Mexico remained three years.

The data of both sources allow affirming that the age difference between sexes shows that greater the age difference, the lesser is the number of married couples, and, hence, unions with closer age differences are better seen than those with greater age differences. This goal becomes difficult to achieve in second and subsequent unions since there is an increasing number of separations and divorces in contemporary Mexico which allow predicting a great complexity and dynamism of the marriage and union market in the following decades.

In line with this scenario, I shall approach the meaning of age difference in three generations of Mexican heterosexual men and women from their subjectivity and intimacy to see how their ideas on the age difference were perceived. Their perceptions are explored through three age groups. The data show that amid a vigorous and strong trend of unions between older men and younger women where great gender inequalities may persist, there are signs of cultural change that show the discomfort and stigma of such differences. Rather than being a contradiction, this reveals how schooling and social origin affect the resignification of the difference, and moreover, suggests that the power relations in the couple are more equitable. I approach age gap relationships from a qualitative standpoint seeking to analyze how men and women involved in both age-homogamous and age-heterogamus see the age difference and how this could be related to unequal gender relations.

THEORY AND CONCEPTS

Partner choice and family formation have been the focus of interest in demography, anthropology, sociology, economy, and history, amongst other disciplines, and each one has settled their own premises on how to study and approach them. Regardless of their differences, they all agree that the election of a partner is not random and that individuals' attributes and decisions, whether conscious or not, play a key role when matching.

In this discussion, I use partner choice and partner market (Van Bavel, 2021) rather than marriage market[2] since they reflect with better accuracy the nature of my sample and the evolving nature of the partner market. The concept marriage market refers to the dynamics of marital life whilst my analysis comprises the dynamics of both married and cohabiting couples, therefore, the conjugal life. I do so by considering Van Bavel (2021) proposal of partner markets from the needs, preferences, and opportunities individuals have when partnering.

Regarding the needs, it considers that an individual is motivated to find a partner in order to fulfill his/her needs of protection, support, love, economic security, material aid, affect, offspring, kinship, and so on. However, individuals' needs vary to a great extent which makes it complex to explain why while some choose a partner earlier, some postpone it or even some others continue in the partner market after they engage. This shows that the discussion of partner choice must also consider his/her preferences and opportunities to grasp a more solid understanding of the market.

As for the preferences, the partner market reveals that individuals "like some traits more than others" (Van Bavel, p. 221) and such traits involve both parts, i.e., are bidirectional and man-driven. In this sense, the preference could be understood as the attractiveness of the individuals or their marriageability (Lichter, McLaughlin, Kephart, & Landry, 1992). Such desirability inclines individuals to choose a partner with specific features, characteristics, properties, or peculiarities such as race, beauty, income, and so on.

In relation to opportunities, finding a partner has a limit, that is, individuals cannot meet all the potential partners in the market; they are forced to select someone from their inner social networks which significantly reduces the size of the group to whom they have access. Broadening the market to increase their chances to find a more desirable match is expensive both in terms of time and money which may complicate and delay the entrance to the market. The opportunities individuals have to meet a partner with similar characteristics strongly depends on their level of schooling, the socioeconomic background of their parents, their economic activity, and the place they live as literature shows (Bozon, 1990; Bozon & Heran, 1989; Bozon et al., 2012; Cuevas, 2022; Esteve & McCaa, 2007; Kalmijn, 1998, 2010; Kalmijn, de Graaf, & Janssen, 2005; Solís, 2009).

As partner choice is not random, it is worth studying the traits and attributes that lead the election. One of these traits is the age on which western literature has already pointed out that is age-structured for heterosexual markets: women tend to choose older men and vice versa. Van Poppel et al. (2001, p. 1) posited that individuals tend to choose a partner close in age establishing an age difference that hardly ever goes beyond three years. Literature on homogamy shows this tendency is to consider it as such when the difference is close but hardly ever the same (Mier, 2009; Van Bavel, 2021; Van Poppel et al., 2001). Evolutionary theory posits that a complete gender equality in the age at the moment of selecting a partner will never occur due to the sexual selection.

Strictly speaking, a three-year difference is more to do with heterogamy than with homogamy. However, given the strong tendency of this pattern in the western world and the lack of a more solid theory, I will use the concept of homogamy to refer to unions with up to 3 years of difference, age gap relationships of age-heterogamy for age differences that go from 4 to 10 years and use the age-discrepant concept for unions that comprise 11 or more years of difference.

Age differences are increasingly approached from a gender perspective which consider it as an indicator of gender inequality (Bozon, 1990; Esteve & McCaa, 2007; Solís et al., 2007; Van Bavel, 2021; Van Poppel et al., 2001). However, the evidence from recent studies both in the United States and in Latin America shows that gender inequality is not necessarily weakening as the age difference between the couple reduces since changes do not imply more equality: women depend less from men to secure their economic well-being and share schools and workplaces but remain underpaid (Sweeney & Cancian, 2004; Van Bavel, Schwartz, & Esteve, 2018), men and women divorce and repartner in similar numbers but it is unclear if that reflects equal opportunities (Grow, Schnor, & Van Bavel, 2017; Schnor, Pasteels, & Van Bavel, 2017), and it is also unclear if despite the converging of their sex differences this could be considered more egalitarian (Zentner & Eagly, 2015).

Unions are crossed by power relationships and gender roles regardless of the formality of the link through which couples start a conjugal life. Age difference, schooling levels, social origin, and occupations are all factors that play a key role in power and gender relationships in their daily life. As research shows, women tend to have less power even when they have higher or similar educational schooling, occupation, social origin and/or are older than their partners (Cuevas, 2022; van Bavel, 2021).

It is convenient to look at unions from a gender perspective since partner choice reproduces socioeconomic and cultural inequalities and enacts gender. The election of a partner is a decision influenced by the social norms and the values individuals apprehended since early childhood and through an intensive socialization in later stages of life. Van Poppel et al. (2001, p. 1) state that

> large age differences in favour of the male are thought to reinforce the husband's ability to demand submission from his bride during marriage (Ware, 1981, pp. 92–93) and to lower the standard of marital sexuality (Mitterauer & Sieder, 1982, pp. 126–127). The alleged trend toward smaller age differences between spouses has therefore been interpreted as indicative of a shift toward increasing gender equality (Atkinson & Glass, 1985; Hochstadt, 1982, p. 542; Veevers, 1984).

Gender theory toward age difference considers that homogamy reduces social disparities or systems' arbitration by raising the possibilities of finding a partner with the same status and attributes. Cortina (2007, p. 39) posits in this respect that marriage patterns – here understood more broadly as unions – are more sensitive to reproduce or modify the social hierarchies and inequalities. In this respect, Kalmijn (1998) discusses that partner choice is also influenced by third party interests such as class and family and calls attention to the role they have in the reproduction of homogamy by encouraging unions among equals and by preventing heterogamus unions. For her part Cortina (2007) also discusses that class endogamy is as rigorously determined by the free game of love as it is constrained by explicit family interventions. This reflects that third parties play a key role in partner choice by organizing potential meetings for the couples, accepting courtship, playing as cupid, giving opinions on the attributes and status of potential candidates, and withdrawing moral and social support to show disagreement.

Bozon & Heran (1989) has approached age-gap unions from a gender perspective and his discussion provides insightful explanations on how women and men rate the biological and social age, the resources the couple exchange in marriage – and therefore unions –, and the gender differences at the moment of choosing a partner. He created two useful concepts to assess the evaluation of age difference, regardless of its type, in couple relationships: biological age and the social age. He considers both are crossed by gender inequality. Physical age refers to the chronological age while social age is the subjective and social perception of the biological age. Both concepts are used by common individuals to define a person's status and social autonomy of any person in the partner market.

Bozon (1990, p. 581) postulates that women's valuation of men's age in general is "perceived, classified and judged according to their social age which is independent of their real biological age." He also considers (1990, p. 583) that more than the objective age gap between the man and themselves, women value the social age gap, at least when the couple is formed. Particularly sought after are values linked to social maturity such as the man's experience, knowledge, and support. When the couple is formed, women are clearly afraid of dominating the partner with their social maturity. Even when the real ages of the two are very close, it seems that they want to assert a male superiority. In short, it is as if a man's liking for a woman could not be born without a perception of her superiority, which higher age helps to bring out.

Bozon's discussion focuses on women's valuation of men's social age but I strongly believe men use the same cultural criterion to choose a partner as they also form part of the social system. The fundamental distinction between women and men's valuation is that the former are educated to subordinate to men whilst the later are educated to exercise this power before women.

Finally, I would like to call the attention on the resource theory to understand why relationship power vests in one partner over the other and I will focus on the analysis of schooling levels, social class, and age. The theory suggests, broadly speaking, that the partner bringing the most resources to the relationship will have more power. The analysis of power and gender in husband-older marriages such as that of Pyke and Adams (2010) shows that most studies oversee the contribution women make to the family even when their resources are more important than those provided by men. These resources can be money and work but only since beauty and youth are also attributes highly valued when men unite to younger women.

Researchers agree that the increasing participation of women in the family economy grant them more power, but literature shows that has not been the case (see Pyke, 1994). Studies show that couples have unequal access to the economic resources because of persistent gender discrimination at the workplace (Hakim, 1996). The resource theory has also failed to see how gender norms, individual ideology and affect diminish women's contribution to the household even in the cases where their money is the basis of the household economy (Pyke, 1994; Pyke & Coltrane, 1996).

METHOD AND PROCEDURE

The men and women interviewed were chosen by locating people known among the research group,[3] and the snowball technique allowed us to locate cases through the population being interviewed. The sample was selected according to their age, having lived as a couple for at least seven years, whether married or cohabitating, having had children with their current or former partner, and having lived in any of the zones of study. We worked with three age groups. The first consisted in young adults between 32 and 48 years of age; the second, adults between the ages of 50 to 63, and the third group consisted in the generation of senior adults of 65 years and older. The interviews were conducted between September 2019 and June 2020 in the Colima Metropolitan Zone[4] (ZMC) and the Guadalajara Metropolitan Zone[5] (AMG) located in the states of Colima and Jalisco respectively, which are part of the Western Mexican region.

A total of eighty-one (81) interviews were conducted, 32 in the ZMC, and 49 in the AMG, of which 46 correspond to women and 35 to men of different socio-economic levels: 29 of low class, 26 of middle class, and 26 of middle upper class. These were transcribed verbatim in Word and systematized and encoded in the Maxqda2020 Proanalytics program. At the first level of systematization, the content was divided according to the five axes of research which were the marital trajectories – from what this analysis shows –, the couple's roles, mutual care, sexuality, and the use of technologies in the couple. Secondly, each researcher analyzed the data of her own axe. In the axe of marital trajectories, I worked specifically on the couple formation through the age difference and this was done by generation, from the gender perspective, and by the number of unions. At the third level of analysis, we worked on age gap to know their meanings in the 81 interviews. To achieve this, we followed Flick's proposal (2007) which gave us particularly useful coordinates to oversee so many cases. The author suggests that before such a large corpus of interviews, it is more important to understand the general structure of the problem and to contextualize the specific case of each one. This contextualization considered the age of both members of the couple, their marital state, their schooling, their social class, and the number of couple relationships with which they were able to provide denser explanations. This analysis produced 126 categories and sub-categories of analysis on age differences between men united to younger women and between women united to younger men of the three generations of study. All the interviewees agreed that the information be used totally or partially in the research.

The aim of the research was to produce empirical data on the five axes mentioned above and their interconnections to intimacy in an effort to elaborate a theoretical discussion on intimate life based on Mexican and Latin American literature. We deliberately sought to discuss how intimacy had been understood and worked in the numerous works we found considering the specific historical, political, and socioeconomic contexts in which these discussions took place. We assumed that the research on intimacy must clearly consider the spatial and cultural coordinates that frame their analysis in order to be able to understand how late modernity had impacted upon the decisions and dynamics of the couples. We departed from the work of Giddens (1998), Bauman (2004) and Beck (1999), and Beck and Beck-Gernsheim (1995) to see how their work had influenced the way intimacy had been understood and worked at an empirical level.

RESULTS

The findings related to the meaning of the age-difference, age-gap, and age-discrepant relationships indicate two simultaneous processes that cross the three generations of men and women interviewed: the high persistence of unions of older men with younger women, and the discomfort and conflicts in both sexes given the age difference. There were three main findings. The first shows that in 9 out of 10 couple relationships, men were older than women and the age distances ranged between 1 and 40 years. Regardless of the difference, data suggest that both the couples and third parties accepted such differences. The second finding shows that most men and women with higher education and middle to upper middle class, perceived age-discrepant unions negatively. The third finding is that in most couple relationships in which the woman was older than the man, she occupied a subordinate position. This allows me to say that the older age of women does not reduce the inequality vis-à-vis their partner, and that age alone does not explain such subordination. In these couple relationships, the age difference was between 1 and 13 years.

THE AGE-GAP AND AGE DISCREPANCY IN THE THREE GENERATIONS OF STUDY

One of the main findings regarding the age difference was that in nine out of ten relationships men were older than their partners and the age difference was between 1 and 40 years. The results indicate that as second and subsequent unions are made, the gap increases, and the broadest difference of 40 years was found in the generation of older adults. Women and men's narrative on this type of relationships shows that in most of the cases, the couples and their families accepted the age difference and that the education and social class marked significant differences in the dynamics of the relationship and gender inequality in the relationship.

Gamaliel is 52 years old, divorced, belongs to the upper-middle class, has a bachelor's degree and two children from his first marriage. He remarried for a second time with a woman seven years younger who belonged to the middle class, was college-educated and divorced with two children. The age-gap between them was of no concern for them or their families when they married.

> Next, we started having a relationship. The truth is that our courtship was supercool; we travelled, we did lots of things, and I really kind of saw myself determined to, to that this is the place where I should be [...] I would say our relationship is excellent...because there is trust, understanding, respect, shared dreams, there is, I mean, it is not the same that when you are twenty something years old and can choose a woman with whom you plan to stay your entire life and where she is going to, you need to stay together because you don't know if she is going to be the same person in 10 years, in 15 or 20. That person is chosen by you when you have a certain level of, first of all, a life lived to the full, and experiences and many other things that have changed the perspective you have; when you're 47 it is a moment when you have more elements to choose [a woman] and to identify yourself with someone because you know what you like and what you don't like [...] Our relationship is quite good on a daily life basis: we got up, she generally gets up, we wake up more or less at the same time, she goes and prepares the coffee, takes the coffee to the room, we drink it and accompany it with a biscuit or something sweet and then after that we shower and go to work. I arrive home by lunch time, and she has the meal ready, we eat and the two of us tidy up the kitchen...the truth is that working with her is cool, she's funny, she's easy going, we get along quite well.

The absence of a narrative on the intervention of third parties in the relationship of Gamaliel during courtship and married life shows age-gap had no relevance in their conjugal life. Likewise, following his narrative it is possible to posit that despite he and his wife assumed a traditional role at home, sharing some domestic activities helped them to bond. It also stands out that his consideration of having made a better choice of partner in his second marriage was linked to a positive valuation of his previous marital life.

In other narratives, we can also clearly see that the age difference favorable to men was not a reason for concern and that the goal was set on the future of the relationship; hence, age played a key role as a stabilizing element of power relationships between both. The case of Benito and his second wife exemplifies this situation well. He was 28 years old, mason, with a high school education, had a daughter from a previous relationship, in addition to two children outside wedlock when he decided to rebuild his life with a woman eight-year younger, with elementary education, single and without children who worked as an employee in a shoe store. Both were of low class.

> [...] In the course of our courtship, I decided whether to marry well. One also throws the imagination, one starts to think forward and imagine the future; I also imagined myself with children, I imagined myself living happily, and this completed the illusion of getting married; and we married well, we had a civil and religious marriage, like all her family [...] We decided to marry because we had been courting for four years and it was a nice relationship with her family and with her and said to myself "what else are we looking for?." And we wanted to unite, we aimed to formalise a family, to become a couple [...] Well, it is a pretty family, she's a pretty woman, I mean, having children is what I dreamed of [...] I met her at a shoe shop, she was a clerk there [...] because I have always disagreed that if the man earns a good living to support the house, well the woman has to stay at home, if she has any career that justifies [she is not at home], if she has an occupation and has no duties at home, I always assumed she would do the house chores, but there is a housewife and there is a professional, there are only two categories, a housewife and a professional.

The previous case supports the argument of the acceptance of age-gap relationships by third parties and the couple itself. Likewise, from the narrative we can infer that their social origin and level of schooling helped them to define the roles each assumed at home and in their relationship: he as a breadwinner and she as a housewife, a role her husband expected her to do on the grounds, she lacked a college degree that prevent it her of doing so. Benito's wife also quitted her job before they marry as a signal of respect and recognition of his capability to support her. In this exchange of needs, she subordinated to his authority not because she was younger but because she was educated to do so, a position reinforced by her low schooling.

In other cases, we can see that in middle-class families, parents approve the courtship and thus, the relationship goes forward, as is the case of Isadora. She was 19 years old when she met her future husband at a family party. She was an undergraduate student and he, a 25-year-old college graduate employed in his parents' business, both middle-class.

> [...] Unlike now, one had to ask permission by making eye contact because my parents were in front of me, then he stood beside me and asked me if I wanted to dance, he was very kind, a real gentleman. And my mother, I turned to my parents, then until my parents gave permission, I could dance. And from [there onwards in the courtship they told me] "Well, now it's okay." [...] Let me put it this way, I have always been there [in the family business] but lately, since he became independent, he got independent from his brothers, not from the business,

then as he got more independent, then I focused more thoroughly on his work since three years ago; but I have always been there [in the family business] but well, well [full time] it's been like three years [...] Well, I didn't have...logically I do think differently now that I did back then [...] I get along quite well with my husband, with Peter, [we are] very cool. In what sense? We have evolutionized in our sexual life, we do very different things, very cool things [laughter]. We spent lots of time together, we chat a lot, he's my best pal. I mean, it's a change, a very good change, I get along with him quite well, right? He's, how to say it? He's my best friend now.

Isadora's narrative shows that she was first subordinated to her parents' authority, particularly her father's, and later, during the first years of her marriage, to her husband's. It is important to note that even though the cultural and economic levels of both were identical, this did not play a key role in greater equality in the relationship during their first years of marriage. In this case it cannot be said that age was the ground on which she accepted her subordination but rather the education she received as a woman. Her narrative also shows her position before her husband changed as he managed to become more independent from his family's business, and therefore, from the pressure they might have punt on them to keep a more traditional arrangement. This impacted in a very positive way their marriage as not only opened new spaces to participate in their own business but also helped them to build a strong relationship based on mutual help, communication and a satisfactory sexual life. As in the case of Gamaliel, Isadora and her husband were of middle class and had a college degree, elements that seem to play an important role in a more egalitarian gender relationships.

The narratives also show that in age-discrepant relationships, as in the case of Raquel, an upper middle-class woman, the family's concern was not the age difference but if she was sure she wanted to get married. She was nineteen years old, had a technical career and worked as her father's secretary when she married a 30-year-old man from the same social class, with university education, suffering from diabetes since childhood. Her parents questioned her decision to marry trying to make her see the responsibility her decision entailed considering her fiancé's health condition.

He was 11 years older than me, and I thought he was only four years older, and later I discovered his age. And he also thought I was older, since I was going dancing and I wore makeup, high heels and wore my hair in a bun because I had long hair; hence, he thought I was much older. He thought I was about 20 when I was 16, and I thought he was 23 when he was 27. [...] At the time I got married, my parents made me think a lot, they discussed with me, argued with me, however, I never felt the imposition of "don't marry" or "if you marry," but these discussions were rather rational: "Why do you want to marry?," "Measure the consequences"... etc. etc. etc. [...] My grandparents were like parents to me [...] I never felt like a daughter-in-law, I felt more like a daughter; they, my parents-in-law, supported me more than they supported him, I felt completely supported [by them] [...] His health continued weakening, had two heart attacks, he started having health problems linked to the circulatory system [...] So, I went to study but there were murmurs, that I went out every day and left him with the children [...] He could move on his own and all that but obviously I was full of life and his health was weakening. He never said to me "don't study," never! I didn't ask him for permission either nor did he say no. Let's say he accepted that someone had to stay at home and take care of the children, and I left the care of the children to him so I could study; and I never had the slightest problem... I didn't have a husband, father or grandparents who told me "This shouldn't be happening, you're the woman," but on the contrary.

Raquel's narrative reflects that what worried both her family and her parents-in-law was her husband's health rather than the age-gap. Even though during their first years of marriage she and her husband organized the domestic work according to traditional norms, the weakening of her husband's health inverted the traditional roles: she continued her education to prepare to be the breadwinner while her husband stayed home looking after the children. Her case sheds light, once more, on the relevance of social class and education in the establishment of more egalitarian relationships when couples face hardship.

Broadly speaking it can be said that in most interviews third parties did not intervene before age-gap and age-discrepant unions. However, the language used by some interviewees suggests a clear awareness of this difference both on their part and on the part of their partners. The narratives of some of them indicate an emotional distancing of the interviewees from their couples. This is visible in the way women narrated the age-gap and age-discrepancy: they showed emotional distancing, neutrality, and skepticism before the question of the age difference.

Teresa's case illustrates this situation quite well. She was a 21-year-old woman with three children, with elementary education, and employed as a house cleaner, when she began her second relationship with a 60-year-old widower with four children from a previous relationship. He had a high school education and worked as a bartender and as a farmer when he was unemployed. Both were poor. None of the two families, particularly hers, objected to the relationship.

> He was already a mature man, the people even asked me if he was my father [laughter], he was already a mature man [...] He never told me [his age], I think he was ashamed, he must have been 60, yes 60 [...] I lived there [in his house] with him, but I worked to make a living. He got mad, didn't want me to go out to work but what he gave didn't allow me to make ends meet and that's how all started, the fights, and well, we left each other. The problem was the money, the thing is when you have a family you need it, you need money [...] He told me [not to work] but the money wasn't enough to support all [three] children. He did help with the baby that was on the way, but it didn't allow me to feed them all [...] I cooked his meals, I washed his clothes, I cleaned the house. I did everything before going to work [...]

The causes that led Teresa to end her relationship were economic rather than age-based issues despite the 39 years that separated them. In her case, as in Benito's case, the division of work followed a rigid pattern based on gender values that translated into long working hours for her and lately, on strong disagreements with her partner. The strong views of her husband on his role as breadwinner and his resistance to accept the relevance of Teresa's income for the well-being of the children troubled their relationship. It is also worth noting that although he held a high school degree this did not seem to make any difference in his attitude toward domestic and paid work. Regarding the language used by Teresa to refer to the age-discrepancy it stands out she detached from him by calling him "a mature man" and "he" instead of calling him by his name. On his part, the age difference seemed to have been a matter of concern for her partner as he refused to tell her his age.

Laura's case also illustrates how women of low social class and low schooling see the union with an older man as a route to gain independence from their father's authority and a false way out of poverty. She was a poor teenager with a high school education and was 19 years old when she met her first partner, a middle-class man with a bachelor's degree, divorced, and 16 years older than her, with whom she cohabitated for 10 years.

> And then… I met him because I needed to work, I needed the money. I always wanted, wanting to have to protect my mother and help her […] he courted me for six years, six years wanting […] I stood up for myself, I didn't want to go out with him, I wanted to get married to my boyfriend, but it didn't work out, it was a cruel breakup for me, and he was there, and well […] I saw him as an older man, and I as a girl, can you imagine? A 19-year gap! Well, as they say, the devil was tempting me, and I said: "Well. If he asks me to marry him, I will get married." And I told him: "Everything is all right. All in order."

Age-discrepant unions are not exclusive to any particular social class or level of education. Fernanda, a divorcee, began a second relationship at the age of 55 with a widower twenty years older than her. Both were middle-class and had a college degree. As in most cases analyzed so far, age-discrepancy was not the concern, at least for her, but rather the opinion of third parties on their relationship. Her narrative also shows a detachment caused by the fear of her partner to the reaction of his children toward his relationship. The memory also reflects on her partner's worry for the age-discrepancy.

> I met a person, because I did not want to have problems with divorcés, or with a… widower. Then, he was 20 years older than me… […] We lived together for a while, but that person was a coward, very coward to…he was a widow, it was common back then that out of respect for the children they didn't make up their mind. I mean, "what would my children say?," "my children will get mad at me," and that's how I ended the relationship, it didn't work any longer […] This partner, well, he…he had a heart attack and freed me, he said: "you're too young for me, you better go home." He got touchy and wanted me to live with his daughters, well, not really, right?

In this case, notwithstanding the similarity of cultural and economic resources, she was subordinated to the authority of her partner by the very fact of being a woman evident in the passive role she played before her partner's decisions on the conditions of their relationship and the importance he gave to his children's opinion. It is also worth mentioning that as in Teresa's case, Fernanda's partner was also worried by the age difference despite her being willing to continue the relationship. It seems to be that the only way out for her to regain emotional stability was to end the relationship before the lack of commitment of her partner to their relationship.

THE ROLE OF SCHOOLING AND SOCIAL CLASS IN THE SIGNIFICANCE OF THE AGE-GAP AND AGE-DISCREPANCY RELATIONSHIPS

The second finding is that for men and women with higher education and middle and upper-middle class, age-gap had a negative connotation. In some cases, even though the age-gap was not significant, it was clear that the interviewees themselves felt uncomfortable with the difference. This contrasts with the attitudes of the partners of some interviewees who felt awkward with the gap. Such is the case of Jimena who considered it crazy to cohabitate with a man she saw as much older than her. She was nineteen and had just finished high school when she met a man with a college degree and a job. Both were middle class and had no children at the time of cohabiting.

> Well, [I was] 19 [...] Yes, yes, [Laughter] I was crazy [...] He was 24 [...] I was finishing high school, he had already finished his BA. Really, at this point, I say, it wasn't that many years the difference, but, at that point, it was because he already had a stable job, had just finished his BA and all that. He, as a man, was my role model both in terms of love and as a man.

Alejandra also felt that way with a four-year age-gap with her boyfriend. She was 19 and was a fresher when she met her future husband. She was from the upper-middle class and he, middle class. They were college classmates.

> [He was] three and a half [older than I was]. But I felt as if he was a geezer! That is, I was going out with an old man [...] Yes, I was in my second university semester [...]

> He was also studying Law. But he had just entered university. He took his time before going to college, and when he entered university, he was in my high school friend's classroom, and that is how I met him [...]

Carolina's narrative also accounts for this and suggests that she perceived that despite the five-year-age-gap with her husband, he was very playful. She was 25 when she met him, and he was her second marital partner. Both had college education, were upper-middle class and had no children.

> It must be also for my husband's personality, how he is, even though he's older than I, not so much, five years older, but he still behaves as a child, very playful; then, no, well it is always fun, we always have something to talk about.

In other cases, the age-discrepancy shakes off the couple's intimate life since the biological difference translates into different sexual needs. This, unlike people of lower classes and little schooling, led the couples with higher education to deal with the problem to stabilize the relationship. This was the case of Braulio, 55 years old with a doctorate degree, civilly married with a 42-year-old woman, also with a doctorate degree, both middle-class.

> I believe that given my age, I am the most, and I also thought of it and said that if I were to die ...our sexual relation has been very open, I rather believe it is her, because in my case, my sexual appetite has waned in the last five or six years, and she is very young, then we have to come to some agreements, such as activities that do not necessarily have to do with penetration because part of my libido has diminished, then, we need to resort to pills.

The age difference, when it is very discrepant, may generate conflicts in the couple for fear of social criticism. This is the case of Carolina who, at the age of 19 started courting a man 16 years older than her. It was her first marital partner. She was in college, and he had already a stable job, and they had problems making public their life as a couple.

> Uncomfortable given the age difference, that is, suddenly you are no longer the girlfriend, they introduce you as "Oh, Carolina" [bitter tone], right? "Oh no! Me, going out with her? She could be my daughter!." And yes. They go out with you! Then, when you are young, you put up with a lot, and then, I started to grow and I said: "that's it, I'm done, that is, I'm getting older, I don't see where this is going," so I left him.

The narratives above show that the level of schooling and social class played a key role in how women and women made sense of the age-gap and age-discrepancy. Among lower social classes and people with elementary and high school level education, age-discrepant marriages and unions were not questioned by the couple or third parties – particularly their families – even when the discrepancy reached 40 years. These cases show that poverty and the family context in which interviewees lived encouraged them to marry and unite to older men hoping to gain autonomy and escape poverty. Conversely, among the interviewees of higher schooling and middle and upper-middle classes, it was obvious that the age-gap was perceived negatively, even in the cases with a 4-to-5-year gap. This questioning occurred mainly in generations of middle-aged and young adults. The above shows that the age-gap and age-discrepancy acquired significance for the interviewees according to their levels of schooling and their social class, and that the gender relationships in both scenarios were different and with greater equity insofar as schooling and social class were higher.

GENDER INEQUALITY IN COUPLE RELATIONSHIPS

The third finding of this research revolves around women's subordinate position in couple relationships in which they are older than men. This suggests that the age-difference, the age-gap, or the age-discrepancy do not explain the subordination of most women to their partners. We need to look at how schooling, social class and occupation interplay with the age difference to be able to understand how gender inequality operates.

The dynamics of Octavio's second union gives a clear account of this. He became a widower at the age of 28 and had to take care of his two young daughters. He had elementary schooling and worked as a laborer. He was facing a desperate situation since he did not know how to solve the dilemma of working and taking care of his daughters. This prompted him to marry a second time with a woman two years older than him, with elementary studies, mother of a three-year-old daughter, who worked as a house cleaner, and as poor as he.

> [...] I only waited one year, after this, I looked for another [partner] to go on with my life. At that time, as my children were very young, I went back to my parents' house, [...] well, because my children were very young and the eldest [inaudible], only women. For a single man with very young daughters and having to work, it is very hard [...] I remember having met her somewhere and [...] she was working [...] after marrying her, she became a housewife, right? But when I met her, she was working as a house cleaner.

This division of labor was also evident in other cases, such as Arturo, a 36-year-old man united to a woman 13 years older than him, both in their first marriage, with college education and low social class. She worked during the first years of their marriage, took care of the household and their two daughters whilst he devoted himself to his job. When Arturo changed jobs, she left hers to dedicate herself full-time to the household and the care of their daughters.

> [...] My previous job was from Monday to Friday in the city, with a relatively stable schedule; but with my current job, in which I have been working for seven years approximately, I need

to travel a lot; they can call me suddenly, I don't know, now, and tell me: "Listen, something happened, you have to come right away because we have a meeting in an hour," and I have to attend a meeting and I don't know if it will last half hour, two hours, and at the best, they'll tell me: "go for your suitcase because you're going right now," and I have to travel for three, four, five days. And I believe that this has also made the situation more complicated, I say, Adela is quite aware of my work, and she supports me a lot. But her workload is quite heavy, taking care of the family, the household chores as well as our daughter, and this, I also believe, is quite exhausting for her.

Some other times, inequality is the result of the excessive freedoms and abuse of authority of men which in the case of Jeremias is expressed through the euphemism "the too many undue things". He is a 50-year-old married man, an entrepreneur with a master's degree, married to a woman two years older than him, with college education and the same social class; both their first marriage.

[...] We travelled since we were very young, since we were children, and this...I believe that at the beginning, it was more out of habit of being together, right? Um... and as both of us were becoming more mature... in what it was... that it had been the best decision we had taken, um, you're a woman, a woman matures more rapidly than a man [...] Um, but I was ... I was beginning and I believe that because I worked at the Attorney General's Office, um... Young, with money and power, um... you do um... too many undue things and I landed well at that time, and, um, I don't believe, I don't believe having made a mistake, right? I made mistakes afterwards, but my decision of living with Lidia, I believe, was not a mistake.

When the woman is older than the man, and belongs to a higher social class, the relationships can become very violent as in Berenice's case. She is a middle-class woman, divorced, 11 years older than her partner, who faced several other challenges in her couple relationship besides age; she had a higher income, greater work stability, and a higher education than her partner. This resulted in great resentments from him; he was a middle-class man, with incomplete college education.

[...] after I began going out with the kiddo. This was a terrible decision [Laughter]. [...] It lasted two years, but well, I was eleven years older, [...] Because he was also bipolar [Laughter]. But he was more... He never did me anything, but we screamed at each other. [...] He, at that time, I was doing better at work than now, and he was earning almost nothing, and it was always his ego, that a woman was earning more. [...] He said I was showing off, that, that, that I, that money, it showed that I had more than him. [...] Well, of course, of course I did. He didn't even have a career.

DISCUSSION

The results suggest that age difference itself – regardless of whether it is an age-homogamus or age-heterogamus relationship – cannot explain gender inequality. We must also look at how other resources or attributes the couple bring into relationship such as education, occupation, and social class interlink and affect gender relations. Bozon (1990), Pyke and Adams (2010), and Esteve and McCaa (2016) support this position.

A first finding in this respect is that among women of low social class and low schooling was more likely that the couples and their families of origin accepted the age-difference, the age-gap and the age-discrepancy. A second finding was that among the interviewees with higher education and higher social status, the narratives were more judgmental, but in those of poor women with lesser education there were also elements that reflected a clear awareness of the age differences on the part of men. In both groups, it was obvious that their partners were concerned about the age difference and feared facing stigma (Goffman, 2006). A third finding is the difference between women and men when re-entering the partner market: for men the age-gap widened significantly in second and subsequent unions whilst the opposite happened to women. The fourth and last finding shows that in regardless of the age difference, age-gap or age-discrepancy when women were older than men tended to leave their jobs, do all the domestic work and look after the children; hence losing their economic independence and becoming more subordinate to their partner's authority. In these relationships couples also faced more difficulties than couples in which men were older than women because the age difference, social origin and schooling differences all combined to affect the couple's stability.

The analysis of the narratives on age differences points out that poor women with little schooling did not accept courtship and the age-gap immediately and that their families not always rejected the relationship. Courtships took time and the women resisted to marry and unite not because the age-discrepancy – that sometimes reached 40 years – but because they yearned for a family and a relationship based on romantic values. However, for poor women whose lives were marked by harshness and sometimes violence these conditions prompted them to marry or unite partners they initially rejected. These results are in line with what Cuevas (2013) and Riquer (1996) found in Mexico in relation to the meaning of motherhood as a way out to poverty and family difficulties.

Regarding the second finding on the role of schooling and social class in perceiving the biological and social age, it is possible to see that poor and less schooled women have a more veiled stance about the age difference, the age-gap and the age-discrepancy than middle and upper-middle class women. By observing the narratives of both groups carefully, it is evident that the paucity of poor and less schooled women narratives such as Teresa or Laura, shows elements of analysis that reveal a more veiled assessment of the differences. The language used reveals certain awareness elaborated as an emotional distance which contrasts with the expressive accounts of middle and upper-middle class women with high schooling such as Raquel, Alejandra or Jimena that were open and critical to their partners biological age even when these were much closer.

Among poor and low schooling women, the social valuation of the biological age was expressed in sentences such as "he was old" or "he was ashamed of revealing his age" as in the case of Teresa, or "he was a mature man" in the case of Laura. In the group of middle-class and highly educated women, the biological difference caused awkwardness expressed in valuations such as "I was crazy" as Jimena stated, "I felt as if he was a geezer" as Alejandra put it, or "I thought he was only four years older, and later I discovered his age" as Raquel expressed it. It is worth saying none of them rejected the marriage or cohabitation because of their partners' biological age.

The narratives of these two groups of women suggest that their partners were concerned by the age-gap and age-discrepancy and feared social criticism and stigma (Goffman, 2006). The narrative of Fernanda's second partner supports this view "You're too young for me." Also the memory of Teresa whose partner "wouldn't tell his age." These cases show that despite the age-gap or age-discrepancy women overlooked the biological difference and married and cohabitated with their partners. The reasons for which they did so speak of how they fulfilled their needs that ranged from wanting a partner, being in love or needing moral, economic, and/or material support.

As for men and women re-entering the partner market, I observe that the age distance in favor of men increased in second or subsequent unions, while the difference for women decreased. This finding coincides with that reported by demographics and sociodemographics. Cabré (1993) states that the marriage and partner market is complex, and its hierarchies are determined by the civil state and age of the women and men circulating in said pool. As can be seen, among men in second marriages and unions, the market neither restricted their value nor their circulation at the time of starting their second unions. The resources they offered to their partners allowed them to play the role of breadwinner and head of the family, as in the case of Gamaliel, Benito and Octavio.

Regarding women re-entering the marriage and partner market, we observe that two of them, Fernanda and Teresa, started second unions with men older than themselves. Nevertheless, in both cases, these women occupied a subordinated position in their relationship even when their social class and education was identical or close to that of their partners. In their relationships prevailed gender inequality since age gender relations operated as a complex system of oppression that subordinated women for the simple fact of being women. Pyke (1994), Pyke and Coltrane (1996), and Pyke and Adams (2010), also found similar evidence.

The gender inequality becomes even more visible among poor and little schooled women given men's machismo and their refusal to relax their gender ideology on domestic work, women's paid job and their sexual life. Laura's case illustrates this process very well. She was a poor and little schooled woman united to a middle-class and high schooled divorcé with whom she established an unequal exchange of cultural, social, and economic resources. This exchange of capitals, as Bozon (1990) calls this type of asymmetries in the formation of couples and marital negotiation, translated into social, cultural, and economic disadvantages for her even when she traded youth and beauty. This unequal exchange of attributes places women in clear disadvantage vis-à-vis their partners, as literature points out.

Quilodrán and Arrieta's study (2022) provides a wealth of information on the weight education, social class, and gender has in second unions. Some of their most relevant findings for my personal discussion show that men in general and women with little schooling and low social origin are the most satisfied with their second unions, as Laura's case shows. The contrary is the case as the narratives of highly educate and upper middle-class Jimena and Fernanda show.

The findings on couple relationships in which women were older than men point out that regardless the age difference in general – which went from 2 to

11 years in the case of women versus 20 to 39 in the case of men – women had the tendency to leave their job to devote themselves to the rearing of children or faced conflicts with their partner given the disparity of income and patrimony. In both cases – Octavio's spouse, two years older than him, and that of Arturo's, nine years older than his wife – these women had paid work at the time of their union and left their jobs to take care of their stepchildren and/or the children from their own relationship hence becoming dependent of their partner's income which weakened their decision making.

Bozon (1990) states that when ages are close, women prefer to assert male superiority. However, as we have seen, this also happened in age-homogamus and age-heterogamus relationship. A key factor in accepting such subordination is the gender-driven education women receive. They are educated and encouraged to submit to the male figure as a sign of respect to his authority and alleged moral superiority regardless of their age, social origin, and education.

Interestingly, the remaining results on relationships in which women were older than their partners – as in the cases of Jeremias and Berenice – point to the same scenario of gender inequality between partners and to the detriment of women. In the case of Jeremias, he acknowledged maturity of her partner before the many bad things he did. In this case both had the same social origin and level of education. While there were no structural differences in their relationship in this regard, gender differences operated at a more intimate level. In Berenice's case, the exchange of resources was unequal and problematic. She was better educated, had a stable job and income, and belonged to a higher social class than her partner. This situation made him hold resentment toward her, caused them a lot of tension between them and led them to break up. As we have seen, when men have these resources in their favor the relationship is more likely to work. This shows that women are more likely to achieve upward social mobility through their partners in these scenarios.

NOTES

*. The results presented here are part of the Project titled Intimidad y relaciones de pareja en el México contemporáneo: desafíos socioculturales [Intimacy and Couple Relationships in Contemporary Mexico: Socio-cultural Challenges] financed by Conacyt through the CB-2016-01 call number 245227/CB284023.

1. As data from my research show, the age gap in cohabitation follows the same logic of the age gap in marriage. However, the nature of the bond, the stability of the relationships and the duration varies as literature from around the globe shows. Therefore, I consider it convenient to add the concept of cohabitation whenever it is needed to distinguish the two of them in the analysis since the population interviewed were both married and living together couples.

2. I initially used the concept marriage market to discuss the election of partners (Cabré, 1993; England & McClintock, 2009; Kalmijn, 1998) but later on moved on to use partner choice and partner market since this discussion provides a broader explanation on union dynamics of the interviewed population which was both married and cohabiting.

3. The work group is made up by Tania Rodríguez Salazar and Zeyda Rodríguez Morales (technical leader) from Universidad de Guadalajara; by María del Rocío Enríquez Rosas from ITESO; and by Ana Josefina Cuevas Hernández from Universidad de Colima.

4. The Colima-Villa de Álvarez Metropolitan Zone consists of five suburban municipalities which are Colima, Comala, Coquimatlán, Cuauhtémoc and Villa de Álvarez and

comprised a population of 380,575 inhabitants in 2020. (https://es.wikipedia.org/wiki/ Zona_metropolitana_de_Colima-Villa_de_%C3%81lvarez, consulted on June 12, 2022).
5. The Guadalajara Metropolitan Zone consists of 10 suburban municipalities which are Guadalajara, Zapopan, San Pedro Tlaquepaque, El Salto, Tonalá, Juanacatlán, Tlajomulco de Zúñiga, Acatlán de los Membrillos, Zapotlanejo, and comprised a population of 5 268 642 habitantes en el 2020. (https://es.wikipedia.org/wiki/Zona_metropolitana_de_ Guadalajara, consulted on June 12, 2022).

REFERENCES

Atkinson, M. P., & Glass, B. (1985). Marital age heterogamy and homogamy, 1900 to 1980. *Journal of Marriage and the Family*, 47(3), 685–700. doi:10.2307/352269

Bauman, Z. (2004). *Modernidad líquida*. México: FCE.

Beck, U. (1999). *Un nuevo mundo feliz. La precariedad del trabajo en la era de la globalización*. Barcelona: Paidós.

Beck, U., & Beck-Gernsheim, E. (1995). *The normal chaos of love*. Cambridge: University Press.

Bozon, M. (1990). Les femmes et l'écart d'âge entre conjoints: une domination consentie. I. Types d'union et attentes en matière d'écart d'âge. *Population*, 45(2), 327–360. doi:10.2307/1533376

Bozon, M., & Heran, F. (1989). Finding a spouse: A survey of how French couples meet. *Population: An English Selection*, 44(1), 91–121. https://www.jstor.org/stable/2949076

Bozon, M., Rault, W., & Dutreuilhm, C. (2012). From sexual debut to first union. Where do young people in France meet their first partners? *Population*, 67(3), 377–410. doi:10.3917/pope.1203.0377

Cabré, A. (1993). *Tensions inminents en els mercats matrimonials*. España: Centro de Estudios Demográficos.

Cabré, A., Cortina, C., & Esteve, A. (2007). Un segle d'ajustos per edat en els mercats matrimonials: Espanya 1922-2004. *Paper de demografia*, (317), 1–20. https://ddd.uab.cat/record/220825

Casterline, J., Williams, L., & McDonald, P. (1986). The age difference between spouses: Variations among developing countries. *Population Studies*, 40(3), 353–374. doi:10.1080/0032472031000142296

Cortina, C. (2007). *¿Quién se empareja con quien?* Doctoral dissertation, University of Catalunya. Retrieved from https://www.tesisenred.net/bitstream/handle/10803/4981/cct1de1.pdf?sequence=1&is Allowed=y

Cosse, I. (2008). Del matrimonio a la pareja. Continuidades y rupturas en el modelo conyugal en Buenos Aires (1960-1975). *Anuario IEHS*, 23, 431–458.

Cowan, G. (1984). The double standard in age-discrepant relationships. *Sex Roles*, 11(1/2), 17–23. doi:10.1007/BF00287436

Cuevas, A. (2013). Contexto familiar y elección de pareja: una aproximación a través de madres solas. *Estudios Sociológicos*, 92, 471–509. doi:10.24201/es.2013v31n92.68

Cuevas, A. (2019). Conyugalidad e intimidad en América Latina: un panorama regional. In A. Cuevas (Coord.), *Intimidad y relaciones de pareja: exploraciones de un campo de investigación* (pp. 66–109). Ciudad de México: Juan Pablos Editores.

Cuevas, A. (2022). *La formación de parejas: emociones, homogamia y brechas de edad*. Guadalajara: Universidad de Guadalajara.

England, P., & McClintock, A. (2009). The gendered double standard of aging in US marriage markets. *Population and Development Review*, 35(4), 797–816. doi:10.1111/j.1728-4457.2009.00309.x

Esteve, A., & McCaa, R. (2007). Homogamia educacional en México y Brasil, 1970– 2000: pautas y tendencias. *Latin American Research Review*, 42(2), 56–85. doi:10.1353/lar.2007.0020

Fernández, M. (2010). Estudios sobre las trayectorias conyugales de las mujeres del Gran Montevideo. *Revista Latinoamericana de Población*, 4(7), 79–104. doi:10.31406/relap2010.v4.i2.n7.2

Flick, U. (2007). *Introducción a la investigación cualitativa*. España: Editorial Morata.

Gayet, C. (2002). Los matrimonios de los hombres de más de 35 años: ¿la búsqueda del rejuvenecimiento?. Una perspectiva a partir de las diferencias de edades entre cónyuges. *Estudios Demográficos y Urbanos*, 17(1), 217–234. doi:10.24201/edu.v17i1.1138

Giddens, A. (1998). *La transformación de la intimidad. Sexualidad, amor y erotismo en las sociedades modernas*. Madrid: Cátedra/Teorema.

Goffman, I. (2006). *Estigma. La identidad deteriorada*. Buenos Aires: Amorroru.

Grow, A., Schnor, C., & Van Bavel, J. (2017). The reversal of the gender gap in education and relative divorce risks: A matter of alternatives? *Populations Studies, 71*(1), 15–S34. doi:10.1080/00324 728.2017.1371477

Hakim, C. (1996). *Key issues in women's work: Female heterogeneity and the polarization of women's employment*. London: Athlone.

Hochstadt, S. (1982). Appendix: Demography and feminism. In P. Robertson (Ed.), *An experience of women. Pattern and change in nineteenth-century Europe* (pp. 541–560). Philadelphia: Temple University Press.

INEGI. (2021). *Comunicado de prensa núm. 549/21, 30 de septiembre de 2021. Estadística de matrimonios*. Mexico: Instituto Nacional de Estadística, Geografía e Informática.

Kalmijn, M. (1994). Assortative mating by cultural and economic occupational status. *American Journal of Sociology, 100*, 422–452.

Kalmijn, M. (1998). Intermarriage and homogamy: Causes, patterns, trends. *Annual Review of Sociology, 24*, 395–421. doi:10.1146/annurev.soc.24.1.395

Kalmijn, M. (2010). Educational inequality, homogamy, and status exchange in Black-White intermarriage: A comment on Rosenfeld. *American Journal of Sociology, 115*(4), 1252–1263. doi:10.1086/649050

Kalmijn, M., de Graaf, P. M., & Janssen, J. P. G. (2005). Intermarriage and the risk of divorce in the Netherlands: The effects of differences in religion and in nationality, 1974-94. *Population Studies, 59*(1), 71–85. doi:10.1080/0032472052000332719

Lichter, D., McLaughlin, D., Kephart, G., & Landry, D. J. (1992). Race and the retreat from marriage: A shortage of marriageable men? *American Sociological Review, 57*(6), 781–789. doi:10.2307/2096123

Mazzeo, V., Martínez, R., Gil, A., & Lascano, V. (2015). Análisis de los cambios en la situación conyugal. Una aplicación de la metodología de panel. *Población de Buenos Aires, 12*(22), 85–96. https://www.redalyc.org/articulo.oa?id=74042520008

Mier, M. (2009). El proceso de formación de parejas en México. In C. Rabell (coord.), *Tramas familiares en el México contemporáneo. Una perspectiva sociodemográfica* (pp. 199–256). México: El Colegio de México.

Mitterauer, M., & Seider, R. (1982). *The European family*. Chicago, IL: University of Chicago Press.

Parrado, E., & Zenteno, R. (2002). Gender differences in union formation in Mexico: Evidence from marital search models. *Journal of Marriage and Family, 64*(3), 756–773. doi:10.1111/j.1741-3737.2002.00756.x

Pyke, K. (1994). Women's employment as a gift or burden? Marital power across marriage, divorce, and remarriage. *Gender and Society, 8*, 73–91. doi:10.1177/089124394008001005

Pyke, K., & Adams, M. (2010). What's age got to do with it? A case study analysis of power and gender in husband-older marriages. *Journal of Family Issues, 31*(6), 748–777. doi:10.1177/0192513X0935

Pyke, K., & Coltrane, S. (1996). Entitlement, obligation, and gratitude in family work. *Journal of Family Issues, 17*, 60–82. doi:10.1177/019251396017001005

Quilodrán, J. (1993). La dinámica de la población y la formación de las parejas. In P. Bedolla Miranda et al., (Comp.), *Estudios de género y feminismo II* (pp. 303–315). Mexico: Fontamara and UNAM.

Quilodrán, J., & Arrieta, A. (2022). Segundas Uniones Conyugales: rematrimonios y reemparejamientos en México. *Revista Latinoamericana de Población, 16*, 1–30. doi:10.31406/relap2022.v16.e202128

Riquer, F. (1996). La maternidad como fatalidad. In T. Lartigue & H. Ávila (Comp.), *Sexualidad y reproducción humana en México* (pp. 195–218). Mexico: Plaza y Valdéz and Universidad Iberoamericana.

Rodríguez, S. (2016). *Conformación de parejas y desigualdad social. Un análisis comparativo del Área Metropolitana de Buenos Aires y la Ciudad de México*. Doctoral dissertation, Mexico: El Colegio de México.

Schnor, C., Pasteels, I., & Van Bavel, J. (2017). Sole physical custody and mother's repartnering after divorce. *Journal of Marriage and Family, 79*(3), 879–90. doi:10.1111/jomf.12389

Solís, P. (2009). Los nuevos senderos de la nupcialidad: cambios en los patrones de formación y disolución de las primeras uniones en México. In C. Rabell (coord.), *Tramas familiares en el México contemporáneo. Una perspectiva sociodemográfica* (pp. 179–199). Mexico: El Colegio de México.

Solís, P. (2010). Entre un "buen partido" y un "peor es nada": selección de pareja en la Ciudad de México. *Revista Latinoamericana de Población, 7*, 57–78. doi:10.31406/relap2010.v4.i2.n7.7

Solís, P. (2016). Movilidad intergeneracional de clase en América Latina: una perspectiva comparativa. In P. solís & M. Boado (Coords.), Y, sin embargo, se mueve... Estratificación social y movilidad intergeneracional de clase en América Latina (pp. 75–132). Editorial Centro de Estudios.

Solís, P., Pullum, T., & Bratter, J. (2007). Homogamy by education and migration status in Monterrey, Mexico: Changes and continuities over time. *Population Research and Policy Review*, 26, 279–298. doi:10.1007/s11113-007-9032-y

Sura, C. (1990). Research and theory on mate selection and premarital relationships in the 1980. *Journal of Marriage and Family*, 52(4), 844–865. doi:10.2307/353306

Sweeney, M., & Cancian, M. (2004). The changing importance of white woman's economic prospects for assortative mating. *Journal of Marriage and Family*, 66(4), 1015–1028. doi:10.1111/j.0022-2445.2004.00073.x

Van Bavel, J. (2021). Partner choice and partner markets. *Population Studies*, 1, 219–231. doi:10.4337/9781788975544.00023

Van Bavel, J., Schwartz, C., & Esteve, A. (2018). The reversal of the gender gap in education and its consequences for family life. *Annual Review of Sociology*, 44, 341–60. doi:10.1146/annurev-soc-073117-041215

Van Poppel, F., Liefbroer, A., Vermunt, J. K., & Smeenk, W. (2001). Love, necessity and opportunity: Changing patterns of marital age homogamy in the Netherlands, 1850-1993. *Population Studies*, 55(1), 1–13. http://www.jstor.org/stable/3092920

Veevers, J. (1984). Age-discrepant marriages: Cross-national comparisons of Canadian-American trends. *Social Biology, 31*(1–2), 18–27. doi:10.1080/19485565.1984.9988559

Vera, H., Berardo, D., & Berardo, F. (1985). Age heterogamy in marriage. *Journal of Marriage and Family*, 47(3), 553–566. doi:10.2307/352269

Ware, H. (1981). *Women, Demography and Development*. Demography Teaching Notes. Australian National University, Canberra.

Wheeler, R., & Gunter, B. (1987). Change in spouse age difference at marriage: A challenge to traditional family and sex roles? *The Sociological Quarterly*, 28(3), 411–421. doi:10.1111/j.1533-8525.1987. tb00303.x

Zentner, M., & Eagly, A. (2015). A sociocultural framework for understanding partner preferences of women and men: Integration of concepts and evidence. *European Review of Social Psychology*, 26(1), 328–373. doi:10.1080/10463283.2015.1111599

CHAPTER 5

PREDICTORS OF MARITAL QUALITY: WHAT MAKES A HAPPY MARRIAGE IN CROATIA?

Josip Obradović and Mira Čudina

ABSTRACT

This chapter aims to verify predictors of marital quality in Croatia. As a theoretical starting point, the Huston Socio-ecological model was used. Huston's so-called "wide-angle and close range" variables were included in to study as predictors of marital quality. A two-level hypothetical model was created consisting of Six groups of predictor variables: Level 1 predictors included Partners' demographic variables, Partners' personality, Partners' value system, Marital processes or dynamics, and Partners' wellbeing. Level 2 predictors included four Marriage characteristics. Altogether at both levels, 42 variables represented predictors. Marital quality in the marriage was a dependent variable. Eight hundred and eighty-four marital couples from 14 counties in various parts of Croatia and from Zagreb, the country's capital, were included in the study. Factor analysis, Maximum likelihood with Promax rotation was used to extract factors. Eight factors were extracted: Marital harmony, Distress, Partners' personality, Negative spillover from work, Traditionalism, Engagement in child care, Participation in decision-making, and Economic hardship. Multilevel analysis using the Mix model in Statistical Package for Social scientist, version 20 was used in data analysis. Predictive on Marital quality in a marriage turned out variables: Marital harmony, Distress, Partners' personality, Traditionalism, Engagement in child care, and Participation in

Conjugal Trajectories: Relationship Beginnings, Change, and Dissolutions
Contemporary Perspectives in Family Research, Volume 22, 81–107
Copyright © 2023 by Emerald Publishing Limited
ISSN: 1530-3535/doi:10.1108/S1530-353520230000022005

decision-making as level 1 and Marriage duration (Marriage stages) as a level 2 variable. Huston's Ecological model proved to be adequate and useful in explaining marital quality.

Keywords: Socio-ecological model; marital harmony; distress; partners personality; marital quality; Croatia

It is important to study marital quality. Poor marital quality creates problems, decreases marital stability (Karney & Bradbury, 1995), damages the physical and mental health of both partners (Kiecolt-Glaser & Newton, 2001; Marcenes & Sheiham, 1996), and finally instigates divorce (Karney & Bradbury, 1995). Thus, we believe that studying marital quality is of significant scientific importance as well as serious practical consequences.

Marital quality can be defined: as individual satisfaction or as mutual adjustment. It can be measured, as global marital quality, or as an assessment of satisfaction in different life domains. An impressive number of studies on the predictors of marital quality exists, but most of these studies were conducted in the United States and some in Western Europe, i.e., societies that are very individualistic (Clement & Swensen, 2000; Karney & Bradbury, 1995; Kaufman & Taniguchi, 2006). Studies on marital quality in societies with different structures and value systems than those that can be found in the United States and Western Europe are very rare (Allendorf, 2012; Esmaeli & Schoebi, 2017). Consequently, we know little about the predictors of marital quality in non-western societies. Are the predictors of marital quality in non-western societies the same, similar, partially, or completely different from those in western societies? For example, in Islam countries, studies show that as far as personal characteristics of the marital partners are concerned there are no major differences between Muslim and Western countries. The differences exist as far as marital processes are concerned (Esmaeli & Schoebi, 2017).

However, even in western societies, there are opinions and theoretical elaborations about the appropriate way of studying marital quality, generally suggesting that present approaches to studying marriage are not satisfactory (Huston, 2000). The same author considers that most studies only cover some predictor variables; and although the results of these studies give valuable insights into the problem, they have some limitations. Huston (2000) defines those studies as either "wide-angle" representing societal and marriage variables (for instance, Value system shared by population or the level of urbanization of the particular county and marriage or dyad variables like marriage duration, number of children in the family, and, cohabitation before marriage). "Close range" variables represent marital partners characteristics and interactions without an association between these two groups. He continues

The historical, multilayered-interdependent causal pathways that produce, maintain and modify marital behavior create enormous analytic problems that must be overcome by scholars who wish to understand why marriages function the way they do. (Huston, 2000, p. 298)

Some other authors (Kelley et al., 1983) studying both marriages and human development (Bronfenbrenner, 1986) share the same opinion and propose a more complex multilevel socio-ecological approach including "wide-angle and close range variables."

MARRIAGE AS A BEHAVIORAL ECOSYSTEM

According to Huston (2000), if we want to study how marriages function one must include variables representing three levels in the analysis: Societal, Individual, and Marital. Those three levels are interrelated, they operate simultaneously and change according to context and time. The societal level represents macro-level variables and the ecological niches within which particular marriages exist. The individual level presents physical and psychological marital partners' character- istics such as personality, attitudes, beliefs, or value systems. The marital level represents marriage as a behavioral system in a larger social environment. This model represents a broad theoretical framework, which can be used as a starting point in studying marriages in different societies and different cultures, and cross-cultural ones. In comparison to the previous one-level studies in Croatia on mari- tal quality predictors (Kamenov, Jelić, Tadinac, & Hromatko, 2008), this study is two or dyad-level satisfying Socio-ecological model assumptions.

PRESENT STUDY

In this study, the Socio-ecological model (Huston, 2000) was used as a starting point. However, there is an issue in regard to which variables should be included in the study. So, we were very careful in deciding which variables should be included in the model. The decision was to include three groups of variables. The first and by far largest group were variables we assumed could fit the Socio-ecological model about marriage functioning. The second group was variables Huston (2000) did not mention, which proved in previous studies to be predictive of marital quality. In the last group, we included in the model variables based on previous ethnological studies on Croatian traditional society. We included this group because we assume that they reflect some elements of traditionalism still present in the Croatian family. Some statistical data on the structure of the Croatian family and public opinion survey results show that Croatian families from the eighteenth until almost the mid-twentieth century were multigenera- tional with a collectivistic system of values, featuring mutual help and solidarity among family members (Erlich, 1964; Leček, 1996; Rihtman-Auguštin, 1984).

Industrialization, urbanization, and the socialistic sociopolitical system dis- mantled traditional families largely after the Second World War. Nevertheless, some elements of collectivism in Croatian families are still present today (Aračić & Nikodem, 2000). Also, the lower divorce rate (30 divorces per 100 new mar- riages in 2017) compared to Other European countries represent a traditional aspect of the Croatian family. Most divorced persons never remarry, which is not the case for many who divorce in North American society (Statistical Yearbook, 2018). The number of children born out of wedlock is 15% (Statistical Yearbook, 2018) which is a relatively small percentage in comparison to other European countries and North America. However, a modern trend is also present in the Croatian family. The number of new marriages has been decreasing over the last several decades and the number of newborn children is also dropping (Statistical Yearbook, 2018). In addition, more young people tend to stay single than previously (24.6% in 2018) and if they marry, they tend to marry later. In 2017, mean age of the groom was 31.3 and the bride 28.6 years (Statistical Yearbook, 2018). In spite of these tendencies, some studies show that marriage as an institution is not obsolete.

According to these studies, 89.6% of the Croatian population consider marriage very important which is a much higher percentage than in most other European countries (Aračić & Nikodem, 2000). It is interesting to note that employed women represent 47% of all employed persons in private and public companies (Statistical Yearbook, 2018), at the same time studies show (Kamenov et al., 2008), that housework and childcare are almost completely the responsibility of women. So, the Croatian family and marriage although westernized share some traditional tendencies that are in accordance with some globalization theories (Pieterse, 2020). It seems that the process of modernization has accelerated since Croatia became a European community member. But nevertheless, some elements of traditionalism are still present that should be taken into consideration together with the Socio-ecological model (Huston, 2000) when studying marriage in Croatia. We could say that generally, the distinctive characteristic of the value system in Croatia is a mixture of modernism and traditionalism.

THE AIMS OF THE STUDY

1. To verify if it is possible to explain marital quality in Croatian marriage using the Socio-ecological model.
2. If yes, the specific aim is to check what group of variables representing Socio-ecological the model is the best predictor of marital quality in Croatia?

MODEL

Accepting the Socio-ecological model as a starting point, we have included two sets of variables as potential predictors of marital quality in Croatia. The first set or group represents variables that turned out to be predictive of marital quality in previous studies conducted elsewhere which we might call universal predictors (love-passion, intimacy, and commitment, marriage duration, and children in the family) while the second set or group is variables specific for the Croatian socio-cultural context (patriarchy, economic hardship). Universal and specific variables were grouped into level 1 and level 2 groups presented in Fig. 1.

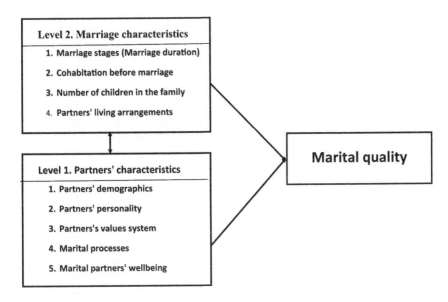

Fig. 1. Socio-Ecological Hypothetical Model of the Relationship Between Predictors and Marital Quality.

The model consisted of 5 groups of level 1 variables and 1 group representing level 2 predictor variables and we assume that two groups are interrelated and both groups of predictors are associated with the variable marital quality in marriage.

Partners' Characteristics or Level 1 Predictor Variables

1. **Demographics.** In this group are predictor variables: Employment status, Gender, and Structure of the family of origin. Education, Frequency of contraceptive use, Marriage order, and Perception of class belonging. All these variables turned out to be single or one of the variables predictive as in the previous studies except the variable Frequency of contraceptive use, but we assume that this variable might be also predictive of marital quality (Atkinson, Liem, & Liem, 1986; Berry & Williams, 1987; Lichter & Carmalt, 2009; Vannoy & Cubbins, 2001; Zhang & Tsang, 2010).
2. **Partners' personality.** In this group are Extraversion, Agreeableness, Emotional Stability, and Self-esteem. These all tend to predict higher marital quality (Botwin, Buss, & Shackelford, 1997; Cundiff, Smith, & Frandsen, 2012; Miller, Caughlin, & Huston, 2003), except in some studies (Robins, Caspi, & Moffit, 2000) in which they tend to predict lower quality marriages. However, since most of these studies were conducted in the United States, it is interesting to investigate if they are also predictive in another social-cultural context.

3. **Partners' value system.** Variables in this group are Patriarchy, Perceptions of gender roles, Participation in religious rituals, Materialism, and Religiosity. These variables were included in the study because they might be specific predictors of marital quality in the Croatian socio-cultural context. Although Croatia has been changing rapidly in the last 30–40 years, various studies show traditional gender roles and the dominance of the husband is still present as a family orientation (Kamenov et al., 2008). It is also known that Croatia is predominantly a catholic society with more than 80% of its population claims to be religious to a certain degree. The variable Materialism was included as a value orientation because Croatia has been in an economic crisis recently for several years. Those variables were also included in this group because they were previously widely used as predictors of marital quality (Fincham & Bradbury, 1993; Sussman & Alexander, 1999; Wiik, Keizer, & Lappegard, 2012).

4. **Marital processes.** The Socio-ecological model (Huston, 2000) hypothesizes that everything that is going on in a marriage can affect marital quality. So, the following variables were included in the study: Sexual satisfaction, Satisfaction with income, Satisfaction with the distribution of household work, Participation in key decision-making, Participation in everyday routine decision-making, Negative spillover from work to marriage and household, Three dimensions of love (Passion, Intimacy and Commitment), Physical attraction, Perceived partner's support, Marital strain, Partners' and Somebody else's engagement in the routine household work and Partners' and Somebody else's engagement in child care. The relationship between most of those variables and marital quality was previously studied (Aron & Henkenmeyer, 1995; Cutrona, 1996; Greeff & Malherbe, 2001; Karney & Bradbury, 1995; Perry-Jenkins, Repetti, & Crouter, 2001) and proved to be a predictor of marital quality.

5. **Marital partners' wellbeing.** This group represents variables: Economic hardship, Depression, Perceived global stress, Positive and Negative affectivity. All these Variables also turned out to be predictors of marital quality in previous studies (Cohan & Bradbury, 1997; Hraba, Lorenz, & Pehaceva, 2000; Perren et al., 2003; Scherwitz & Rugulies, 1992).

Marriage Characteristics or Level 2 Variables

In this group, we have included variables that were very predictive in previous studies. These are Marriage duration (Marriage stages), Cohabitation before marriage, and Number of children in the marriage (Belsky, & Kelly, 1994; Shapiro, Gottman, & Carrere, 2000; Wiik et al., 2012), and variable Living arrangements which is specific for Croatia because of tradition, especially in rural areas, or because of housing problem some marital partners live together with their or their partner's parents.

Altogether we have included 45 variables predictors in the model. The inclusion criterion of variables incorporated those variables in previous studies that proved to be predictors of marital quality, or that might be relevant in the

Croatian cultural context. We wanted to cover a wide area of potential predictors as required by the Socio-ecological model. However, we should point out that Huston's (2000) model also includes societal or level 3 variables as a potential predictor of marital quality. In difference to Huston's (2000) assumption, our study is two levels or Level 3 variables like a system of population values were not included. Because data about those variables were not available.

Hypotheses

H1. Partners' demographic characteristics (level 1 variables) are predictive of marital quality in a marriage.

H2. After mutual adjustment between predictors, the group of variables representing marital processes is the best predictor of marital quality in a marriage.

H3. Marriage characteristics (level 2 variables) are predictive of marital quality after controlling for the effects of level 1 variables.

METHOD

Sample

This study was conducted in 14 counties (there are 20 županija or counties in Croatia), as well as Zagreb, the capital of Croatia. In total, 884 couples or 1,768 marital partners were included in the study. Although it would have been optimal that this study was conducted in all counties, with a probability sample, this was not feasible due to financial constraints. The first step was to consult internal documents about the population educational structure in each county. After getting that information, we decided to use a quota sample as a method of data collection. The criterion for selecting couples was the husband's educational level. Our goal was to have approximately the same share of couples with a particular level of husband's education in the sample, as registered in the particular county. For example, if 20% of husbands had a high school education in County X, our goal was to have approximately 20% of similar couples representing County X in our sample. In cases where one or both partners refused to participate, a new couple with a husband's same educational level was found. The correlation between husbands' and wives' education in the sample was $r = 0.54$, $p < 0.001$. The fieldwork was done by a psychologist or graduate student in psychology and sociology. Interviewers had special training on how to conduct interviews successfully. Marital partners were interviewed separately to secure independence in answering questions. The educational structure of the sample for both marital partners is presented in Table 1.

In addition to the husband's education as a criterion for selecting couples, we also took into account marriage duration, the number of children in the family, couples' living arrangement, and cohabitation before marriage. The mean marriage duration in the sample is $M = 15.90$ years, (SD = 11.42), with a minimum of 1 and a maximum of 53 years. The number of children in the family is $C = 2$ with a minimum of 0 and a maximum of 6. In relation to the living arrangement, 22% of couples live together with one of the partners' parents, 35.8% live separately

Table 1.   The Educational Structure of the Sample.

Years of Schooling	Wives (%)	Husbands (%)
Elementary school (8 years of schooling)	13.6	8.9
Vocational school (11 years of schooling)	15.3	21.6
High school (12 years of schooling)	36.0	31.9
Community college degree (15 years of schooling)	13.8	15.2
University degree (16 years of schooling).	21.3	22.4

Note: Wives $N = 884$; Husbands $N = 884$.

but near parents with their help, and 42.2% live separately and independently from their parents' Cohabitation before marriage was also present; 44.8% of couples cohabitated before getting married. On most of the variables, less than 2% of the data was missing. In terms of organization, fieldwork was very demanding. Firstly, the interviewers were required to ask some sensitive questions about intimate aspects of life, which is a very delicate process, especially in some traditional parts of the country. Secondly, both marital partners were interviewed so it was rather difficult to organize their independent participation and to ensure conditions of privacy so that they were able to freely express their most intimate feelings about marriage without their partner's knowledge of their answers. After receiving special training, a group of psychologists and graduate students in psychology and sociology interviewed husbands and wives separately, either in their homes or at their places of work. Partners were given a questionnaire consisting of different scales. They had to read every question or item and encircle a number showing how much they agree with a particular statement. On average, working with a marital partner lasted 80 minutes.

VARIABLES AND MEASURES

Six groups of variables included in the study as predictors of marital quality are presented in Table 2.

A specific predictor variable in Table 2 is Marriage duration. This variable was measured as a continuous scale but according to the Family life course theory (White & Klein, 2008) as a level 2 variable, it was transformed into five categories each one representing specific one stage of the family course. "A family stage is an interval of time in which the structure and interactions of role relationships in the family are noticeably and qualitatively distinct from other periods of time (Aldous, 1996, p. 130).

Dependent Variable

Marital quality. This variable represents the global subjective evaluation of one's satisfaction in marriage (Norton, 1983). The variable was measured by QMI (Quality of Marriage Index) developed by Norton (1983). "A higher total score on the scale indicated higher marital quality. The scale has been used and validated previously in many studies (Funk & Rogge, 2007; Heyman, Sayers, &

Table 2. Level 1 and Level 2 Predictors of Marital Quality.

Variable	Definition	Scale	Items	Sample of Items	α
		Partners' Characteristics or Level 1 Variables			
		Characteristics of Partners' Demographic Variables			
Employment status	Position in workforce	Nominal	4 categories	1 (Unemployed), 2 (Temporary employed), 3 (Permanently employed), 4 (Retired)	
Gender	Sex of partner	Dummy	2 categories	Wife = 0, Husband = 1	
Structure of the family of origin	Family structure	Nominal	6 categories	1 (With both parents), 2 (With mother with contact with father), 6 (Without both natural parents)	
Education	Educational achievement	Ordinal	From elementary to a university degree (five levels)		
Frequency of contraceptive use	Frequency of birth control	Likert type single item	Five-point format, from 1 (never) to 5 (very often)		
Marriage order	Marriage in succession	Nominal	Three categories: first, second, and third		
Perception of class belonging	One's evaluation of class belonging	Nominal	Three categories: lower, middle, and upper		
		Characteristics of Partners' Personality Variables			
Extraversion	A wide interest and engagement in different social activities	Continuous, IPIP; Mlacic & Goldberg (2007)	Ten items scale with 10 bipolar antinomies, nine-point format	"Open – closed," or "without confidence – with confidence"	0.93
Agreeableness	Concern for social harmony	Continuous, IPIP; Mlacic & Goldberg(2007)	Ten items scale with 10 bipolar antinomies, nine-point format	"Unpleasant – pleasant" or "selfish – unselfish"	0.94
Emotional stability	Stable and a less reactive response to stress	Continuous, IPIP; Mlacic & Goldberg(2007)	Ten items scale with 10 bipolar antinomies, nine-point format	"Full of tension – relaxed" or "unstable – stable"	0.93
Self-esteem	Emotional evaluation of one's own worth	Continuous (Rosenberg, 1995)	Six items scale with the five-point format: 1 (strongly disagree) to 5 (strongly agree)	A person's subjective emotional evaluation of one's own worth	0.71

(Continued)

Table 2. (*Continued*)

Variable	Definition	Scale	Items	Sample of Items	α
Characteristics of Partners' Value System Variables					
Patriarchy	Husbands hold primary power	Continuous (Obradović, 2009)	Nine items scale with the five-point format: 1 (strongly disagree) to 5 (strongly agree)	It is natural that wives in some areas have less freedom than their husbands	0.85
Perception of gender roles	Partners' attitudes toward gender roles	Continuous (Obradović, 2009)	Eight items scale with the five-point format: 1 (strongly disagree) to 5 (strongly agree)	Mothers with small children should stay at home instead of being employed	0.72
Materialism	How much material goods are salient in person's life	Continuous (Richins & Dawson, 1992)	Seven items scale with the five-point format: 1 (strongly disagree) to 5 (strongly agree)	I like luxury in everyday life	0.70
Religiosity	Ideological or as a beliefs system	Continuous (Faulkner & DeJong, 1979)	Five items scale with the five-point format: 1 (strongly disagree) to 5 (strongly agree)	The end of the world will come to God willing	0.94
Participation in religious rituals during the last three months	Frequency of religious behavior		Single item scale with 4 categories, from 1 (never) to 4 (every day)		
Characteristics of Marital Processes Variables					
Sexual satisfaction in marriage	Partner's evaluation of one's sexual experience in marriage		Single item scale with the five-point format: 1 (strongly disagree) to 5 (strongly agree)		
Satisfaction with income	Partner's evaluation of one's satisfaction with income		Single item scale with the five-point format: 1 (strongly disagree) to 5 (strongly agree)		
Satisfaction with the distribution of household work	Partner's evaluation of one's activity in household work		Single item scale with the five-point format: 1 (strongly disagree) to 5 (strongly agree)		
Participation in key decision-making	Decisions that have major consequences for family life like changing a place of dwelling		Single item scale with the five-point format, from 1(very rarely) to 5 (very often)		

Variable	Description	Type (Source)	Scale format	Example item	
Participation in everyday routine decision-making	Decisions with minor consequences for family life like food shopping				
Negative spill-over from work to marriage	The transition of stress experienced in work to the marriage relationship	Continuous (Small & Riley 1990)	Single item scale with the five-point format, from very rarely to 5 very often	My job keeps me from spending time with my spouse.	0.71
Negative spill-over from work to housework (home management)	The transition of stress from work to household	Continuous (Small & Riley 1990)	Five items scale with the five-point format, from 1 (very rarely) to 5 (very often)	My job makes it difficult for me to get household work done.	0.93
Love (Intimacy)	Refers to feelings of closeness, and bondedness in loving relationships	Continuous (Sternberg, 1997)	Five items scale with five-point format from 1 (very rarely) to 5 (very often)	I have a warm and comfortable relationship with my partner.	0.97
Love (Passion)	Refers to the drives that lead to romance and sexual consummation	Continuous (Sternberg, 1997)	Twelve items scale with the five-point format, from 1 (very rarely) to 5 (very often)	I cannot imagine another person making me as happy as my marital partner does	0.96
Love (Commitment to partner)	Refers, in the long term, to one's commitment to maintaining relationship	Continuous (Sternberg, 1997)	Twelve items scale with the five-point format, from 1 (very rarely) to 5 (very often)	I can't imagine ending my relationship with my partner	0.97
Companionate love	Intimate non-passionate type of love	Continuous (Grote & Frieze, 1994)	Nine point scale with a five-point format, from 1 (strongly disagree) to 5 (strongly agree)	The companionship I share with my partner is an important part of my love for him/her	0.96
Physical attraction	Partner's evaluation about one's liking other partner's physical characteristics		Single item scale with the five-point format, from 1 (not at all) to 5 (very much)	I find my partner physically attractive	
Perceived partner's support	Perception of partner's responsiveness to one's needs	Continuous (Turner & Marino, 1994)	Six items with a five-point format, from 1 (strongly disagree) to 5 (strongly agree)	When I am with my partner, I feel completely able to relax and be myself	0.96
Marital strain	Long-lasting marital stress as a consequence of deteriorated marital relationships	Continuous (McCubbin, Thompson, & McCubbin, 1994)	Four items with 1 = yes and 0 = no format	Recently I had some difficulties in my sexual relationship with my marital partner	0.71

(Continued)

Table 2. (Continued)

Variable	Definition	Scale	Items	Sample of Items	α
Perception of own engagement in routine household work	Engagement in housework		Six items continuous scale from 0 to 50 hours a week	Meal preparation, house cleaning, going to the market, dishwashing, laundry, and ironing	0.86
Perception of partner's engagement in routine household work	Housework		Six items continuous scale from 0 to 50 hours a week	Meal preparation, house cleaning, going to the market, dishwashing, laundry, and ironing	0.86
Perception of someone else's engagement in routine household work	Housework		Six items continuous scale from 0 to 50 hours a week	Meal preparation, house cleaning, going to the market, dishwashing, laundry, and ironing.	0.85
Perception of own engagement in childcare	Engagement in childcare		Three items continuous scale from 0 to 50 hours a week	Feeding and bathing, teaching, instructions, and playing with a child.	0.79
Perception of partner's engagement in child care	Engagement in childcare		Three items continuous scale from 0 to 50 hours a week	Feeding and bathing, teaching, instructions, and playing with a child	0.80
Perception of someone else's engagement in childcare	Engagement in childcare		Three items continuous scale from 0 to 50 hours a week	Feeding and bathing, teaching, instructions, and playing with a child	0.86
Characteristics of Marital Partners' Wellbeing Variables					
Economic hardship	The chronic form of household stress that creates fears about one's ability to pay bills	Continuous (Obradović, 2009)	Seven items scale with 2 categories: 1 = yes and 0 = no format	Do you have enough money to buy appropriate food for yourself and your family?	0.76
Depression	Depression is manifested by symptoms of depressive mood, low energy, and lack of concentration	Continuous, The CES-D Inventory (Radloff, 1997)	Twenty items with a four-point interval format, from 1 (rarely) to 4 (often or every day)	I had trouble keeping my mind on what I was doing	0.91
Perceived global stress	Perception of the degree to which situations in one's life are appraised as stressful	Continuous (Cohen, Karkarck, & Mermelstein, 1983)	Thirteen item scale with a five-point format, from 1 (never or very rarely) to 5 (very often)	In the last month, how often have you been upset because of something that happened	0.75

Variable	Description	Type / Source	Measurement / Coding	Items / Stages	Reliability
Positive affectivity	Reflects the extent to which a person feels enthusiastic, active, and alert	Continuous (Watson, Clark, & Tellegen, 1988)	Ten items-words representing positive motions, with a five-point format, from 1 (very rarely) to 5 (very often)	Words include: excited, strong, proud, and interested	0.88
Negative affectivity	The general dimension of subjective distress and unpleasurable engagement	Continuous (Watson et al., 1988)	Ten items-words representing negative emotions, with a five-point format, from 1 (very rarely) to 5 (very often)	Irritable, ashamed, jittery, and afraid	0.83
Marriage Variables Characteristics or Level 2					
Marriage duration (Marriage stages)		Continuous, ranging from 1 to 53	Continuous scale which was transformed according to Family life course theory (White & Klein, 2008) in five categories	1 (Beginning of marriage, first two years; 2 (Period with preschool children); 3 (Marriage with children from 8 to 18 years); 4 (Marriage with adult children from 19 to 26 years living with parents); 5 Marriage with adult children not living with parents.	
Cohabitation before marriage		Dummy	Yes coded as 1 and No coded as 2		
Number of children in the family			Continuous, from 0 (No children) to 6 (Six children)		
Partners' living arrangement	Various types of living arrangements are more or less independent and separate from both partners' parents	Six categories variable	1 (Living in the same household with my parents), 2 (With partner's parents), 3 (In the same house but not the same household with my parents), 4 (With partner's parents), 5 (Living separately with parents help), 6 (Living separately)		
Dependent Variable					
Marital quality	The global concept consists of satisfaction with interaction, adjustment, and partner relationships	MQI (Marital Quality Index) Norton (1983)	Six items scale with 5 point format: 1 (strongly disagree) to 5 (strongly agree)	My relationship with my partner makes me happy.	0.98

Bellack, 1994; Ledermann & Macho, 2009). The scale consists of six items with 5-point format ranging from 1 (strongly disagree) to 5 (strongly agree). Sample of items: "We have a good marriage," or: "My relationship with my partner makes me happy." A higher total score indicated higher marital quality. Internal consistency in this study Cronbach α for both marital partners was 0.98.

Most of the variables were translated from the English language. Native-speaking English language translator together with the authors of this chapter translated and linguistically adjusted scales avoiding Croatian colloquial language. The Croatian version of the scale was first used in the pilot study ($N = 160$ couples) before being used in the final one.

RESULTS

Descriptive Statistics

Item scores on every variable were summed up for all continuous variables In addition, we verified for multicollinearity. Out of 45 predictor variables listed and described as predictors, Tolerance and VIF parameters indicated multicollinearity for 3 variables. Those were: Love (passion), Love (intimacy), and the age of the partners. For all other variables, tolerance was higher than 0.10 and VIF was smaller than 5. So in the analysis, 42 predictor variables and dependent variable Marital quality were included. First, we shall present correlations between all groups of predictors and the dependent variable Marital quality for the whole sample ($N = 1,768$). Results are presented in Table 3.

Correlation coefficients in Table 3 clearly show a high positive association between groups of variables Marital processes (Perceived partners' support, Love-commitment, Sexual satisfaction in marriage, and Physical attraction) and a negative association of Marital strain with dependent variable Marital quality. Somewhat lower correlation coefficients are for variables representing Marital partners' wellbeing. And still, lower correlations for Personality variables. Demographic variables are positive or negative predictors but of very small correlations.

The highest positive correlation is between Perceived partner's support and marital quality which is specific to Croatian society. Mutual help, solidarity between partners, and dependency on the partner are characteristics of still present elements of the traditional value system in Croatian society The rest of the correlations between other marital processes variables like Love-commitment, Sexual satisfaction, or Physical attraction present universal associations which can be most probably found in most other societies. The same explanation is for the high but negative correlation between Marital strain and Marital quality. Most probably in all societies, Marital strain creates problems in partners' relationships and consequently, decreases marital quality.

Analytic Strategy

Having such a large number of variables there was a dilemma whether to use all variables as predictors separately or perform the factor analysis and use obtained

Table 3. Correlations Between Variable Predictors and Marital Quality for a Whole Sample.

Predictor Variables		*r*
Partners'	Gender	0.059*
demographics	Marriage order	−0.012
variables	Structure of the family of origin	−0.040
	Employment status	0.015
	Frequency of contraceptive use	−0.092**
	Perception of class belonging	−0.040
	Education	−0.073**
Partners' personality	Extraversion	0.191**
	Agreeableness	0.134**
	Emotional stability	0.276**
	Self-esteem	0.227**
Partners' value	Patriarchy	0.033
system	Perception of gender roles	0.047*
	Materialism	−0.039
	Religiosity	0.229**
	Participation in religious rituals in the last three months	0.136**
Marital processes	Sexual satisfaction	0.657**
	Satisfaction with income	0.110**
	Satisfaction with the distribution of household work	0.383**
	Participation in key decision making	0.250**
	Participation in everyday routine decision-making	0.162**
	Negative spillover from work to marriage	0.083**
	Negative spillover from work to housework (home management)	−0.013
	Love (commitment to partner)	0.856**
	Physical attraction	0.495**
	Perceived partner's support	0.909**
	Marital strain	−0.576**
	Perception of own engagement in routine household work	−0.035
	Perception of partner's engagement in household work	0.101
	Perception of someone else's engagement in household work	−0.051
	Perception of own engagement in child care	−0.055
	Perception of partner's engagement in child care	0.031
	Perception of someone else's engagement in childcare	0.009
Marital partners'	Economic hardship	−0.123**
wellbeing	Depression	−0.282**
	Perceived global stress	−0.176**
	Positive affectivity	0.230**
	Negative affectivity	−0.308**
Marriage characteristics	Marriage duration	0.009
	Cohabitation before marriage	0.093
	Number of children in the family	0.092
	Living arrangement	0.044

Note: $N = 1,764$; * $p < 0.05$, ** $p < 0.01$.

factor scores as predictors. Because of clarity, we decided on using the factor scores as predictors. Thirty-one level 1 continuous variables representing partners' personality, value systems, marital processes, and wellbeing were included in the Factor analysis.

Factor analysis Maximum likelihood with Promax rotation was used for extracting factors and items loaded more than 0.40 were selected to represent particular factors. Criteria were eigenvalue greater than 1 and Scree plot. The analysis yielded 8 factors with eigenvalues greater than 1 and explained 57% of the total variance. Obtained results are presented in Table 4.

As can be seen in Table 4 Factor 1 *Marital harmony* represents Love (commitment to partner), Perceived partners' support, Physical attraction Sexual satisfaction, and absence of Marital strain in a marriage. Factor 2 *Distress* represents: Perceived global stress, Depression, and Negative affectivity, and low Self-esteem, *Factor* 3 represents the marital partners' personality: Agreeableness Extraversion, and Emotional stability. Factor 4 *Negative spillover from work* represents Negative spillover from work to marriage and household. Factor 5 *Traditionalism* represents Patriarchy and traditional gender roles. Factor 6 represents the *Perception of own, partner and someone else engagement in child care*. Factor 7 represents the Perception of own participation in key and routine decision-making and eventually Factor 8 represents Economic hardship marital partners' experience.

To test the hypotheses, we used Multilevel linear regression modeling using the Statistical package for social scientists (SPSS version 20) with Maximum likelihood as an estimation. There are several advantages of a Multilevel analysis over single-level approaches including greater accuracy in calculating standard errors associated with parameter estimates (Hox, 2002). Multilevel level modeling also allows the use of continuous, ordinal, and categorical variables of different levels as predictors, mutually adjusted. In our study Level, 1 variable included partners' demographics and 8 individual scores of Promax factors, while Level 2 variables were: Marriage characteristics: Partners' living arrangement, Cohabitation before marriage, The number of children younger than 18 years, and Marriage durations, or marriage stages as dyad variables. Level 1 variables are nested in level 2 or couples variables. Marital quality was a dependent or outcome variable.

The first step in Multilevel level analysis is to develop a so-called Null model without predictors. This model also provides an estimate of dependence within each level 2 unit in terms of an Intraclass correlation (ICC) which describes the proportion of variance that is common to each unit or couple (Heck, Thomas, & Tabata, 2014). Obtained ICC = 0.717 with Intercept = 30.638, Wald Z test = 17.013, $p < 0.001$ and Residual = 12.049, Wald test = 20.565, $p < 0.001$, and -2 Log-likelihood = 10780.805 as the fitting estimate shows that there is a lot of variations between partners and marriages or couples in relation to the marital quality. The obtained ICC suggests that a multilevel analysis is required. In the next step Model 1 with level 1, followed by level 2 was developed. Level 1 represents partners' demographics and Level 2 represents marriage characteristics variables. The obtained results are related to *H1* and are presented in Table 5.

Table 4. Factor Loadings from Principal Component Factor Analysis with Promax Rotation and Percentages of Variance for Predictors of Marital Quality.

Variables	1	2	3	4	5	6	7	8
				Factor Loadings				
1. Extraversion	-0.046	-0.103	**0.854**	0.201	0.010	0.048	0.032	0.017
2. Agreeableness	0.004	0.079	**0.953**	-0.061	0.005	-0.112	-0.148	0.078
3. Emotional stability	-0.011	-0.347	**0.752**	0.009	0.090	-0.078	-0.028	0.079
4. Self-esteem	0.020	**-0.449**	0.246	-0.100	-0.043	0.105	0.086	-0.147
5. Patriarchy	-0.031	0.172	-0.093	0.354	0.037	-0.026	-0.171	0.052
6. Perception of Gender roles	-0.070	-0.262	-0.133	0.303	**0.467**	-0.041	-0.077	0.129
7. Materialism	0.012	0.198	0.264	0.018	**0.499**	0.064	0.112	-0.297
8. Religiosity	0.186	0.120	0.150	0.048	**0.761**	0.049	-0.056	-0.034
9. Participation in religious rituals	0.035	0.001	0.001	-0.134	**0.755**	0.073	0.043	-0.153
10. Sexual satisfaction Marriage	**0.748**	-0.026	-0.008	-0.097	0.100	0.022	0.060	0.021
11. Satisfaction with income	-0.006	-0.110	-0.010	0.122	0.094	0.030	-0.189	**-0.880**
12. Satisfaction with the distribution of household work	0.357	-0.245	-0.053	0.118	-0.042	-0.049	0.155	-0.079
13. Participation in key decision-making	0.097	-0.188	-0.065	0.198	-0.129	0.002	**0.855**	0.065
14. Participation in everyday routine decision-making	0.006	0.013	0.043	0.041	0.030	-0.003	**0.850**	0.080
15. Negative spillover from work to marriage	-0.072	0.387	0.173	**0.885**	0.022	0.060	0.145	-0.110
16. Negative spill-over from work to housework (home management)	-0.026	0.301	0.120	**0.935**	0.024	0.018	0.166	-0.077
17. Love (Commitment to partner)	**0.899**	0.080	0.032	-0.011	0.065	-0.041	-0.049	0.003
18. Physical attraction	**0.735**	0.121	0.121	-0.072	-0.109	0.102	-0.228	-0.093
19. Perceived partner's support	**0.860**	-0.065	-0.005	-0.005	0.046	-0.027	0.096	0.024
20. Marital strain	**-0.660**	0.010	0.179	-0.032	-.133	0.118	0.091	-0.057
21. Perception of own engagement in routine household work	-0.018	0.290	0.084	-0.374	0.312	0.190	0.099	0.186
22. Perception of partner's engagement in routine household work	0.166	-0.254	-0.028	0.312	-0.239	0.230	-0.195	0.174

(Continued)

Table 4. (*Continued*)

Variables				Factor Loadings				
	1	2	3	4	5	6	7	8
23. Perception of someone else's engagement in routine household work	−0.083	−0.088	−0.108	0.075	0.024	0.111	0.314	0.126
24. Perception of own engagement in childcare	−0.063	0.095	−0.011	−0.059	0.104	**0.859**	0.037	0.001
25. Perception of partner's engagement in child care	0.063	−0.059	−0.050	0.183	−0.080	**0.866**	−0.044	0.021
26. Perception of someone else's engagement in child care	−0.089	−0.120	−0.155	−0.023	0.113	**0.488**	0.096	−0.049
27. Economic hardship	−0.008	0.134	0.092	−0.076	−0.042	−0.044	0.059	**0.861**
28. Depression	0.003	**0.777**	0.003	0.030	0.049	−0.128	0.109	−0.113
29. Perceived global stress	0.116	**0.864**	−0.005	−0.029	−0.014	−0.057	0.119	0.010
30. Positive affectivity	0.054	−0.126	0.377	−0.088	0.112	0.114	0.038	0.224
31. Negative affectivity	−0.075	**0.791**	0.012	−0.184	0.075	0.075	0.102	−0.041
% of variance	17.07	9.08	6.72	6.190	5.742	5.035	4.303	3.809
Reliability α	0.69	0.79	0.83	0.75	0.76	0.78	0.70	0.71

Notes: N = 1,768 marital partners. Factor: 1 = Marital harmony, 2 = Distress, 3 = Partners' personality, 4 = Negative spillover from work, 5. Traditionalism, 6. Engagement in child care, 7. Participation in decision-making. 8. Economic hardship.

Table 5. Estimates of Fixed Effects on Partners Marital Quality.

Variables		Model 1			Model 2		
		Estimates of Partners' Demographic Fixed Effects			Estimates of All Fixed Effects		
		Coefficient	Std. Error	t	Coefficient	Std. Error	t
		Partners' demographic or level 1 effects			All partners' variables or level 1 effects		
Intercept		28.85	3.35	6.38**	22.40	2.06	10.89**
Gender	Wives	−0.76	0.25	−3.08**	0.33	0.21	1.57
	Husbands	0	0		0	0	
Marriage order	First marriage	0.42	3.08	0.140	0.92	0.57	0.46
	Second marriage	0.43	3.07	1.38	1.90	1.94	0.98
	Third marriage	0	0		0	0	
Structure of the family of origin	With both natural parents	1.65	0.94	1.93	0.92	0.57	2.11*
	With mother and contact with father	1.58	1.08	1.47	1.37	0.66	2.08*
	Only with mother	2.13	1.09	1.96**	0.69	0.64	1.05
	With father and contact with mother	2.73	−2.08	1.31	−1.02	1.26	−0.81
	Only with father	1.06	1.48	0.72	0.94	0.92	1.02
	Without both natural parents	0	0		0	0	
Employment status	Unemployed	0.95	0.57	1.67	0.43	0.33	1.29
	Temporary employment	0.18	0.66	0.27	−0.18	0.39	−0.46
	Permanent employment	0.22	0.54	0.42	−0.16	0.31	−0.51
	Retired	0	0		0	0	
Frequency of contraceptive use		−0.11	0.10	1.05	−0.05	0.05	−0.97
Perception of class belonging		1.34	0.40	3.37**	−0.28	0.22	−1.27
Education		−0.16	0.08	−2.04*	0.06	0.05	0.97
Marital harmony					5.51	0.09	65.82**
Distress					−0.23	0.09	−2.63*
Personality					−0.22	0.08	−2.62*
Negative pill over					0.05	0.09	−0.59
Traditionalism					−0.39	0.06	4.59**
Engagement in child cares					0.40	0.08	−3.58**

(Continued)

Table 5. (*Continued*)

Variables	Model 1			Model 2		
	Estimates of Partners' Demographic Fixed Effects			Estimates of All Fixed Effects		
	Coefficient	Std. Error	t	Coefficient	Std. Error	t
	Partners' demographic or level 1 effects			All partners' variables or level 1 effects		
Participation in decision-making				-0.07	0.08	4.79**
Economic hardship				0.01	0.09	0.142
Marital or level 2 effects						
Partners' living arrangement						
Living in same household with my parents	-1.75	0.57	-3.05**	0.08	0.31	0.26
Living in same household with partners' parents	-0.65	0.66	-0.98	0.18	0.35	0.50
Living in same house with my parents but in a separate household	0.35	0.62	0.57	0.18	0.34	0.55
Living in same house with partners' parents but in a separate household	-1.17	0.64	-1.82	-0.13	0.34	-0.38
Living separately from parents but with their assistance	-0.20	0.31	0.67	-0.07	0.20	-0.36
Live separately from parents	0	0		0	0	
Cohabitation before marriage						
Cohabitate before marriage	-0.93	0.38	-2.46**	-0.17	0.17	-0.96
Not cohabitated before marriage	0	0		0	0	
Children in the family younger than 18 years	0.07	0.23	0.29	0.03	0.10	0.33
Marriage duration (Marriage stages)						
Beginning (first two years-no children)	0.86	1.02	0.85	-0.78	0.45	-1.74
Preschool children up to 7 years	1.95	0.72	-2.70**	-0.92	0.32	-2.85**
Children from 8 to 18 years	-2.63	0.76	-3.49**	-0.72	0.33	-2.17*
Adult children from 19 to 26 years living with parents	-0.35	0.70	-0.50	-0.31	0.30	-1.01
Adult children not living with parents	0	0		0	0	
R^2		0.05			0.53	
-2Loglikehood		9753.682			7726.188	

Note: $N = 884$ marital couples, Coefficient represents the value of a particular predictor variable after adjustment with the rest of the predictor variables.

Results Related to the H1

Results for model 1 will be described first and after that those for model 2. Intercept estimates (28.85 and $t = 6.38$, $p < 0.001$) show that couples significantly vary in Marital quality. Wives' marital quality is lower than their husbands ($t = -3.08$, $p < 0.001$). Also, the perception of class belonging variable turned out to be predictive. In couples who perceive themselves as belonging to a higher class, marital quality is higher ($t = 3.37$, $p < 0.001$). The level of education is negatively predictive of marital quality ($t = -2.04$, $p < 0.05$). Three out of four level 2 variables representing marriage characteristics turned out to be predictive of marital quality: Living arrangement. Living in the same household with one's parents turned out to be negatively predictive of marital quality ($t = -3.05$, $p < 0.001$). These results are very important because in Croatia living with parents is frequent, because of traditional or economic reasons. The results also show that partners cohabitating before the marriage have a lower level of marital quality ($t = -2.46$, $p < 0.001$), and that Marital quality varies in different marriage stages: the stage. Partners with preschool and school children have the lowest marital quality. Estimates of the covariance parameter for model 1 such as Residual representing variation between partners is 10.73, with Wald Z test $= 16.96$, $p < 0.001$. Intercept representing variation between couples $= 28.69$ with Wald Z test $= 18.56$ $p < 0.001$, shows that there are significant variations between partners and marital couples on the marital quality variable. The fitting estimate for the model is -2 Log-likelihood $= 9753.682$. Level 1 variables or partners' demographics and level 2 variables representing marriage characteristics explained a small percentage of variance $R^2 = 0.06$, $p < 0.001$ of marital quality.

Results Related to the H2

In model 2 all level 1 and level 2 predictors were included in the analysis: First demographic variables and then variables representing eight factors. In model 2 there are radical changes in comparison to model 1. Intercept is significant ($t = 10.89$, $p < 0.001$) but there is no significant difference in marital quality between wives and husbands ($t = 1.57$, $p > 0.05$). The Variable Structure of the family of origin is predictive of marital quality in marriage: Significantly, higher marital quality was evident in marriages where partners spent their childhood with both parents ($t = 2.16$, $p < 0.95$) or lived with their mother and had contact with their father ($t = 2.26$, $p < 0.05$). Fixed effects for most of the factor variables representing level 1 were predictive of marital quality in marriage. Marital harmony ($t = 65.82$, $p < 0.001$) turned out to be the most predictive, confirming H2. Other factor variables: Distress ($t = -2.63$, $p < 0.05$), Personality ($t = -2.62$, $p < 0.001$), Traditionalism ($t = 4.59$, $p < 0.001$), Engagement in child care (-3.58, $p < 0.001$), and Participation in decision-making ($t = 4.79$, $p < 0.001$) were also predictive but in different directions. Marital quality in marriage will be higher when more traditionalism is shared by marital partners and when they participate in decision-making more. However, it is lower if partners experience distress and are more engaged in child care. Interesting results were obtained in relation to partners' personalities. Marital quality in a dyad will be higher when partners are less extroverted, agreeable, and emotionally stable ($t = -2.62$, $p < 0.05$). Those results are different than in previous studies (Karney & Bradbury, 1995) and probably specific to the Croatian socio-cultural context.

Results Related to the H3

Marriage duration (Marriage stages) is the only level 2 variable predictive of marital quality. Marital quality is lower in stages with preschool children ($t = -2.85$, $p < 0.001$), and school children ($t = -2.17$, $p < 0.001$) than in stages with adult children. Obtained results partly confirmed H3. For the model obtained estimates of covariance parameters are Residual = 5.53, with Wald Z test = 18.49, $p < 0.001$, and Intercept = 2.57 with Wald Z test = 7.03, $p < 0.01$, and Fitting estimates -2 Log-likelihood = 7726.188 proving better fit of the Model 2 than Model 1. A relatively high percentage of the variance of the dependent variable Marital quality was explained ($R^2 = 0.53$, $p < 0.001$) by model 2.

DISCUSSION

Discussion Related to H1

In model 1 wives' marital quality was lower than their husbands'. Such results have already been obtained in previous studies in the United States and other countries (Ragsdale, 1996). Working outside the home and engagement in domestic work as well as child care are possible reasons, but also higher aspirations and expectations from marriage are often frustrated by the ongoing pace of social change in Croatia. In contrast to other countries (Heejeong & Marks, 2013), partners with a lower level of education experience a higher level of marital quality. The reason could be a higher level of expectation from marriage shared by better educated marital partners which are not carried out. However, partners who consider themselves as belonging to a higher social class have higher marital quality. Those results probably indicate that other dimensions of class structure such as social prestige, income, and power affect the experience of marital quality independently from education. Results concerning the relationship between the marital living arrangement and marital quality are very relevant in Croatian society because many partners especially in nonurban settings live together with parents. Results show that these partners experience lower marital quality indicating a tendency for the independence of the younger generation. Similar to previous studies (Jose, O'Leary, & Moyer, 2010), results of this study show that partners who cohabitated before marriage experience lower marital quality. This might be because they spent the most romantic part of their time together before getting married.

Discussion Related to H2

In Model 2, when all predictor variables are included testing the Socio-ecological model, many changes occurred. The only demographic variable Structure of the family of origin turned out to be predictive. Arrangement living in childhood with both parents and arrangements living with mother with contact with the father was positively predictive of marital quality. Expectedly, after mutual adjustment between predictors, level 1 variable (factor) Marital harmony (commitment, support, sexual satisfaction, physical attraction, and absence of marital strain) turned out to be the strongest predictor for marital quality, confirmed in previous studies (Karney & Bradbury, 1995). We identified those variables as universal predictors of marital quality for different socio-cultural contexts. Other level 1 variables (factors): such as Traditionalism and Participation in decision-making probably specific to the Croatian socio-cultural context also turned out to be positively predictive of marital quality. However, Distress and Engagement in child care turned out to be negative predictors. Following predictors, after mutual adjustment were not predictive of marital quality: Gender, Marriage order, Employment status, Frequency of contraceptive use, Perception of Partners' class belonging, Negative spillover from work, Partners' living arrangement, Cohabitation before marriage, and Children in the family younger than 18 years.

The great change presented in Model 2 shows that demographic variables seem to be less important predictors of marital quality than partners' characteristics such as partners' attitudes, values, or experience of marital relationships. Using Model 1, our intention in this study was to show how only demographic variables predict marital quality. In comparison, by using Model 2, we tested how the Socio-ecological model explained marital quality. By comparing the results of those two models, it seems that Huston's (2000) recommendation to include "Wide-angle" and "Close range" variables was correct. Thus we should focus on both models giving precedence to the Socio-ecological model's explanation documented by the percentage of explained variance of the variable marital quality and -2 Log-likelihood Fitting estimate.

Discussion Related to H3

Marriage duration as a predictor of marital quality has been intensively studied in the United States. Most of these studies have shown that marital quality starts decreasing after several years and that previous high quality is never recovered (Shapiro et al., 2000). In this study, Family life course theory (White & Klein, 2008) was used according to which marriage duration is classified in specific stages so we grouped couples in several categories or stages as presented in Tables 2 and 5. Obtained results show that the relationship between marriage duration (marriage stages) and marital quality is curvilinear (The individual scores on the two variables increase up to a certain point, after that scores on the one variable increase and the other start to decrease) what is different from studies conducted previously (Shapiro et al., 2000). These results are probably a consequence of the persisting traditional attitudes among the older generation of marital partners in Croatia. The older generation was socialized in childhood while patriarchy was absolutely dominant.

What could be generally said about predictors of marital quality in Croatia? The results of the present study are in many respects similar to studies in other social contexts, although some specific variables are predictors of marital quality in Croatia. Marital harmony (perceived partner's support, commitment, sexual satisfaction, physical attraction, absence of marital strain) was a very important predictor, similarly observed in the United States and some other countries (Brock & Lawrence, 2009). The same is valid for the variable Distress. It seems that these variables are universal marital quality predictors irrespective of socio-cultural context. However, Traditionalism, Marital partners' personalities, and Engagement in child care are some variables specific to the socio-cultural context in Croatia.

Results of this study show that the group of "universals" are salient predictors of marital quality in Croatia but together with a group of variables specific to the Croatian socio-cultural context. It seems that generally, not only in Croatia, the combination of "universal" and "specific" groups of predictors can provide an adequate explanation of marital quality. Marital partners live in various cultural contexts, which cannot be ignored. Using Huston's Socio-ecological model (2000) and including "wide-angle" and "close range" variables represent better insight into the predictors of marital quality proved by the high percentage of explained variance of marital quality.

CONCLUSIONS AND STUDY LIMITATIONS

This is the first complex or two-level study that attempts to establish predictors of marital quality in Croatia. Two models were tested. The first model represents marital partners' socio-demographic variables as level 1 predictors and marriage characteristics as level 2. The second one is the Socio-ecological model consisting of five groups of level 1 predictors plus marriage characteristics as level 2. Firstly, the results of model 1 demonstrated wives' experience of lower marital quality. Secondly, marital quality proved to be higher for partners of lower educational levels who perceived themselves as belonging to a higher social class. Marital quality was lower for partners living with their parents and also for partners who cohabitated before getting married as well as for partners who had preschool and school children.

Results of model 2 demonstrated no difference between husbands' and wives' marital quality. Marital quality was higher for partners who lived in childhood with both parents and who lived with their mother but had contact with the father, than for partners who lived only with a father or without both biological parents. Also, it was higher, if there was more marital harmony in marriage, and the more they participated in decision-making. In contrast, marital quality will be lower if there is distress in marriage and, more partners are engaged in child care.

We believe that this study clearly shows the salience of social and cultural context in studying marital quality. It also shows that the Socio-ecological model is an adequate theoretical framework for studying marital functioning. However, there are also some study limitations. Its main objectionable feature is that it is cross-sectional. Finally, we believe that this study is of global interest: In studying marital quality, in addition to universal predictors probably present in all societies, it seems indispensable to include variables specific to a particular society.

REFERENCES

Aldous, J. (1996). *Family careers: Rethinking of the developmental perspectives*. Thousand Oaks, CA: Sage.

Allendorf, K. (2012). Marital quality from a rural Indian context in comparative perspective. *Journal of Comparative Family Studies, 67*, 311–322.

Aračić, P., & Nikodem, K. (2000). Važnost braka i obitelji u hrvatskom društvu (Salience of family and marriage in Croatian society). *Bogoslovna smotra, 2*, 291–311.

Aron, A., & Henkenmeyer, L. (1995). Marital satisfaction and passionate love. *Journal of Social and Personal Relationship, 12*, 139–146.

Atkinson, T., Liem, R., & Liem, J. (1986). The social costs of unemployment: Implications for social support. *Journal of Health & Social Behavior, 3*, 317–331.

Belsky, J. I., & Kelly, Y. J. (1994). *The transition to parenthood: How first child changes a marriage. Why do some couples grow closer and others apart?* New York: Dell Publishing.

Berry, R., & Williams, F. (1987). Assessing the relationship between quality of life and marital and income satisfaction: A path analytic approach. *Journal of Marriage & Family, 49*, 107–117.

Botwin, M. D., Buss, D. M., & Shackelford, T. K. (1997). Personality and mate preferences: Five factors in mate selection and marital satisfaction. *Journal of Personality, 65*, 107–136.

Brock, R. L., & Lawrence, E. (2009). Too much of a good thing: Under provision versus overprovision of partner support. *Journal of Family Psychology, 23*, 181–192.

Bronfenbrenner, U. (1986). Ecology of the family as a context for human development: Research perspectives. *Developmental Psychology, 22*, 723–742.

Clement, R., & Swensen, C. H. (2000). Commitment to one's spouse as a predictor of marital quality among older couples. *Current Psychology: Development, Learning, Personality, 19*, 110–119.

Cohan, C. L., & Bradbury, T. N. (1997). Negative life events, marital interaction, and longitudinal course of newlywed marriage. *Journal of Personality and Social Psychology, 79*, 224–237.

Cohen, S., Karkarck, T., & Mermelstein, R. (1983). A global measure of perceived stress. *Journal of Health and Social Behavior, 24*, 385–396.

Cundiff, J. M., Smith, T. W., & Frandsen, C. A. (2012). Incremental validity of spouse ratings versus self-reports of personality as predictors of marital quality and behavior during marital conflict. *Psychological Assessment, 24*(3), 676–684.

Cutrona, C. (1996). *Social support in couples*. Thousand Oaks, CA: Sage Publications.

Erlich, V. (1964). *Porodica u transformaciji (The family in transformation)*. Zagreb: Školska knjiga.

Esmaeli, N. S., & Schoebi, D. (2017). Research on correlate of marital quality and stability in Muslim countries: A review. *Journal of Family Theory Review, 9*, 69–92.

Faulkner, J. E., & DeJong, G. F. (1979). Religiosity in 5 D. An empirical analysis. In R. Wuthnow (Ed.), *Concept and indicators of religious commitment: New directions in quantitative research* (pp. 246–254). New York: Academic Press.

Fincham, D., & Bradbury, T. N. (1993). Marital satisfaction, depression, and attributions: A longitudinal analysis. *Journal of Personality and Social Psychology, 64*, 442–452.

Funk, J. L., & Rogge, R. D. (2007). Testing the ruler with items response theory: Increasing precision of measurement for relationship satisfaction with the Couples Satisfaction Index. *Journal of Family Psychology, 21*, 572–583.

Greeff, A. P., & Malherbe, H. L. (2001). Intimacy and marital satisfaction in spouses. *Journal of Sex and Marital Therapy, 27*, 247–257.

Grote, N., & Frieze, I. (1994). Measurement of friendship-based love in intimate relationships. *Personal Relationships, 1*, 275–300.

Heck, R. H., Thomas, L. N., & Tabata, L. N. (2014). *Multilevel and longitudinal modeling with IBM SPSS* (2nd ed.). New York: Routledge.

Heejeong, C., & Marks, N. F. (2013). Marital quality, socioeconomic status, and physical health. *Journal of Marriage and Family, 75*, 903–919.

Heyman, R., Sayers, S., & Bellack, A. (1994). Global marital satisfaction versus marital adjustment: An empirical comparison of three measures. *Journal of Family Psychology, 8*, 432–452.

Hox, J. (2002). *Multilevel analysis: Technique and application*. Mahwah, NJ: Lawrence Erlbaum Associates.

Hraba, J., Lorenz, F. O., & Pehaceva, Z. (2000). Family stress during the Czech transformation. *Journal of Marriage and the Family*, *62*, 520–531.

Huston, T. L. (2000). The social ecology of marriage and other intimate unions. *Journal of Marriage and the Family*, *62*, 298–320.

Jose, A., O'Leary, K., & Moyer, A. (2010). Does premarital cohabitation predict subsequent marital stability and marital quality? A meta-analysis. *Journal of Marriage and the Family*, *72*, 105–116.

Kamenov, Z., Jelić, I., Tadinac, M., & Hromatko, I. (2008), Quality and stability of the relationship as a function of distribution of housework, financial investment, and decision making. In *15th Psychology Days in Zadar: Book of Selected Proceedings* (pp. 133–151). Zadar: University of Zadar.

Karney, B. R., & Bradbury, N. T. (1995). The longitudinal course of marital quality and stability: A review of theory, method and research. *Psychological Bulletin*, *118*, 3–34.

Kaufman, G., & Taniguchi, H. (2006). Gender and marital happiness in later life. *Journal of Family Issues*, *27*, 735–757.

Kelley, H. H., Berscheid, E., Christensen, J. H., Harvey, T. L., Huston, G., Levinger, E., ... Peterson, D. R. (Eds.). (1983). *Close relationships* (pp. 486–503). New York: Academic Press.

Kiecolt-Glaser, J. K., & Newton, T. I. (2001). Marriage and the health: His and hers. *Psychological Bulletin*, *127*, 472–503.

Leček, S. (1996), Seljačka obitelj u Hrvatskoj 1918-1960. Metoda usmene povijesti (Peasant Family in Croatia 1918-1960: The Oral history Method). *Radovi Zavoda za hrvatsku povijest Filozofskoga fakulteta Sveučilišta u Zagrebu*, *29*, 249–265.

Ledermann, T., & Macho, S. (2009). Mediation in dyadic data at the level of the dyads: A structural equation approach. *Journal of Family Psychology*, *23*, 661–670.

Lichter, D. L., & Carmalt, J. H. (2009). Religion and marital quality among low-income couples. *Social Science Research*, *38*, 166–187.

Marcenes, W., & Sheiham, A. (1996). The relationship between marital quality and the oral health status. *Psychology and Health*, *11*, 357–369.

McCubbin, H. I., Thompson, A. I., & McCubbin, M. A. (1996). *Family assessment: Resiliency, coping, and adaptation: Inventories for Research and Practice.* Madison, WI: University of Wisconsin Publishers.

Miller, P. C., Caughlin, J., & Huston, T. (2003). Trait expressiveness and marital satisfaction: The role of idealization processes. *Journal of Marriage and Family*, *65*, 978–995.

Mlacic, B., & Goldberg, L. R. (2007). An analysis of a cross-cultural personality Inventory: IPIP big-five factor markers in Croatia. *Journal of Personality Assessment*, *88*, 168–177.

Norton, R. (1983). Measuring marital quality .*Journal of Marriage and the Family*, *47*, 141–151.

Obradović, J. (2009). *The scales for measuring marital processes in couples.* Unpublished Project Report, Zagreb.

Perren, S., Von Will, A., Simoni, H., Stadlmayr, W., Burgin, D., & Klitzing, K. (2003). Parental psychopathology, marital quality, and the transition to parenthood. *American Journal of Orthopsychiatry*, *73*, 55–64.

Perry-Jenkins, M., Repetti, R. L., & Crouter, A. C. (2001). Work and family in 1990. *Journal of Marriage and the Family*, *62*, 981–998.

Pieterse, J. N. (2020). *Globalization and culture: Global melange* (4th ed.). New York: Rowman & Littlefield.

Radloff, S. R. (1997). The CES-D scale: A self–report depression scale for research in the general population. *Applied Psychological Measurement*, *1*, 385–401.

Ragsdale, J. D. (1996). Gender satisfaction level and use of relational maintenance strategies in marriage. *Communication Monographs*, *63*, 354–369.

Richins, M. L., & Dawson, S. (1992). A consumer values orientation for materialism and its measurement: Scale development and validation. *Journal of Consumer Research*, *19*, 303–316.

Rihtman-Auguštin, D. (1984). *Struktura tradicijskog mišljenja (The structure of traditional thinking).* Zagreb: Školska knjiga.

Robins, R., Caspi, A., & Moffit, T. (2000). Two personalities, one relationship: Both partners' personality traits shape the quality in their relationship. *Journal of Personality and Social Psychology*, *79*, 251–259.

Rosenberg, M. (1965). *Society and the adolescent self-image*. Princeton, NJ: University Press.

Scherwitz, K. A., & Rugulies, R. (1992). Lifestyle and hostility. In H. S. Friedman (Ed.), *Coping and health* (pp. 77–98). Washington, DC: American Psychological Association.

Shapiro, A., Gottman, J., & Carrere, S. (2000). The baby and the marriage: Identifying factors that buffer against decline in marital satisfaction after the first baby arrives. *Journal of Family Psychology, 14*, 59–70.

Small, S. A., & Riley, D. (1990). Towards a multidimensional assessment of work spillover into family life. *Journal of Marriage and the Family, 52*, 51–61.

Statistical Yearbook. (2018). Zagreb: Croatian Bureau of Statistics.

Sternberg, R. (1997). Construct validation of triangular love scale. *European Journal of Social Psychology, 27*, 313–335.

Sussman, L. M., & Alexander, C. M. (1999). How religiosity and ethnicity affect marital satisfaction for Jewish-Christian couples. *Journal of Mental Health Counseling, 21*, 173–185.

Turner, R. J., & Marino, F. (1994). Social support and social structure: A descriptive epidemiology. *Journal of Health and Social Behavior, 35*, 193–221.

Vannoy, D., & Cubbins, L. (2001). Relative socioeconomic status of spouses, gender attitudes and attributes, and marital quality experienced by couples in metropolitan Moscow. *Journal of Comparative Family Studies, 32*, 195–217.

Watson, D., Clark A. C., & Tellegen, A. (1988). Development and validation of brief measures of positive and negative affect: The PANAS scales. *Journal of Personality and Social Psychology, 54*, 1063–1070.

White, J., & Klein, D. M. (2008). *Family theories*. Los Angeles, CA: Sage.

Wiik, A. K., Keizer, R., & Lappegard, T. (2012). Relationship quality in marital and cohabiting unions across Europe. *Journal of Marriage and Family, 74*, 389–398.

Zhang, H., & Tsang, K. (2010). The influence of urban wives' relative income and education on marital quality. *Chinese Journal of Clinical Psychology, 18*, 632–634.

CHAPTER 6

MARRIAGE FORMATION IN VIETNAM: CHARACTERISTICS AND CHANGES

Nguyen Huu Minh and Bui Thu Huong

ABSTRACT

This chapter analyzes characteristics and changing patterns of marriage formation in Vietnam over the past 50 years, from various aspects including the motives underpinning marriage decision-making, the process of mate acquaintance, the criteria for mate selection, and marriage decision-making rights. The chapter is based on a review of data derived from the Vietnam Family Survey 2006 (MOCST et al., 2008) and the Vietnam Marriage Survey 2017 (Minh, 2021). It shows that the pattern of marriage formation in Vietnam has changed significantly in the past decades under the influence of various socio-economic and legal factors. Marriage is increasingly associated with the value of personal happiness. People today have many more opportunities to meet and get to know each other before marriage than older generations in the past. Adolescents spend more time getting to know their future spouse and have more options when choosing future partners before marriage. Marriage based on a partner's individual qualities is preferred, gradually replacing mate selection based on family background. Parents' power over their children's marriage has decreased, while young people are becoming more and more independent in making decisions about their lives. In other words, today, it is the interests of the people involved in the marriage that matters, not only the interests of the family and kinship that determines marriages. However, despite these new marriage formation patterns, the belief that children's marriage is an important

Conjugal Trajectories: Relationship Beginnings, Change, and Dissolutions
Contemporary Perspectives in Family Research, Volume 22, 109–127
Copyright © 2023 by Emerald Publishing Limited
All rights of reproduction in any form reserved
ISSN: 1530-3535/doi:10.1108/S1530-353520230000022006

affair for the whole family is still maintained. The general pattern is that there is a mix of personal factors and family circumstances regarding the marriage choices.

Keywords: Marriage formation; marriage choices; changes; individualism; Vietnam; mate selection

1. BACKGROUND

Vietnam is located in Southeast Asia, bordered by China to the north, Laos and Cambodia to the west, and by the East Sea to the east. With a population of around 98.8 million in April 2022, Vietnam is the third most populous country in Southeast Asia, surpassed only by Indonesia and the Philippines, and it is the 15th most populous country in the world. The population of Vietnam is largely concentrated in the Red River Delta (in the North) and in the Mekong River Delta (in the South). With about 62% of the population living in rural areas, Vietnam is primarily an agricultural country.

In the context of Vietnam, the network of kinship relations and family, usually classified as patrilineal, plays an indispensable part in the organization of each individual's life and the society as a whole (Barbieri & Belanger, 2009, p. 10). The patrilineal feature of Vietnamese kinship is explicitly illustrated in the privilege that a man is granted, and simultaneously expected to perform, in order to sustain the paternal side of the family. Moreover, the reflection of a male-oriented lineage system in Vietnam can also be found in bifurcate collateral kinship administration (Spencer, 1945). Furthermore, as a member of a family group, each individual does not have any personal interests other than those which are subsumed under or shown in the welfare and continuity of the family group (Wesner & Hitchcock, 2009). As such, any decision that a member makes in regard to his/her own good or household, if any, reflects the influence and interests of the family at large.

In term of marriage, the male-oriented model of kinship stresses the male-centered continuity of the lineage, which in itself underlines the importance of this union and reproduction. In this view, the most important objective of marriage is to produce male offspring to assure continuity of the patrilineage and to perform the rites of ancestor worship, which are the highest expression of Confucian filial piety. Because of the importance of marriage to the family and kin, marriage was seen primarily as a transaction between two families, rather than a matter between the couple. The intervention of the family of origin into the marriages of young couples was even acknowledged by feudal laws, from the Le Code in the fifteenth century and the Gia Long Code in early nineteenth century, to the three Civil Codes applied in the three regions of Vietnam before 1945 (Mau, 1962).

Indeed, in the traditional pre-socialist society of Vietnam, the level of the natal family's involvement in decision-making regarding children's marriage manifested in various aspects. Marriage was early and arranged by the parental generation.

The selection process for a son-in-law/daughter-in-law was conducted through intermediaries when a child assumedly reached the age of sexual maturity. As such, most of the time the bride and groom did not meet and/or know each other until marriage. The concept of love before marriage did not exist and love was generally thought to "develop naturally between husband and wife following marriage" (P. T. V. Anh & Thuy, 2003, p. 205). The parents' choice of spouse was primarily based on considerations regarding *môn đăng hộ đối* [compatibility between the two families] in terms of social and economic status (Belanger & Hong, 1999). For those families who had sons, the selection of daughters-in-law required serious attention because the future bride could bring about bad luck or unhappiness to the in-laws. In addition to the consideration of her family background, the desirable qualities of a woman for marriage were gentleness and delicacy (i.e., a woman with good ethics), her ability to produce a male heir, and her potential contribution to household production (Chi, 1993).

The introduction of the 1960 Law of Marriage and Family can be read as an attempt by the socialist government in northern Vietnam to *quét sạch* [sweep clean] the "old morality" and therefore the old regime it legitimized. The policy aimed to

develop and consolidate the socialist marriage and family system, shape a new type of man, and promote a new socialist way of life, eliminating the vestige of feudalism, backward customs or bourgeois thoughts about marriage and family. (Goodkind, 1996, p. 719)

The socialist-oriented reform of the marriage and family system, which is strictly heterosexual, was based on four fundamental tenets: (1) individual freedom in all matters relating to marriage; (2) monogamy; (3) gender equality; and (4) protection of women's and children's rights, prohibiting forced marriage, concubinage and abuse (National Assembly of Vietnam, 1960). The revolutionary state hoped the new regime would produce "happy, democratic, and harmonious families, in which all members were united, loved each other and helped each other in a progressive manner" (Malarney, 2002, p. 149). For the first time, the age of marriage was regulated by law, whereby only men from 20 years of age and older and women from 18 years of age or older are allowed to get married. Regulations regarding the age of marriage are the first condition to ensure that married people are physically and mentally mature, capable of fully performing the basic functions of the family and, more importantly, to ensure human rights in Vietnamese marriage and family.

One remarkable feature of the voluntary marital regime advocated by the socialist government is that it embraced the notion of *tình yêu* [love]. Together with mutual assistance for progress, reciprocal love was clarified as the precondition of a happy marriage (Malarney, 2002, p. 153). However, the socialist ideal of love promoted by the party during the 1960s and up until the mid-1980s was not about the kind of romance that intellectuals advocated in the colonial context of Vietnam in the first decades of the twentieth century (Phinney, 2008, p. 330). Instead, it was channeled toward the goal of "reunification of the country" (Phinney, 2008, p. 341). Furthermore, in the search for a modern version of love-based marriage, Vietnamese people were still upholding the "old" traditions of marriage, with an emphasis on the dominance of parents' approval and moral characteristics of a future spouse in the selection process (Locke, Tam, & Hoa, 2014). In addition, having children is given priority within marriage and thought to be the foundation on which marital love grows (Van Bich, 1999).

A constellation of changes in values pertaining to gender and family relations has been documented as results of Doi Moi (renovation) and openness policies instigated in Vietnam since 1986. Alongside the increased level of education and economic independence, the accessibility to a wider range of family planning services and information under market-socialist Vietnam has been a critical determinant of women's agentic decisions-making capacity regarding sexual and reproductive choices (Huong, 2010). The importance of sexuality is no longer limited to biological connections and reproductive output, but has expanded to include other aspects of this form of intimacy such as bodily pleasure and disclosure. In the same sense, whilst the primacy of the family continued to be inscribed in state discourses, cohabitation, the postponement or avoidance of marriage, and single parenting by women are all visible and, indeed, on the rise (Chien, 2011; Martin, 2010). The prevalence of these practices can be perceived as an outcome of a more liberal attitude displayed by young people as compared with their parental generations. Furthermore, being freed from a strict regimentation of marriage, sexuality and childbearing are now equated with individual freedom of choice and a greater tolerance of diversity in a fast globalizing context such as Vietnam.

Against this background, this chapter aims to investigate the distinctive features and emergent trajectories of marriage in Vietnam over the past 50 years with the main focus on several aspects of family formation such as the reasons for marriage, the process of acquaintance and courtship, the criteria of mate selection, and the marriage decision-making capacity.

2. DATA

The data on which this chapter is based were drawn from a review of several data sets of the large-scale studies on Vietnamese families conducted over the past few decades, especially those from the Vietnam Family Survey 2006 (VFS, 2006) and the Survey on Basic Characteristics of Marriage in Vietnam today and Influencing Factors between 2017 and 2018 (VMS, 2017). Alongside the national census, these two studies have arguably added more to the very scant prior sociological knowledge surrounding family formation and characteristics in Vietnam. Both studies utilized random sampling techniques. The selected households were representative of both urban and rural areas in the country's key regions and economic zones. The rural–urban ratio of participants was based on the research design and findings of the 2001 Vietnam Household Living Standards Survey (VFS, 2006) and the 2016 Vietnam Population and Housing Survey (VMS, 2017).

In reality, VFS 2006 recruited 9,300 households, of which 26.2% were from urban areas and VMS 2017 recruited 1.819 households, of which 44.4% were urban. Household questionnaires covered wide range of marriage and family issues and were administered by well-trained researchers. The analysis presented in this chapter relates to data that pointed out the reasons of marriage, the process of acquaintance and courtship, the criteria of mate selection, and the marriage decision-making capacity. In addition, the tables and graphs included in this article are the results of bivariate analysis with Chi-square test (for crosstabulation) and *T*-Test for mean comparison. Multivariate analysis was used, however, given the framework of the article, the results were not fully presented other than some brief references in some sections of what follows.

3. FINDINGS

3.1. Reasons for Getting Married

As stated earlier, in the traditional Vietnamese family, marriage was compulsory for the continuation of lineage. When asked to give the three most important reasons to decide to get married, more than 50% of respondents (the highest percentage) in the VMS 2017 said that because they love each other, which is meant for personal happiness rather than family's or lineage's interest. It is noteworthy that there is no difference between men and women in terms of marrying for love, while newly-wed people in urban areas emphasized the reason of love more than the counterpart groups (Table 1). Nearly 50% of the participants thought that mature people should get married like everyone else, and for this reason there is no difference between population groups, implying that the common norm of marriage age has a universal effect on social groups.

The data in Table 1 also illustrate that nearly 50% of respondents said that marriage is for emotional support, and women and the group who married in the

Table 1. Percentage of Reason for Getting Married by Gender, Residence Area, and Year of Marriage (First Marriage, N = 1792).

Characteristics	For Love	Right Age for Marriage	Emotional Help	Caring for Family	To Have Children	Parent's Demand	Material Help
Total	54.8	47.8	43.9	43.4	23.8	18.9	11.6
Gender			**	***	*	*	***
Male	55.7	48.5	40.6	47.6	26.1	16.8	8.4
Female	54.0	47.3	46.8	39.5	21.7	20.8	14.6
Residence area at marriage	***			***	*	***	*
Urban	59.7	47.6	44.4	38.4	21.8	12.6	9.7
Rural	50.9	48.0	43.5	47.6	25.3	23.9	13.2
Marriage year	***		**			***	*
Before 1976	34.2	50.7	43.8	43.8	26.0	35.6	12.3
1976–1986	49.0	50.7	40.8	45.1	28.8	24.4	9.6
1987–1999	52.7	47.7	39.7	44.9	23.0	18.3	13.0
2000–2009	56.6	50.0	50.4	42.7	21.8	16.5	13.0
2010–2017	67.7	42.2	44.9	38.4	22.4	12.9	7.1

Source: VMS 2017.
Notes: Statistical significance levels: $*p < 0.05$; $**p < 0.01$; $***p < 0.001$.

period 2000–2009 emphasized this more than other groups. Regarding the reason for getting married to help the family, the percentage of men admitting this was higher than that of women, showing the role of women in the family, and rural people also emphasized this reason more than urban dwellers.

There are differences between population groups in terms of the remaining reasons such as having children, to fulfill the wishes of parents, or to rely on each other for material life. Getting married to have children was the reason cited by about a quarter of people surveyed. Having a child has an important meaning in terms of continuing the lineage and is also a source of security in old age. Men more clearly expressed the desire to have children to continue the lineage and rural people preserved the tradition of having to marry to have children more so than urban people.

As mentioned above, in a traditional society, getting married is not only mean-ingful to the individuals involved, it is also the fulfillment of parents' responsibili-ties in the process of raising children. The trend of changing the concept of the meaning of marriage is evident as there was a lower percentage of people who gave as a reason for getting married to "meet the needs" of their parents in urban areas and among those who married recently. Women cited this reason higher than men, indicating that the pressure to get married is much higher among women than men, supporting the view that the meaning of women's life exists only within the framework of marriage (Marr, 1981) and the reproductive period of women is shorter than that of men. The need to marry for material support is also more evident in women than men and in rural areas more than in urban areas, while it was at the lowest percentage in the recently married group, 2010–2017.

In comparison with the results of the VFS 2006, although the specific results are different, the overall view of the reasons is quite close. Taking marriage for granted and getting married as a result of falling in love are still the most impor-tant reasons for marriage. Next is about taking care of family members and is a material base for individual life (Ministry of Culture, Sport and Tourism [MOCST], General Statistics Office, Institute for Family and Gender Studies, & UNICEF, 2008).

Further analysis (Minh, 2021) shows that educational factors are impor-tant in explaining the pattern of people's motivation to get married. The more educated group often had a significantly higher proportion than the lower-educated group, giving reasons related to personal desire to get married, and a lower percentage citing reasons related to parental needs and economic interdependence.

In summary, compared to the past, when the majority of the population lived in rural areas and worked in agriculture, marriage mainly carried mean-ings associated with succession, additional labor for the family, and insurance for old age. At the present time, evidence of fundamental changes in the pur-poses and meanings of marriage are documented in the way that individual factors are more pronounced than family and lineage factors. However, the interplay of tradition and modernity is still evident. Indeed, a significant pro-portion of people still get married mainly because of their parents, sometimes for security in old age.

3.2. Getting Acquainted and Courtship Before Marriage

3.2.1. Ways of Getting Acquainted

Each person or generation usually has their own way of becoming acquainted with each other before marriage. In earlier marriage cohorts, the percentage of those introduced by relatives and family when they reach the age of marriage accounted for a higher percentage. People today have more opportunities to meet and get to know each other before marriage than their parent's generations (Hong, 1994). According to a study by Nguyen H. Minh (1999) in the Red River Delta, the percentage of people who "don't know each other" before marriage had decreased significantly when compared with the group of people who got married in the period 1946–1960 to the period 1986–1995. The role of the family in the pre-marital meeting of individuals was also markedly reduced. Instead, the role of friendship groups and recreational groups increased.

The VMS 2017 confirms that the rate of self-acquaintance before marriage is high. In general, for those in the survey sample, the rate of meeting each other for the first time without arrangement or introduction is more than 80% (Fig. 1). The remaining nearly 20% (322 people) is through arrangement and introduction, possibly through parents or family members, friends or other people. The number of people getting to know each other through matchmakers accounts for a very low percentage of these people (5.6% out of 322 people).

There is a fundamental difference in the rate of self-acquaintance across socio-demographic groups. In particular, men who lived in the city when married, and who married more recently, have a higher rate of self-acquaintance (Fig. 1). For those of self-acquaintance, the environment is quite conducive: studying together, working together, getting to know each other in the same circumstances, getting to know each other quite randomly, etc. The social environment of communication and acquaintance is extended, and young people are different from their

Fig. 1. Self-Acquaintance Before Marriage by Gender, Residence Area, and Year of Marriage (First Marriage, $N = 1,792$). *Source*: VMS 2017.

parents or grandparents, who lived in "village bamboo huts"; today, they go to school, to work, go out... and there they get to know each other.

As for those getting acquainted themselves, the main foundation is still having a common environment, especially living, studying and working together or through common friends. Within self-acquaintance situations, studying, working or living together accounted for the highest percentage (52.6%), followed by common friends (28.3%). The rate of meeting randomly through sporting or cultural activities, or simply by chance, is relatively low (6.8% and 11.3%, respectively).

The precise circumstances of self-acquaintance vary across social groups (Table 2). People living in cities have a more diversified living environment, so the rate of casual self-acquaintance is higher than people living in rural areas. Meanwhile, people in the countryside have a higher percentage of self-acquaintance because of living in the same locality. People who married after Doi Moi (since 1987) were more likely to meet each other through common friends, while those who married before Doi Moi were more possible to get to know each other thanks to living in the same area or studying and working together. Further analysis also shows that people with higher education were more likely to be introduced to others through mutual friends (Minh, 2021).

3.2.2. Time of Courtship Process

On average, for the people surveyed in the VMS 2017, it took 22.7 months from the time they started the courtship to the point of marriage. About 50% of these respondents had 1 year or less and about 26% had more than 2 years. With this length of courtship, more than 80% of respondents shared that they had known each other by the time of marriage. Those who had a longer duration of courtship were more likely to assert that they understood each other better.

The duration of courtship itself differs among several social groups as well (Table 3). People who reported living in the city at the time of their marriage

Table 2.   Self-Acquaintance Situation by Gender, Residence Area, and Year of Marriage (First Marriage, $N = 1,477$).

Characteristics		Studying, Living, Working Together	Common Friends	Sports-Cultural Activity	By Chance
Total[1]		52.6 (777)	28.3 (418)	6.8 (100)	11.3 (167)
Gender*	Male	51.8	28.6	8.8	10.1
	Female	53.5	28.0	4.8	12.5
Residence area at marriage***	Urban	46.9	29.7	5.7	16.4
	Rural	56.5	27.3	7.5	7.9
Marriage year***	Before 1976	67.3	16.3	6.1	10.2
	1976–1986	62.0	19.0	7.7	11.3
	1987–1999	52.5	30.7	5.1	11.5
	2000–2009	48.3	31.3	7.1	12.6
	2010–2017	46.5	31.0	8.6	9.4

[1]*Percentage of getting acquaintance through internet only 1%, therefore the results were not shown here.*
Source: VMS 2017.
Notes: Statistical significance levels: $*p < 0.05$; $**p < 0.01$; $***p < 0.001$.

Table 3. Time Duration of Courtship Before Marriage by Gender, Residence Area, and Year of Marriage (First Marriage, $N = 1{,}792$).

Characteristics		0–6 Months	7–12 Months	13–24 Months	25 or More Months	Mean Time of Acquaintance (Months)	N
Total		20.9	27.2	25.7	26.2	22.7	1,792
Gender**	Male	18.2	25.9	28.1	27.9	23.2	858
	Female	23.4	28.4	23.6	24.6	22.2	934
Residence	Urban	11.7	21.7	28.5	38.1	29.8***	709
area***	Rural	27.0	30.7	23.9	18.4	18.1	1,083
Year of	Before 1976	34.2	34.2	24.7	6.8	13.0***	73
marriage***	1976–1986	29.2	24.5	24.0	22.3	19.0	359
	1987–1999	21.4	28.8	23.4	26.4	22.8	594
	2000–2009	16.5	28.1	25.8	29.6	25.2	466
	2010–2017	13.4	24.0	32.9	29.8	25.6	292

Source: VMS 2017.
Notes: Statistical significance levels: *$p < 0.05$; **$p < 0.01$; ***$p < 0.001$.

and those who got married more recently had the longest average duration of courtship. The need to secure housing and economic conditions for independent living among urban populations, as well as being younger people, make them spend more time on the mate selection process. Further analysis also showed that the group with college-university education and above took a significantly longer time in courtship than lower-educated groups (Minh, 2021).

3.2.3. Number of Potential Partners

Another factor associated with the variation in youth dating patterns is the number of partners with whom respondents had courtships before marrying their current spouses. In traditional society young people often did not have the opportunity to find out about their partner because their parents had done it for them. In modern society, one of the key indicators of freedom of marriage is the individual ability to look for a partner and decide who will be his/her future spouse. Indeed, the dating process itself can more easily cause individuals to change potential partners for different reasons. The results of the analysis (Fig. 2) show that men have a higher rate of multiple courtships with other people before marrying their current partners. People living in urban areas have a higher rate of dating others prior to marriage than people living in rural areas, and among the more recently married group, the higher the percentage of people who have dated others before marriage. This result reflects a much more modern lifestyle trend toward people having a more open outlook in regard to mate selection.

3.3. Criteria of Mate Selection

Associated with changes in the courtship process, people's criteria for mate selection have also changed. The traditional pattern of choosing a daughter-in-law/ son-in-law, based on similar social and economic family backgrounds, is now

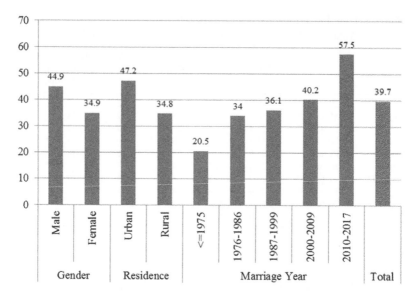

Fig. 2.   Percentage of Getting Courtship Others Before First Marriage
(First Marriage, $N = 1,790$). *Source*: VMS 2017.

being replaced by a match between individual characteristics in terms of behavior, ethics, emotions, and lifestyle. Today's young people are much more concerned with the suitability of their potential partners rather than just the status
of their two families.

Both the VFS 2006 and the VMS 2017 confirmed the tendency to appreciate
some moral values and individual behaviors rather than aspects of education,
occupation or family background. For example, according to the VFS 2006, for
the 18–60 age cohort, the three most important criteria for choosing a partner
were: (1) "good behavior/ethics" (62.6%); (2) "hard working, resourceful work"
(33.9%); and (3) "good health" (33.5%) (Fig. 3). These criteria were selected by
both men and women and were relatively stable across marriage groups in different marriage cohorts, from before 1976 to 2006.

Meanwhile, as released by the VMS 2017, the three most important characteristics of potential partners were: (1) good behavior/ethics; (2) hard working,
resourceful work; and (3) shared similar lifestyle, followed by the criterion of
good health. This results show the stability of some traditional mate selection
criteria such as morality, behavior or hard work and resourcefulness to ensure
a good life. Physical health is also very important because it is not only related
to the family's economic activity, but also a condition for women to give birth
to healthy children. A view of similar lifestyles shows relatively clear modern
characteristics, reflecting the need to be in harmony with the soul and life in the
marriage (Fig. 4).

However, mate selection is not entirely based on individual characteristics. A
percentage of the population continues to emphasize criteria regarding family

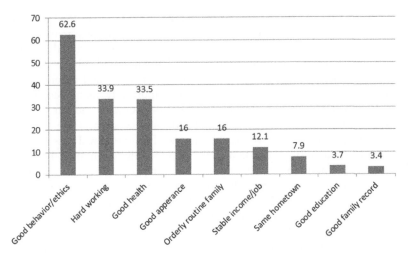

Fig. 3. Percentage of Mate Selection Criteria in the VFS 2006 (18–60 Years Old; *N* = 8,573). *Source*: MOCST et al. (2008; Table 5.3).

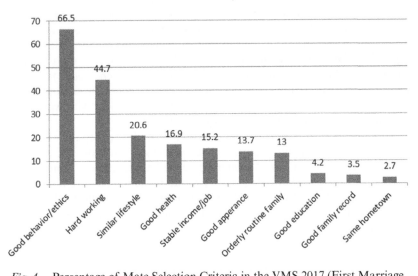

Fig. 4. Percentage of Mate Selection Criteria in the VMS 2017 (First Marriage, *N* = 1,780). *Source*: VMS 2017.

and village relationships. For example, nearly 30% of respondents in the VFS 2006 were concerned with conditions related to their partners' families or hometowns such as "orderly routine/harmonious family", "same hometown" or "good family record" (Fig. 4). This percentage decreased in the VMS 2017, but still stood at about 20% of people making this choice. This suggests personal characteristics and family circumstances are still at the forefront of people's concern when choosing a future spouse.

There are socio-economic reasons behind the appreciation of the family factor in individual decisions when choosing a spouse. The pervasive nature of marriage and its important role in Vietnamese society forces individuals to make a careful choice in order to maintain long-term happiness and enhance the quality of their family life. Family support in economic matters and parenting is still crucial to personal success these days. More importantly, many people believe that an individual's qualities are nurtured and developed in the family environment. A harmonious, orderly family often educates children to live in harmony with everyone, and a family with a stable financial condition will pass on effective business methods to their children to develop the family economy. In addition, the expected support of family and relatives for personal success, as encapsulated in the traditional saying *"one person in the kinship becomes a mandarin, a whole kinship can get benefits,"* has not completely disappeared in modern society. Therefore, the family background of the spouse, especially the economic condition and networks in the family, carries with it potential factors that can positively, or negatively, affect the whole individual's life expectations in the future.

There are certain differences between social groups regarding the criteria for mate selection. Table 4 of the VMS 2017 results shows that the traditional gender concept that emphasized women's behavior/ethics, and men's responsibility to take care of the family economy is evident in the percentage of men who put more emphasis on the "good behavior/ethics" (understood as a good gentle, well-mannered) characteristics of the spouse than women. At the same time, women emphasized the "stable income/job" characteristics of the spouse more than men. The traditional concept *"Girls are greedy for talent, boys are greedy for beauty,"* is also preserved in part of the population. There is evidence from both the VFS 2006 and the VMS 2017 (Table 4) indicating that, compared with women, men continue to be more concerned with physical appearance.

As for the difference between urban and rural people's conception of marriage, city people pay less attention to the characteristics of "hardworking, resourceful at work," "good health" and "good appearance," but emphasize more the criterion of "stable income/job" than rural people. These results were also found in the VFS 2006 (MOCST et al., 2008). Comparing marriage cohorts, the marriage cohort before 1976 tend to put less emphasis on "stable income/job" traits than other groups.

3.4. Marriage Decision-Making Rights

As stated above, in traditional Vietnamese society, marriage was usually decided by parents and the elderly. Today, with great socio-economic changes, this power dynamic has changed. Studies over the past three decades in Vietnam have shown a strong trend of shifting from marriages arranged by parental generations to those based on individual freedom, and confirms that the majority of newlyweds have marital autonomy (Barbieri & Huy, 1995; Goodkind, 1996; Minh, 1999; Van, 2007; etc.). The VFS 2006 showed a decreasing trend of parents' decision-making power over their children's marriage. For people aged 61 and over, 28.5% of their marriages were completely decided by their parents,

Table 4. Criteria for Marriage Selection (First Marriage, $N = 1,780$).

Characteristics		Good Behavior/ Ethics	Hard-working, Resource-ful at Work	Similar Lifestyle	Good Health	Stable Income/ Job	Good Appear-ance	Orderly Routine/ Harmony Family	N
Total		66.4	44.6	20.5	16.9	15.2	13.7	13.0	1,780
Gender	Male	72.6***	43.4	23.3**	12.0***	11.8***	16.6***	14.6*	856
	Female	60.7	45.8	18.2	21.4	18.4	11.0	11.6	924
Residence at	Urban	65.4	40.1**	17.3**	8.9***	18.8**	11.6*	12.6	707
marriage	Rural	67.1	47.6	22.8	22.2	12.9	15.1	13.3	1,073
Year of first	Before 1976	54.8*	47.9*	14.1	16.9	6.8***	8.5	16.9*	71
marriage	1976–1986	67.7	39.3	20.4	18.7	13.4	15.9	17.8	353
	1987–1999	63.4	49.1	20.8	16.9	11.8	13.0	11.7	592
	2000–2009	68.7	44.2	20.7	17.3	16.5	13.4	9.9	463
	2010–2017	69.9	41.1	20.5	12.3	23.3	14.4	13.4	292

Source: VMS 2017.
Notes: Statistical significance levels: *$p < 0.05$; **$p < 0.01$; ***$p < 0.001$.

while for 18–60 years old, only 7.3%. Meanwhile, the percentage of people aged 61 and over having their marriage decided by themselves or with parents' consultation was about 46% and the percentage for people aged 18–60 was about 78% (MOCST et al., 2008).

Data from VMS 2017 (Fig. 5) pointed to the prevailing pattern of young people making decisions by themselves, or in conjunction with their parents (82.4%). The percentage of children deciding to get married with parental consent is the second highest, accounting for approximately 70%.

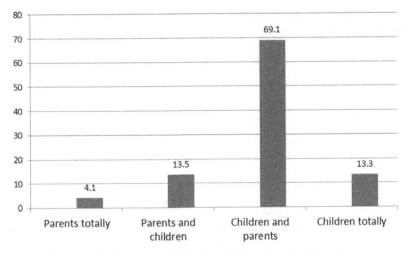

Fig. 5. Marriage Decision-Making Pattern in VMS 2017 (First Marriage, at Least One Parent Was Alive at the Time of Marriage, $N = 1,778$). *Source*: VMS 2017.

Although children's freedom to choose a partner is increasing, the role of parents and families in children's marriage is still important. The VFS 2006 demonstrated that the percentage of marriages that are completely decided upon by the respondents themselves (age 18 and older) without consulting their parents was less than 10% and decreased very slowly, from 10.5% for the age group 61 and older to 6.3% for the 18–60 age group, and remained stable in the marriage cohorts from 1975 and earlier to the later cohorts (MOCST et al., 2008). The VMS 2017 also shows that while the proportion of young people who make decisions in consultation with their parents has increased significantly across the marriage cohorts, especially after the 2010 cohort compared to earlier cohorts (the difference with the pre-1976 cohort is more than 20 percentage points and with the 1976–1986 cohort is about 13 percentage points), the proportion of young people making their own decisions has risen slowly (Table 5).

Some people argue that arranging a marriage for young people is a "natural" parental right, because the parents have been responsible for bringing up their child themselves. Respecting the opinions of parents and other family members helps create a consensus in the new life, between the new members, being the daughter-in-law, son-in-law and the husband's and wife's family. Up to now, the pattern of living with the husband's family after marriage is still common. Therefore, if there is parental arrangement, the post-marital relationship between a daughter-in-law and her parents-in-law and other family members will be more favorable (Minh, 2008; Minh & Hirschman, 2021; MOCST et al., 2008).

Our analytical review of the VFS 2006 and VMS 2017, alongside previous studies (Goodkind, 1996; Minh, 1999), shows that in general men are more capable of making their personal decisions given their prior consultation with parents than women, which reflects a greater level of passivity among women in

Table 5.   Marriage Decision-Making Right by Gender, Residence, and Year of Marriage (First Marriage, at Least One Parent Was Alive at the Time of Marriage, $N = 1,778$).

Characteristics		Totally Decided by Parents	Parents Decided with Child's Consultation	Child Decided with Parent's Consultation	Totally Decided by Child	N
Total		4.1	13.5	69.1	13.3	1,778
Gender**	Male	2.5	11.9	73.1	12.5	854
	Female	5.5	14.9	65.5	14.1	924
Residence at marriage***	Urban	3.0	9.4	71.3	16.3	700
	Rural	4.7	16.1	67.7	11.4	1,078
Year of marriage***	Before 1976	12.5	20.8	56.9	9.7	72
	1976–1986	6.5	15.9	65.7	11.9	353
	1987–1999	3.7	15.1	68.4	12.8	588
	2000–2009	2.2	12.5	68.1	17.2	464
	2010–2017	2.7	7.2	78.8	11.3	292

Source: VMS 2017.
Notes: Statistical significance levels: *$p < 0.05$; **$p < 0.01$; ***$p < 0.001$.

terms of marriage. Young people's individual decision-making power in marriage is also higher in the group of people living in urban areas or getting married in later cohorts. In addition, the data in Table 5 and previous findings show that marriage decision-making power transferred from parents to young people was most pronounced in the pre-1976 period compared with later periods. After 1975, that trend continued, but the visibility of change was not significant (Minh, 1999; MOCST et al., 2008).

Other factors are involved in changing the pattern of the individual's freedom in marriage from earlier periods. First is the role of factors that characterize the modernization process, such as the increase in educational attainment and the expansion of off-farm career opportunities. People's educational attainment is considered to be the most important factor explaining the population's tendency to significantly increase marriages based on freedom of choice. Occupational factors are confirmed to be extremely important in explaining the population's pattern of freedom to choose a partner, especially for women who previously worked only within close proximity to their families and mostly agriculture (Minh, 1999, 2018; MOCST et al., 2008).

The state has significant influence over the marriage decisions of individuals in Vietnam, through policies directly related to marriage and family. The influence of the state is often reflected in changes in the proportion of people who have the freedom to choose their spouse in the process of policy implementation in different marriage cohorts (Table 5) and through differences in the freedom of mate selection among a group of people working or not working in state-owned socio-economic organizations (Goodkind, 1996; Minh, 1999).

4. DISCUSSION

From a cultural approach, the chapter is interested in the way the features of the traditional marriage institution shaped the current marriage pattern. The pattern of marriage formation in Vietnam, from a process of getting to know each other, having a period of courtship, to criteria for choosing a partner and the right to decide on individual's marriage, has changed significantly in the past few decades, under the influence of economic and social factors, as well as laws and policies. Marriage is increasingly associated with the value of personal happiness, although the meaning of family interest is still very important. People today have more opportunities to meet and get to know each other before marriage than in their parent's generations.

The studying and working environments as well as entertainment activities have gradually become a common place to meet and get to know a potential partner, and that is replacing the traditional family and village space. Adolescents spend more time on courtship, and have more options for choosing a future partner before deciding to marry. Marriage based on partner's individual characteristics is now preferred, gradually replacing mate selection based on suitability of family background. Parents' power over their children's marriage has decreased, while young people are becoming more and more independent in making decisions about their lives. In other words, it is the interests of the people involved in the marriage, not the interests of the family and lineage, that determine marriages today. This trend is consistent with the general pattern of mate selection observed in countries in Asia and the world (Mäenpää & Jalovaara, 2014; Sheng, 2005; Xenos & Gultiano, 1992; Xu, 2021).

However, the new marriage pattern has not completely broken with the past. Marriage still has a very important meaning for the Vietnamese people; the majority of Vietnamese people are still actively looking for marriage. Some traditional marital values in choosing a partner are still preserved. The increase in individual freedom to choose a mate in recent cohorts of marriage does not mean that young people are now completely in charge of their marriage. The concept that children's marriage is an important affair for the whole family is still maintained. The general pattern is that there is a mix of personal factors and family circumstances in the choice of marriage.

In other words, even though the personal dimension is emphasized, the core elements of the family building process are still preserved, which is the attachment/linkage of individual's and family's interests. All these characteristics show the interweaving of characteristics of modern life along with the preservation of traditional values, when there is a gap between the higher speed of socio-economic development and the slower transformation of cultural values. In the context of a country that has just achieved an above average level of economic development, with a medium level of industrialization and modernization, the impact of cultural factors is even greater. Family participation in children's marriage not only reflects the social pressure to maintain traditions, but it also demonstrates the rationality of individuals' decisions taking into account the importance of marriage in Vietnam. It is believed that the continuity and unity of the extended family will be better maintained if all important members of the extended family share decisions about the mate selection of each member. This trend harmonizes the interests of parents, other family members and those who get married, so it will certainly persist for a long time in Vietnam, especially in rural areas.

Important factors affecting the formation of marriage in Vietnam include: the positive changes seen in the education system; a developing level of both industrialization and urbanization, with the spread of urban lifestyles and expanding off-farm occupational opportunities; the preservation of cultural patterns; individual and household characteristics. The past few decades have marked the tireless efforts of the Vietnam government and the whole society in improving the educational level of the population, especially for women, helping young people become less dependent on their parents. New job opportunities outside of agriculture for people generally, and especially women, gives young people a better opportunity to be financially self-supporting, and enrich their communication outside the family. It is a meaningful turning point for young people to be more active in deciding their choices. The urban environment provides residents with greater exposure to new ideas emphasizing the individual's freedom in their marriage and more opportunities to make contact with people outside the living area. These findings are consistent with research findings on the same topic in a number of countries and regions that, due to the strong impact of increasing education and expanding occupations outside of family, individuals' marriages will become less dependent on families, and young people have greater autonomy (Jones & Yeung, 2014; Thornton, Axinn, & Xie, 2007; Thornton, Chang, & Lin, 1994; Thornton, Chang, & Yang, 1994; Pew Research Center, 2010; Xenos & Gultiano, 1992).

The trend of changing patterns of marriage formation over time also shows the role of the government through the legal and policy system. This directly creates the legal framework for young people's right to freely choose a spouse. The impact of the state factor is similar to what has been found in China, a neighboring country that shares many similarities with Vietnam in its development, that marriage and family law, and advocacy movements to implement the law, is an important factor in accelerating a tendency to move from marriage arranged by family and parents to voluntary marriage (Davis & Harrell, 1993; Xu, 2021).

Along with structural transformations such as higher educational attainment, more off-farm occupation, urbanization, etc., the increased tendency to freely choose a mate and the criteria of mate selection becoming more closely aligned with the new socio-economic context in the recent marriage cohorts shows a real shift in perception toward individual decision-making power and the personal traits of their spouse. New modern lifestyles, changes in marriage and family laws, efforts by government agencies and mass organizations to enforce these laws through administrative measures, communication systems, and widespread discussion among the population can also play an important role in this cultural transformation.

Given the nature of a review article as well as the limited availability of data, the authors could only analyze the differences in the pattern of marriage formation among some social groups using variables of gender, place of residence and year of marriage. Other variables such as religious beliefs or ethnic cultural characteristics can also modify marriage patterns. The division of courtship over time or whether to get to know someone else before the current marriage has only slightly been touched upon. The process of reconciling the interests between parents and children in deciding their children's marriage as well as the multidimensional influence of state factors on individuals' choice of life partner have not been explained in much detail. These issues may be the subject of future studies on the pattern of marriage formation in Vietnam.

REFERENCES

Anh, P. T. V., & Thuy, P. T. (2003). Let's talk about love: Depictions of love and marriage in contemporary Vietnamese short fiction. In B. W. L. Drummond & M. Thomas (Eds.), *Consuming urban culture in contemporary Vietnam* (pp. 202–218). London: Routledge Curzon.

Barbieri, M., & Belanger, D. (2009). *Reconfiguring families in contemporary Vietnam*. Stanford: Stanford University Press.

Barbieri, M., & Huy, V. T. (1995, November). Impacts of socio-economic changes on Vietnamese family: A case study in Thaibinh Province. Paper presented in the Workshop "Family, Economic Change, and Fertility", Hanoi, Vietnam.

Belanger, D., & Hong, K. T. (1999). Single women's experiences of sexual relationships and abortion in Hanoi, Vietnam. *Reproductive Health Matters, 7*(14), 71–78.

Chi, N. T. (1993). The traditional Viet village in Bac Bo: Its organizational structure and problems. In H. L. Phan et al. (Eds.), *The traditional village in Vietnam* (pp. 44–142). Hanoi: The Gioi Publishers.

Chien, N. D. (2011). Bien doi khuon mau tinh yeu xuat hien song chung truoc hon nhan (Transformation of love and premarital cohabitation). Paper presented at the Hoi thao quoc te ve Dong gop cua Khoa hoc Xa hoi–Nhan van trong phat trien kinh te–xa hoi [International Conference on Contributions of Social Sciences and Humanities in Socio–Economic Development], Hanoi. Retrieved from http://tainguyenso.vnu.edu.vn/jspui/handle/123456789/3896

Davis, D., & Harrell. S. (1993). Introduction: The impact of post-Mao reforms on family life. In D. Deborah & S. Harrell (Eds.), *Chinese families in the post-Mao era* (pp. 1–24). Berkeley, CA: University of California Press.

Goode, W. J. (1963). *World revolution and family patterns.* Glencoe: Free Press.

Goodkind, D. (1996). State agendas, local sentiments: Vietnamese wedding practices amidst socialist transformations. *Social Forces, 75*(2), 717–742.

Hong, K. T. (1994). Rural family formation in the new socio-economic situation. *Sociological Review, 46*(2), 76–84.

Huong, B. T. (2010). 'Let's Talk about Sex, Baby': Sexual Communication in Marriage in Contemporary Vietnam. *Culture, Health & Sexuality, 12*(Suppl 1), S19–S29.

Jones, G. W., & Yeung, W.-J. J. (2014). Marriage in Asia. *Journal of Family Issues, 35*(12), 1567–1583.

Locke, C., Tam, N. T. T., & Hoa, T. N. N. (2014). Mobile householding and marital dissolution in Vietnam: An inevitable consequence? *Geoforum, 51,* 273–283.

Mäenpää, E., & Jalovaara, M. (2014). Homogamy in socio-economic background and education, and the dissolution of cohabiting unions. *Demographic Research, 30,* 1769–1792.

Malarney, K. S. (2002). How to marry? The consequences of the campaign to reform marriage and weddings. In K. S. Malarney (Ed.), *Culture, ritual and revolution in Vietnam* (pp. 148–171). Honolulu: University of Hawai'i Press.

Marr, D. G. (1981). *Vietnamese tradition on trial, 1920–1945.* University of California Press.

Martin, P. (2010). 'These days virginity is just a feeling': Heterosexuality and change in young urban Vietnamese men. *Culture, Health & Sexuality, 12*(S1), 5–18.

Mau, V. V. (1962). *Review of Vietnam civil codes. Volume 1, family.* Saigon: National Ministry of Education.

Minh, N. H. (1999). Marriage-selection freedom in the Red River Delta: Tradition and changes. *Sociological Review, 65*(1), 28–39.

Minh, N. H. (2008). Post-marital residence rotation custom: Tradition and contemporary situation in Vietnam rural. *Family and Gender Studies, 18*(4), 3–13.

Minh, N. H. (2009). Changes of marriage making decision in Vietnam and determinants. *Family and Gender Studies, 19*(4), 3–17. Hanoi.

Minh, N. H. (2021). *Marriage and Marital Experiences in Vietnam.* Hanoi, Vietnam: Social Sciences Publishing House.

Ministry of Culture, Sport and Tourism (MOCST), General Statistics Office, Institute for Family and Gender Studies, & UNICEF. (2008). Result of the Survey on the Vietnamese Family 2006. Hanoi, Vietnam: MOCST Publishing House.

National Assembly of Vietnam. (1960). *Luat Hon nhan va Gia dinh [the Law of Marriage and Family].* Hanoi: National Assembly of Vietnam.

Pew Research Center. (2010). *The decline of marriage and rise of new families* (A social and demographic trends report). WA, DC: Pew Research Center Publisher.

Phinney, M. H. (2008). Objects of affection: Vietnamese discourses on love and emancipation. *Positions: East Asia Cultures Critique, 16*(2), 329–358.

Sheng, X. (2005). Chinese families. In B. N. Adams & J. Trost (Eds.), *Handbook of world families.* Thousand Oaks, CA: Sage Publications.

Spencer, R. F. (1945). The Annamese kinship system. *Southwestern Journal of Anthropology, 1*(2), 284–310.

Thornton, A., Axinn, W. G., & Xie, Y. (Eds.). (2007). *Marriage and cohabitation.* Chicago, IL: The University of Chicago Press.

Thornton, A., Chang, J.-S., & Lin, H.-S. (1994). From arranged marriage toward love match. In A. Thornton & H.-S. Lin (Eds.), *Social change and the family in Taiwan* (pp. 148–177). Chicago, IL: The University of Chicago Press.

Thornton, A., Chang, J.-S., & Yang, L.-S. (1994). Determinants of historical changes in marital arrangements, dating, and premarital sexual intimacy and pregnancy. In A. Thornton & H.-S. Lin (Eds.), *Social change and the family in Taiwan* (pp. 178–201).Chicago, IL: The University of Chicago Press.

Van, L. N. (2007). Pattern of introductions, engagements and making marriage decision in Vietnamese rural areas in the Doi Moi period. *Sociological Review, 99*(3), 24–36.

Van Bich, P. (1999). *The Vietnamese family in change: The case of the Red River Delta.* Surrey: Curzon.

Wesner, S., & Hitchcock, M. (2009). Vietnamese values, networks and family businesses in London. *Asia Pacific Business Review, 15*(2), 265–282.

Xenos, P., & Gultiano, S. A. (1992). *Trends in female and male age at marriage and celibacy in Asia* (Papers of the program on population). Honolulu, Hawaii: East-West Center. No. 120.

Xu, A. (2021). Mate selection: Analysis of changes and causes during the past five decades. In O. Emiko & P. Uberoi (Eds.), *Reprint in English in the Volume 3 of the Four Volume Set "Asian Families and Intimacies"* (pp. 51–74). Sage Publishing. ISBN: 9789353286200.

CHAPTER 7

EDUCATION, MARRIAGE COHORTS, AND DIFFERENT PATHWAYS TO MARRIAGE IN EAST ASIAN SOCIETIES

Shichao Du

ABSTRACT

The literature on marriage formation neglects different pathways to marriage. This study focuses on arranged marriage, introduced marriage, and self-initiated marriage as three main marriage pathways in East Asia and examines how people's marriage pathway choices are associated with education and change over time in mainland China, Japan, South Korea, and Taiwan. Using data from the East Asian Social Survey, this study finds that education is associated with fewer arranged marriages and more self-initiated marriages and that more recent marriage cohorts also witness a decline in arranged marriages and an increase in self-initiated marriages. However, how introduced marriage is associated with education and change over time varies in four East Asian societies. The findings support the "developmentalism-marriage" framework that developmental idealism leads to modern marital practices.

Keywords: Pathway to marriage; education; marriage cohort; developmental idealism; East Asia; arranged marriage

Conjugal Trajectories: Relationship Beginnings, Change, and Dissolutions
Contemporary Perspectives in Family Research, Volume 22, 129–149
Copyright © 2023 by Emerald Publishing Limited
All rights of reproduction in any form reserved
ISSN: 1530-3535/doi:10.1108/S1530-353520230000022007

INTRODUCTION

Family scholars have been turning their attention to East Asian societies for their special family cultures and different marital practices from those in the West (e.g., Atoh, Kandiah, & Ivanov, 2004; Chen & Li, 2014; Frejka, Jones, & Sardon, 2010; Jones & Yeung, 2014; Kan, Hertog, & Kolpashnikova, 2019; H. Park, 2021; Raymo, Park, Xie, & Yeung, 2015; Suzuki, 2013). All of the studies cited above agree that East Asia is experiencing a family transition toward fewer and later marriages. For instance, marriage has been delayed overall and certain groups of young adults even forgo marriage in East Asia. Age at first marriage began to climb in the 1970s–1980s and recently reached 30 for men and 28 for women in Japan, South Korea, and Taiwan, making them some of the latest-marrying societies in the world (Raymo et al., 2015). The percentage of those who never married at age 50 increased between 1980 and 2010 from 2.6% to 20.2% in Japan, from 0.4% to 5.8% in South Korea, and from 5.0% to 10.1% in Taiwan (Raymo et al., 2015). The change in mainland China is more recent and less pronounced, but the gap between mainland China and its neighboring East Asian societies is narrowing (Jones & Yeung, 2014; Yeung & Hu, 2013). In this vein, researchers conclude that the marriage market in East Asia is changing much more dramatically than in the West.

In their annual review paper, Raymo et al. (2015) point to the changes as well as the continuity in East Asia families. The traditional features, expectations, and obligations of East Asia families have rarely changed. The tension between rapid transformations in the marriage market and limited alternations in family norms shapes unique marital practices in East Asian societies. However, what are these unique practices has seldom been discussed in the literature.

Following this annual review paper, a special collection on family changes in East Asia appeared in *Demographic Research* (H. Park, 2021). This special collection, with eight empirical studies, collectively demonstrates the continuity of gender inequality within families in East Asia societies. Although this collection is an important supplement to our limited knowledge of the changing demographic trends in the region, the eight studies included in this special collection separately focus only on one of the East Asian societies. Comparison or synthesized research is needed to understand the within-region variation as well as similarities among East Asian societies.

For these reasons, this study focuses on different pathways to marriage, a concept challenging the Western idea of love-based companionate marriage,[1] and examines its correlates in four East Asian societies: mainland China (hereafter China), Japan, South Korea (hereafter Korea), and Taiwan. Three marriage pathways are specified in this study: arranged marriage, introduced marriage, and self-initiated marriage. I scrutinize how education influences East Asian people's marriage pathway choice and how the educational effect varies across different societies in East Asia. I also investigate how various pathways to marriage change in different marriage cohorts, as more recent marriage cohorts have more developmental ideologies. Under the "developmentalism-marriage" framework, hypotheses are proposed. Data are from East Asia Social Survey 2006 and 2016.

Although this study is not among the first to examine the educational effect on marriage in East Asia, it is the first, to my knowledge, to specify various pathways to marriage and compare the educational effect among East Asian societies. Practically, knowing people's marriage pathway choices can have implications for policy intervention to boost the low marriage rates in East Asia. Theoretically, the investigation of different pathways to marriage in East Asia can challenge the Western-based "companionate marriage" ideal and the "Standard North American Family" (Cohen, 2021; Powell, Hamilton, Manago, & Cheng, 2016; Smith, 1993). Besides self-initiation, marriage may also be arranged or introduced by social relations in East Asian societies, suggesting that families are embedded in social networks (Rindfuss, Choe, Bumpass, & Tsuya, 2004). Therefore, although this study focuses on localized marital practices in a non-Western setting, the findings can contribute to the broader literature and be applied to other social contexts as well.

LITERATURE REVIEW

Different Pathways to Marriage

Pronounced similarities across China, Japan, Korea, and Taiwan can be traced back to the common origin of the Confucian tradition of families (e.g., Chen & Li, 2014; I. Park & Cho, 1995). The expectations and obligations of the family, according to the Confucian tradition, are parallel in all these societies. For example, the culture of family lineage and filial piety – which requires children and grandchildren to obey and care for their older generations – is the core of family behavior (Chu & Yu, 2010; Tu, 2000). Although some well-educated women and men in East Asia are now resisting their parents' intervention by showing indifference to the marriage market, marriage as a package of family expectations and obligations has never been altered (Bumpass, Rindfuss, Choe, & Tsuya, 2009; Martin, 1990; Rindfuss et al., 2004). Therefore, marriage cannot be understood as a merely private choice in East Asia societies. Instead, it is highly public and embedded in social relations (Davis & Friedman, 2014). In this vein, different mate selection strategies besides self-initiation should be taken into consideration. In this study, I focus on three main strategies, historically or currently, for mate selection. They are arranged marriage, introduced marriage, and self-initiated marriage. These three marriage pathways reflect different levels of modernization, with the first one being the least modern and the last one being the most modern.

Arranged marriage is the marital practice of parents, along with other senior family members, choosing spouses for their unmarried children on the basis of religion, social and economic standing, and other characteristics of prospective spouses and their families (Bennett, 1983; Uberoi, 2006). It emphasizes the importance of parental intervention and intergenerational relationships and is thought to be related to marital happiness and social benefits beyond the family (Allendorf & Thornton, 2015). Prevalent in Hindu societies, arranged marriages have drawn wide scholarly attention (e.g., Allendorf, 2013; Allendorf & Thornton, 2015; Epstein, Pandit, & Thakar, 2013; Ghimire, Axinn, Yabiku, & Thornton, 2006; Harkness & Khaled, 2014; South, Trent, & Bose, 2016; Y. Zhang & Axinn, 2021). Although "strict" arranged marriage – where couples-to-be did not meet each other until the wedding day (South et al., 2016) – no longer exist in East Asian societies,[2] "loose" arranged marriage – where young adults follow their parents' marriage arrangements without consent – was historically popular in Confucian societies and is still practiced in some regions (Xu & Whyte, 1990). Indeed, the practice of arranged marriage is less insightful for understanding contemporary marriage in East Asia, a close look at its historical trend can help explain the modernization of marriage in the region.

Different from but related to arranged marriages, introduced marriages take new forms of parental (as well as other social relations') involvement in unmarried adults' mate selection. In this marital practice, unmarried adults are introduced to other marriage candidates by their social relations (e.g., parents, friends, or professional matchmakers) and they decide whether to date and ultimately marry each other (Gui, 2017; Riley, 1994). Although in introduced marriages, couples-to-be are arranged to meet, their subsequent partnership is based on free will. Parents and other family authorities have lost absolute control over couples-to-be, although they continue to exert influence on the final marital decision (Blair & Madigan, 2019; J. Zhang & Sun, 2014). This introduced marriage is frequently practiced by those who are anxious about marriage in East Asian societies, including China, Japan, Korea, and Taiwan (Applbaum, 1995; Chuang & Wolf, 2010; Huang, Jin, & Xu, 2012; Jiang, Zhang, & Sanchez-Barricarte, 2015; Mathews & Straughan, 2016; Peterson, Kim, McCarthy, Park, & Plamondon, 2011). For instance, Chinese parents actively scout for a potential spouse for their unmarried adult children through activities like "matchmaking" when their unmarried children reach a mature age (Gui, 2017; J. Zhang & Sun, 2014). Such marital practice is different from the Western understanding that a family is a personal issue "characterized by the mutual affection, sympathetic understanding, and comradeship of its members" (Burgess, 1963, p. vii). Although around 7% of heterosexual couples in the United States met each other through family ties in 2017, this number is estimated to have sharply decreased from almost 30% in the 1950s (Rosenfeld, Thomas, & Hausen, 2019). This dramatic decline suggests the dominant modern idea of "companionate marriage" that love is the basis for a mutual relationship and its subsequent marriage in Western societies (Cohen, 2021, p. 57). Diverging from the faith in love-based companionate marriages, which are free of parental intervention, introduced marriages in East Asia serve as an alternative pathway to marriage formation. An investigation of introduced marriage can produce fruitful insights for understanding the dynamics of marriage as well as the interaction between social relations and marriage formation, even beyond East Asia.

Mating and marriage for recent cohorts in East Asian societies are more and more based on free will (Davis, 2014b; Schneider, 2014). In modern idealism, love and romance are perceived as the ground for marriage (Giordano et al., 2006; Tillman et al., 2019). This type of modern marriage pathway that is based on romantic relationships, individual selection, or elopement is free from parental involvement and intervention of other social relations (Allendorf, 2013; Clignet & Sween, 1969). Research shows that co-residence with parents delayed young adults' relationship formation, indicating the nature of self-management of modern relationships among young adults (Yu, Lin, & Su, 2019). Self-initiated relationship formation is now trending in all East Asian societies. For example, although the interest in a romantic relationship is shown to be declining in Japan (Ghaznavi et al., 2020), romantic relationship *per se* is becoming more self-based (Kanemasa, Hertog, & Kolpashnikova, 2004). Similar findings are also found in Taiwan (Yu, Lin, & Su, 2019). One study surprisingly finds that Korean young adults involve their family and friends less in their romantic relationships than Americans do (Jin & Oh, 2010). The story in China is a bit different. Although the idea of self-initiated partnership is increasing among young adults, their mating process is still more likely to be intervened by their social relations like peers and parents than young adults in North America (Blair & Madigan, 2019; Li, Connolly, Jiang, Pepler, & Craig, 2010).

A close examination of different pathways to marriage (arranged, introduced, or self-initiated) can reflect different forms of intergenerational relationships, various levels of family embeddedness in social networks, as well as the extent of modern idealism regarding marriage formation in East Asian societies. It also adds nuanced knowledge to the existing literature on marriage and family that is dominated by the Western model of "companionate marriage."

Education as the Developmental Idealism Generator

The relationship between education and marriage has been well documented in a wealth of research pointing to the delaying effect of education on union formation and childbearing (e.g., Axinn & Barber, 2001; Blossfeld & Huinink, 1991; Glick, Handy, & Sahn, 2015; Kalmijn 2013; Perelli-Harris & Lyons-Amos, 2016). The life course perspective suggests that the existence of a relatively rigid sequencing of demographic events in early adulthood determines the delayed family formation following prolonged education (Skirbekk, Kohler, & Prskawetz, 2004). Although college-educated individuals are found to have higher possibilities of getting married than their less-educated counterparts (Cherlin, 2010; Kalmijn, 2013; Schoen & Cheng, 2006; Torr, 2011), they have always married later than others because of extended schooling years and the tendency not to marry while in school (Blossfeld & Huinink, 1991; Goldstein & Kenney, 2001; Thornton, Axinn, & Xie, 2007).

Despite the well-studied delaying effect of education, how education influences people's marriage pathway choice is less known. The "developmentalism-marriage" framework – that developmental idealism leads to modern and later marriage – can guide the investigation of the relationship between education and various pathways to marriage (Thornton, 2001, 2005; Thornton et al., 2012). Here, developmentalism (or developmental idealism) refers to the values and beliefs that modernized culture is preferred over traditional culture because the former indicates development (Allendorf & Thornton, 2015; Thornton, 2005). In one famous study, Allendorf and Thornton (2015) point to the family-related developmentalism that choosing one's own spouse, living in a nuclear family, and having a small number of children are desirable. In a series of studies regarding marriage in Nepal, researchers treat education as a nonfamily experience that enhances developmental idealism and consequently modernizes people's marriage behavior (Allendorf & Thornton, 2015; Allendorf, Thornton, Mitchell, & Young-DeMarco, 2019; Compernolle & Axinn 2019; Ghimire et al., 2006; Yabiku, 2005). They reveal that people (especially females) with a higher level of developmental idealism are more likely to delay their marriage and make marital decisions by themselves (without parental control) (Allendorf, 2017; Allendorf et al., 2019; Ghimire et al., 2006).

This "education-developmentalism-marriage" trajectory also applies to East Asian societies. Developmental idealism is found to be correlated with modern family values as well as modern family practices, including the favor for choosing a spouse by themselves (Lai & Thornton, 2015). In democratic East Asian societies of Japan, South Korea, and Taiwan, education is also found to delay people's entry into marriage partly through the mechanism of developmental idealism cultivated (Cheng, 2014; Raymo, 2003; Yoo, 2016). For these reasons, it is reasonable to speculate that well-educated individuals in East Asia are more likely to take on modern marital practices. In particular, they are more likely to find a spouse on their own and less likely to be arranged for marriage. Few studies have directly examined this question in East Asian settings although some scholarly attention has been paid to Hindu societies (e.g., Allendorf & Thornton, 2015). In this vein, I propose the hypothesis that,

H1a. Individuals with more years of education are more likely to have a self-initiated marriage, compared with an arranged marriage and an introduced marriage.

H1b. Individuals with more years of education are less likely to have an arranged marriage, compared with a self-initiated marriage and an introduced marriage.

Developmental Idealism Evolving with Marriage Cohorts

While education indicates the individual level of developmental idealism, cohort evolution reflects changes in the aggregated level of developmental idealism. The second demographic transition framework casts primary emphasis on ideational change as an explanation for fewer marriages and lower fertility in Europe and other Western societies (e.g., Surkyn & Lesthaeghe, 2004; Zaidi & Morgan, 2017). This perspective can be appropriated to understand various marriage pathways in East Asian societies.

As the first East Asian country to modernize, Japan has been strongly influenced by Western policies and ideals (including developmental idealism) since the late nineteenth century. These influences reached Taiwan and South Korea later after World War II, under the paradigm of modernization and economic development (Raymo et al., 2015). Although Western impacts did not enter China until the past three decades, developmental idealism has been increasing since then (Thornton & Xie, 2016). In the family domain, these Western influences are dominated by the developmental idealism that emphasizes the modern forms of the family, low fertility, late marriages, as well as self-determination in marriage (Raymo et al., 2015). Even though many features of the traditional East Asian culture remain intact, this developmental idealism is visibly increasing and evolving with cohorts (Cai, 2010; Mobrand, 2020; Thornton et al., 2012). If more recent cohorts (I focus on marriage cohorts in this study) are encultured with more developmental idealism, they are also more likely to take on modern marital practices rather than traditional ones. In this vein, I also propose that,

H2a. More recent marriage cohorts are more likely to have a self-initiated marriage, compared with an arranged marriage and an introduced marriage.

H1b. More recent marriage cohorts are less likely to have an arranged marriage, compared with a self-initiated marriage and an introduced marriage.

DATA AND METHOD

Data

Data for this study are from the 2006 and 2016 East Asian Social Survey (EASS). EASS is a biennial project with a different theme every two years. The themes for EASS2006 and EASS2016 were both "Family Life." EASS was conducted in four East Asian societies: mainland China, Japan, South Korea, and Taiwan. The surveys conducted in each society all used multi-stage sampling. The Chinese survey was conducted by Renmin University; the Japanese survey was conducted by Osaka University of Commerce; the South Korean survey was conducted by Sungkyunkwan University; and the Taiwanese survey was conducted by the Institute of Sociology, Academia Sinica.

In this study, I pooled the 2006 and 2016 surveys and restricted the sample to once-married couples. After data restriction and casewise deletion of missing values, there were 5,066 records left in the Chinese sample, 3,455 in the Japanese sample, 1,211 in the South Korean sample, and 1,349 in the Taiwanese sample. It is noteworthy that the South Korean and Taiwanese surveys in 2016 did not ask respondents about their marriage pathways, so the sample sizes were smaller for these two societies than those for China and Japan.

Dependent Variable

The dependent variable is the pathway to marriage. The survey asked married respondents about how they met their spouses in their first and current marriages. Possible answers included "met by arrangement," "met by introduction," and "met by self." I coded respondents who answered "met by self" as self-initiated marriage and those who answered "by arrangement" and "by introduction" as arranged marriage and introduced marriage respectively. I only used information about respondents' first marriage to avoid the effect of previous marital experiences on peoples' marriage pathway choices.

Independent Variable

The independent variables are education and marriage cohort. Education was measured in two ways. First, it was measured by the years of education as a continuous variable. Second, it was measured by the highest degree ever obtained as a categorical variable, with three possible attributes of less than high school, high school, and college and above. I used the first measure as the key predicting variable in the main analysis because continuous variables can be illustrated more intuitively. I also used the second measure in the robustness test.

Marriage cohort was measured by the year when respondents got married. Possible attributes included "pre-1969," "1970–1979," "1980–1989," "1990–1999," and "post-2000." Although a proportion of respondents married after 2010, the number is relatively small. Thus, they were categorized into the "post-2000" cohort. The age at marriage was also included in model estimations. Since marriage cohorts and the age at marriage together reflect respondents' current age, I did not control for respondents' age in model estimations to avoid multicollinearity.

Control Variable

Control variables included gender, age at marriage, whether being religiously affiliated, place of residence at age 15, parental years of education, and attitudes toward marriage. All these variables happened before the year of marriage. Possible attributes of the place of residence included big city, medium- or small-sized city, town, and rural village. Since the survey did not ask respondents about their SES before marriage, I used parental education as the proxy. Attitudes toward marriage were measured by the question "do you agree that married men are happier than their unmarried counterparts?" and "do you agree that married women are happier than their unmarried counterparts?" I added scores for the two questions and got the value for marital attitudes. The survey also specified respondents' district of residence by identifying their primary sampling unit (PSU). I also controlled for PSU in all model estimations to fix the regional effect.

Analytic Strategy

I employed multiple logistic regression models to estimate the relationship between education and different pathways to marriage in four East Asian societies respectively. The models compared the odds of each marriage pathway with one another. Based on the model estimation results, I illustrated the predicted relationships between education and marriage pathways by plots for the four societies to show similarities and differences. Then I also conducted two robustness tests by examining gender heterogeneity and using a categorical independent variable.

It is noteworthy that the analytic strategy employed in this study could not demonstrate causality. Endogeneity problems such as unobserved confounders possibly existed. For example, personality and life experiences can influence both respondents' educational achievements and their pathways to marriage. For this reason, I was cautious about the use of "causal effect." Instead, I used "correlation" or "association" to indicate the relationship between key variables.

FINDINGS

Descriptive Findings

Table 1 exhibits variable distributions in four East Asian societies respectively. Arranged marriage was relatively prevalent in South Korea. Slightly more than 35% of Korean respondents met their spouses by arrangement. Meanwhile, another 35% of Korean respondents met their spouses by self-initiation and the remaining met their spouses by introduction. Mainland China and Taiwan were similar in people's marriage pathway choices. In China, around 11% of the respondents had an arranged marriage; slightly less than 60% of the respondents had an introduced marriage; the left 30% had a self-initiated marriage. In Taiwan, around 18% of the respondents had an arranged marriage; 43% of the

Table 1.   Descriptive Statistics.

Variables	China	Japan	South Korea	Taiwan
	% / Mean (S.D.) [min., max.]	% / Mean (S.D.) [min., max.]	% / Mean (S.D.) [min., max.]	% / Mean (S.D.) [min., max.]
Pathway to marriage				
Arranged	11.01	20.64	36.04	17.79
Introduced	59.34	29.34	28.81	43.14
Self-initiated	29.65	50.01	35.15	39.07
Marriage cohort				
-1969	10.66	28.86	18.82	26.98
1970–1979	16.30	22.20	12.58	19.27
1980–1989	28.25	15.17	23.64	21.87
1990–1999	23.11	15.34	38.87	20.24
2000-	21.67	18.44	14.09	11.64
Years of education	8.71 (4.27) [0, 21]	12.48 (2.51) [6, 18]	11.77 (4.58) [0, 23]	9.79 (4.74) [0, 23]
Male (1=yes)	45.68	44.60	41.21	46.85
Place of residence at age 15				
Big city	16.29	13.72	28.10	10.08
Medium- or small-sized city	29.71	38.73	20.07	13.86
Town	10.74	34.10	10.97	18.98
Rural village	43.27	13.46	40.86	57.08
Religious affiliation (1 = yes)	10.56	34.07	62.62	84.88
Age at marriage	23.92 (3.73) [16, 53]	26.13 (4.18) [16, 56]	26.17 (3.99) [16, 40]	25.28 (4.84) [16, 55]
Attitudes toward marriage	8.52 (2.17) [2, 14]	8.59 (1.97) [2, 14]	9.99 (2.74) [2, 14]	8.36 (2.60) [2, 14]
Parental years of education	4.86 (4.55) [0, 16]	8.57 (3.41) [6, 18]	7.56 (5.12) [0, 23]	5.30 (4.57) [0, 18]
N	5,066	3,455	1,121	1,349

Note: Data are from East Asian Social Survey 2006 and 2016.

respondents had an introduced marriage; less than 40% of the respondents had a self-initiated marriage. Relatively, Japan had the most modern marriage market among the four. Around half of the respondents had a self-initiated marriage; around 30% of the respondents met their spouse by introduction; the left 20% met their spouse by arrangement. However, it is noteworthy that the Chinese and the Japanese samples included 2006 and 2016 surveys, while the Korean and the Taiwan samples only included the 2006 survey.

I also broke down different marriage pathways to various marriage cohorts in four East Asian societies and illustrated the distributions in Fig. 1. Although which marriage pathway was dominant varied across marriage cohorts and societies, two major patterns were found. Mainland China and Taiwan represented one pattern that arranged marriage and introduced marriage steadily declined and self-initiated marriage increased over marriage cohorts. Japan and South Korea represented the other pattern that introduced marriage and self-initiated marriage increased and arranged marriage sharply declined over marriage cohorts.

Consistent with the common agreement on modernization, China had the lowest level of education and Japan had the highest level of education among the four East Asian societies. The average years of education were 8.7 years, while this number was 9.8 in Taiwan, 11.8 in South Korea, and 12.5 in Japan. Notably, no respondents in Japan had fewer than 6 years of education.

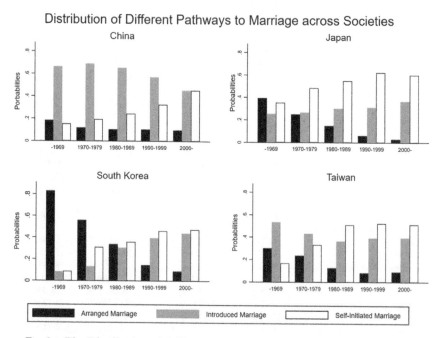

Fig. 1. The Distribution of Different Pathways to Marriage in Four East Asian Societies.

Model Estimations

Table 2 displays the results of model estimations in four East Asian societies. Supporting the "developmentalism-marriage" assumption, education was estimated to result in more modern marriage pathways in East Asian societies. In China, although years of education were not significantly associated with the odds ratio of introduced marriage to arranged marriage, they are positively associated with the odds ratio of self-initiated marriage to arranged marriage and the

Table 2. Predicting Different Pathways to Marriage in Four East Asian Societies: Education and Marriage Cohort.

	Introduced Marriage vs Arranged Marriage	Self-Initiated Marriage vs Arranged Marriage	Self-Initiated Marriage vs Introduced Marriage
Panel A: Chinese Sample (N = 5,066)			
Years of education	0.015	0.112***	0.097***
	(0.013)	(0.015)	(0.011)
Marriage cohort (ref. -1969)			
1970–1979	0.519**	0.704***	0.184
	(0.164)	(0.207)	(0.159)
1980–1989	0.553***	0.812***	0.258+
	(0.152)	(0.189)	(0.146)
1990–1999	0.456**	1.089***	0.632***
	(0.161)	(0.196)	(0.148)
2000-	0.377*	1.617***	1.240***
	(0.018)	(0.211)	(0.154)
Controls added?	YES	YES	YES
PSU effect fixed?	YES	YES	YES
Constant	1.131*	–0.366	–1.497***
	(0.476)	(0.528)	(0.348)
Panel B: Japanese Sample (N = 3,455)			
Years of education	–0.006	0.089***	0.095***
	(0.023)	(0.022)	(0.194)
Marriage cohort (ref. -1969)			
1970–1979	0.579***	0.740***	0.160
	(0.137)	(0.125)	(0.125)
1980–1989	1.341***	1.464***	0.123
	(0.177)	(0.165)	(0.141)
1990–1999	2.371***	2.624***	0.253+
	(0.232)	(0.222)	(0.143)
2000-	3.491***	3.617***	0.126
	(0.289)	(0.283)	(0.145)
Controls added?	YES	YES	YES
PSU effect fixed?	YES	YES	YES
Constant	2.494***	3.916***	1.422***
	(0.548)	(0.525)	(0.412)

(Continued)

Table 2. (*Continued*)

	Introduced Marriage vs Arranged Marriage	Self-Initiated Marriage vs Arranged Marriage	Self-Initiated Marriage vs Introduced Marriage
Panel C: South Korean Sample (N = 1,121)			
Years of education	0.124***	0.113***	−0.122
	(0.029)	(0.028)	(0.028)
Marriage cohort (ref. -1969)			
1970–1979	0.598	1.641***	1.043*
	(0.387)	(0.333)	(0.448)
1980–1989	1.605***	2.114***	0.509
	(0.345)	(0.340)	(0.399)
1990–1999	2.622***	3.215***	0.593
	(0.370)	(0.369)	(0.402)
2000-	3.537***	4.243***	0.706
	(0.507)	(0.511)	(0.439)
Controls added?	YES	YES	YES
PSU effect fixed?	YES	YES	YES
Constant	−1.074	1.440	2.515***
	(0.884)	(0.827)	(0.795)
Panel D: Taiwanese Sample (N = 1,349)			
Years of education	0.025	0.126***	0.102***
	(0.022)	(0.025)	(0.021)
Marriage cohort (ref. -1969)			
1970–1979	−0.067	0.693**	0.761***
	(0.223)	(0.261)	(0.226)
1980–1989	0.306	1.586***	1.280***
	(0.226)	(0.292)	(0.231)
1990–1999	0.653*	1.998***	1.345***
	(0.318)	(0.343)	(0.251)
2000-	1.143**	2.733***	1.590***
	(0.436)	(0.461)	(0.293)
Controls added?	YES	YES	YES
PSU effect fixed?	YES	YES	YES
Constant	2.087*	3.153***	1.066
	(0.834)	(0.913)	(0.633)

Standard errors in are shown in parentheses.
$^{†}p < 0.1$, $^{*}p < 0.05$, $^{**}p < 0.01$, $^{***}p < 0.001$.
Notes: Data are from East Asian Social Survey 2006 and 2016.

odds ratio of self-initiated marriage to introduced marriage. Specifically, for each additional year of education, the odds ratio of self-initiated marriage to arranged marriage increased by 12% ($e^{0.112} - 1 = 0.118$) and the odds ratio of self-initiated marriage to introduced marriage increased by 10% ($e^{0.097} - 1 = 0.102$).

The relationship between education and marriage pathways was similar in China, Japan, and Taiwan. There was no sufficient evidence for the assumption that education is associated with fewer arranged marriages, but it was evidenced to be associated with more self-initiated marriages. In Japan, for each additional year of education, the odds ratio of self-initiated marriage to arranged marriage increased by 9% ($e^{0.089} - 1 = 0.093$) and the odds ratio of self-initiated marriage to introduced marriage increased by 10% ($e^{0.095} - 1 = 0.099$). In Taiwan, for each additional year of education, the odds ratio of self-initiated marriage to arranged marriage increased by 13% ($e^{0.126} - 1 = 0.134$) and the odds ratio of self-initiated marriage to introduced marriage increased by 10% ($e^{0.107} - 1 = 0.099$).

In South Korea, the relationship between education and marriage pathways was different from that in other East Asian societies. Education was estimated to be associated with fewer arranged marriages, but not with more self-initiated marriages. For each additional year of education, the odds of introduced marriage to arranged marriage increased by 13% ($e^{0.124} - 1 = 0.132$) and the odds of self-initiated marriage to arranged marriage increased by 12% ($e^{0.113} - 1 = 0.119$). The odds ratio of self-initiated marriage to introduced marriage did not significantly vary with any additional year of education.

I then predicted the relationship in each society and illustrated them in Fig. 2. Although the predicted probabilities of different marriage pathways varied across societies, two major patterns were revealed in the figure. In China, Japan, and Taiwan, individuals with more years of education were less likely to have an arranged marriage or an introduced marriage, while they were more likely to have a self-initiated marriage. In South Korea, individuals with more years of education were less likely to have an arranged marriage, whereas they were more likely to have an introduced marriage or a self-initiated marriage.

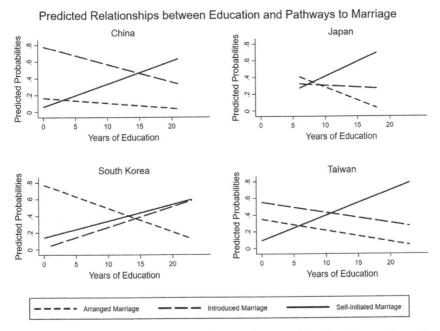

Fig. 2. Predicted Probabilities of Different Pathways to Marriage Across Years of Education in Four East Asian Societies.

Fig. 3 shows the predicted probabilities of different pathways to marriage in each marriage cohort from pre-1970 to post-2000. Similar to the distribution shown in Fig. 1, there were also two patterns of association found. In China and Taiwan, the probability of having an arranged marriage or an introduced marriage slightly decreased over marriage cohorts, while the probability of having a self-initiated marriage increased. In Japan and South Korea, the probability of having an arranged marriage sharply decreased over marriage cohorts, whereas the probability of having an introduced marriage or a self-initiated marriage increased. In more recent cohorts, people were predicted to be most likely to meet their spouse by themselves and least likely by arrangement in Japan, South Korea, and Taiwan. However, in China, introduced marriage had always been the most popular pathway to marriage and arranged marriage the least.

I also examined whether the educational effect on marriage pathways varied across marriage cohorts, but no heterogeneous effects were found (I did not show the results in the paper). The relationship between education and marriage pathways was robust in all marriage cohorts.

Despite nuances, the general pattern detected in the model estimations is that education was associated with fewer arranged marriages and more self-initiated marriages. In addition, the use of arranged marriage declined, and the use of self-initiated marriage increased over marriage cohorts in all East Asian societies. The hypotheses were supported while little was known about how the use of introduced marriage changed with education or marriage cohorts.

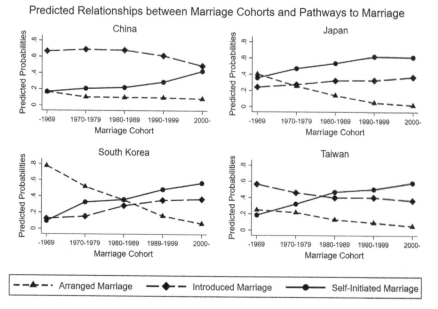

Fig. 3. Predicted Probabilities of Different Pathways to Marriage Across Marriage Cohorts in Four East Asian Societies.

Robustness Test

I conducted two batteries of robustness tests. First, I examined the relationship between education and different pathways to marriage for males and females respectively. The results in Table 3 showed that the educational effects for males and for females were very similar, although it seemed that education had a stronger effect on females. In addition, the general pattern shown in Table 3 resembled the one found in the main analysis.

Then, I used the level of education as the independent variable and examined the educational effect. Again, the general pattern that well-educated people were more likely to meet their spouse by themselves and less likely by arrangement was similar to what was found in the main analysis. The tests together evidenced the robustness of the findings (Table 4).

CONCLUSIONS AND DISCUSSIONS

Marriage and family researchers have been interested in the educational effect on marriage formation. Much attention has been paid to the timing of marriage, neglecting the pathways to marriage. The rapid change in the marriage market and various marital practices in East Asian societies provide opportunities to examine different pathways to marriage and their correlates. Motivated by the "developmentalism-marriage" framework, this study focuses on education and cohort as proxy variables for individual-level and aggregated-level developmental idealism. Model estimations support the assumption that developmental idealism leads to more modern marriages and inhibits traditional marriage pathways.

Table 3. Robustness Test I: Gender Heterogeneity.

	Males			Females		
	IM vs AM	SM vs AM	SM vs IM	IM vs AM	SM vs AM	SM vs IM
Panel A: China						
Years of Education	0.030	0.123***	0.094***	0.008	0.114***	0.107***
	(0.021)	(0.023)	(0.016)	(0.018)	(0.021)	(0.014)
Panel B: Japan						
Years of Education	0.038	0.114***	0.076**	–0.051	0.072*	0.122***
	(0.032)	(0.031)	(0.026)	(0.036)	(0.034)	(0.030)
Panel C: South Korea						
Years of Education	0.092*	0.027	–0.065	0.158***	0.204***	0.046
	(0.043)	(0.042)	(0.039)	(0.043)	(0.042)	(0.043)
Panel D: Taiwan						
Years of Education	0.046	0.123***	0.076*	0.031	0.152***	0.121***
	(0.035)	(0.039)	(0.030)	(0.033)	(0.038)	(0.316)

Standard errors in are shown in parentheses.
†$p < 0.1$, * $p < 0.05$, ** $p < 0.01$, *** $p < 0.001$.
Notes: AM = arranged marriage; IM = introduced marriage; SM = self-initiated marriage.
All models are with control variables added, PSU effect fixed, and marriage cohort effect fixed.
Data are from East Asian Social Survey 2006 and 2016.

Table 4.   Robustness Test II: Levels of Education as the Independent Variable.

	IM vs AM	SM vs AM	SM vs IM
Panel A: China			
Level of Education (rf. Less than high school)			
High school	0.121	0.655***	0.534***
	(0.120)	(0.130)	(0.082)
College and above	0.412†	0.779***	0.367*
	(0.241)	(0.239)	(0.102)
Panel B: Japan			
Level of Education (rf. Less than high school)			
High school	0.056	0.460***	0.404***
	(0.135)	(0.130)	(0.125)
College and above	0.051	0.652***	0.602***
	(0.188)	(0.178)	(0.146)
Panel C: South Korea			
Level of Education (rf. Less than high school)			
High school	0.738**	0.458†	−0.279
	(0.278)	(0.145)	(0.290)
College and above	1.036***	0.695*	−0.342
	(0.321)	(0.298)	(0.310)
Panel D: Taiwan			
Level of Education (rf. Less than high school)			
High school	0.009	0.648**	0.639***
	(0.213)	(0.223)	(0.163)
College and above	0.180	1.284***	1.104***
	(0.344)	(0.348)	(0.163)

Standard errors in are shown in parentheses.
†$p < 0.1$, *$p < 0.05$, **$p < 0.01$, ***$p < 0.001$.
Notes: AM = arranged marriage; IM = introduced marriage; SM = self-initiated marriage.
All models are with control variables added, PSU effect fixed, and marriage cohort effect fixed.
Data are from East Asian Social Survey 2006 and 2016.

Specifically, education is estimated to be associated with fewer arranged marriages and more self-initiated marriages in all four East Asian societies, although the association between education and introduced marriage varies. In addition, more recent cohorts are also estimated to be more likely to have a self-initiated marriage and less likely to have an arranged marriage. The use of introduced marriage also varies across societies. It is beyond the scope of this study to explain why differences in introduced marriages occur among East Asian societies, given their common Confucian tradition in families. However, based on the literature and the findings, I speculate that the different patterns may be caused by the current marriage rates in the four societies. In South Korea and Japan where the marriage rates are relatively low,[3] an introduced marriage is regarded and practiced as a possible way to deal with the low marriage prospect. In contrast, it is regarded as a traditional martial practice and not accepted by people with higher developmental idealism in mainland China and Taiwan where the marriage rates are relatively high. Future studies are encouraged to examine whether the local marriage rate matters.

The findings should be read with caution. First, although general patterns were found, the variation within the pattern (i.e., how introduced marriage changed over education levels and marriage cohorts) was under-discussed and under-explained. With the data available, I could not interpret the similarities and differences between East Asian societies. Future studies are expected to provide refined explanations for them. Second, there was no direct measure for developmental idealism. Education and cohorts were used as proxy variables for it, but they were also possible to influence marriage through mechanisms other than developmental idealism. Future surveys are expected to include questions regarding developmental idealism. Third, because of the survey design, the samples of the four East Asian societies were imbalanced. The Chinese and the Japanese sample included both 2006 and 2016 surveys, while the Korean and the Taiwanese samples only included the 2006 survey. Therefore, I carefully examine the marriage cohort effect to avoid possible biases. Last, the models I employed in this study could not imply causality. More casual inference designs are needed if causality is expected to be detected.

Despite the limitations, this study contributes to the literature by extending the educational effect from delayed marriage to various marriage pathways in non-Western settings. Due to the common Confucian tradition, East Asian societies share similarities in marital attitudes and marital practices (Greenhalgh, 1985; Raymo et al., 2015). Moreover, these marital attitudes and marital practices are different from those in the West (Atoh et al., 2004; Jones & Yeung, 2014; H. Park, 2021; Raymo et al., 2015). Therefore, a close look at the marriage market in East Asian societies can open a fruitful avenue for new research on marriage (Hoelter, Axinn, & Ghimire, 2004). Theoretically, the investigation of marriage pathways can expand family research beyond its classical agenda. Since researchers have recently been aware that almost half (44.5%) of the couples in Western societies like the United States met their partners through non-individualized pathways (Rosenfeld & Thomas, 2012), more scholarly attention is called for to understand "how" people get married instead of "when" they married (Armstrong & Hamilton, 2021). The findings of this study are believed to have insights beyond the region of East Asia. Practically, by examining different marriage pathways employed by people with various educational backgrounds and in various cohorts, we can have a better understanding of young adults' changing marital preferences. This understanding is believed to imply and warrant future policy interventions which can effectively boost the marriage rates in East Asian societies where the marriage market is entering a "recession" (Raymo et al., 2015).

NOTES

1. Companionate marriage refers to marriages based on affection, friendship, and sexual gratification. In the development of forms of marriage in the West, companionate marriages represent a shift away from institutional marriages and parental intervention (Burgess, 1963). Different from some parental-intervened marriage forms, love is the basis for mutual relationships and its subsequent individualized companionate marriages (Cohen, 2021).

2. For example, arranged marriage was legally abolished in the 1930s before the People's Republic of China was established (Davis, 2014a). Moreover, in the working definition of arranged marriage, Ghimire et al. (2006) highlight the parental control over adult children's

SHICHAO DU

marriage, with no involvement of the husband- and wife-to-be in the choice of spouse. Although Chinese couples did not have complete freedom over their marital decisions in Mao's era (because of the state control [Davis, 2014b]), they were involved in the choice of spouse and at least had the right to say no.

3. According to the statistical annual reports in the four societies, South Korea and Japan have relatively lower marriage rates. The marriage rate in South Korea was 6.8 marriages per 1,000 population in 2006, 5.5 in 2016, and 4.2 in 2020. The marriage rate in Japan was 5.7 in 2006, 5.0 in 2016, and 4.3 in 2020. Mainland China and Taiwan have relatively higher marriage rates. The marriage rate in mainland China was 7.2 in 2006, 8.3 in 2016, and 5.8 in 2020. The marriage rate in Taiwan was 6.2 in 2006, 6.3 in 2016, and 5.2 in 2020. In terms of the marriage rate, South Korea and Japan are alike, while mainland China and Taiwan are similar.

ACKNOWLEDGMENTS

The research is supported by the Chinese National Social Science Funding on the project "Understanding Social Values and Behavioral Patterns of the New Generation from An Intergenerational Perspective [19ZDA145]."

REFERENCES

Allendorf, K. (2013). Schemas of marital change: From arranged marriages to eloping for love. *Journal of Marriage and Family, 75*(2), 453–469.

Allendorf, K. (2017). Conflict and compatibility? Developmental idealism and gendered differences in marital choice. *Journal of Marriage and Family, 79*(2), 337–355.

Allendorf, K., & Thornton, A. (2015). Caste and choice: The influence of developmental idealism on marriage behavior. *American Journal of Sociology, 121*(1), 243–287.

Allendorf, K., Thornton, A., Mitchell, C., & Young-DeMarco, L. (2019). The influence of developmental idealism on marital attitudes, expectations, and timing. *Journal of Family Issues, 40*(17), 2359–2388.

Applbaum, K. D. (1995). Marriage with the proper stranger: Arranged marriage in Metropolitan Japan. *Ethnology, 34*(1), 37–51.

Armstrong, E. A., & Hamilton, L. T. (2021). Classed pathways to marriage: Hometown ties, college networks, and life after graduation. *Journal of Marriage and Family, 83*(4), 1004–1019.

Atoh, M., Kandiah, V., & Ivanov, S. (2004). The second demographic transition in Asia? Comparative analysis of the low fertility situation in East and South-East Asian countries. *The Japanese Journal of Population, 2*(1), 42–75.

Axinn, W. G., & Barber, J. S. (2001). Mass education and fertility transition. *American Sociological Review, 66*(4), 481–505.

Bennett, L. (1983). *Dangerous wives and sacred sisters: Social and symbolic roles of high-caste women in Nepal.* New York: Columbia University Press.

Blair, S. L., & Madigan, T. J. (2019). Dating, marriage, and parental approval: An examination of young adults in China. *Social Science Quarterly, 100*(6), 2351–2368.

Blossfeld, H.-P., & Huinink, J. (1991). human capital investments or norms of role transition? How women's schooling and career affect the process of family formation. *American Journal of Sociology, 97*(1), 143–168.

Bumpass, L. L., Rindfuss, R. R., Choe, M. K., & Tsuya, N. O. (2009). The institutional context of low fertility: The case of Japan. *Asian Population Studies, 5*(3), 215–235.

Burgess, E. W. (1963). *The family: From institution to companionship.* New York: American Book Co.

Cai, Y. (2010). China's below-replacement fertility: Government policy or socioeconomic development?*Population and Development Review, 36*(3), 419–440.

Chen, Y.-C. C., & Li, J.-C. A. (2014). Family change in East Asia. In J. Treas, J. Scott, & M. Richards (Eds.), *The Wiley Blackwell companion to the sociology of families* (pp. 61–82). Chichester: Wiley.

Cheng, Y.-h. A. (2014). Changing partner choice and marriage propensities by education in post-industrial Taiwan, 2000–2010.*Demographic Research, 31*, 1007–1042.

Cherlin, A. (2010). Demographic trends in the United States: A review of research in the 2000s. *Journal of Marriage and Family, 72*(3), 403–419.

Chu, C.Y. C., & Yu, R.-R. (2010). *Understanding Chinese families: A comparative study of Taiwan and Southeast China*. New York: Oxford University.

Chuang, Y.-C., & Wolf, A. P. (2010). Marriage in Taiwan, 1881–1905 an example of regional diversity. *Asian Studies, 54*(3), 781–795.

Clignet, R., & Sween, J. (1969), Social change and type of marriage. *American Journal of Sociology, 75*(1), 123–145.

Cohen, P. N. (2021). *The family: Diversity, inequality, and social change* (3rd ed.). New York: W. W. Norton & Company.

Compernolle, E. L., & Axinn, W. G. (2019). Mass education, international travel, and ideal ages at marriage. *Demography, 56*(6), 2083–2108.

Davis, D. S. (2014a). On the limits of personal autonomy: PRC law and the institution of marriage. In D. S. Davis & S. L. Friedman (Eds.), *Wives, husbands, and lovers: Marriage and sexuality in Hong Kong, Taiwan, and Urban China* (pp. 41–61). Redwood City: Stanford University Press.

Davis, D. S. (2014b). Privatization of marriage in post-socialist China. *Modern China, 40*(6), 551–577.

Davis, D. S., & Friedman, S. L. (2014). Deinstitutionalizing marriage and sexuality. In D. S. Davis & S. L. Friedman (Eds.), *Wives, husbands, and lovers: Marriage and sexuality in Hong Kong, Taiwan, and Urban China* (pp. 1–38). Redwood City: Stanford University Press.

Epstein, R., Pandit, M., & Thakar, M. (2013). How love emerges in arranged marriages: Two cross-cultural studies. *Journal of Comparative Family Studies, 44*(3), 341–360.

Frejka, T., Jones, G. W., & Sardon, J.-P. (2010). East Asian childbearing patterns and policy developments. *Population and Development Review, 36*(3), 579–606.

Ghaznavi, C., Sakamoto, H., Nomura, S., Kubota, A., Yoneoka, D., Shibuya, K., & Ueda, P. (2020). The Herbivore's dilemma: Trends in and factors associated with heterosexual relationship status and interest in romantic relationships among young adults in Japan – Analysis of national surveys, 1987–2015. *PLoS ONE, 15*(11), e0241571.

Ghimire, D. J., Axinn, W. G., Yabiku, S. T., & Thornton, A. (2006). Social change, premarital nonfamily experience, and spouse choice in an arranged marriage society. *American Journal of Sociology, 111*(4), 1181–1218.

Giordano, P. C., Longmore, M. A., & Manning, W. D. (2006). Gender and the meanings of adolescent romantic relationships: A focus on boys. *American Sociological Review, 71*(2), 260–287.

Glick, P., Handy, C., & Sahn, D. E. (2015). Schooling, marriage, and age at first birth in Madagascar. *Population Studies, 69*(2), 219–236.

Goldstein, R. J., & Kenney, C. T. (2001). Marriage delayed or marriage forgone? New cohort forecasts of first marriage for U.S. women. *American Sociological Review, 66*(4), 506–519.

Greenhalgh, S. (1985). Sexual stratification: The other side of "growth with equity" in East Asia." *Population and Development Review, 11*(2), 265–314.

Gui, T. (2017). 'Devalued' daughters versus 'appreciated' sons: Gender inequality in China's parent-organized matchmaking markets. *Journal of Family Issues, 38*(13), 1923–1948.

Harkness, G., & Khaled, R. (2014). Modern traditionalism: Consanguineous marriage in Qatar. *Journal of Marriage and Family, 76*(3), 687–603.

Hoelter, L. F., Axinn, W. G., & Ghimire, D. J. (2004). Social change, premarital nonfamily experiences, and marital dynamics. *Journal of Marriage and Family, 66*(5), 1131–1151.

Huang, F., Jin, G. Z., & Xu, L. C. (2012). Love and money by parental matchmaking: Evidence from urban couples in China. *American Economic Review: Papers & Proceedings, 102*(3), 555–560.

Jiang, W., Zhang, Y., & Sanchez-Barricarte, J. J. (2015). Marriage expenses in rural China. *The China Review, 15*(1), 207–236.

Jin, B., & Oh, S. (2020). Cultural differences of social network influence on romantic relationships: A comparison of the United States and South Korea. *Communication Studies, 61*(2), 156–171.

Jones, G. W., & Yeung, W.-J. J. (2014). Marriage in Asia. *Journal of Family Issues, 35*(12), 1567–1583.

Kalmijn, M. (2013). The educational gradient in marriage: A comparison of 25 European countries. *Demography, 50*(6), 1499–1520.

Kan, M.-Y., Hertog, E., & Kolpashnikova, K. (2019). Housework share and fertility preference in four East Asian countries in 2006 and 2012. *Demographic Research, 41*(35), 1021–1046.

Kanemasa, Y., Taniguchi, J., Daibo, I., & Ishimori, M. (2004). Love styles and romantic love experiences in Japan. *Social Behavior and Personality: An International Journal, 32*(3), 265–281.

Lai, Q., & Thornton, A. (2015). The making of family values: Developmental idealism in Gansu, China. *Social Science Research, 51*, 174–188.

Li, Z. H., Connolly, J., Jiang, D., Pepler, D., & Craig, W. (2010). Adolescent romantic relationships in China and Canada: A cross-national comparison. *International Journal of Behavioral Development, 34*(2), 113–120.

Martin, L. G. (1990). Changing intergenerational family relations in East Asia. *The ANNALS of the American Academy of Political and Social Science, 510*(1), 102–114.

Mathews, M., & Straughan, P. T. (2016). Single Singaporeans and their hesitation to use commercial matchmaking services. *Journal of Comparative Family Studies, 47*(2), 247–266.

Mobrand, E. (2020). Developmental citizenship, symbolic landscapes, and transformation in China and South Korea. *Citizenship Studies, 24*(7), 950–957.

Park, H. (2021). Introduction to the special collection on family changes and inequality in East Asia. *Demographic Research, 44*(40), 979–992.

Park, I. H., & Cho, L.-J. (1995). Confucianism and the Korean family. *Journal of Comparative Family Studies, 26*(1), 117–134.

Perelli-Harris, B., & Lyons-Amos, M. (2016). Partnership patterns in the United States and across Europe: The role of education and country context. *Social Forces, 95*(1), 251–281.

Peterson, B. E., Kim, R., McCarthy, J. M., Park, C. J., & Plamondon, L. T. (2011). Authoritarianism and arranged marriage in Bangladesh and Korea. *Journal of Research in Personality, 45*(6), 622–630.

Powell, B., Hamilton, L., Manago, B., & Cheng, S. (2016). Implications of changing family forms for children. *Annual Review of Sociology, 42*, 301–322.

Raymo, J. M. (2003). Educational attainment and the transition to first marriage among Japanese women. *Demography, 40*(1), 83–103.

Raymo, J. M., Park, H., Xie, Y., & Yeung, W.-j. J. (2015). Marriage and family in East Asia: Continuity and change. *Annual Review of Sociology, 41*, 471–492.

Riley, N. E. (1994). Interwoven lives: Parents, marriage, and Guanxi in China. *Journal of Marriage and Family, 56*(4), 791–803.

Rindfuss, R. R., Choe, M. K., Bumpass, L. L., & Tsuya, N. O. (2004). Social networks and family change in Japan. *American Sociological Review, 69*(6), 838–861.

Rosenfeld, M. J., & Thomas, R. J. (2012). Searching for a mate: The rise of the internet as a social intermediary. *American Sociological Review, 77*(4), 523–547.

Rosenfeld, M. J., Thomas, R. J., & Hausen, S. (2019). Disintermediating your friends: How online dating in the United States displaces other ways of meeting. *Proceedings of the National Academy of Sciences, 116*(36), 11753–11758.

Schneider, M. M. (2014). *The ugly wife is a treasure at home: True stories of love and marriage in communist China.* Lincoln, NE: Potomac Books.

Schoen, R., & Cheng, Y.-h. A. (2006). Partner choice and the differential retreat from marriage. *Journal of Marriage and the Family, 68*(1), 1–10.

Skirbekk, V., Kohler, H.-P., & Prskawetz, A. (2004). Birth month, school graduation, and the timing of births and marriages. *Demography, 41*(3), 547–568.

Smith, D. E. (1993). The standard North American family: SNAF as an ideological code. *Journal of Family Issues, 14*(1), 50–65.

South, S. J., Trent, K., & Bose, S. (2016). Demographic opportunity and the mate selection process in India. *Journal of Comparative Family Studies, 47*(2), 221–246.

Surkyn, J., & Lesthaeghe, R. (2004). Value orientations and the second demographic transition (SDT) in northern, western and southern Europe: An update. *Demographic Research, 3*(3), 45–86.

Suzuki, T. (2013). *Low fertility and population aging in Japan and Eastern Asia.* New York: Springer.

Thornton, A. (2001). The developmental paradigm, reading history sideways, and family change. *Demography, 38*(4), 449–465.

Thornton, A. (2005). *Reading history sideways: The fallacy and enduring impact of the developmental paradigm on family life.* Chicago, IL: University of Chicago Press.

Thornton, A., Axinn, W., & Xie, Y. (2007). *Marriage and cohabitation.* Chicago, IL: The University of Chicago Press.

Thornton, A., Binstock, G., Yount, K. M., Abbasi-Shavazi, M. J., Ghimire, D., & Xie, Y. (2012). International fertility change: New data and insights from the developmental idealism framework. *Demography, 49*(2), 667–698.

Thornton, A., & Xie, Y. (2016). Developmental idealism in China. *Chinese Journal of Sociology, 2*(4), 483–496.

Tillman, K. H., Brewster, K. L., & Holway, G. V. (2019). Sexual and romantic relationship in young adulthood. *Annual Review of Sociology, 45*, 133–153.

Torr, B. M. (2011). The changing relationship between education and marriage in the United States, 1940–2000. *Journal of Family History, 36*(4), 483–503.

Tu, W. (2000). Implications of the rise of 'Confucian' East Asia. *Daedalus, 129*(1), 195–218.

Uberoi, P. (2006). *Freedom and destiny: Gender, family, and popular culture in India.* Oxford: Oxford University Press.

Xu, X., & Whyte, M. K. (1990). Love matches and arranged marriages: A Chinese replication. *Journal of Marriage and Family, 52*(3), 709–722.

Yabiku, S. T. (2005). The effect of non-family experiences on age of marriage in a setting of rapid social change. *Population, 59*(3), 339–354.

Yeung, W.-j. J., & Hu, S. (2013). Coming of age in times of change: The transition to adulthood in China. *The Annals of the American Academy of Political and Social Science, 646*, 149–171.

Yoo, S. H. (2016). Postponement and recuperation in cohort marriage: The experience of South Korea. *Demographic Research, 35*(35), 1045–1078.

Yu, W.-h., Lin, Z., & Su, K.-h. (2019). Parent-child coresidence and experiences of romantic relationships: Evidence from young adults in Taiwan. *Chinses Sociological Review, 51*(2), 173–206.

Zaidi, B., & Morgan, S. P. (2017). The second demographic transition theory: A review and appraisal. *Annual Review of Sociology, 43*, 473–492.

Zhang, Y., & Axinn, W. G. (2021). Marital experiences and depression in an arranged marriage setting. *American Journal of Sociology, 126*(6), 1439–1486.

Zhang, J., & Sun, P. (2014). 'When are you going to get married?' Parental matchmaking and middle-class women in contemporary urban China. In D. S. Davis & S. L. Friedman (Eds.), *Wives, husbands, and lovers: Marriage and sexuality in Hong Kong, Taiwan, and Urban China* (pp. 118–144). Redwood City: Stanford University Press.

CHAPTER 8

LIFE TRAJECTORIES AND REPRODUCTIVE STRATEGIES OF COSTA RICAN HOUSEHOLDS: AN INTERGENERATIONAL PERSPECTIVE

Natalia Carballo Murillo

ABSTRACT

This research aims to analyze, from the perspective of family life trajectories, the intergenerational changes in the reproductive strategies of Costa Rican households. The four strategies explored are fertility and marriage, educational, economic, social and symbolic. Pierre Bourdieu's theory of social reproduction strategies is the frame of reference to study these strategies. Also, the second demographic transition (SDT) is used to contextualize intergenerational changes. The family life trajectories of three generations in different geographic locations and socioeconomic contexts were reconstructed through interviews. A generational triad was chosen for the interviews; the generational triad refers to three generations of the same consanguineous family. One interview was conducted per generation in each triad, 3 per triad, and 15 in total. Generationally, changes in the types and forms of households are identified; they are dynamic households that change their composition as part of the kinship and family support networks undertaken. The first generation with a single marriage, secondary economic role, not least, but within the priority household. Second generations of one or more unions, in the cases of second unions, unlike the first ones, are unions with shared responsibilities. And the third generation

Conjugal Trajectories: Relationship Beginnings, Change, and Dissolutions
Contemporary Perspectives in Family Research, Volume 22, 151–173
Copyright © 2023 by Emerald Publishing Limited
All rights of reproduction in any form reserved
ISSN: 1530-3535/doi:10.1108/S1530-353520230000022008

with an independent life, living in an apartment with roommates, or who at their parents' age still live in the dwelling with them, at ages when they already had families and independent life. Finally, this work seeks to discuss whether the dynamics of household transformations are influenced by the socioeconomic context of each household and each generation.

Keywords: Costa Rica; family life trajectory; fertility; intergenerational; reproductive strategy; socioeconomic context

INTRODUCTION

The household is a living being born, reproduced, and transformed in its temporal dimension. It is transformed to the rhythm of the socioeconomic context, demographic patterns, and its members' decisions; that is to say, it is dynamic and not static. But its dynamics are not unidirectional; the household also transforms the socioeconomic context and demographic patterns, astounding us with its capacity for change, adaptation, and survival.

This bidirectionality gives it its own dynamism, a dynamism that has been studied with concepts such as tactics, representations, capacity for individual or collective agency, kinship networks or systems, family networks, survival and reproduction strategies, among others, concepts that will be used in this research to analyze from the perspective of family life trajectories the changes in the reproductive strategies of Costa Rican households, to achieve an intergenerational view of the phenomenon.

Through qualitative sources, fertility and marital, educational, economic, social, and symbolic strategies were described and analyzed, defined based on Pierre Bourdieu's strategies of social reproduction. These four categories are used to explain the intergenerational changes in these reproductive strategies from the perspective of family life trajectories.

To achieve this, interviews were conducted with three generations of households, allowing us to contrast quantifiable and numerical data, without faces or life histories, with the family life trajectories of the three generations of households interviewed, with their life stories and experiences. The research question to be answered is: how do Costa Rican households change from one generation to the next according to fertility and marital, educational, economic, social, and symbolic strategies?

For this purpose, a reconstruction by generations of the life trajectories of the people in the interviewed households was carried out to understand the households' conformation, especially the strategies, agency capacity, and networks within each. Economic, political, and social changes led households to make decisions, implement strategies and organize family networks that allowed them to survive and reproduce, demonstrating their capacity for collective agency.

In the population-household relationship, the transformation of the population structure in Costa Rica as of 2015 affects the configuration of households, which, together with the changes attributed to the so-called SDT, in terms of marriage and fertility, translates into homes where different generations live together. Generations that show the increase in schooling levels, the decrease in the number of children, the family arrangements as, for example, obtaining housing and individual and collective maintenance of the group.

LITERATURE REVIEW AND THEORETICAL FRAMEWORK

The central concept of this research is that of the household. The household, as the primary unit of analysis, refers to the group of people who live together in the same physical space and carry out tasks to achieve the economic and non-economic maintenance of the group (Barquero & Trejos, 2005). This group of people may or may not be linked by kinship ties. Still, regardless of this, they share housing (physical space), budget, consumption, production, services, and activities of daily life (Ariza & de Oliveira, 2003), and in some cases, biological reproduction (Ariño, 2007).

The household is made up of one or several families, determined by kinship, either by filiation (consanguinity) or by alliance (marriage systems) (Segalen, 1992), are the institutions that channel not only the kinship relations and networks that allow the identification in the community, as well as access to it but also the subjective and socialization elements that define the way in which consumption and production are carried out in the household (the socio-structural and economic). Among its primary functions are the teaching and reproduction of values and beliefs, which are projected, represented, and coexisted in society.

Families go through various phases or stages,

from the constitution of an initial nucleus through different moments of change according to the growth of the initial group and the ages of its members, to the dissolution of said nucleus or its dispersion into new nuclei. (Barquero & Trejos, 2005, p. 333)

These stages are defined as the family life cycle. They must be understood in terms of the life cycle of its members: This approach, based on the life course, links personal and family development with historical events thanks to comparisons of age and cohort, achieving

that the analysis and interpretation have gone from being a simple examination of the different stages of the family cycle, to becoming an analysis of the chronological evolution of family and individual transitions. (Hareven, 1995, p. 115)

In addition to the life cycle of its members, the stages are defined by the composition, size and structure of the families, the structure "is revealing of a certain form of organization that regulates the transmission of cultural practices and values, articulating family and work, family and power, family and wealth" (Segalen, 1992, p. 43), in "relation to the conditioning factors of their society" (Hareven, 1995, p. 111), be they cultural, social or economic.

As Ariño explains, as the dynamic units that they are, they are conditioned "by demographic dynamics, particularly marriage and fertility (…) the population by sex and age and its distribution in the territory, together with economic, social, cultural patterns" (Ariño, 2007, p. 255). But also due to the cumulative result of retrospective trends in fertility, mortality, and migration and the influence of socioeconomic and political processes (Pérez, 2010).

The reproduction strategies of households depend on the social stratum in which they find themselves as members; in that social world, they are constructed and reconstructed; on this depends the distribution and acquisition of economic and social capital, the mechanisms and dispositions of reproduction, and they seek the material, biological and immaterial reproduction of the family or families that make up the household (Bourdieu, 2013) in order to ensure biological reproduction, preserve life and develop all practices "indispensable for the optimization of the material and non-material conditions of existence of the household and of each of its members" (Torrado, 2003, p. 28). Therefore, the behavior of the social agents of the household contributes to the "reproduction of the social position, to the reproduction of their social class of belonging and, therefore, to the reproduction of the global structure of social classes" (Torrado, 2003, p. 28).

Similarly, strategies are complex responses to economic, material, cultural, and ideological conditions determined by the type of social and biological reproduction, taking into account that each social group implements its own reproduction strategy (Chacón, 1995) in a given context and time. In other words, strategies are conditioned

> by the style of development in force in a given society (…), which determines the characteristics of the labor and consumption market, the actions of the State and the living conditions of the population. (Ariño, 2005, p. 258)

For this research, the strategies of households for their reproduction are actions of social agents oriented by the socioeconomic stratum to which they belong and the life cycle of their members, both of which determine the basic needs of each household and how they are met. At the same time, these strategies depend on their social condition or position to obtain and transmit the necessary goods that allow guaranteeing or improving the household's own economic and social capital, in a feedback relationship with society, and on the limits imposed by the State in a given time, space and context.

The family and the household must exist for such strategies to be possible; at the same time, those strategies are a requirement to perpetuate the family and the household (Bourdieu, 2013). Moreover, strategies are conditioned by the juridical-political, the cultural-ideological, the socio-economic "and are deployed throughout the family life cycle through a set of behavioral dimensions" (Street, 2004, p. 47).

In analyzing the bidirectional relationship between context and household and its members and reproductive strategies, we use the theory of the SDT.

This theory, proposed by Ron Lesthaeghe and Dirk van de Kaa in 1987, suggests that the main changes are sustained fertility below replacement level, a multiplicity of marital arrangements other than marriage, a disconnection between marriage and marriage and procreation, and a non-stationary population (Lesthaeghe, 2010). Lesthaeghe explains that from 1950 onwards, a series of changes related to nuptiality took place that revealed the first signs of the emergence of the SDT:

- The rapid weakening of social control exercised by institutions correlates to the increase in the autonomy of individual morality.
- Greater social acceptance of sexuality outside of marriage.
- The accentuation of individual aspirations within the couple.
- The development of more symmetrical exchange patterns within the unions.
- The discovery of opportunity costs resulting from women's economic autonomy.
- The merging of the domestic and spouses' careers in domestic transactions.
- The availability of efficient contraceptives, which help women control their reproduction. Lesthaeghe (cited by Quilodrán, 2011).

The idea behind this theory is related to the change in preferences; it is proposed that the First Demographic Transition (FDT) is anchored to the fulfillment of basic material needs, while the second is the expression of the development of a higher order, non-material needs and expressiveness of values (Lesthaegue, 2010), in which greater equality in gender relations is included.

Collective behavior no longer obeys the norms based on the ideology of the family supported by the Church and the State. Instead, the new regime is governed by the primacy of individual choice (Lesthaegue, 2010), characterized "above all by changes in the behaviors of individuals at the level, basically, of family formation and stability" (Quilodrán, 2011, p. 69).

Other changes consistent with this question are increased free unions, divorce and remarriage, children out of wedlock, and childless marriages. In this sense, the SDT refers to demographic elements that interfere with and shape households and cultural, social (with an essential weight of education), and economic aspects linked to them.

METHODOLOGY

This chapter provides an experiential analysis of household strategies to understand generational decisions and changes. The family life trajectories of three generations in different geographical locations and socioeconomic contexts are reconstructed through interviews.

The perspective of family life trajectories will help us to study the relationship between the strategies implemented, the family life cycle, and the life cycle of household members, determining the generational trajectory and by type of household (Torrado, 2005). The objective is to provide an experiential context and to understand households, specifically their reproduction and survival strategies from their protagonists.

For the interviews, a generational triad was chosen as follows: Guanacaste (1 triad), Puntarenas (1 triad), Limón (1 triad), San José (1 triad), Cartago (1 triad). The generational triad refers to three generations of the same consanguineous family (elderly mothers, daughters, daughters, or sons of their daughters[1]), which make up the study population.

One interview was conducted per generation in each triad, 3 per triad, and 15 interviews in total. For the sample selection (the triads), the snowball sampling technique was used: meet some informants and get them to introduce us to others (Taylor & Bogdan, 1987).

The number of households is not representative since the theoretical sampling strategy was used, where the number of cases studied is relatively unimportant.

What is important is the potential of each case to assist the researcher in developing theoretical understandings of the studied area of social life (Taylor & Bogdan, 1987) and, in our case, of the household and the life course.

The interviews allowed encounters aimed at understanding the informant's perspectives on their lives, experiences, or situations, as expressed in their own words (Taylor & Bogdan, 1987). The programmed standardized interview was carried out; that is, the wording and order of all the questions were the same for each person since these should be comparable so that when variations appear among interviewees, they can be attributed to fundamental differences in response, and not to the instrument (Valles, 1999). The questions made it possible to reconstruct the trajectory of first and second unions (when there were any), of the different generations, by geographic area.

The information obtained in the interviews was analyzed with the ATLAS. ti software according to the strategies of fertility and marital, educational, economic investment, social and symbolic investment, for which the information was classified as follows:

- Fertility and marriage strategy: number of children, marriage-related and husband-related questions.
- Educational strategy: the interviewee's schooling level, children, spouse, or partners.
- Economic investment: questions about income, facilities to buy and obtain essential and non-essential goods, the type(s) of jobs of the interviewee and other household members, extra work, or various ways of getting money.
- Social and symbolic investment: related to housing tenure and what I observed when I conducted the interviews.
- Type of household: questions related to the division of tasks, parenting, household economic decisions, type of headship, or other elements that help to reconstruct the kind of household.

The process of coding and establishing relationships was based on the analysis of the sociodemographic characteristics of each interview. The type of household experienced gives importance to the aspects that determine the trajectories of the unions and the family life of the households and their members, as well as the strategies carried out by each of the generations for the survival and reproduction of the households since the stages of the family life course "do not respond only to the evolution of chronological age, but also to the patterns and meanings that define the institutions in each society and historical moment" (Raimondi & Street, 2005, p. 80).

The information will be compared between generations; attention will be paid to generational behavior and the reconstruction of household types to understand the dynamics of household transformations from the trajectories of family life. To maintain anonymity and respect for their private and family lives, pseudonyms will be used when referring to the persons interviewed.

RESULTS

Profile of Persons and Households Interviewed

As shown in Table 1, the first generation of interviewees was born between 1928 and 1952. They are women between 93 and 69 years old with an educational level that did not reach higher education. In some cases, they did not even finish primary school; only 20% completed high school. From the one who never lived with a partner to those who were married until death separated them from their husbands. Widows or currently in a union, without separations, ruptures, or divorces, with between 2 and 6 children, for a total of 20 children. The common thing in all of them is to be Catholics who declare themselves believers.

The second generation is between 65 and 50 years old, born between 1956 and 1971. With high school or higher education, 80% graduated from high school. Unlike the generation that preceded them, the phrase "until death do them part" did not echo in them, separated or divorced, with two and even three relationships and between three and four children, that is, there is a decrease of four children about the total number of children born by the first generation. But like their mothers, they are all Catholics and believers. The predominant type of household in both generations is the conjugal nuclear household with children or extended household.

The third generation, the youngest, were between 42 and 28 years old at the interview, born between 1979 and 1993, and all with higher education. Generationally they are different from their grandmothers and mothers; they are in a union, dating, or single, and only one has been married with a child or none. The total number of children decreased by 14 compared to their mothers' generation and by 18 children to their grandmothers' generation. Believers and Catholics declare themselves non-practicing or non-believers at all. In a single-parent or compound home, they visit home on weekends or still live at home with their parents and siblings.

Marriage and Fertility Strategy. The family life trajectory of most of these women born in the first half of the twentieth century begins with religious marriage. Married at a very young age and underage or in their early twenties. With courtships of two, six years, or two-month visits interceded by the father. They confess that their husband was the first man in their lives, and in some cases, the only one, and as is to be expected, in an era so much more conservative than the present one, above all, because of the value of women's virginity, they did not live together before marriage. Their husbands were older than they were.

Ms C: Yes, and only that man I met as well. I slept with only one; neither before nor after has there been another.

I: So you never lived with other people; you were only with your husband?

Ms C: Yes (M. Castillo, January 5, 2019).

Pregnant very soon after or before marriage, they had their first child within the first year of marriage. In the decade in which they have them, the total fertility rate in Costa Rica was approximately six children, consistent with this figure; they had between six and two children. The number of children was the result of their

Table 1. Profile of Persons and Households Interviewed.

Generation	Age	Finish High School	Married	Total Number of Children
First	Between 93 and 69 years old	20%	80%	20
Second	Between 65 and 50 years old	80%	80%	16
Third	between 42 and 28 years old	100%	20%	2

youth and the life of their husbands; some stopped having children when their husbands died due to contraceptives or operations: "all three were born in three years, by the time I was 21 years old, I already had three" (K. Moreno, January 14, 2019).

And those children so close to the marriage and between them, were they wanted? They agree that they became aware of the pregnancies when they were already several months pregnant; that is, most of them were not planned but desired, even in such adverse conditions as the one explained by Mrs Lopez:

> My eldest daughter's father was married and was a friend, but he went beyond friendship as a friend. The past men are very macho; if they don't want to do it the easy way, they go the hard way (...) Yes, and just as it happened to me with the first one, it occurred with the second one. I don't know, but I tell them: "God knows what he does" because if I hadn't had them that way, I wouldn't have them. (N. López, March 1, 2020)

Like their mothers, the family life trajectory of this second generation begins with a religious marriage; however, for some, this marriage was the first of several unions. Married or united between the ages of 18 and 27 with men older than themselves, their courtships lasted between 7 months and 8 years. They had between three and four children; some were planned, others were not, but they mentioned they were wanted.

Even though they did not live with their husbands before marriage, when I asked them if "before getting married it is convenient to live together for a while, to try living together," most of them answered that they agreed. For example, Mrs Carrillo comments:

> I think so, of course, although I never really, holy God! But not at that time, but it hasn't bothered me with any relationship that my daughters have had, not at all because no, it's the same if they last longer than maybe (...) and they are happier than a marriage. (V. Carrillo, February 2, 2019)

Unlike their mothers, Mrs Abarca and Mrs Carrillo divorced after almost 20 years of marriage and began their second marriage, both civil, almost in their fifties or early fifties; their husbands, unlike them, had no children. In this second relationship, they live with them before getting married. They say they had other relationships between the divorce and the second marriage.

On the other hand, Mrs Alpízar separates after almost 10 years of relationship, a relationship she calls open, after which she comments that she has not had anything, not even a boyfriend.

Ms A: Well, actually, there was no marriage. It was an open relationship
I: an open relationship, what do you mean?

Ms A: Open in the sense that I allowed it because I was not getting used to living in his house, with the environment, I don't know, with the environment that he provided, so for me, it was like having love and having freedom.

I: OK. How many years were you with him like that?

Ms A: About nine years.

I: And after that relationship, have you had any other relationships?

Ms A: No.

I: Boyfriend? Nothing?

Ms A: No (R. Alpízar, March 1, 2020).

The family life trajectory of the third generation of interviewees is different in each of the cases, but they have in common that most of them have not married. Only Mrs Herrera, after almost five years of cohabitation, got married in a civil marriage shortly after the first and only birth, a pregnancy that was not planned but desired.

Mr Jiménez does not plan for his first child, but he does want one and explains that the reason for living with his partner, after almost five years of dating, is his son:

I: You moved in together because of the baby?

Mr J: You can say. Yes, because the baby is five months old and I decided, let's say, how to live about five months ago (H. Jiménez, March 3, 2020).

Unlike their mothers, their children and relationships are in their near thirties or thirties. Mr Marin and Mr Cascante still live in their mothers' house, both in a dating relationship, but they explain that neither marriage nor children are a priority.

Mr M: No, it is not in my plans to get married or have children at the moment. I still have other plans in mind.

I: Like what?

Mr M: Like ah well, like making one's house first, making one's things, car, traveling... (G. Marín, February 9, 2019).

In the case of Mr Cascante, his priority is to continue studying. Mrs Brenes explains,

I see myself having a partner, but not getting married because I don't believe in marriage (…) but not having children. I am very clear about that; I don't want to have children. (V. Brenes, March 1, 2020)

The decrease in married people, and the increase in divorces and separations, are exemplified in the previous paragraphs. Ladies of the first generation are all married by religious marriage, while the ladies of the second generation, although married by religious marriage, speak about divorces and separations. There is a decrease in the number of children if we take the maximum number of children per generation, going from six children in the first generation to one child in the third generation.

Educational Strategy. The highest level of schooling of the first-generation women is high school. Mrs Castillo explains that until old age, she went to the university to receive free courses,

> my daughter was there when they opened those groups (for older adults), she tells me "mommy go, go! And you go with me," and then I went there to Bellas Artes. (M. Castillo, January 5, 2019)

Mrs López studied accounting until the fourth year of high school. "I did book technology and accounting" (N. López, March 1, 2020), and Mrs Moreno, first year. Mrs Morales has completed primary school, while Mrs Rojas only spent a "little while" in first grade. However, she knows how to read and write:

Ms R: I tell you why, because of the first child. He was going to school, and I didn't know anything.

Ms R: I had forgotten everything, and then they sent me one, oh! Plus those, what do they call them? Subtractions, ones you put in and take out, ones, oh! That you have to put here, and you have to put a subtraction here. It is like a...

I: Fractions? Divisions?

Ms R: Divisions!

Ms R: Oh, dear! I "oh my God! How do I do?" Well, I took the booklet away, and I put it like this, and in my opinion, he took it with him, and the next day he arrived with a scratch like this. A scratch [of incorrect answer], oh what the hell! What do I do? How do I learn? I said. And then, in the evening, I prayed to the Lord.

Ms R: Because I don't beat around the bush.

I: Really?

Ms R: Yes, as they tell me, "take two from four" is that so? And another day I come and make a sum and take away, I put four on top and four on the bottom, and I go and take out two, or I don't know, the thing is that I see and I say: Ah yes! Then that's the way it has to be. Another day I waited until they sent me something else with my son nothing; they sent me other things. Oh, shit!

I: Right when you had mastered it.

Mr R: Yes, see, they sent me one the other day, and I started. I was the one who did it and sent it back to them, and when it came back with the note -excellent. I was so happy, and that's how I learned (S. Rojas, March 3, 2020).

Ms Carrillo comments:

> I have been studying since, well, since I was 20 years old. I started with engineering, but I had to quit when I got pregnant (...), and well, I don't know, life helped me, I went through schools, experience and then, the last [daughter] gave me time to study little by little. (V. Carrillo, February 2, 2019)

Similar situation to that of Mrs Carrillo, Mrs Alpízar:

I: Did you study as a grown-up?
Ms A: Already old, already had given birth.
I: Why? Because of your children?
Ms A: Well, I was already a high school graduate; I went to study as a mid-level technician; I studied for two years and something. I finished, and then I returned home and went to work in a business that needed someone reliable, and I met my daughter's father and my oldest daughter was in her way (R. Alpízar, March 1, 2020).

And that of Mrs Abarca

yes, it happened to me that I was with my degree, working and with a small baby, with pregnancy, impossible. I took up my studies again, in another university, and in another career. (L. Abarca, January 14, 2019)

Mrs Chavarría's example tells us about the lack of opportunities and motherhood:

I: did you study late because you did not want to stud or because you did not have opportunities to study?
Ms C: I did not have opportunities to study.
I: Even older?
Ms C: Because there was only one school there.
I: Ah, yes.
Ms C: I dropped out of school in the fifth grade because I was already 15 years old, and all the kids were bullying me.
I: So, how long ago did you take the ninth grade?
Ms C: About three, four years.
I: Did you go back to school? Let's say, to education after your children had grown up?
S.C: Ah, yes.
I: You had them first and then decided to continue studying?
S.C: Oh yes, well, about four years (J. Chavarría, March 3, 2020).

The husbands or partners of these women, for the most part, have higher education, as do their sons and daughters. All the people interviewed in the third generation have completed higher education, in some cases, two university degrees, the first already completed, the second in progress. The increase in the levels of schooling of one generation concerning the other is evident.

Economic Investment Strategy. Where household reproduction and survival strategies, individual agency, tactics, and family networks are most evident is in the economic investment strategy. This is where the first-generation women relate their experiences and the strategies implemented to survive as a family and household. In this sense, the first thing to point out is the household income; they recognized their husbands as the leading economic contributors; they worked in agricultural work, construction, vendors, or miscellaneous while in charge of the home and the family.

In some cases, the money given by the husband was not enough, and even if it was, they all carried out activities, demonstrating their capacity for agency, to increase the household's economic capital as a strategy for survival. For example, Mrs Morales, when I asked her if her husband's money was enough for her, she told me that not always, that there were times when the money he gave her was not enough to live on; when that happened, she made candies to help her buy things for the house and to be able to buy food and what she needed to survive (B. Morales, February 8, 2019).

In the case of Mrs Castillo, she explains:

Ms C: When I was trying to work, I don't know, he indeed felt like, like I was not happy, or I don't know what, no, no.

I: And he didn't let you?

Ms C: No, then I worked making bread; I made bridal cakes and anything like that, decorating.

Ms C: But he wasn't pleased about it; I could see that he didn't like it.

I: But, were you still doing it?

Ms C: Ah, yes, let's say, every Saturday, the bread. I used to make batches of sweet and salty bread.

I: And did you sell it?

Ms C Ah, yes, yes, among the acquaintances.

I: And, what did you do with that money?

Ms C: Well, it was so little that it would go away; it would go away in anything.

I: In anything?

Ms C: I never did any special savings.

I: No, but did you invest it in the house? Or in you?

S. C: In whatever was needed (M. Castillo, January 5, 2019).

However, in some cases, the money given to them by their husbands was limited:

Ms R: No, let's put it this way. He would come by and pay if we took it out on credit. He would only give me money when I went somewhere, like the hospital or insurance company.

I: That is when he gave you money?

Ms R: Uh-huh.

I: But wasn't it like a monthly income?

Ms R: No, what the bus fare was worth, that he gave me.

I: What if you wanted to buy something?

Ms R: Oh no, I couldn't buy anything because I had no money (S. Rojas, March 3, 2020).

Their husbands had higher incomes and were the main financial contributor to the household impacted their pensions. Most of them receive a stipend, but only one receives it through the contributory system; the others are pensions from the non-contributory system,[2] through the husband's pension when he dies, or because their husbands cannot manage it themselves due to health issues. In all cases, they explain that their sons and daughters help them financially.

Most of them have their daughters living in their homes, a sign of the family support network since it is an economic benefit for their daughters, but also for them because they take care of them; an example is the case of Mrs Castillo:

Ms C: The thing is that my daughter arrives and tells me one day, "Oh mommy, I am tired of paying for such expensive apartments or houses." The little girl had a doggie that had been given to her, and she said: "I am not allowed to have the dog there," she says: "What do I do?" and said, "I have…; they each have a piece [a piece of land that they will inherit]."

Ms C: And she says "don't you think I could build a house here?" And I tell her, of course! Build it if it's yours, and she says: "but I'll be stuck in debt," and I tell her, let's do something, get a car; because she was traveling by bus, and I tell her, get a car, and you live with me, if it's good for you, then you build the house, and well, she never built the house.

Ms C: And it worked for me.

I: Yes, yes, of course, because you have company (M. Castillo, January 5, 2019).

In cases where the daughters live at home, they collaborate with the work or household economy, as Mrs Moreno commented:

I: Does the one who still lives with you contribute anything to the household?

Ms M: Yes

I: Does he help you?

Ms M: Yes.

I: And was it because he wanted to, or because you asked him to contribute with something?

Ms M: Oh, no, since he has a nice income, he takes us everywhere; takes us to eat and everything.

I: Ah, ok, but does he also give you like, to buy food, to pay for…?

Ms M: He asked for a credit card for me (K. Moreno, January 14, 2019).

In the homes of most second-generation women, their children still live with them, but unlike their mothers, they live with all their children, minors, and university graduates with jobs. This is also a sign of the family support network, but in these cases, they are more extensive networks since, as Mrs Abarca explains, there are more members:

I: And then, the other very interesting question is why do you think your children still live here?

Ms A: Because this is a 5-star hotel. And I think that, well, as long as you don't bother them because, for example, the older one contributes. In the beginning, I felt that it was like they were giving me something for myself, and my older brother made me see that no, that here he had internet, telephone, hot water, food, someone to iron, to do laundry, so I said well it's okay. The other one, for example, just started a business, so I understand him; it is still taking off, so I do not bother him, nor do I demand from him (L. Abarca, January 14, 2019).

Or the case of Mrs Alpízar, she comments that one of her sons "says that first, he studies so he can work after" (R. Alpízar, March 1, 2020). But it also allows them to have a greater capacity for collective agency within the household; for example, Mrs Chavarría states that one of her sons is the primary economic support of the household.

Household income is different in the five cases. In the case of Mrs Chavarría, the son is the main contributor because he is the one who gives the most money. Although she defines herself as a housewife, she explains that she occasionally works with an uncle, and the husband works in whatever he can.

In the case of the women with more than one union, they agree that in the first union, they were the main economic contributor to the household; in one of the cases carrying out different jobs to be able to have or increase household capital, a situation that changes in the later unions, since, in the current ones, they explain that their husband is the primary breadwinner. Mrs Quesada explains that her husband has been the primary breadwinner in the 30 years of marriage.

Mrs Alpízar comments that while in the relationship, she dedicated herself to raising the children. The partner contributed when he visited them or when she or the children asked for money. After the separation, she lives on alimony and catalog sales. At the time of the interview, she said that she and her mother are the prominent financial supporters of the household. She finished her university studies and managed to get a stable job; her mother is a pensioner.

The third-generation people who live in their mothers' houses contribute to the household economy according to their possibilities, paying bills, and buying food. Still, they explain that they have never asked for a specific or monthly amount. In the case of Mrs Herrera, she works on her own, supporting herself and her son, with occasional help from her ex-partner. For his part, Mr. Jiménez gives a specific amount of money a week to help support his son.

Social and Symbolic Investment Strategy. Regardless of the material condition of the houses observed during the interviews, some of which were more basic in design than others, all the first-generation women received me in their homes, in their own houses. The housing tenure ranged from land inherited from the husband, or the brother, to the house bought with the sale of the first one, by the husband, or with the daughters' help.

But specifically, what were the family support networks and tactics that made it possible to build and obtain the house? Mrs Morales explains that she buys the place where she welcomes me with the sale of the first one, which she gets in the following way:

When the husband died, he had everything ready; he had the wood and other materials needed for that first house. When the husband dies, one of the aunts who loved her husband very much starts to build the house; she tells me so, but the lady also dies and cannot finish it. As this house is next to the back of where the Bank is currently located, she says that when they start to build the Bank, the builders arrive, and she makes a business deal with them. They rent the house to her; instead of paying her rent, they pay her in kind, that is to say, building the house, and thus she finishes building it. This is how Mrs Morales spends building her house and buying her current house (B. Morales, February 8, 2019).

For her part, Mrs Rojas, when I ask her if she has the house because of a loan or housing bond, she explains:

Ms R: No, it's made of wood. No, well, we went down there to get the wood.
I: And did you put it together?
Ms R: And we put it together, yes.
I: And the lot?
Ms R: Eh, this lot belonged to my brother. My brother, all this here belonged to him, but when he died, he told his wife: "Rosita, he says, this little piece up here, you give it to Soledad."
I: You?
Ms R: Yes (S. Rojas, March 3, 2020).

Different strategies were put to work during the house's tenure and construction. The case of Mrs Moreno is an example of the family support network for the construction of housing; in addition to a loan, the husband, his brother, and her brother participated in the building; in the case of her brother, she comments that "he came to help for free" (K. Moreno, January 14, 2019).

Ms M: He told him, you should see that there, they sell a little house, like this and like that, and he came to see it, and you should know that I made a novena to the Holy Spirit, and everything, and out of nowhere the bank lent us, they lent him everything in a week, everything, they lent us twenty one thousand pesos, look at that.
I: So he [the husband] bought this house, but he built it too. Did he build it?
Ms M: Oh, yes, what we had was a slum, imagine that only the window bars and some planks for wooden formworks, nothing else, the rest was useless, and the sewer of the toilet was here, it was in the kitchen until they threw the pipe to the street. It lasted from May until the first of December when we came, working with him, his brother, and one of my brothers (K. Moreno, January 14, 2019).

Most of the second-generation women interviewed own their own homes; they rented or lived with relatives before owning. But the purchase or construction strategies and the tactics put in place differ. These range from family help to pay the loan premium, demonstrating the capacity for the collective agency:

We rented and here, always, always, always, we always rented, there was never enough money to even think about buying anything, then when he left I got a loan and everything (...) I think I am very punctual, and I pay my debts. First, we did not eat rather than not paying, and I went to all the banks, and they told me, "no, you woman alone, with your salary, we cannot give you a loan," and I was already earning well when I went to see them. And I used to say, "hell, I wouldn't even miss half a month's payment," but that's how it is, that's how loans are and look, several members of the family lent me for the down payment, and I was left with the debt, and I started paying the ones that were in dollars first because that's how it was. (V. Carrillo, February 2, 2019)

Permission to remodel the house:

I invested here, and I told my children that with the investment I made, the remodeling of the house, I could have bought another place, but to update the house, let's say, because the house was not like that, it was smaller, simpler, so I acquired a loan there, but there we go. (R. Alpízar, March 1, 2020)

Or help from the state:

We were on a piece of land that belonged to my father-in-law and a bit of land that belonged to the street. My father-in-law's lot was his, but the rest was street property. So... my father-in-law sold it to a brother-in-law and, well, he didn't want to give us the water, so we had no way to get the water, then I realized that here, an uncle told me that they were going to distribute some lots, so I came and left some letters, and they gave us a lot. (J. Chavarría, March 3, 2020)

They build the house, and Mrs Chavarría lives there with her family, then they go to live with her mother, Mrs Rojas. And it is in that house where Mr Jiménez (third generation), his partner, and the baby sometimes stay since they live in her mother's house with her mother's partner and her brother. In the case of the other people of the third generation, Mrs Herrera and Mrs Brenes rent an apartment, and Mr Marín and Mr Cascante live with their parents and siblings.

The different strategies, translated into tactics, family networks, and capacity for collective agency, to build and obtain housing mentioned in this section exemplify the use of the space or land already available or to carry out strategies that would allow them to have or get accommodation with minimal or no expenses.

Household Types. The family life trajectory of the women of the first generation begins with a religious marriage with men older than them or of the same age; continues with sons and daughters before that marriage, previous ones, or between them. This leads them to use tactics to put their family and kinship networks to work and their capacity for the agency to survive and reproduce in their homes and with their families. In this section, we will reconstruct this trajectory and the strategies implemented from an experiential point of view.

Their family life trajectories were mostly in conjugal homes with children; in these cases, they were their husbands, sons, and daughters. They recognized themselves as housewives, in charge of the money given to them by their husbands (when was the case), the purchases, the cleaning when they did not have a maid, the kitchen, and the children's upbringing. In some cases, parenting and household decisions or decisions regarding their children were shared. However, they mentioned that their husbands did not know what it was like to go to a school or college meeting or to speak "harshly" to their children.

In the case of their husbands, the economic strategies for the survival and reproduction of the household involved dedicating themselves to various tasks or having several jobs; as the husband of Mrs Moreno in this regard, she comments:

> Look, he worked at the Ministry [as a janitor], and he used to go, he was a house painter, and in two days, he earned what he earned in a month at the Ministry; and when he arrived, he would tell me: "keep this for me." (K. Moreno, January 14, 2019)

Or Mrs Morales when she explains that indeed the head of the household was him, that he was the one who contributed most economically to the household, working in carpentry, tractors, or plowing land (B. Morales, February 8, 2019).

Despite indicating that the husbands were the ones who contributed the most to the household, they do not know how much they earned; they only stated that they gave the money or came with the groceries. Most of them agreed that they had enough money to live on but not enough for trips or vacations, and they also commented that they made bread, candies, or raffles to "help themselves." Their sons and daughters studied, got married, or are still at home; in fact, the reasons for the departure of their sons and daughters from home obey practically two reasons: education or marriage.

The above description should not lead us to think that the family life trajectories of these women were static and linear; this would be a severe mistake. They were dynamic household trajectories, where mobility, kinship, and family networks played an important role. For example, Mrs Morales, when her husband dies, goes to live with her in-laws; once they die, she goes to live with her mother and sister, then builds a house, which she then rents for a while so that her mother could have money to help support her daughters. At the same time, she works in Panama since she goes to Panama for a job opportunity, leaving her daughters with her grandmother (her mother) here in Costa Rica. Already in her second union, she sets up a shoe store with her partner (B. Morales, February 8, 2019).

Or Mrs Moreno, who:

> We've always lived alone since we got married. We did live there in Barrio, his [her husband's] father had two houses and a patio, small rooms, we lived in one of those rooms for a long time, then we moved to a bigger house, and then he bought this, here. (K. Moreno, January 14, 2019)

In the case of Mrs Rojas, the changes in strategies and the shape of the household were marked by the death of her husband, the old age of her parents, and the departure of her sons and daughters from the household:

I: In the first years of marriage, you live with your husband and children? Only?

Ms R: Uh-huh, yes.

I: Ok. Then you lived with your mom and dad to care for them in their old age?

Ms R: Aha, yes, yes. At old age.

I: Ok, the first years with your children and husband, seven years with your father, and 24 years with your mother. Did your father live with you, your husband, and your children?

Ms R: Yes.

I: Those who had not left.

Ms R: Yes.

I: But your mother lived with you and your husband for a while, and then only with you?

Ms R: Yes, with me (S. Rojas, March 3, 2020).

Mrs López's home is an extended household, where she, her mother, nieces, nephews, daughters, and grandchildren have lived together over the years. This is a household that highlights the different strategies (tactics and networks) that families carry out to reproduce themselves educationally, economically, and symbolically.

Ms L: My mother moved in then, and other grandchildren moved in. We rented a house, and my mother made food for us and helped us.

I: Was it your mom, you, and your oldest daughter?

Ms L: And the other grandchildren, nephews, two older ones came; they lived with us. Then they all came, and we were one family. After we became independent, each one of us took a house here.

I: So it was your mom, your oldest daughter, and your two nephews or cousins?

Ms L: The two nephews, but the whole family joined us after that.

I: The home was already like that; the family, while they were settling in, were they studying?

Ms L: Meanwhile, yes, yes, yes, exactly. Afterward, my sister came.

I: Oh, I get it. They were more like the temporaries while they were getting settled in, and you always remained.

Ms L: Always, yes.

I: How did they help each other? I mean, financially, did everyone put in a bit of money? Do you remember how they managed it?

Ms L: When we lived there, they sent us rice, beans, bananas, and oranges. If not, my brother used to take us there, because there is a small farm and my father was there too. My dad would come and go and send us things, and then, after that, the nephew would work a little bit and help us.

I: Okay. So they sent them, and how did you do with the money? With what you worked and what they worked?

Ms L: That was for the house, for everything, yes.

I: And with the housework...? How did you do it? Do you remember your mother was the one who mostly helped around the house, and you helped her?

Ms L: Yes.

I: If you had to name the leading financial supporter of the household, who would you say it was? You, your nephew...?

Ms L: Me.

I: And then, from what you received, you were able to pay the loan for the house, and eat well, and pay the electricity and water bills.

Ms L. Yes, electricity, water. (N. López, March 1, 2020).

The family life trajectory of Mrs Alpízar, daughter of Mrs López and the second generation interviewed, starts from the extended household portrayed in the previous quote. During their almost ten-year relationship, Mrs Alpízar was between her partner's place of residence and her mother's house, stating that the upbringing fell mainly on her. She resumed her university studies during her last pregnancy, and these studies have allowed her to have a stable and permanent job. Together with her mother, Mrs Lopez, they are the primary breadwinners in the household, while her children, who still live at home, study and work.

At the time of the interviews, the family life trajectories of the second generation of women are based on extended, compound, conjugal households with children and without children; their households have been dynamic and changing over time.

From a first union that begins with religious marriage, in which they have all their children, declare themselves the primary breadwinners; in charge of child-rearing and household decisions, as well as material goods such as the house or the car, for example. Intermediate unions where they live together or go out with others, second marriages where their husbands are the primary breadwinners, and household decisions and housework are shared.

In the case of Mrs Quesada, two years after her marriage, she had her first child, and this nuclear household with children continues more than thirty years later, with her three children living with her and her husband. She has a degree but has only practiced for a few years to dedicate herself to raising her children and managing the household:

> He gives me, let's say, he always, well, at the beginning when we were just married, let's say, I used to ask him and everything, but then a time came when he was kind of messy. He decided to give me everything, let's say, he comes, he gives me all the money, then I manage it, let's say, I come, I make the payments for everything in the house, the groceries, and everything. (H. Quesada, February 9, 2019)

She has always had someone to help her with the housework, while parenting and other household decisions are made on a shared basis.

Mrs Chavarría's nuclear household with children becomes an extended household, showing the family support network. "They called me to come and help, so that's why I'm here. Before it was because of my grandmother, for not leaving my mom alone, and now for not leaving her alone" (J. Chavarría, March 3, 2020). Regarding parenting, she comments that it has been both of them (referring to her and her husband), but she is the stricter one. When I ask her how the division of tasks has been, she explains:

I: Regarding the family and all the logic, how is the division of tasks? Since your husband sometimes works, sometimes he doesn't, and you are here. Sometimes he helps you clean or in the kitchen.

Ms C: Ah, yes.
I: Or is it all up to you?
Ms C: Ah no, no, no, if I tell him "pick up those clothes," he picks them up. We always divide everything. Let's say, if I work and earn a little more than him, he gives me whatever he can give me; together we pay, like the electricity, water, telephone, everything (J. Chavarría, March 3, 2020).

There are various households of third-generation individuals outside their mothers' homes, whether in a single-parent household, a compound household, or renting an apartment with roommates. Mr Jimenez has been living with his partner's family for the past few months, constituting a composite household. He explains that the household chores and raising his baby fall on his partner. However, he clarifies that the decisions and the headship are shared.

Mrs Herrera comments that she has been responsible for the upbringing. At the same time, household decisions were divided according to the workload, stating that the headship was shared and that at some times, the primary economic support was provided by the couple and at other times in a shared manner.

Finally, Mrs Brenes' independent life shows that living in an apartment with roommates also entails organization and division of the group and personal tasks:

I: Do you divide the cleaning?
Ms B: uh-huh, we clean twice weekly but take turns.
I: and the food?
Ms B: everyone buys their food. (V. Brenes, March 1, 2020).

In addition, she says that she helps out at her grandmother's house, Mrs Lopez, when she has cash flow "because I have to pay my fares, pay the rent, buy food, and so far I'm doing a savings plan" (V. Brenes, March 1, 2020).

CONCLUSIONS

The generational change from the first to the third generation reconstructed through family life trajectories (across the four chosen strategies and household types) validates the SDT theory, the theoretical basis of this manuscript. There is a decline in fertility, below replacement level in the case of the third generation, marital arrangements other than marriage, and the disconnection between marriage and childbearing.

In the case of the third generation, not being practitioners of the religion in which they were raised and of which their mothers and grandmothers declare themselves believers and practitioners shows how their ideology and representation of the family and the home are not based on the religious or state, and in some cases, highlights individual aspirations within the couple.

The selected questions on the level of schooling of the spouse or partner allow us to determine that marriages or unions are, for the most part, between equivalent groups in terms of education. Generally, the partners of the second and third-generation interviewees, like themselves, have higher education. For the first generation, according to the information from the interviews, it seems that the marriage was more because it was meant to be; however, their husbands are of equivalent socioeconomic status.

Regardless of socioeconomic stratum, all women in the first and second generations married through a religious marriage. Free unions do not seem to depend on the socioeconomic stratum but marital status and experience before the free union. In the case of the third generation, singleness and lower fertility predominate, but this is also not dependent on the socioeconomic stratum.

The study of the educational strategy evidences the increase in people's academic level from one generation to the next. In the case of some of the ladies of the second generation, studying was a tactic after having their children that allowed them economic independence from their partners or ex-partners. Socioeconomic status does not define educational level per se; it restricts access to the opportunity to continue studying, to have a scholarship, or to be able to pay for college.

The strategy of each household, of each generation, to perpetuate or increase its economic capital depended on the financial contribution of the husband, the tactics of the women interviewed to improve it, the family support networks, and their capacity for individual and collective agency, regardless of whether they were the primary breadwinners.

Through the interviews, it was impossible to identify the income gap by the declared head of household. However, it can be concluded that household income depended on the socioeconomic stratum to which the household belonged, not on the region.

The kind of support of the first generation depended on their husbands and, at present, on the help of their daughters and sons. In the case of the second generation, most women will rely on their jobs, although it can be assumed, taking into account the information from the interviews, that they will also depend on their husbands and sons.

Analyzing the social and symbolic investment strategy from the tenure and way of obtaining housing allows us to understand the importance of housing. All the women of the first generation, and most of the second generation, have their own homes. To achieve this, they put into practice different tactics, family support networks, and their capacity for the collective agency as a family.

The strategies for obtaining and holding a house depended on the socioeconomic status of the women, their families, and their husbands. Whether it was the land inherited from the husband or brother, the house was bought with the sale of the first one, with the help of the husband, the daughters, or other relatives. It is clear that obtaining housing also depended on the capacity of indebtedness or the support of the State.

The reconstruction of the family life trajectory of the ladies of the first generation and their strategies exemplifies how the social and reproductive systems put in place to survive as a household take the form of tactics, putting their family and kinship networks into operation, demonstrating their capacity for individual and collective agency.

Generationally, changes in the types and forms of households are identified; they are dynamic households that change their composition as part of the kinship and family support networks. The first generation with only one marriage, a secondary economic role, although no less important, but within the priority household. Second generations of one or more unions, in the cases of second unions, are unions with shared responsibilities, unlike the first ones. And the third generation with an independent life, living in an apartment with roommates, or who at their parents' age still live in the dwelling with them, at ages when they already had families and independent life.

Households change generationally; the same household goes through different types of households over time, depending on the life cycle of its members and according to their socioeconomic stratum and context. In this temporal dimension of households, the vertical dimension (practices and intergenerational transmission) intersects with the horizontal dimension, which, understanding the household as a unit of input and production, makes it possible to observe the exchanges, what enters and leaves the household, through practices and generational transmission.

NOTES

1. Must have attained the age of majority, over 18 years old in Costa Rica.
2. This is a welfare pension granted by the social security without the need to have contributed to the system

REFERENCES

Ariño, M. (2005). Composición de la familia en la Argentina actual: allegamiento de núcleos conyugales secundarios. In S. Torrado (Ed.), *Trayectorias nupciales, familias ocultas (Buenos Aires, entresiglos)* (pp. 257–286). Buenos Aires: Ciepp, Cátedra Demografía Social FCS-UBA, Miño y Dávila.

Ariño, M. (2007). Familias tradicionales, nuevas familias. In S. Torrado (Ed.), *Población y bienestar en la Argentina del primero al segundo centenario* (pp. 255–284). Buenos Aires: Edhasa.

Ariza, M., & de Oliveira, O. (2003). Acerca de las familias y los hogares: estructura y dinámica. In C. Wainerman (Ed.), *Familia, trabajo y género. Un mundo de nuevas relaciones* (pp. 19–54). Argentina: Fondo de Cultura Económica de Argentina.

Barquero, J., & Trejos, J. D. (2005). Tipos de hogar, ciclo de vida familiar y pobreza en Costa Rica, 1987-2002. In R. Chinchilla (Ed.), *Población y salud en Mesoamérica* (pp. 323–357). San José: Centro Centroamericano de Población.

Bourdieu, P. (2013). *Las estrategias de la reproducción social* (Primera, 1a reimpr. ed.). Buenos Aires: Siglo Veintiuno Editores.

Chacón, F. (1995). La historia de la familia. Debates metodológicos y problemas conceptuales. *Revista Internacional de Sociología, 11*, 5.

Hareven, T. (1995). Historia de la familia y la complejidad del cambio social. *Revista de Demografía Histórica-Journal of Iberoamerican Population Studies, 13*(1), 99–150.

Lesthaeghe, R. (2010). The unfolding story of the second demographic transition. *Population and Development Review, 36*(2), 211–251.

Pérez, H. (2010). *La población de Costa Rica, 1750-2000: una historia experimental*. Costa Rica: Editorial Universidad de Costa Rica.

Quilodrán, J. (2011). La familia, referentes en transición. In J. Quilodrán (Ed.), *Parejas conyugales en transformación: una visión al finalizar el siglo XX* (pp. 53–98).México: El Colegio de México, Centro de Estudios Demográficos, Urbanos y Ambientales.

Raimondi, M., & Street, M. C. (2005). Cambios y continuidades en la primera unión de las mujeres hacia fines del XX. In S. Torrado (Ed.), *Trayectorias nupciales, familias ocultas* (Buenos Aires, entresiglos) (pp. 75–117). Buenos Aires: Ciepp, Cátedra Demografía Social FCS-UBA, Miño y Dávila.

Segalen, M. (1992). *Antropología histórica de la familia.* Madrid: Taurus.

Street, M. (2004). Disolución conyugal, organización familiar y condiciones de vida. Aportes para su comprensión. *Revista Argentina de Sociología, 2*(2), 43–66.

Taylor, S., & Bogdan, R. (1987). *Introducción a los métodos cualitativos de investigación. La búsqued de significados.* España: Paidós.

Torrado, S. (2003). *Historia de la familia en la Argentina moderna (1870–2000).* Buenos Aires: Ediciones de la Flor.

Torrado, S. (2005). Algunas precisiones metodológicas. In S. Torrado (Ed.), *Trayectorias nupciales, familias ocultas (Buenos Aires, entresiglos)* (pp. 21-34). Buenos Aires: Ciepp, Cátedra Demografía Social FCS-UBA, Miño y Dávila.

Valles, M. (1999). *Técnicas cualitativas de investigación social. Reflexión metodológica y práctica profesional.* España: Síntesis.

CHAPTER 9

WHAT DIFFERENCE DOES MARRIAGE MAKE? LIFE COURSE TRAJECTORIES AND THE TRANSITION TO MARRIAGE FOR GAY MEN AND LESBIANS

Aaron Hoy

ABSTRACT

Research on same-sex marriage has suggested that the transition to marriage is a symbolically meaningful experience that significantly changes sexual minority lives. This chapter draws upon semi-structured, in-depth interviews with 28 married gay men and lesbians to examine how the life course trajectories they took en route to marriage shaped their experiences transitioning to marriage. A description of the short and direct and long and winding trajectories to marriage is provided. Subsequently, it is demonstrated that, although those who took the former report experiences much like those documented by research thus far, those who took the latter had smaller wedding ceremonies to which they attach relatively little meaning, and they report that getting married has done little to change their family relationships. These findings paint a more nuanced picture of the transition to same-sex marriage than has been documented to-date, and point to important directions for future research.

Keywords: Gay; lesbian; life course trajectory; marriage; meaning; relationship formation

Conjugal Trajectories: Relationship Beginnings, Change, and Dissolutions
Contemporary Perspectives in Family Research, Volume 22, 175–194
Copyright © 2023 by Emerald Publishing Limited
All rights of reproduction in any form reserved
ISSN: 1530-3535/doi:10.1108/S1530-353520230000022009

INTRODUCTION

During the campaign for marriage equality in the United States, scholars and activists often advocated for equal marriage rights by highlighting the many ways that marriage would positively impact sexual minorities. For instance, liberal, rights-based arguments often emphasized that marriage would allow sexual minorities to access crucial legal rights, including those related to taxation, inheritance, healthcare, and parenting (Eskridge & Spedale, 2006; Sullivan, 1996). Proponents even popularized the fact (which others disputed) that there are 1,049 specific rights attached to marriage (Cherlin 2009a). In addition, many marriage equality advocates argued that because marriage is associated with better psychological, physical, and financial well-being, extending equal marriage rights would improve the lives sexual minority individuals (e.g., Chauncey, 2004; Eskridge & Spedale, 2006; Herdt & Kertzner, 2006; Wolfson, 2005). To be sure, others were critical of this framing, arguing that a narrow focus on the individual benefits of marriage obscures the fundamental issue of equality before the law (see Herdt & Kertzner, 2006; Kitzinger & Wilkinson, 2004). Still, the argument was "recycled on LGBT websites and in equal marriage campaigning documents and regularly [made] an appearance in media and political debate" due in large part to the fact that it was "rhetorically effective" (Kitzinger & Wilkinson, 2004, p. 186).

In 2015, the US Supreme Court legalized same-sex marriage nationwide with its decision in *Obergefell v. Hodges*. Following this, scholars have begun to examine the ways that sexual minorities are impacted by the transition to marriage, generally finding that as predicted, marriage benefits sexual minority individuals in various ways. In addition to offering many legal rights, research suggests that marriage also strengthens same-sex relationships (Rosenfeld, 2014) and leads to deeper levels of commitment (Green, 2010; Schecter, Tracy, Page, & Luong, 2008). In addition, getting married can lead to improved family relationships for sexual minorities, many of whom struggle with distant or hostile relationships with biological family (Green, 2010; Schecter et al., 2008; but see Ocobock, 2013). Early research also shows that marriage is associated with better psychological well-being, including lower levels of depression and internalized homophobia (LeBlanc, Frost, & Bowen, 2018; Wight, LeBlanc, & Badgett, 2013).

Given these findings, it is likely unsurprising that the transition to marriage appears to be a deeply meaningful, even profound experience for most sexual minority individuals (Kimport, 2014; Schecter et al., 2008). For instance, Kimport (2014) shows that gay men and lesbians who married during the Winter of Love in 2004 were emotionally overwhelmed, often in ways they did not expect, by the wedding ceremony and the support they received from others upon marrying. In addition, Schecter et al. (2008) report that same-sex couples often use words like "powerful" and "profound" to describe the ways that getting married impacted them, revealing "the deep emotional scaffolding underlying the social and legal legitimacy, recognition, and protection that marriage affords" (p. 413). Overall, with relatively few exceptions, the existing research supports the conclusion that the transition to marriage is a significant life-course transition that instigates many meaningful changes in the lives of sexual minority individuals.

Still, given the short history of marriage equality in the United States, research on same-sex marriage is only beginning to develop, and such research has yet to fully explore the complexity and diversity of sexual minority individuals' experiences with marriage. In this chapter, I seek to draw a more nuanced picture of how sexual minority individuals experience the transition to marriage. Drawing on semi-structured, in-depth interviews with 28 currently married gay men and lesbians, I highlight the key role that participants' relationship trajectories played in shaping their transitions to marriage. Informed by the life-course perspective, I show that those who took relatively short and straightforward trajectories *en route* to marriage – what I term a *short and direct trajectory* – did experience the transition to marriage as profoundly meaningful and impactful. I show that for these participants, the wedding ceremony was often a lavish and symbolically meaningful event and that getting married often led to, among other things, closer family relationships. However, I also show that those who took longer and more complex trajectories – what I term a *long and winding trajectory* – tended to experience the transition to marriage as relatively insignificant and unable to or unnecessary for transforming how others, including family members, see and treat them. This latter group demonstrates that although the transition into a same-sex marriage can be the profound experience early research has documented, these experiences are far from universal. I argue that by drawing attention to the ways that marital experiences are patterned – in this case, by life-course trajectories – the findings I present below offer a useful direction for future research on same-sex marriage.

LITERATURE REVIEW

Transitioning into a Same-Sex Marriage

It is important to recognize that not all sexual minority individuals choose to marry. In fact, many actively resist the heteronormativity and sexism they associate with the institution of marriage (e.g., Bernstein & Taylor, 2013), although such resistance does appear to have been tempered somewhat by legal marriage equality (Humble, 2013; Ocobock, 2018a). Still, among those who do marry, early research shows that the transition to marriage often brings with it significant improvements in the lives of sexual minority individuals. For instance, research shows that getting married is associated with increased feelings of inclusion and acceptance as well as decreased feelings of stigma and discrimination among sexual minorities (e.g., Badgett, 2011; Green, 2010; Kimport, 2014; LeBlanc et al., 2018; Schecter et al., 2008). As noted above, marriage is also associated better overall psychological well-being, including decreased internalized homophobia and depression (LeBlanc et al., 2018; Riggle, Rostosky, & Horne, 2010; Wight et al., 2013). Based on a sample of sexual minorities in Texas, Sutton and Scotch (2020) show that compared to those who remain unmarried, married sexual minorities also report higher quality of life, including greater financial security and access to healthcare. Even following the legalization of same-sex marriage, stigma against sexual minorities remains pervasive and thus may mitigate the extent to which sexual minority individuals benefit from the transition to marriage (Reczek, Liu, & Wilkinson, 2020). However, research does suggest that these benefits are significant enough to help offset longstanding inequalities between sexual minorities and heterosexuals in terms of well-being (Wight et al., 2013).

To date, qualitative research has suggested that the transition to marriage is an emotionally intense, even overwhelming experience for sexual minorities (Green, 2010; Kimport, 2014; Richman, 2014). Historically excluded from the institution, sexual minority individuals who marry often find the experience very meaningful, sometimes surprisingly so. For instance, Kimport's (2014) research reveals that many are surprised by how emotional they become during and immediately after getting married. Furthermore, Kimport (2014) shows that many have such a reaction because getting married leads them to feel accepted and included in society, often for the first time. For this reason, Kimport (2014) argues that for sexual minorities, the transition to marriage often reveals "the hidden injuries of homophobia."

Related, research also suggests that the transition to marriage can change how sexual minority individuals are seen and treated by others (Kimport, 2014; Ocobock, 2013). In particular, much of the research thus far focuses specifically on family members, given that relationships with biological family members are often difficult or distant for sexual minorities as a result of homophobia (Reczek, 2016). For instance, based on qualitative interviews with gay men in Iowa, Ocobock (2013) shows that getting married often leads to improved family relationships as family members offer increased support and greater inclusion in family activities following the transition to marriage. Research also suggests that sexual minority individuals receive increased support from friends (Ocobock, 2018a), co-workers (Kimport, 2014), and those working in the wedding industry (Humble, 2016) during and immediately after the transition to marriage.

Thus far, scholars have tended to argue that the emotional experience of getting married and the changes in how others see and treat sexual minorities both reflect the symbolic significance attached to the institution of marriage (Green, 2010; Kimport, 2014; Ocobock, 2013). Although marriage rates are declining overall, marriage is still culturally constructed as the most esteemed relationship form (Cherlin, 2004, 2009b), and as a result, the transition to marriage can often legitimize intimate relationships, making them seem more serious and therefore respectable to others (Cherlin, 2009b; Rosenbury, 2013). From a critical perspective, some scholars argue that such experiences reflect the workings of heteronormativity (Green, 2010; Kimport, 2014). That is, the experience of acceptance and support upon marrying is predicated on the normativity associated with marriage, which has historically been a heterosexual relationship form. As Kimport (2014) puts it, the way sexual minority individuals experience the transition to marriage "demonstrates the potency of marital status to cue the legitimacy of family relationships, and thus the deep connection between heteronormativity and marriage" (p. 105).

However, it is important to note that marriage is likely a more complex and varied experience than early research on same-sex marriage has documented thus far. In this chapter, I focus specifically on the transition to marriage – that is, the time period immediately before and after a same-sex couples gets married – and explore how this transition varies based on the life- course trajectories that sexual minority individuals take *en route* to marriage. I explore how these trajectories shape the transition to marriage because same-sex marriage was only recently legalized nationwide and as a result, many same-sex couples who are married today were in a relationship with their spouse for many years prior to getting married. For instance, Rothblum, Balsam, and Solomon (2008) report that in a sample of 101 sexual minority men and 120 sexual minority women who married in California, the men had been with their spouse for an average of almost 15 years prior to getting married, and the women had been with their spouse for an average of almost 9 years before they married. In comparison, heterosexual couples typically marry after having been together for an average of two to three years (Frances-Tan & Mialon, 2015). As such, many sexual minority individuals make the transition to marriage following life- course trajectories that were often much longer than is typical for married couples overall.

Furthermore, many sexual minorities enter into legal marriage after having already had their relationship legally recognized in one way or another. In the lead-up to legal marriage equality in the United States, many states offered alternative forms of legal relationship recognition such as domestic partnerships or civil unions, which granted same-sex couples many of the same rights that come with marriage (Rothblum et al., 2008; Willetts, 2011). In addition, these forms of relationship recognition offered couples some degree of legitimacy, despite being legally separate from marriage (Wienke & Hill, 2009). Either as a way of celebrating legal relationship recognition or not, many sexual minorities marry after having had a commitment ceremony, as well. Prior to marriage equality, these ceremonies, which often borrow elements from traditional, heterosexual weddings, allowed same-sex couples to publicly declare their commitment to the relationship outside of marriage (Hull, 2006; Lewin, 1999). To be sure, these experiences are likely to be somewhat unique to the first cohort of same-sex marriages in the United States, but for the same-sex couples in that cohort, they likely shape how they experience the transition to marriage.

Life-Course Trajectories and Transitions

As stated above, my objective in this article is to use qualitative data from in-depth interviews to paint a nuanced picture of the transition to marriage for sexual minority individuals by documenting the decisive role that life-course trajectories play in shaping the experience and meaning of this transition for a sample of currently married gay men and lesbians. Although the results I present here do raise key questions for future research, my goal is not to build on or refine existing theories. Still, my focus on both the transition to marriage and life-course trajectories is informed by the life-course perspective (e.g., Elder, Johnson, & Crosnoe, 2003). In particular, the life-course concept of "trajectories" refers to the patterns of stability and change over time within individual lives (Clipp, Pavalko, & Elder, 1992; Elder 1985). Elder (1998) argues that lives are comprised of multiple, overlapping trajectories across various domains. For instance, an individual's trajectory within the domain of family might involve forming a committed relationship, cohabitation, getting married, and/or getting divorced. Thus, life-course trajectories can involve multiple, sequentially ordered transitions, defined as key life events that chart the course of life course trajectories (Elder, 1985; George, 1993). Especially significant transitions, such as the transition to marriage, are often described as "turning points" in the life course perspective (Elder, 1985, 1998; Elder et al., 2003).

Here, I strike a distinction between two trajectories. The first is what I term the *short and direct trajectory*. Along this trajectory, an individual's relationship moves swiftly to marriage, following a common, even normative path from the initial formation of the relationship to marriage. For this article, I conducted qualitative interviews with 28 currently married gay men and lesbians. Of these 28 participants, 11 took the short and direct trajectory. These 11 participants were with their spouses 3.9 years, on average, prior to getting married, which is comparable to the national average for all married couples (see Frances-Tan & Mialon, 2015). To the extent that getting married within the first several years of a relationship is expected and normative (see Carlson, 2012; Sharp & Ganong, 2007), participants who took the short and direct trajectory adhered to this norm. For them, getting married was, in general, a very meaningful and impactful experience. Many describe the transition to marriage as one that brought them great happiness and continues to hold meaning for them today. Even further, many claim that getting married brought about changes in their relationships with others. For instance, nearly all participants who took the short and direct trajectory also described the transition to marriage as one that strengthened their family relationships, even those that had weak or distant beforehand. Thus, for these participants, the experience of getting married was quite like those documented in the existing research.

However, I compare these experiences to those of participants who took the long and winding trajectory. This is a trajectory along which a relationship passes many milestones. In total, 17 of the 28 participants took this trajectory. These individuals had been with their spouses an average of 16.3 years prior to getting married, although some had been together for as many as 41 years (Leonard). Again, such lengthy trajectories to marriage appear more common among sexual minorities given the fact that until recently, they were legally barred from the institution of marriage. Furthermore, taking the long and winding trajectory often involved experiences with legal relationship recognition of one sort or another. Among participants who took this trajectory, eight had registered a domestic partnership before legal marriage was an option in their home state; by comparison, no one who took the short and direct trajectory had registered a domestic partnership prior to getting married. Doing so granted participants and their partners (now spouses) legal rights as well as recognition and legitimacy from others. Ten participants who took the long and winding trajectory also had a commitment ceremony prior to getting married; no participants who took the short and direct trajectory did so. Having a commitment ceremony was a way for participants to publicly commit to the relationship and to garner at least some degree of recognition and legitimacy for the relationship. Altogether, experiencing a domestic partnership, a commitment ceremony, or both prior to getting legally married made these participants' trajectories to marriage not only longer but also more complex.

Compared to participants who took the short and direct trajectory, the transition to marriage was less meaningful for those who took the long and winding trajectory. To be sure, most described getting married as a positive experience. Many said that they married for legal rights and tax benefits, which they did receive upon marrying. However, for these participants, the transition to marriage did not carry the same symbolic weight that it did for others. In fact, many described the experience as a formality, a positive and fun experience that was, in the end, mostly unnecessary. Thus, for these participants, the transition to legal marriage did little to initiate change in their family relationships.

In the sections below, I compare how participants who took these two different trajectories experienced the transition to marriage. In the first section, I show how they had unique wedding experiences. According to existing research, because the wedding ceremony formally initiates the transition to marriage, it is often a deeply meaningful, even overwhelming experience for heterosexual and sexual minority individuals alike (Kimport, 2014; Otnes & Pleck, 2003). In general, those who took the short and direct trajectory had much larger, even lavish weddings that, in some cases, continue to hold deep symbolic meaning. By contrast, those who took the long and winding trajectory had much smaller weddings that tended to carry less meaning. In the second section, I examine the different ways in which the transition to marriage did, or did not, transform participants' lives. For those who took the short and direct trajectory, getting married strengthened their family relationships. However, those who took the long and winding trajectory found that marriage made few differences for them, and for some, this was a source of disappointment or hurt. Based on these findings, I argue that the transition is a more complex and varied experience than research has documented thus far, and that these findings point to important directions for future research.

METHODS

As noted above, in this chapter, I take a qualitative approach by drawing upon semi-structured, in-depth interviews with a non-random convenience sample of 28 currently married gay men and lesbians. By focusing on "where they live imaginatively," in-depth interviews allow researchers to see how participants experience and make sense of social phenomena (Lamont & Swidler, 2014, p. 159). In this chapter, I focus specifically on how participants experience and make sense of the transition to marriage, and how this is shaped by the life course trajectories that participants took leading into marriage. Anyone 18 years of age or older who currently married to a same-sex spouse was invited to participate in an interview. After receiving Institutional Review Board approval, I distributed recruitment materials through my personal and professional networks and through the assistance of non-profit and advocacy organizations that serve sexual minorities. I also posted recruitment materials in coffee shops, grocery stores, hair salons, and community centers in several cities across Upstate New York.

In total, 28 individuals agree to an interview, all of which were conducted between February and September of 2017. Of these, 22 were conducted over the telephone; six were conducted in-person at a location chosen by the participant. Although in-person interviews are often considered preferable given that they allow researchers to observe facial expressions and other non-verbal ques, telephone interviews do give participants greater anonymity, which can be important to members of stigmatized groups, including sexual minorities (Pfeffer, 2010). During the interview, participants were asked about a broad range of topics, including their relationship history (both before and after getting married), what they see as the strengths and weaknesses of their marriage, various marital arrangements and dynamics (e.g., the distribution of housework, decision-making, sex), and the impact that getting married had on their family-of-origin relationships. Because the interviews were semi-structured, however, participants were also encouraged to talk openly about their experiences with marriage. To improve the accuracy and reliability of the data, participants were also encouraged to talk in specific and concrete terms (see Weiss, 1994). For instance, when participants described a general pattern that they have observed in their relationship, I would often follow-up with, "Can you tell me about a specific time that happened?" I also asked for clarification and confirmation throughout each interview to assess the accuracy of my understanding and interpretations. In the end, interviews lasted, on average, approximately 90 minutes in total.

Of the 28 sexual minority individuals who were interviewed for this article, all identified as either gay or lesbian. For this reason, I refer to "gay men and lesbians," rather than sexual minorities more broadly, when describing my own results below, as they may not apply to a significant number of sexual minorities, including most significantly those who identify as bisexual. In addition, 16 participants are women, and 12 are men; all 28 are cisgender. In terms of race, one participant is Asian American, one is Native American, and the remaining 26 are all White. As such, the results I present here also may not apply to gay men and lesbians of color. In terms of education, the sample is generally well-educated, with 22 of the 28 participants having completed a four-year college degree. In addition, 15 hold an advanced degree such as a MA, Ph.D., or JD. Although participants hold various occupations, the education level of the sample as a whole is another limitation. However, this may reflect the fact that marriage rates, including those among sexual minorities, are increasingly divergent by socioeconomic status, with those who are better off marrying more often than those who are worse off (Cherlin, 2009b; Gates, 2015). In terms of age, the sample is relatively diverse, with participants ranging from 28- to 78- years old at the time of the interview.

In terms of relationship duration, participants had been married, on average, approximately four years at the time of the interview, although a few had been married for less than a year. Although participants had been in a relationship with their spouse, on average, just over 11 years when they married, as I emphasize throughout this chapter, there was significant variation, with some taking a short and direct trajectory to marriage and others taking a long and winding trajectory. Finally, it is worth noting that eight couples are also included in the sample, such that 20 marriages (and not 28) are represented in the results below. However, my unit of analysis remains the individual, not the couple, given that married couples can and often do have unique experiences and understandings of the relationship they share.

All interviews were audio-recorded using a digital recorder and then transcribed verbatim. All identifying information was removed during the transcription process. Because I took an inductive approach loosely informed by grounded theory (Charmaz, 2006), I began analyzing the data before completing data collection. I began by reading through interview transcripts multiple times each, doing several rounds of open coding, and writing memos on emergent themes. Early in the analysis, relationship histories became a significant theme, and as a result, I incorporated additional questions about the history of the participant's relationship into the interview guide. Through subsequent interviews and analysis, including additional coding and memo-writing, the short and direct trajectory and the long and winding trajectory both emerged as native concepts. Once data collection was complete, participants were categorized as having followed one of the two trajectories, and through a final round of focused coding and memo-writing, the different ways that each experienced the transition to marriage came into focus.

RESULTS

Wedding Ceremonies on the Short and Direct Trajectory

During their interviews, participants who took the short and direct trajectory recalled their weddings with fondness. Many said that the experience brings them happiness and joy even today. In general, they described weddings that were of considerable size and sophistication, often using words like "big," "beautiful," and "gorgeous." For example, after being in a relationship for two years, Charity (28) proposed to her then-girlfriend, and when she accepted, the couple quickly began planning their wedding. According to Charity, it was lavish. It was held at a new, upscale events center in a major Midwestern city. Hundreds of guests attended, and they all celebrated her marriage by singing and dancing at the reception afterward. "It was so big and beautiful," Charity said. "It was the happiest day of my life."

Similarly, James (42) talked at length about his wedding, which took place at a historic church in the downtown area of his home city. Hundreds of people attended the ceremony, after which they relocated to a nearby hotel for the reception. "Our wedding was absolutely beautiful," he said.

> And we had this big, huge, beautiful reception at a hotel downtown right next to the church. There were a lot of people, good food, and drinks. Everybody had a really good time. It was very special.

Although nearly all participants who took the short and direct trajectory described their weddings in this way, the one exception was Martin (40), who holds a high school diploma and works in retail. Given his limited income, he and his husband were unable to afford the larger, more elaborate weddings that other participants had. But even so, Martin recalled his more modest wedding with fondness. "It was a really great time," he said. "I know for me, it was very special." Thus, all participants who took the short and direct trajectory, including Martin, described wedding experiences that were quite positive. For most, the wedding even exceeded their expectations.

Furthermore, participants who took this trajectory attached significant meaning to their weddings. For some participants, the wedding was meaningful because family members, including some who had previously been either distant or hostile, agreed to attend. For these participants, the wedding made them feel accepted and supported by their families. For instance, Charity had had a difficult relationship with her step-father prior to her wedding. He had been emotionally distant, and at times, he struggled to accept her identity as a lesbian. But after a discussion with Charity's mother, with whom Charity has always felt close, he agreed to attend. Having both her mother and step-father in attendance made the wedding very meaningful to her. As she put it,

> For my mom to be there, crying and supportive, was great. It meant the world to me. And my step-dad was there, too, and he was very supportive. That was kind of a big deal to me, and it meant a lot.

Martin attached significant meaning to his more modest wedding for similar reasons. His parents are devoutly religious, and when Martin came out as gay many years ago, they reacted with hostility. As he explained,

> Early on, they would definitely make remarks like, "Oh, our son's soul is in jeopardy." And you know, "This will cause him to go to hell." And they would email me like, "We didn't raise you this way."

Given these experiences, Martin did not expect his parents to attend his wedding, but they did. "You know, just a few years ago, they were all about the Bible or their religious beliefs," he said.

> And that prevented them from supporting me or my relationship...But they showed up to the wedding. I couldn't believe it. It just blew me away. I was, like, in shock.

Although she does not focus on her family members specifically, the fact that so many people attended Diana's (47) wedding made it a meaningful experience for her, too. Like other participants who took the short and direct trajectory, Diana had a wedding that was extravagant. "Even today," she said, "there are times when I wake up and it's like, 'Did that really happen? Did we really have that wedding? Or was that some kind of weird dream?'" Looking back, Diana feels as though she attaches such meaning to the experience because so many people agreed to attend and offered their support. She said,

> We kissed each other and we said these vows, and we did it in front of all these people. We were so vulnerable at that moment. But that's what made it such a great experience that sometimes I can't believe it really happened.

Wedding Ceremonies on the Long and Winding Trajectory

In contrast, participants who took the long and winding trajectory had wedding experiences that were positive but less meaningful experiences overall. Most had wedding ceremonies that were relatively small. Often, they did little planning or preparation. For these participants, the bigger, more lavish weddings that those who took the short and direct trajectory had were unnecessary, or even unwanted, precisely because they had been together for so long before they married. For instance, Carol (64) and her wife had been together for 21 years by the time they got married. Because of their lengthy relationship history, Carol did not feel that a large or elaborate wedding was necessary. "The only thing we really wanted was to go to Niagara Falls," she said.

> So we...went to New York and did it. Nobody really came. The wedding itself was just two friends with us. We had a small dinner with some family and our circle of friends when we got back. But we didn't want any more than that.

Similarly, Annabel (45) said that she felt little need to have a large or extravagant wedding. "I've been involved with really big weddings," she said. "And that just didn't feel necessary to me, not after all this time together." In fact, she had been involved with her siblings' weddings, which she remembered requiring a lot of work and help from others, and she knew she did not want such an experience for her own wedding. She said,

> We just kind of said, "Hey, we want to be married, so we're getting married." And then I kind of planned the whole thing myself. I didn't need it to be this big event, so I could do it myself, no problems really.

Like Annabel, Jeff (40) wanted a smaller, more intimate wedding. As he recounted during his interview, when his then-boyfriend entered a drawing to win an all-expenses-paid destination wedding, Jeff sat him down to explain that he did not want such a big and elaborate wedding.

> I told him, like, "I don't want that." We didn't need that anyway. What's the point? I said, "I just want sun on an island alone, by ourselves." I kind of thought, like, "We deserve to get away just the two of us after all these years."

Jeff's husband agreed, and the couple decided to get married in a small ceremony at an island resort. "We got an elopement package for, like, $200...It included everything, and it was a great time. I'm glad we did that, just the two of us."

In addition to having smaller, more modest weddings, participants who took the long and winding trajectory attached less meaning to these experiences. For many, this was because they had felt as though they were married, for all intents and purposes, even before the wedding. For instance, Leonard (78) and his husband had been together for 41 years by the time they married. The couple did very little planning for their wedding and had few guests present for their ceremony at City Hall in New York City. In fact, the only other person in attendance was Leonard's mother-in-law. Leonard said,

We just didn't feel like planning a big ceremony and didn't think we needed to. We'd been together a really long time at that point. We knew our love for one another, and I think most of our friends and family did too. After 41 years, we were basically married anyway.

Similarly, Barry (52) and his husband had been together for 16 years when they finally got married. According to Barry, it was because they had such a long relationship history that they decided to have a small, intimate wedding. He said:

Again, we had it in our minds that we've been married all these years just like any straight couple you know or same-sex couple that could get married…So in talking with Wes' sister who lives in Cape Cod, Massachusetts, she was like, 'Guys, I've been telling you guys for years, just get married here. Get married right on the beach outside my house, and we can have the reception right in my backyard.' So we decided to do that. We went down to Cape Cod and had the ceremony and just a small dinner with a few of our friends from Massachusetts. It was nice but you know, it wasn't practical to get everyone down there from up here.

According to Barry, having been together for so many years prior to marriage, he and his husband had come to feel as if they were married anyway. Because of this, they had, as Barry recounted, a positive wedding experience, but one that lacked significant meaning. Similarly, Dean (46) said,

You know after 13 years, it's kind of funny. Like, after all these years, it was just, like, a little bit more relaxed. You know, we were basically living our lives like we were married anyway. We'd already had our shared checking accounts, shared everything, so by that point, you know, it was kind of about having a legal document.

Thus, according to Dean, his wedding was small and less meaningful because, like Leonard and Barry, he felt that he was already married.

Along the long and winding trajectory, many had also had a commitment ceremony. This, too, led some to have smaller weddings that were, in general, less meaningful. For many, having had a commitment ceremony made the wedding feel unnecessary or even redundant. For instance, Angela (45) and her wife had been together for 10 years before they got married, during which time they had had a commitment ceremony. According to Angela, that experience was big and quite meaningful. She said,

It was huge. We had about 100 people there. Both sets of parents were there, family and friends. We had a big banquet and a dinner, too. It was a really special event. I know it meant a lot to me. It made me feel like I was legitimately married.

However, when I asked Angela about her wedding, she responded simply with, "We eloped." As Angela explained, having another big ceremony, even if it would celebrate their transition into legal marriage, seemed unnecessary. "To me, it was a formality of legality," she said.

It was one of those things where it was now legal to do so. It gave us more rights and benefits, so we went ahead and did the legal thing. But we didn't need to go all out just for that.

In fact, Angela and her wife only told their parents after the fact. She said,

We called both sets of parents after we legally did it, and both of them said, "Why did you do that? It doesn't make any sense, you're already married." And we were. We'd already had the commitment ceremony.

Jessica (39) also said that she and her wife chose to have a "really small wedding" because they had already had a commitment ceremony. "We didn't need a big, huge party," she said.

> So we had a little thing. We had our big celebration several years back, when we had the commitment ceremony. That was the big one, so we didn't need to do that again.

Jessica and her wife had their wedding at their home. A few family members and friends attended, and they had a cake and a small dinner afterward. It was a positive experience, but one to which Jessica attaches little meaning. "I went back to work on Monday," she said.

Overall, then, taking the long and winding trajectory led many to establish long-term relationships that they experienced as marriages even though they were legally excluded from the institution of marriage. In this sense, participants performed marriage culturally (see Hull, 2006), including by having a commitment ceremony. However, once they were granted access to legal marriage, these experiences of already performing marriage led them to have smaller, more intimate weddings to which they attached relatively little meaning. As several of participants explained, their weddings were positive but unnecessary rituals that simply confirmed, in a legal sense, their status as married.

Family Relationships and Dynamics on the Short and Direct Trajectory

Participants who took the short and direct trajectory not only had larger and more meaningful weddings but also felt that getting married led to more significant changes in their lives. In particular, these participants said that as a result of getting married, they developed closer relationships with family members, especially their parents, and that they were more included in their families. As with their weddings, those who took the short and direct trajectory tended to say that such changes in their family relationships and dynamics were very meaningful to them.

For instance, Bethany (28) explained that before getting married, she had a difficult relationship with her father. "My dad really struggled when I came out," she said. "I think, you know, he had this vision that I would end up marrying a man, so he was pretty slow to come around." Despite his desire to see his daughter marry a man, Bethany felt that her father became more accepting of her identity as a lesbian when she announced her plans to marry.

> I think us getting married really helped him. It helped him a lot, actually. He really came around once we started planning the wedding because he could see how happy I was.

This was especially meaningful to Bethany because she values strong family relationships. She said,

> It meant the world to me when he came around. I'm really close with my family…so when my dad came out of that shell, it meant a lot to me. It made everything with my family finally feel right.

Bethany's wife, Charity, had a similar experience with her father. Before they were married, Charity had a somewhat distant relationship with her father, whom she describes as "emotionless." However, as she explained, getting married "opened a door" for their relationship. During a conversation not long after the engagement was announced, Charity's father said that he accepts her relationship and wants her to be happy, no matter what. "To have that as I'm getting ready to get married," Charity said,

> was really special for me. I think he maybe wasn't OK with the marrying a woman thing, but him saying that he wants me to be happy was really special.

Martin said that many members of his family, not only his parents, have become more accepting of him and have welcomed him into the family as a result of his getting married. Before getting married, Martin's family members, who are all religious, had frequently expressed homophobic views, which caused a rift between Martin and his family. Upon getting married, though, his family changed. "They've been great ever since then," he said. "They've been very supportive." This has allowed Martin to feel like a part of his family for the first time. He is especially happy that he now gets to spend time with the children in his family. He said,

> I feel like we've created a whole new family. I mean, I guess that some people would call their family their best friends. I'm one of them now. Some of the kids in the family call me Uncle Marty now, which they never did before. That's really cool. That means a lot to me.

Similarly, Diana explained that after getting married, she and her wife were included in one another's family for the first time. She said,

> My mother-in-law views me as her other daughter basically. And my mom views my spouse as her daughter-in-law but also, you know, like part of the family. And my step-father, also…we've been very included.

Diana attributes these changes to her family relationships and dynamics to marriage and its ability to change the way others see and treat others and their relationship. She said,

> Getting married and you know, the wedding, was a big part of that. Like, that helped them understand that, like, we are making this commitment, and it's not just a commitment to each other – it's, like, a commitment to being a part of this family and our community together.

Life Changes on the Long and Winding Trajectory

Compared to those who took the short and direct trajectory, participants who took the long and winding trajectory felt that marriage led to far fewer changes in their lives. As they explained it, their longer and more complex relationship histories rendered the transition to marriage less impactful. Unlike those who took the short and direct trajectory, these participants found that their families were generally supportive of their marriage but were less vocal or enthusiastic about their support. For instance, Brad (46) said that his family reacted positively when he and his husband married. However, most felt as though they should have married long before they did. "I think everyone was really happy for us," he said.

But at the same time, you know, they all thought it was a long time coming. My mother said, "It's about time." And you know, my cousins were all, you know, "It's about time." My whole family was very much that way, yeah. His family was, too.

Similarly, Kim (60) said,

Everybody wondered why it took so long. They were happy for us, but seriously, they were like, "Oh, great surprise!" Like, "Who didn't see that coming?" So, they all knew it was coming."

Given such reactions, it is likely unsurprising that getting married did not lead to significant changes in their family relationships or dynamics.

According to some participants, this reflects the fact that others had already begun to see them as married, even prior to their legal marriage. For instance, Susan (42), who had been with her wife 11 years before they married, explained that her family had almost no reaction to her getting married. "They had no reaction whatsoever," she said. "Like, none." When asked why, Susan said,

It was because for all these years, in their eyes, we'd been a married couple anyway. So, like, "Who cares if you're legally married now? If you have this piece of paper?"

Barry said that his family's initial reaction to his marriage was quite supportive but that it did not change his relationships with them or the dynamics between them in any way. "I don't think it really changed anything," he said.

Again, we'd been together for many years at that point. Everybody treated us like we were married before we went down [to get married]. So, they were happy we were finally married, but it didn't make any difference in their eyes, I don't think.

Some of the participants who had had a commitment ceremony pointed to these ceremonies when explaining why getting married led to few changes for them. For instance, Jane (44) said that getting married did not change anything for her, least of all her family relationships. "I mean, [my family] didn't have any response, which I thought was bizarre." According to Jane, this was because she and her wife had had a commitment ceremony several years before they married. The ceremony was a big event, and one that carried significant meaning for her and her family. However, as a result, getting married led to few changes in her family relationships or dynamics. As she explained,

So when we did our commitment ceremony, it was a big hairy deal, and everybody came in for it. And I really just think they thought, "Well, you're doing this one just for the thought of it." So, this is just a formality. We ended up having all our friends there but not our family because they all just thought, "You've done this already."

A few participants who took the long and winding trajectory also said that the fact that getting married seemed to mean relatively little to others was disappointing and hurtful for them. For instance, Kim said that she was hurt by the unenthusiastic response she received from her family after she finally got married. She said,

It was disappointing to be honest with you. We kinda thought it would be a much bigger deal to people, especially our families – our parents and siblings...I mean, getting married is still a big deal, even though we'd already had the commitment ceremony at that point. But when they didn't really say anything...that was disappointing. That was hurtful.

Similarly, when I asked Susan if she wished that her family had responded more enthusiastically to her marriage, she replied,

Oh, for sure. It was a little bit of a let-down. I mean, we'd been together for a long time, but we'd never been *married* married, you know? So, when it finally happened...I kinda hoped in the back of my mind that people would be more excited for us.

Overall, then, participants who took the long and winding trajectory found that the transition to marriage initiated few significant changes in their lives and in their relationships with others, especially their families. Many reported that others responded positively but in a way that was restrained or subdued, even less than what some had hoped for. Indeed, others seemed to attach little significance to their getting married. For some, this was because they had been together for so long before marriage. During this time, many had been seen by others as married for all intents and purposes. Others had commitment ceremonies. Whatever the reason, taking the long and winding trajectory prevented the transition to marriage from creating significant changes for them.

CONCLUSION

To date, research on same-sex marriage has portrayed the transition to marriage as a deeply meaningful experience that profoundly impacts the lives of sexual minorities (e.g., Green, 2010; Kimport, 2014; LeBlanc et al., 2018; Richman, 2014; Riggle et al., 2010; Wight et al., 2013). However, given that same-sex marriage was only legalized across the United States in 2015, research in this area is only beginning to develop and has not yet explored how the transition to marry might vary for sexual minority individuals. In this chapter, I draw upon in-depth interviews with 28 currently married gay men and lesbians to explore how the life course transitions that participants took *en route* to marriage shaped their experiences with the transition to marriage. As I show in the sections above, those who took the short and direct trajectory had experiences much like those documented thus far. They tended to have large, even lavish wedding ceremonies to which they attach significant symbolic meaning, in part because these were well-attended, including by family members who had been either distant or hostile. Furthermore, these participants reported that as a result of getting married, they grew closer to their families, including parents, extended family members, and in-laws, all of whom now include them more fully in the family. In contrast, those who took the long and winding trajectory tended to have much smaller weddings, some of them all but unplanned, to which they attach relatively little meaning either because they felt as though they were married before or because they had already had a commitment ceremony. In addition, these same participants reported that getting married did little to nothing to change how others, including family members, see and treat them. In such cases, participants said that others had seen them as married anyway, either because they had been together for so long or because they had had a commitment ceremony. As such, the transition to marriage did not catalyze the significant changes that others experienced, which some described as disappointing or hurtful. Overall, those who took the long and winding trajectory are similar to those participants in Ocobock's (2018b) research who reported that "because marriage had occurred later in the relationship they experienced little marital transition or change in their relationship dynamics" (p. 373).

It is worth noting that those who took the short and direct trajectory are, on average, younger than those who took the long and winding trajectory. The average age among participants who took the short and direct trajectory is 35.9, compared to 50.6 among those who took the long and winding trajectory. However, some who took the long and winding trajectory were relatively young and still attributed their experiences with marriage to their lengthy relationship history. For instance, Dana took the long and winding trajectory but is only 38. Thus, age may well explain some of the differences I observe, but likely not all. Most importantly, though, participants themselves saw their trajectories to marriage making all the difference; none even mentioned age during their interview.

To be clear, these findings are not meant to suggest that marriage equality is somehow unimportant. In fact, all participants made clear that they believe strongly in their right to marry, and even those who took the long and winding trajectory were adamant that getting married was a positive experience. Not least of all, it has given them legal rights that they could not access otherwise. However, these findings do illustrate that the experience of getting married is more complex and diverse among sexual minorities than has been documented thus far and that for some, the transition to marriage is not the emotionally overwhelming, transformative experience it is for others. To be sure, the long and winding trajectory I describe here likely reflects the unique circumstances of the first cohort of sexual minorities to marry in the United States. Indeed, many participants said explicitly that they would have married sooner had they been legally permitted to do so. In the future, it will likely be that what I call the short and direct trajectory will become the norm for same-sex couples, much as it is now for different-sex couples (Carlson, 2012; Sharp & Ganong, 2007).

Still, these findings are important because they offer a more nuanced picture of how this historically significant cohort has experienced the institution of marriage thus far. Furthermore, these findings are a useful reminder that average differences between married and unmarried populations can mask meaningful differences within those populations, including among sexual minorities. After all, a large and well-established body of research documents that for heterosexuals, marriage is associated with a wide range of positive outcomes, including better physical (Liu & Umberson, 2008; Waite, 1995) and psychological (for a review, see Williams, Frech, & Carlson, 2010) well-being, higher levels of income and wealth (Killewald & Gough, 2013), and longer life expectancies (for a review, see Rendall, Weden, Favreault, & Waldron, 2011). However, as scholars have recently stressed, the benefits of heterosexual marriage vary significantly by sociodemographic factors such as race, social class, and gender. In particular, Whites (e.g., Corra, Carter, Carter, & Knox, 2009), those with higher levels of income and wealth (Carlson & Kail, 2018), and men (e.g., Corra et al., 2009; Killewald &

Gough, 2013) all disproportionately benefit from marriage, relative to racial minorities, those with lower levels of income and wealth, and women, respectively. Research in this area has not yet addressed whether similar dynamics play out within same-sex marriages, too. In this chapter, I show that how married gay men and lesbians experience the transition to marriage varies based on the life course trajectories taken *en route* to marriage, but there are likely other variations that have yet to be accounted for, including perhaps those based on race, social class, and/or gender. Moving forward, scholars of same-sex marriage should be attentive to these possible variations, among others. Early research on same-sex marriages suggests that as with heterosexuals, sexual minority individuals benefit, on average, from the transition to marriage, but what variations lie underneath those averages will be important to uncover in the future.

REFERENCES

Badgett, M. V. L. (2011). Social inclusion and the value of marriage equality in Massachusetts and the Netherlands. *Journal of Social Issues, 67*(2), 316–334.

Bernstein, M., & Taylor, V. (2013). Marital discord: Understanding the contested place of marriage in the lesbian and gay movement. In M. Bernstein & V. Taylor (Eds.), *The marrying kind? Debating same-sex marriage within the lesbian and gay movement* (pp. 1–35). Minneapolis, MN: University of Minnesota Press.

Carlson, D. L. (2012). Deviations from desired age at marriage: Mental health differences across marital status. *Journal of Marriage and Family, 74*, 743–758.

Carlson, D. L., & Kail, B. L. (2018). Socioeconomic variation in the association of marriage with depressive symptoms. *Social Science Research, 71*, 85–97.

Charmaz, K. (2006). *Constructing grounded theory: A practical guide through qualitative analysis.* Thousand Oaks, CA: Sage.

Chauncey, G. (2004). Why marriage? *The surprising history shaping today's debate over gay equality.* New York: Basic.

Cherlin, A. J. (2004). The deinstitutionalization of American marriage. *Journal of Marriage and Family, 66*, 848–861.

Cherlin, A. J. (2009a). *One thousand and forty-nine reasons why it's hard to know when a fact is a fact.* Austin, TX: Council on Contemporary Families.

Cherlin, A. J. (2009b). *The marriage-go-round: The state of marriage and the family in America today.* New York: Vintage.

Clipp, E. C., Pavalko, E. K., & Elder, G. H. (1992). Trajectories of health: In concept and empirical pattern. *Behavior, Health, and Aging, 2*, 159–179.

Corra, M., Carter, S. K., Carter, J. S., & Knox, D. (2009). Trends in marital happiness by gender and race, 1973 to 2006. *Journal of Family Issues, 30*, 1379–1404.

Elder, G. H. (1985). Perspectives on the life course. In G. H. Elder (Ed.), *Life course dynamics: Trajectories and transitions, 1968*–1980 (pp. 23–49). Ithaca, NY: Cornell University Press.

Elder, G. H. (1998). The life course as developmental theory. *Child Development, 69*, 1–12.

Elder, G. H., Johnson, M. K., & Crosnoe, R. (2003). The emergence and development of life course theory. In J. T. Mortimer & M. J. Shanahan (Eds.), *Handbook of the life course* (pp. 3–19). New York: Kluwer Academic/Plenum.

Eskridge, W., & Spedale, D. (2006). *Gay marriage: For better or worse? What we've learned from the evidence.* New York: Oxford University Press.

Frances-Tan, A., & Mialon, H. M. (2015). 'A diamond is forever' and other fairy tales: The relationship between wedding expenses and marriage duration. *Economic Inquiry, 53*, 1919–1930.

Gates, G. J. (2015). *Demographics of married and unmarried same-sex couples: Analyses of the 2013 American Community Survey.* Los Angeles, CA: The Williams Institute.

George, L. K. (1993). Sociological perspectives on life transitions. *Annual Review of Sociology, 19,* 353–357.

Green, A. I. (2010). Queer unions: Same-sex spouses marrying tradition and innovation. *Canadian Journal of Sociology, 35,* 399–436.

Herdt, G., & Kertzner, R. (2006). 'I do, but I can't': The impact of marriage denial on the mental health and sexual citizenship of lesbians and gay men in the United States. *Sexuality Research & Social Policy, 3,* 33–49.

Hull, K. E. (2006). *Same-sex marriage: The cultural politics of love and law.* Cambridge: Cambridge University Press.

Humble, A. M. (2013). Moving from ambivalence to certainty: Older same-sex couples marry in Canada. *Canadian Journal on Aging, 32,* 131–144.

Humble, A. M. (2016). "She didn't bat an eye": Canadian same-sex wedding planning and support from the wedding industry. *Journal of GLBT Family Studies, 12,* 277–299.

Killewald, A., & Gough, M. (2013). Does specialization explain marriage penalties and premiums? *American Sociological Review, 78,* 477–502.

Kimport, K. (2014). *Queering marriage: Challenging family formation in the United States.* New Brunswick, NJ: Rutgers University Press.

Kitzinger, C., & Wilkinson, S. (2004). Social advocacy for equal marriage: The politics of 'rights' and the psychology of 'mental health.' *Analyses of Social Issues and Public Policy, 4,* 173–194.

Lamont, M., & Swidler, A. (2014). Methodological pluralism and the possibilities and limits of interviewing. *Qualitative Sociology, 37,* 153–171.

LeBlanc, A. J., Frost, D. M., & Bowen, K. (2018). Legal marriage, unequal recognition, and mental health among same-sex couples. *Journal of Marriage and Family, 80,* 397–408.

Lewin, E. (1999). *Recognizing ourselves: Ceremonies of lesbian and gay commitment.* New York: Columbia University Press.

Liu, H., & Umberson, D. (2008). The times they are a changin': Marital status and health differentials from 1972 to 2003. *Journal of Health and Social Behavior, 49,* 239–253.

Ocobock, A. (2013). The power and limits of marriage: Married gay men's family relationships. *Journal of Marriage and Family, 75,* 191–205.

Ocobock, A. (2018a). From public debate to private decision: The normalization of marriage among critical LGBQ people. In M. W. Yarbrough, A. Jones, & J. N. DeFilippis (Eds.), *Queer families and relationships after marriage equality* (pp. 59–72). New York: Routledge.

Ocobock, A. (2018b). Status or access? The impact of marriage on lesbian, gay, bisexual, and queer community change. *Journal of Marriage and Family, 80,* 367–382.

Otnes, C. C., & Pleck, E. (2003). *Cinderella dreams: The allure of the lavish wedding.* Berkeley, CA: University of California Press.

Pfeffer, C. A. (2010). Women's work? Women partners of transgender men doing housework and emotion work. *Journal of Marriage and Family, 72,* 165–183.

Reczek, C. (2016). Ambivalence in gay and lesbian family relationships. *Journal of Marriage and Family, 78,* 644–659.

Reczek, C., Liu, H., & Wilkinson, L. (2020). Conclusion: Future directions for research on health of sexual minority couples. In H. Liu, C. Reczek, & L. Wilkinson (Eds.), *Marriage and health: The well-being of same-sex couples* (pp. 254–262). New Brunswick, NJ: Rutgers University Press.

Rendall, M. S., Weden, M. M., Favreault, M. M., & Waldron, H. (2011). The protective effect of marriage for survival: A review and update. *Demography, 48,* 481–506.

Richman, K. D. (2014). *License to wed: What legal marriage means to same-sex couples.* New York: New York University Press.

Riggle, E. D. B., Rostosky, S. S., & Horne, S. G. (2010). Psychological distress, well-being, and legal recognition in same-sex relationships. *Journal of Family Psychology, 24,* 82–86.

Rosenbury, L. A. (2013). Marital status and privilege. *Journal of Gender, Race, and Justice, 16,* 769–791.

Rosenfeld, M. J. (2014). Couple longevity in the era of same-sex marriage in the United States. *Journal of Marriage and Family, 76,* 905–918.

Rothblum, E. D., Balsam, K. F., & Solomon, S. E. (2008). Comparison of same-sex couples who married in Massachusetts, had domestic partnerships in California, or had civil unions in Vermont. *Journal of Family Issues, 29,* 48–78.

Schecter, E., Tracy, A. J., Page, K. V., & Luong, G. (2008). Shall we marry? Legal marriage as a commitment event in same-sex relationships. *Journal of Homosexuality, 54*, 400–422.

Sharp, E. A., & Ganong, L. (2007). Living in the gray: Women's experiences of missing the marital transition. *Journal of Marriage and Family, 69*, 831–844.

Sullivan, A. (1996). *Virtually normal: An argument about homosexuality*. New York: Vintage.

Sutton, K., & Scotch, R. K. (2020). Married in Texas: Findings from an LGBT community needs assessment. In H. Liu, C. Reczek, & L. Wilkinson (Eds.), *Marriage and health: The well- being of same-sex couples* (pp. 188–198). New Brunswick, NJ: Rutgers University Press.

Waite, L. J. (1995). Does marriage matter? *Demography, 32*, 483–507.

Weiss, Robert S. (1994). *Learning from Strangers: The Art and Method of Qualitative Interview Studies*. New York, NY: The Free Press.

Wienke, C., & Hill, G. J. (2009). Does the 'marriage benefit' extend to partners in gay and lesbian relationships? Evidence from a random sample of sexually active adults. *Journal of Family Issues, 30*, 259–289.

Wight, R. G., LeBlanc, A. J., & Badgett, M. V. L. (2013). Same-sex legal marriage and psychological well-being: Findings from the California Health Interview Study. *American Journal of Public Health, 103*, 339–346.

Willetts, M. C. (2011). Registered domestic partnerships, same-sex marriage, and the pursuit of equality in California. *Family Relations, 60*, 135–149.

Williams, K., Frech, A., & Carlson, D. L. (2010). Marital status and mental health. In T. N. Brown & T. L. Scheid (Eds.), *A handbook for the study of mental health: Social contexts, theories, and systems* (pp. 306–320). New York: Cambridge University Press.

Wolfson, E. (2005). *Why marriage matters: America, equality, and gay people's right to marry*. New York: Simon & Schuster.

CHAPTER 10

IDENTIFYING PREDICTORS OF FIRST VERSUS SUBSEQUENT DIVORCE AMONG DIVORCING PARENTS

Joshua J. Turner, Olena Kopystynska, Kay Bradford, Brian J. Higginbotham and David G. Schramm

ABSTRACT

High divorce rates have coincided with higher rates of remarriage. Although remarriages are more susceptible to dissolution than first-order marriages, less research has focused on factors that promote vulnerabilities among remarried couples. In the current study, the authors focused on whether predictors of divorce differ by the number of times someone has been married. The authors examined some of the most common reasons for divorce, as identified by parents who completed a state-mandated divorce education course (n = 8,364), while also controlling for participant sociodemographic characteristics. Participants going through their first divorce were more likely to identify growing apart and infidelity as reasons for seeking a divorce. Conversely, those going through a subsequent divorce were more likely to list problems with alcohol/drug abuse, childrearing differences, emotional/psychological/verbal mistreatment, money problems, physical violence, and arguing. Multivariate analyses indicated that sociodemographic factors were stronger predictors of divorce number than commonly listed reasons for divorce for both male and female participants.

Conjugal Trajectories: Relationship Beginnings, Change, and Dissolutions
Contemporary Perspectives in Family Research, Volume 22, 195–212
Copyright © 2023 by Emerald Publishing Limited
All rights of reproduction in any form reserved
ISSN: 1530-3535/doi:10.1108/S1530-353520230000022010

Implications for remarital and stepfamily stability and directions for future research are discussed.

Keywords: Divorce; subsequent divorce; remarriage; stepfamilies; divorce number; infidelity

INTRODUCTION

Although divorce rates in the United States have leveled off in recent decades (Cohen, 2019; Mayol-Garcia, Gurrentz, & Kreider, 2021), they are still among the highest in the world (Adema & Ali, 2015). Steady divorce rates have coincided with more adults available for remarriage, a union in which at least one partner was previously married (Livingston, 2014). Of notable concern is that, in comparison to first-order marriages, remarriages (also referred to as higher-order marriages) are more vulnerable to relationship dissolution (DeLongis & Zwicker, 2017).

Extensive research has been conducted on distal and proximal factors that predict divorce (Amato, 2010; Amato & Hohmann-Marriott, 2007; Amato & Previti, 2003; Bratter & King, 2008). These include communication issues, incompatibility, and violence, just to name a few (Crabtree, Harris, Bell, Allen, & Roberts, 2018; Hawkins, Willoughby, & Doherty, 2012). Among sociodemographic factors, marrying at a younger age and having lower levels of education have also contributed to an increased risk of divorce (Amato & Previti, 2003; Cohen, 2019). Although prior divorce has been identified as a risk factor for subsequent divorce (Amato, 2010), it is less clear whether the same factors that contribute to first divorces also contribute to subsequent divorces. Considering that remarriages are at a greater risk for dissolution, this area of research warrants attention, especially as programs designed to reduce the likelihood of divorce continue to gain momentum (Lucier-Greer & Adler-Baeder, 2012; Stanley et al., 2020).

The purpose of this study was to identify what factors predict first versus subsequent divorce. Specifically, we evaluated whether commonly identified reasons for divorce (e.g., money problems, communication challenges; Amato, 2010; Dew, Britt, & Huston, 2012; Hawkins et al., 2012; Rodrigues, Hall, & Fincham, 2006) differ for those seeking their first divorce when compared to those seeking a subsequent divorce, while controlling for participants' sociodemographic characteristics. Additionally, we examined similarities and differences in predictors of divorce number by gender.

LITERATURE REVIEW

Remarriage and Divorce

Approximately 40% of new marriages are a remarriage for at least one spouse (Geiger & Livingston, 2019). Furthermore, of those with a marital event in the last 12 months, nearly 28% of men and 27% of women have been married multiple times (Mayol-Garcia et al., 2021). Finally, in comparison to first-order marriages, remarriages have greater levels of instability, with divorce rates for these unions estimated at 60%, which is approximately 10% higher than first-order marriages (Copen, Daniels, Vespa, & Mosher, 2012; DeLongis & Zwicker, 2017).

Despite the prevalence of remarriage (Livingston, 2014), research on remarriage and divorce of remarried couples is relatively limited due to the tendency of extant literature to lump all types of divorces together. Work by Cherlin (1978, 2020) has characterized remarriage as an incomplete institution due to its complexity in terms of role ambiguity and constraints on traditional family life. This complexity and potential for increased conflict, may accelerate the exit from remarriages (Amato, 1996; Falke & Larson, 2007; Gold, 2017; Smock, 2000). This may especially be the case when couples are distressed and lack marital satisfaction (Whitton, Stanley, Markham, & Johnson, 2013).

As suggested by marital search (England & Farkas, 1986) and marriage market hypotheses (Spikic et al., 2021), relationship instability among remarried couples may be attributable to fewer available and attractive partners for remarriage. From this theoretical perspective, the "marriage market" has fewer options and is less attractive for those who have been married previously (Qian & Lichter, 2018), leading to the matching of partners with potentially less compatible social and personality traits. As a result of demographic imbalance, remarrying individuals often marry those who are markedly different from their previous spouse (Choi & Tienda, 2017).

As Qian and Lichter (2018) argue, casting a "wider net" when pursuing potential remarital partners, and the resulting mismatches in compatibility, can leave remarriages in a position of vulnerability. This situation may put remarrying women with younger children in a particularly precarious position, leading them to partner with a spouse out of perceived financial necessity (Sweeney, 1997), with less emphasis being placed on partner quality and compatibility (de Graaf & Kalmijn, 2003). Indeed, marriage market theorists have argued that a smaller pool of available men increases the challenges women face when it comes to repartnering (Kreidl & Hubatková, 2017). Conversely, remarriage for men may be more incentivized, especially in terms of addressing loneliness and promoting healthier behaviors (Willams & Umberson, 2004).

Finally, complex family dynamics, such as children from previous relationships, potentially unresolved legal and personal issues from these relationships, and the stigma attached to stepfamily formation can add instability to remarriages and stepfamilies (DeLongis & Zwicker, 2017; Kopystynska, Bradford, Higginbotham, & Whiteman, 2021). Indeed, issues such as disagreements related to child custody and difficult interactions with ex-partners can make remarriages difficult and may even lead to fewer quality remarital prospects for those wishing to repartner (de Graaf & Kalmijn, 2003; Goldscheider & Sassler, 2006). These considerations, along with the paucity of comparative research on first versus subsequent divorce, present the need to explore which factors are most effective in predicting divorce number, especially considering the increasing prevalence of remarriage (Geiger & Livingston, 2019; Livingston, 2014; Raley & Sweeney, 2020).

Common Reasons for Divorce

Extensive research has been conducted on the reasons divorcing individuals attribute to the dissolution of their marriage (Amato & Previti, 2003; Crabtree et al., 2018; de Graaf & Kalmijn, 2006; Hawkins et al., 2012; Pearce Plauche, Marks, & Hawkins, 2016). Hawkins et al. (2012) found that growing apart and communication issues were the most prevalent reasons for pursuing a divorce, while also showing that these "soft" reasons for divorce were more common than destructive (or "harder") reasons, such as infidelity, substance abuse, and physical violence. Other studies have corroborated these findings, with most tending to identify "softer" reasons as the primary reasons that contributed to the decision to pursue a divorce (Al Gharaibeh & Bromfield, 2012; Johnson et al., 2001). The propensity for divorcing individuals to attribute less destructive reasons to their divorce is consistent with the tendency for individuals to place more emphasis on relational issues as opposed to behavioral problems when seeking a divorce (Crabtree et al., 2018; de Graaf & Kalmijn, 2006). However, those divorcing are not a homogeneous group and reasons for seeking a divorce may differ based on certain factors, such as household income (Williamson, Nguyen, Rothman, & Doss, 2020).

Sociodemographic Predictors of Divorce

Research on the sociodemographic factors associated with the susceptibility to divorce have yielded some common themes (Amato & Previti, 2003; Cohen, 2019; Pearce Plauche et al., 2016; Williamson et al., 2020). From a sociodemographic perspective, major predictors or risk factors associated with divorce include presence of children, age, education level, income level, race and ethnicity, and length of marriage (Amato & Hohmann-Marriott, 2007). A review of literature outlining each of these sociodemographic factors is presented below.

Presence of Children

Generally, the presence of children results in more contextual stress (Williamson et al., 2020). The presence of children in the home is often associated with other motives for seeking divorce, such as infidelity and financial concerns (de Graaf & Kalmijn, 2006). The existence of these factors in the home may give motivation, especially for mothers, to seek divorce in order to remove children from negative environments (Amato & Previti, 2003).

A large percentage of remarriages (approximately 65%) involve children from previous relationships (Zeleznikow & Zeleznikow, 2015), which has been found to increase the risk for a subsequent divorce (Amato, 2010; Booth & Edwards, 1992; Bramlett & Mosher, 2001). Indeed, the presence of stepchildren and greater stepfamily complexity has been associated with lower perceived marital quality among remarried couples (Falke & Larson, 2007). Detriments to remarital quality, as they relate to the presence of children, are often attributed to poor stepparent-stepchild relations (DeLongis & Zwicker, 2017).

Age

Age at marriage has been identified as a strong predictor of marital longevity (Amato & Hohmann-Marriott, 2007, England, Allison, & Sayer, 2016).

In particular, entering into marriage at a younger age has been associated with greater marital problems, such as incompatibility or growing apart, conflict, and substance abuse (Amato & Previti, 2003; Bumpass, Martin, & Sweet, 1991). Conversely, marrying at older ages has been found to reduce the odds of marital dissolution, as the aforementioned problems have been found to be less of an issue among older couples (Isen & Stevenson, 2010; Lundberg, Pollak, & Stearns, 2016).

Education
Research consistently shows that individuals with higher levels of education have higher levels of marital stability on average than individuals with lower levels of education (Bramlett & Mosher, 2001; Cohen, 2019). Amato (2010) noted that divorce rates for college-educated couples have shown consistent decline, while divorce rates for couples without college educations have remained constant. Some researchers posit that higher levels of education promote better communication between couples, which better equips them to resolve marital disputes (Amato & Previti, 2003). Recent scholarship also suggests that highly educated couples are motivated to stay together to protect their wealth, and to invest in the long-term well-being of their children (Raley & Sweeney, 2020).

Income
Household income and financial resources have also been found to be associated with marital stability (Conger et al., 1990; Crapo, Turner, Kopystynska, Bradford, & Higginbotham, 2021), although some studies find no association (Raley & Sweeney, 2020). Research has pointed to how differences in socioeconomic status (SES) is related to the types of problems that couples experience, with higher levels of income more often associated with relationship-centered problems, such as incompatibility (Amato & Previti, 2003). Conversely, couples with low SES have been found to be more susceptible to what Hawkins et al. (2012) identified as "harder" reasons for divorce, such as physical violence and substance abuse, which have been shown to increase vulnerability to marital instability and disruption (Williamson et al., 2020). Other contextual factors must also be considered, as lower-income couples are more likely to cohabit before marriage (Hemez & Manning, 2017), have more children in the home (Doss, Rhoades, Stanley, & Markman, 2009), and bring children from previous relationships (Lamidi, 2016), all of which can contribute to more contextual stress, lower marital satisfaction, and subsequent divorce.

Race and Ethnicity
Research comparing the divorce rates of different racial and ethnic groups has shown that White/Caucasian and Hispanic couples experience a lower risk for divorce when compared to African American couples (Aughinbaugh, Robles, & Sun, 2013; Cohen, 2019). However, higher educational attainment has been identified as a protective factor against divorce among African Americans (Sweeney & Phillips, 2004). Asian and foreign-born Hispanic women have low divorce rates, but African-American, US-born, and Native American women have high divorce rates (Raley & Sweeney, 2020).

Length of Marriage

As a life course variable, length of marriage can be telling in terms of predicting divorce and divorce number (Cohen, 2019; Williamson et al., 2020). When looking at the impact of length of marriage on the likelihood of divorce, multiple examples point to the link between marriage length and marital satisfaction, with mixed results. Earlier research has consistently found that on average, marital satisfaction declined for couples over time (Johnson, Amoloza, & Booth, 1992; Kamp Dush, Taylor, & Kroeger, 2008; VanLaningham, Johnson, & Amato, 2001). However, in their recent reviews of research on marriage length and marital satisfaction, Karney and Bradbury (2020) noted that whereas some couples experienced declines in marital satisfaction, others did not. Couples who experienced declines in marital satisfaction tended to report lower initial satisfaction with their relationships (Karney & Bradbury, 2020; Proulx, Ermer, & Kanter, 2017).

CURRENT STUDY

Considering the consistent and relatively high divorce rates in the United States, particularly among remarried couples, the current study sought to identify what factors best predict divorce number among parents who completed a divorce education course. The following research questions were posed:

1) What are the strongest predictors (common reasons or sociodemographic) of divorce number (i.e., first vs subsequent divorces)?
2) What are the similarities and differences (in predictors of divorce number) by gender?

Exploring such questions may hold implications for addressing remarital and stepfamily stability, while also informing practitioners of stepfamily education programs of the unique challenges faced by remarried individuals and why these unions are more susceptible to dissolution, which has been identified as a limitation of current interventions for this group (Adler-Baeder & Higginbotham, 2020).

METHOD

Procedure

Data were collected from divorcing parents who participated in a state-mandated, online divorce education course in a Western state between January 2019 and December 2020. The Court contracted with University-based family life specialists to develop the online course. Per underlying legislation, the course was designed to sensitize parents to their children's needs during and after the divorce process. After program completion, participants were presented an optional, anonymous online survey related to course effectiveness and reasons they were seeking a divorce. Data on participant sociodemographic characteristics were also collected. No incentives were offered for survey participation.

SAMPLE

Between January 2019 and December 2020, 18,828 divorcing parents participated in the course, and 8,364 parents completed the post-course survey, yielding a 44.4% participation rate. Female participants comprised 55% of the sample. Mean age was 38.01 years ($SD = 8.09$). The average marriage length for the sample was 12.1 years ($SD = 7.22$). On average, participants had 2.5 children ($SD = 1.44$). In terms of education, 34% had a Bachelor's degree or higher. Thirty per cent of the sample reported household incomes between $30,000 and $59,999. Eighty-two per cent of the sample identified as White or Caucasian. The majority (nearly 83%) of the sample were seeking their first divorce (see Table 1).

Table 1. Participant characteristics ($n = 8,364$).

	N	%
Gender		
Male	3,733	44.63
Female	4,631	55.37
Age Group		
18–24	395	4.72
25–34	2,932	35.05
35–44	3,485	41.67
45–54	1,396	16.69
55 and older	156	1.87
Race/Ethnicity		
White or Caucasian	6,876	82.20
Hispanic/Latino	761	9.10
Asian/Pacific Islander	192	2.30
American Indian or Alaska Native	100	1.20
Black or African American	67	0.80
Two or more races	368	4.40
Education		
Less than high school	308	3.68
High school diploma/GED	1,515	18.11
Some college	2,079	24.85
Associate's/Technical degree	1,649	19.72
Bachelor's degree or higher	2,813	33.64
Household Income		
Less than $30,000	2,168	25.92
$30,000–$59,999	2,482	29.68
$60,000–$89,999	1,464	17.50
$90,000–$119,999	965	11.54
$120,000–$149,999	521	6.23
$150,000 or more	764	9.13
Number of Children		
1 child	2,075	24.81
2 children	2,719	32.51
3 or more children	3,570	42.68
Marriage Number		
1 marriage	6,909	82.61
2 marriages	1,223	14.62
More than 2 marriages	232	2.77

Measures

Common Reasons for Divorce

Participants were presented with a list of 14 common reasons for divorce (e.g., growing apart, communication issues) which was informed by the work of Amato (2010), Dew et al. (2012), and Rodrigues et al. (2006). As the course and survey were conducted under contract with the State's Court system, Court officials' recommendations and input regarding the number and naming of the "common reasons" were honored. For example, questions did not ask participants to allocate blame or admit fault. Rather, for each of the 14 reasons, participants were asked generally: "how much has each played a role in the decision to divorce?" Items were rated on a scale from "1" (*none*) to "4" (*a lot*). Table 2 displays the averages for the entire sample and comparisons between those seeking their first divorce versus those seeking a subsequent divorce.

Sociodemographic Characteristics

Data were collected on the number of children living in the home, participant age, education, household income, minority status, and length of marriage. All variables were continuous, with the exception of minority status, which was coded into a dichotomous variable, with White participants being assigned a code of "0" and all other participants being assigned a code of "1." Those in this group included participants of Hispanic/Latino ethnicity, as well as participants who reported their race as Asian/Pacific Islander, American Indian or Alaska Native, Black

Table 2. Common reasons for divorce (First vs. Subsequent Divorces).

Variable	M	SD	First Divorces	Subsequent Divorces	t
Communication	3.45	0.84	3.45	3.47	−0.78
Growing apart	2.87	1.09	2.89	2.80	2.58*
Emotional/psychological/ verbal mistreatment	2.84	1.19	2.82	2.91	−2.41*
Arguing	2.63	1.19	2.60	2.76	−4.60***
Mental Health	2.40	1.20	2.40	2.41	−0.55
Infidelity	2.35	1.31	2.36	2.29	1.90
Money problems	2.23	1.14	2.22	2.29	−2.26*
Childrearing differences	2.17	1.09	2.12	2.40	−8.62***
Working too much	1.82	1.05	1.81	1.83	−6.72
Extended family	1.80	1.04	1.80	1.82	−0.69
Alcohol/drug abuse	1.73	1.12	1.70	1.86	−4.79***
Online addiction	1.71	1.10	1.72	1.68	1.29
Working too little	1.62	1.01	1.62	1.64	−0.71
Physical violence	1.44	0.90	1.41	1.57	−5.72***

Note: $*p < .05$, $**p < .01$, $***p < .001$.

or African American, and participants claiming two or more races. A detailed breakdown of participants by race/ethnicity is provided in Table 1.

Divorce Number

The outcome measure for this study was a dichotomous variable that indicated a participant's number of divorces (i.e., divorce number). This variable was converted from the original continuous variable. First divorces were assigned a code of "0," while subsequent (multiple) divorces were assigned a code of "1."

Data Analyses

Hierarchical logistic regression models were employed to predict group membership (i.e., first or subsequent divorce) for male and female participants. Models consisted of two steps. In Step I, common reasons for divorce were entered, while Step II introduced sociodemographic characteristics. For each model, Nagelkerke R^2 displayed how the amount of explained variance changed with each step.

RESULTS

Descriptive Results and Comparisons

Table 2 reports reasons for divorce, comparing first versus subsequent divorces. For the overall sample, communication ($M = 3.45$, $SD = 0.84$) was the strongest reason for seeking a divorce, followed by growing apart ($M = 2.87$, $SD = 1.09$), and emotional/psychological/verbal mistreatment ($M = 2.84$, $SD = 1.19$). Independent samples t-tests revealed several statistically significant differences between those seeking a first divorce and those seeking a subsequent divorce. For instance, those seeking a first divorce reported that growing apart played a more significant role in their decision to divorce when compared to those seeking a subsequent divorce. For those seeking a subsequent divorce, alcohol/drug abuse, childrearing differences, emotional/psychological/verbal mistreatment, money problems, physical violence, and arguing played a more significant role in their decision to divorce when compared to those seeking a first divorce.

Predictors of Divorce Number by Gender

Female Participants

Common Reasons for Divorce. Females who identified growing apart ($e^\beta = 0.87$, $p = 0.000$) and working too little ($e^\beta = 0.91$, $p = 0.042$) as their reason for seeking a divorce were more likely to be classified in the first divorce group. Childrearing differences ($e^\beta = 1.34$, $p = 0.000$) increased the likelihood that a female participant fell into the subsequent divorce group by 34%. Other common reasons that increased the likelihood that a female participant would fall into the subsequent divorce group included physical violence ($e^\beta = 1.14$, $p = 0.004$) and alcohol/drug abuse ($e^\beta = 1.10$, $p = 0.009$). Step I explained 4.4% (Nagelkerke R^2) of the variance in divorce number for female participants, correctly classifying 82.4% of cases.

Sociodemographic Characteristics. Female participants with higher levels of education ($e^\beta = 0.86$, $p = 0.000$), coming from longer marriages ($e^\beta = 0.76$, $p = 0.000$), and those of minority status ($e^\beta = 0.65$, $p = 0.003$) were more likely to fall into the first divorce group. Older female participants ($e^\beta = 1.29$, $p = 0.000$) and those with greater numbers of children ($e^\beta = 1.27$, $p = 0.000$), were significantly more likely to fall into the subsequent divorce group. Working too little ($e^\beta = 0.86$, $p = 0.003$) remained as a significant reason for females seeking a first divorce, while childrearing differences ($e^\beta = 1.21$, $p = 0.000$), physical violence ($e^\beta = 1.15$, $p = 0.010$), and working too much ($e^\beta = 1.10$, $p = 0.046$), increased the likelihood of a female participant seeking a subsequent divorce. Step II explained 37.3% (Nagelkerke R^2) of the variance in divorce number for female participants, correctly classifying 85.3% of cases (see Table 3).

Male Participants
Common Reasons for Divorce. Mental health ($e^\beta = 0.90$, $p = 0.032$) and online addiction ($e^\beta = 0.88$, $p = 0.042$) increased the likelihood that male participants

Table 3. Logistic Regression Results Predicting Divorce Number
(Female Participants).

Variable	Step I			Step II		
	β	SE	e^β	β	SE	e^β
Common Reasons for Divorce						
Alcohol/drug abuse	.09**	.04	1.10	.04	.04	1.04
Communication	−.05	.06	.95	−.11	.08	.90
Childrearing differences	.30***	.04	1.34	.19***	.05	1.21
Emotional/psych/verbal mistreatment	−.02	.05	.98	.04	.06	1.04
Extended family	−.06	.04	.94	−.05	.05	.95
Growing apart	−.14***	.04	.87	−.03	.05	.97
Infidelity	−.06	.03	.94	−.03	.04	.97
Mental Health	−.03	.04	.97	−.00	.05	1.00
Money problems	.03	.04	1.03	.05	.05	1.05
Online addiction	−.01	.04	.99	.01	.05	1.01
Physical violence	.13**	.04	1.14	.14**	.05	1.15
Arguing	.06	.05	1.06	.03	.05	1.03
Working too much	.04	.04	1.04	.10*	.05	1.10
Working too little	−.09*	.04	.91	−.15**	.05	.86
Sociodemographic Characteristics						
Number of children	–	–	–	.24***	.04	1.27
Age	–	–	–	.26***	.01	1.29
Education	–	–	–	−.16***	.03	.86
Income	–	–	–	.05	.04	1.05
Minority status	–	–	–	−.42**	.14	.65
Length of marriage	–	–	–	−.27***	.01	.76
Nagelkerke R^2		0.044			0.373	
Correct classification (%)		82.4			85.3	

Note: *$p < .05$, **$p < .01$, ***$p < .001$.

would fall into the first divorce group. Similar to females, childrearing differences ($e^\beta = 1.21$, $p = 0.000$) increased the likelihood by 21% that a male participant would fall into the subsequent divorce group. Alcohol/drug abuse ($e^\beta = 1.18$, $p = 0.000$) also increased the likelihood that a male participant would fall into the subsequent divorce group. Step I explained 2.7% (Nagelkerke R^2) of the variance in divorce number and correctly classified 83.2% of cases.

Sociodemographic Characteristics. Male participants with higher levels of education ($e^\beta = 0.87$, $p = 0.000$), who had been married longer ($e^\beta = 0.77$, $p = 0.000$), and who were of minority status ($e^\beta = 0.69$, $p = 0.018$) were more likely to fall into the first divorce group. Conversely, age ($e^\beta = 1.27$, $p = 0.000$) and number of children ($e^\beta = 1.21$, $p = 0.000$) increased the likelihood that a male participant would fall into the subsequent divorce group. After controlling for sociodemographic characteristics, none of the common reasons for divorce were significant predictors of group membership for male participants seeking a first divorce, while childrearing differences ($e^\beta = 1.17$, $p = 0.013$) were predictive of male participants seeking a subsequent divorce. Step II explained 39.3% (Nagelkerke R^2) of the variance in divorce number, correctly classifying 86.2% of cases (see Table 4).

Table 4. Logistic Regression Results Predicting Divorce Number (Male Participants).

Variable	Step I			Step II		
	β	SE	e^β	β	SE	e^β
Common Reasons for Divorce						
Alcohol/drug abuse	.16***	.05	1.18	.04	.06	1.04
Communication	−.09	.06	.92	−.06	.07	.94
Childrearing differences	.19***	.05	1.21	.16*	.06	1.17
Emotional/psych/verbal mistreatment	−.07	.05	.93	−.10	.06	.90
Extended family	−.04	.05	.96	.03	.06	1.03
Growing apart	−.09	.05	.91	−.01	.06	.99
Infidelity	−.06	.04	.94	−.03	.05	.97
Mental Health	−.10*	.05	.90	−.07	.06	.93
Money problems	.04	.05	1.04	.01	.06	1.01
Online addiction	−.12*	.06	.88	−.10	.07	.90
Physical violence	.14	.08	1.15	.07	.09	1.07
Arguing	.06	.05	1.07	.00	.06	1.00
Working too much	−.07	.05	.94	−.09	.06	.91
Working too little	.06	.06	1.06	.10	.07	1.10
Sociodemographic Characteristics						
Number of children	–	–	–	.19***	.04	1.21
Age	–	–	–	.24***	.01	1.27
Education	–	–	–	−.14***	.03	.87
Income	–	–	–	.01	.04	1.01
Minority status	–	–	–	−.36*	.15	.69
Length of marriage	–	–	–	−.26***	.01	.77
Nagelkerke R^2		0.027			0.393	
Correct classification (%)		83.2			86.2	

*Note: *$p < .05$, **$p < .01$, ***$p < .001$.

DISCUSSION

Although multiple studies have looked at predictors of divorce (Amato, 2010; Amato & Hohmann-Marriott, 2007; Amato & Previti, 2003; Bratter & King, 2008), to our knowledge, no studies have examined which factors (common reasons for divorce or sociodemographic characteristics) were most effective in predicting divorce number (first vs subsequent divorce), and what similarities and differences existed by gender. These were the goals of the current study. Evaluations of this study's findings are organized by this study's primary research questions.

Evaluation of Findings

Predictors of Divorce Number

Initial comparisons between participants by divorce number showed that those seeking a subsequent divorce had a wider range of problems than those seeking a first divorce. Specifically, they reported significantly greater difficulties with alcohol/drug abuse, childrearing differences, emotional/psychological/verbal mistreatment, money problems, physical violence, and arguing. Prior research suggests that both men and women more often cite problems such as growing apart and communication issues (de Graaf & Kalmijn, 2006), but this may be an artifact of past research lumping all divorces together. In the current study, results suggest that "harder" reasons for divorce (Hawkins et al., 2012) were more prevalent for those going through a subsequent divorce.

The fact that childrearing differences were more of a problem for subsequent divorce lends support to previous research related to the difficulties encountered in stepfamilies, especially as it relates to the roles parental figures play in the stepfamily household and the negotiation of these roles (Murry & Lippold, 2018). Indeed, research has shown that if left unresolved, issues with childrearing and role ambiguity can lead to tension between remarried couples (Papernow, 2013). Although speculative, the prevalence of physical violence as a more common reason for those seeking a subsequent divorce may serve as a distinguishing factor between the two types of divorce, when considering that research often cites relational, instead of behavioral issues as the primary motives for divorce (de Graaf & Kalmijn, 2006; Hawkins et al., 2012; Williamson et al., 2020). However, it should also be noted that research has found an increased risk for conflict and physical violence in higher-order marriages and stepfamilies (Bester & Malan-Van Rooyen, 2015), especially for women (Brownbridge, 2004). As we will discuss later, women seeking a subsequent divorce were more likely to attribute physical violence as a reason for divorce.

Gender: Similarities and Differences

Separate multivariate analyses for female and male participants revealed similarities and differences in predictors of divorce number. This section discusses the results of these analyses in light of the final model for each group. First, childrearing differences predicted subsequent divorce for both men and women. As mentioned earlier, such a finding lends support to previous research related to the difficulties stepfamilies face in terms of the roles parental figures play in the stepfamily household and the negotiation of these roles (Murry & Lippold, 2018).

Second, the number of children in the home also increased the likelihood of seeking a subsequent divorce for both men and women. This lends further support to the role presence of children and stepchildren play in increasing amounts of contextual stress and possible parent-child difficulties in stepfamily homes (DeLongis & Zwicker, 2017; Falke & Larson, 2007; Turner, Kopystynska, Bradford, Schramm, & Higginbotham, 2021).

Next, older participants from both genders showed a greater likelihood of seeking a subsequent divorce, showing support for research that has found that the likelihood of entering into higher-order marriage (and possible divorce) increases with age (Livingston, 2014).

Finally, regarding gender similarities among those seeking a first divorce, higher levels of education, minority status, and longer marriages increased the likelihood that both men and women would fall into the first divorce group. In terms of education, research has noted the stability and longevity that education can bring to marriages (Wang, 2015), which may help explain why those with higher education levels were more likely seeking their first, rather than a subsequent divorce. The remarriage rate of minorities may provide a plausible explanation for why minority status increased the likelihood of seeking a first divorce. Indeed, those of minority status are less likely to remarry (Livingston, 2014), and thus less likely to be in a position to seek a subsequent divorce. The finding that first divorcees come from longer marriages, is consistent with research describing the higher levels of instability in higher-order marriages (Copen et al., 2012). This is reinforced by demographic research, which found that higher-order marriages ending in divorce tended to have shorter durations than first-order marriages (Aughinbaugh et al., 2013).

In terms of differences by gender, female participants showed a divergence from male participants on specific indicators. For example, females seeking a first divorce were more likely to cite working too little as a reason for seeking a divorce. It is unclear, however, if they associated lack of work with the actions of their husband or themselves. Nonetheless, this may point to financial concerns, a common reason attributed to marital dissolution (Amato & Previti, 2003), and a common motivation for women (especially mothers of young children) to seek remarriage (Sweeney, 1997). Interestingly, female participants seeking a subsequent divorce cited working too much as a reason for seeking a divorce. Operating under the assumption that wives associated working too much with their husbands' behavior, this finding is consistent with past research in which wives attributed their husband's work habits to their unhappiness with the marriage and the perceived inequity in the division of household labor (de Graaf & Kalmijn, 2006; Hawkins et al., 2012). Alternatively, too much time spent at work among husbands may also be exacerbated by financial responsibilities for children or spouses from previous relationships, which has been found to increase marital conflict in remarriage (Falke & Larson, 2007). Physical violence was also more likely to be cited by female participants as a reason for seeking a subsequent divorce. This is consistent with previous research that found increased risks for conflict and physical violence in higher-order marriages (Bester &

Malan-Van Rooyen, 2015), with women being particularly vulnerable (Brownbridge, 2004). This finding may also illustrate an example of partner incompatibility that may be more frequent in remarriage (Choi & Tienda, 2017; de Graaf & Kalmijn, 2003; Qian & Lichter, 2018).

Limitations

The limitations of this study may help inform future research on this topic. First, this sample was less racially and ethnically diverse than national averages due to the state in which the study was conducted. Similar studies should be conducted with more racially and ethnically diverse samples to examine possible differences by race and/or ethnicity.

Next, although the divorce education course was designed for divorcing parents with dependent children, the data used in this study were not coupled, nor was longitudinal data available. Using coupled (or dyadic) data would allow for the matching of responses. Such an approach might reveal more about the inner-workings of the relationship and possibly reveal patterns about the extent to which (ex)-couples share similar or divergent sentiments on key reasons presented in the survey. Being able to match responses at the couple level would also shed light on which partner initiated the divorce process, while also providing insight on the marriage (or divorce) number for each partner. The absence of longitudinal data did not allow us to examine if the reasons for those going through a subsequent divorce were similar to or different from the reasons that influenced their first divorce. A retrospective series of questions for those seeking a subsequent divorce about what they attributed to their first divorce might be telling with respect to predicting divorce number, while helping to increase our understanding as to whether individuals assign similar reasons for multiple divorce. If this is the case, perhaps intervention programs could help individuals get out of "old behavioral patterns."

Finally, due to the structure of the survey questionnaire, it could not be determined if participants were attributing their marital problems to their partner or to themselves. Past research allows us to draw assumptions, but without directly asking whom they believed was to blame for a certain problem, the reasons participants attributed to their decision to divorce had to be approached more generally. Future research may examine specifics about which partner is responsible for which behavior. This would allow researchers to detect patterns in interpersonal problems for those engaged in serial marriage (or divorce).

Practical Implications

This study holds practical implications for both research and interventions for remarried couples. From a research perspective, this is the first study (to our knowledge), to evaluate commonly cited reasons for divorce and sociodemographic characteristics in the context of predicting divorce number (i.e., first versus subsequent divorce), while also looking at similarities and differences by gender. Perhaps the most informative results from this analysis may be the role of sociodemographic factors in predicting divorce number, as these factors were stronger predictors of divorce number when compared to common reasons people attribute to their divorce. The addition of contextual factors (i.e., sociodemographic characteristics) to this body of work may help to inform future studies on this and similar topics.

From an applied perspective, these findings may help practitioners, especially in a preventative sense. In particular, the ability to identify early warning signs (ideally in a pre-marital education, pre-cohabitation context) for remarried couples and stepfamilies may be particularly helpful in that practitioners may be able to illustrate the contextual risk factors associated with subsequent divorce. For example, given that many remarried couples were likely to attribute physical violence as a reason for divorce, relationship education for stepfamilies could include curricula on ways to solve conflict in constructive ways. Such a contribution may be especially helpful, considering the continued growth of stepfamilies and the high percentage of remarriages that involve children from prior unions. Furthermore, given that childrearing differences were the strongest predictor of divorce number among the common reasons for divorce, even after controlling for sociodemographic characteristics, and were more likely to predict a subsequent divorce for both genders, may point to the importance of addressing role ambiguity and parental responsibilities in stepfamilies. In this context, role strain may also be an important issue to address, as the number of children in the home also predicted subsequent divorce for both male and female participants.

As results showed, however, childrearing differences were just one of several issues that appeared to be a problem that warranted possible preventative interventions for those who were going through a subsequent divorce. Difficulties with "harder" reasons for divorce, such as alcohol/drug abuse, physical violence, arguing, mistreatment, and money problems, which those going through a subsequent divorce also had more of a problem with, are additional issues that could be addressed through intervening measures and family life education ideally for couples considering entering into a remarriage. Such educational efforts may help to improve the conditions of remarried couples and stepfamilies and their potential to nurture healthier relationships.

REFERENCES

Adema, W., & Ali, N. (2015). Recent changes in family outcomes and policies in OECD countries: The impact of the economic crisis. *Community, Work, & Family, 18*(2), 145–166. doi: 10.1080/13668803.2015.1013020

Adler-Baeder, B. F., & Higginbotham, B. (2020). Efforts to design, implement, and evaluate community-based education for stepfamilies: Current knowledge and future directions. *Family Relations, 69*(3), 559–576. doi: 10.1111/fare.12427

Al Gharaibeh, F., & Bromfield, N. (2012). An analysis of divorce cases in the United Arab Emirates: A rising trend. *Journal of Divorce & Remarriage, 53*(6), 436–452. doi: 10.1080/10502556.2012.682896

Amato, P. R. (1996). Explaining the intergenerational transmission of divorce. *Journal of Marriage and the Family, 58*(3), 628–640. doi: 10.2307/353723

Amato, P. R. (2010). Research on divorce: Continuing trends and new developments. *Journal of Marriage and Family, 72*(3), 650–666. doi: 10.1111/j.1741-3737.2010.00723.x

Amato, P. R., & Hohmann-Marriott, B. (2007). A comparison of high- and low-distress marriages that end in divorce. *Journal of Marriage and Family, 69*(3), 621–638. doi: 10.1111/j.1741-3737.2007.00396.x

Amato, P. R., & Previti, D. (2003). People's reasons for divorcing: Gender, social class, the life course, and adjustment. *Journal of Family Issues, 24*(5), 602–626. doi: 10.1177/0192513X03254507

Aughinbaugh, A., Robles, O., & Sun, H. (2013, October). Marriage and divorce: Patterns by gender, race, and educational attainment. *Monthly Labor Review.* https://www.bls.gov/opub/mlr/2013/article/marriage-and-divorce-patterns-by-gender-race-and-educational-attainment.htm

Bester, S., & Malan-Van Rooyen, M. (2015). Emotional development, effects of parenting and family structure on. *International Encyclopedia of the Social & Behavioral Sciences, 7*(2), 438–444. doi: 10.1016/B978-0-08-097086-8.23048-1

Booth, A., & Edwards, J. N. (1992). Starting over: Why remarriages are more unstable. *Journal of Family Issues, 13*(2), 179–194. doi: 10.1177/019251392013002004

Bramlett, M. D., & Mosher, W. D. (2001). *First marriage dissolution, divorce, and remarriage: United States. Advance data from vital and health statistics* (No. 323). Hyattsville, MD: National Center for Health Statistics.

Bratter, J., & King, R. B. (2008). But will it last? Marital instability among interracial and same-race couples. *Family Relations, 57*(2), 160–171. doi: 10.1111/j.1741-3729.2008.00491.x

Brownbridge, D. A. (2004). Male partner violence against women in stepfamilies: An analysis of risk and explanations in the Canadian milieu. *Violence and Victims, 19*(1), 17–36. doi: 10.1891/088667004780842903

Bumpass, L. L., Martin, T. C., & Sweet, J. A. (1991). The impact of family background and early marital factors on marital disruption. *Journal of Family Issues, 12*(1), 22–42. doi: 10.1177/019251391012001003

Cherlin, A. (1978). Remarriage as an incomplete institution. *American Journal of Sociology, 84*(3), 634–650. doi: 10.1086/226830

Cherlin, A. (2020). Degrees of change: An assessment of the deinstitutionalization of marriage thesis. *Journal of Marriage and Family, 82*(1), 62–80. doi: 10.1111/jomf.12605

Choi, K. H., & Tienda, M. (2017). Marriage-market constraints and mate-selection behavior: Racial, ethnic, and gender differences in intermarriage. *Journal of Marriage and Family, 79*(2), 301–317. doi: 10.1111/jomf.12346

Cohen, P. N. (2019). The coming divorce decline. *Socius: Sociological Research for a Dynamic World, 5*, 1–6. doi: 10.1177/2378023119873497

Conger, R. D., Elder, G. H., Lorenz, F. O., Conger, K. J., Simons, R. L., Whitbeck, L. B., ... Melby, J. N. (1990). Linking economic hardship to marital quality and instability. *Journal of Marriage & the Family, 52*(3), 643–656. doi: 10.2307/352931

Copen, C., Daniels, K., Vespa, J., & Mosher, W. (2012). *First marriages in the United States: Data from the 2006–2010 National Survey of Family Growth* (National health statistics reports; no. 49). Hyattsville, MD: National Center for Health Statistics.

Crabtree, S. A., Harris, S. M., Bell, N. K., Allen, S., & Roberts, K. M. (2018). The roles of love and happiness in divorce decision making. *Journal of Divorce & Remarriage, 59*(8), 601–615. doi: 10.1080/10502556.2018.1466254

Crapo, J. S., Turner, J. J., Kopystynska, O., Bradford, K., & Higginbotham, B. J. (2021). Financial stress and perceptions of spousal behavior over time in remarriage. *Journal of Family and Economic Issues, 42*(2), 300–313. doi: 10.1007/s10834-020-09697-6

de Graaf, P. M., & Kalmijn, M. (2003). Alternative routes in the remarriage market: Competing-risk analyses of union formation after divorce. *Social Forces, 81*(4), 1459–1498. doi: 10.1353/sof.2003.0052

de Graaf, P. M., & Kalmijn, M. (2006). Divorce motives in a period of rising divorce: Evidence from a Dutch life-history survey. *Journal of Family Issues, 27*(4), 483–505. doi: 10.1177/0192513X05283982

DeLongis, A., & Zwicker, A. (2017). Marital satisfaction and divorce in couples in stepfamilies. *Current Opinion in Psychology, 13*, 158–161. doi: 10.1016/j.copsyc.2016.11.00

Dew, J., Britt, S., & Huston, S. (2012). Examining the relationship between financial issues and divorce. *Family Relations, 61*(4), 615–628. doi: 10.1111/j.1741-3729.2012.00715.x

Doss, B. D., Rhoades, G. K., Stanley, S. M., & Markman, H. J. (2009). Marital therapy, retreats, and books: The who, what, when, and why of relationship help-seeking. *Journal of Marital and Family Therapy, 35*(1), 18–29. doi: 10.1111/j.1752-0606.2008.00093.x

England, P., Allison, P. D., & Sayer, L. C. (2016). Is your spouse more likely to divorce you if you are the older partner? *Journal of Marriage and Family, 78*(5), 1184–1194. doi: 10.1111/jomf.12314

England, P., & Farkas, G. (1986). *Households, employment, and gender: A social, economic, and demographic view.* Aldine Publishing Company. doi: 10.4324/9780203789766

Falke, S. I., & Larson, J. H. (2007). Premarital predictors of remarital quality: Implications for clinicians. *Contemporary Family Therapy, 29*(9), 9–23. doi: 10.1007/s10591-007-9024-4

Geiger, A. W., & Livingston, G. (2019). *8 facts about love and marriage in America.* Pew Research Center. Retrieved from https://www.pewresearch.org/fact-tank/2019/02/13/8-facts-about-love-and-marriage/

Gold, J. M. (2017). Assessment for stepfamily marriages: Implications for family counselors. *The Family Journal: Counseling and Therapy for Couples and Families, 25*(4), 322–326. doi: 10.1177/1066480717732171

Goldscheider, F., & Sassler, S. (2006). Creating stepfamilies: Integrating children into the study of union formation. *Journal of Marriage and Family, 68*(2), 275–291. doi: 10.1111/j.1741-3737.2006.00252.x

Hawkins, A. J., Willoughby, B. J., & Doherty, W. J. (2012). Reasons for divorce and openness to marital reconciliation. *Journal of Divorce & Remarriage, 53*(6), 453–463. doi: 10.1080/10502556.2012.682898

Hemez, P., & Manning, W. D. (2017). *Over twenty-five years of change in cohabitation experience in the U.S., 1987–2013* (Family Profiles, FP-17-02). Bowling Green, OH: National Center for Family & Marriage Research. Retrieved from https://www.bgsu.edu/ncfmr/resources/data/family-profiles/hemez-manning-25-years-change-cohabitation-fp-17-02.html

Isen, A., Stevenson, B. (2010). *Women's education and family behavior: Trends in marriage, divorce and fertility.* Working Paper 15725. National Bureau of Economic Research.

Johnson, D. R., Amoloza, T. O., & Booth, A. (1992). Stability and developmental change in marital quality: A three-wave panel analysis. *Journal of Marriage & the Family, 54*(3), 582–594. doi: 10.2307/353244

Johnson, C. A., Stanley, S. M., Glenn, N. D., Amato, P. R., Nock, S. L., Markman, H. J., & Robin Dion, M. (2001). *Marriage in Oklahoma: 2001 Baseline statewide survey on marriage and divorce.* OSU Bureau for Social Research, Oklahoma State University.

Kamp Dush, C. M., Taylor, M. G., & Kroeger, R. A. (2008). Marital happiness and psychological well-being across the life course. *Family Relations, 57*(2), 211–226. doi: 10.1111/j.1741-3729.2008.00495.x

Karney, B. R., & Bradbury, T. N. (2020). Research on marital satisfaction and stability in the 2010s: Challenging conventional wisdom. *Journal of Marriage and Family, 82*(1), 100–116. doi: 10.1111/jomf.12635

Kopystynska, O., Bradford, K., Higginbotham, B., & Whiteman, S. (2021). Impact of positive and negative socioemotional behaviors on remarital instability. *Journal of Family Issues, 43*(12), 3194–3217. doi: 10.1177/0192513X211042851

Kreidl, M., & Hubatková, B. (2017). Rising rates of cohabitation and the odds of repartnering: Does the gap between men and women disappear? *Journal of Divorce & Remarriage, 58*(7), 487–506. doi: 10.1080/10502556.2017.1343580

Lamidi, E. (2016). *A quarter century change in nonmarital births: Differences by educational attainment* (Family Profiles, FP-16-05). Bowling Green, OH: National Center for Family & Marriage Research. Retrieved from http://www.bgsu.edu/content/dam/BGSU/college-of-arts-and-sciences/NCFMR/documents/FP/FP-15-03-birth-trends-single-cohabiting-moms.pdf

Livingston, G. (2014). *Four-in-ten couples are saying "I do," again: Growing number of adults have remarried.* Pew Research Center. Retrieved from https://www.pewsocialtrends.org/2014/11/14/four-in-ten-couples-are-saying-i-do-again/

Lucier-Greer, M., & Adler-Baeder, F. (2012). Does couple and relationship education work for individuals in stepfamilies? A meta-analytic study. *Family Relations: An Interdisciplinary Journal of Applied Family Studies, 61*(5), 756–769. doi: 10.1111/j.1741-3729.2012.00728.x

Lundberg, S., Pollak, R. A., & Stearns, J. (2016). Family inequality: Diverging patterns in marriage, cohabitation, and childbearing. *Journal of Economic Perspectives*, *30*(2), 79–102. doi: 10.1257/jep.30.2.79

Mayol-Garcia, Y., Gurrentz, B., & Kreider, R. M. (2021, April). *Number, timing, and duration of marriages and divorces: 2016*. Report No. P70-167. Retrieved from https://www.census.gov/newsro om/press-releases/2021/marriages-and-divorces.html

Murry, V. M., & Lippold, M. A. (2018). Parenting practices in diverse family structures: Examination of adolescents' development and adjustment. *Journal of Research on Adolescence*, *28*(3), 650–664. doi: 10.1111/jora.12390

Papernow, P. (2013). *Surviving and thriving in stepfamily relationships: What works and what doesn't.* New York, NY: Routledge.

Proulx, C. M., Ermer, A. E., & Kanter, J. B. (2017). Group-based trajectory modeling of marital quality: A critical review. *Journal of Family Theory & Review*, *9*(3), 307–327. doi: 10.1111/jfrt.12201

Pearce Plauche, H., Marks, L. D., & Hawkins, A. J. (2016). Why we chose to stay together: Qualitative interviews with separated couples who chose to reconcile. *Journal of Divorce & Remarriage*, *57*(5), 317–337. doi: 10.1080/10502556.2016.1185089

Qian, Z., & Lichter, D. T. (2018). Marriage markets and intermarriage: Exchange in first marriages and remarriages. *Demography*, *55*(3), 849–875. doi: 10.1007/s13524-018-0671-x

Raley, R. K., & Sweeney, M. M. (2020). Divorce, repartnering, and stepfamilies: A decade in review. *Journal of Marriage and Family*, *82*(1), 81–99. doi: 10.1111/jomf.12651

Rodrigues, A. E., Hall, J. H., & Fincham, F. D. (2006). What predicts divorce and relationship dissolution? In M. A. Fine & J. J. Harvey (Eds.), *Handbook of divorce and relationship dissolution* (pp. 85–112). New York, NY: Lawrence Erlbaum Associates Publishers.

Smock, P. J. (2000). Cohabitation in the United States: An appraisal of research themes, findings, and implications. *Annual Review of Sociology*, *26*(1), 1–20. doi: 10.1146/annurev.soc.26.1.1

Spikic, S., Mortelmans, D., & Van Gasse, D. (2021). More of the same? Comparing the personalities of ex-spouse and new partner after divorce. *Social Sciences*, *10*(11). doi: 10.3390/socsci10110431

Stanley, S. M., Carlson, R. G., Rhoades, G. K., Markman, H. J., Ritchie, L. L., & Hawkins, A. J. (2020). Best practices in relationship education focused on intimate relationships. *Family Relations*, *69*(3), 497–519. doi: 10.1111/fare.12419

Sweeney, M. M. (1997). Remarriage of women and men after divorce: The role of socioeconomic prospects. *Journal of Family Issues*, *18*(5), 479–502. doi: 10.1177/019251397018005002

Sweeney, M. M., & Phillips, J. A. (2004). Understanding racial differences in marital disruption: Recent trends and explanations. *Journal of Marriage and Family*, *66*(3), 639–650. doi: 10.1111/j.0022-2445.2004.00043.x

Turner, J. J., Kopystynska, O., Bradford, K., Schramm, D. G., & Higginbotham, B. (2021). Predicting parenting and stepparenting difficulties among newly remarried parents. *Journal of Divorce & Remarriage*, *62*(7), 511–531. doi: 10.1080/10502556.2021.1925857

VanLaningham, J., Johnson, D. R., & Amato, P. (2001). Marital happiness, marital duration, and the U-shaped curve: Evidence from a five-wave panel study. *Social Forces*, *79*(4), 1313–1341. doi: 10.1353/sof.2001.0055

Wang, W. (2015). *The link between a college education and a lasting marriage.* Pew Research Center. Retrieved from https://www.pewresearch.org/fact-tank/2015/12/04/education-and-marriage/

Whitton, S. W., Stanley, S. M., Markham, H. J., & Johnson, C. A. (2013). Attitudes toward divorce, commitment, and divorce proneness in first and remarriages. *Journal of Marriage and Family*, *75*(2), 276–287. doi: 10.1111/jomf.12008

Willams, K., & Umberson, D. (2004). Marital status, marital transitions, and health: A gendered life course perspective. *Journal of Health and Social Behavior*, *45*(1), 81–98. doi: 10.1177/002214650404500106

Williamson, H. C., Nguyen, T. T. T., Rothman, K., & Doss, B. D. (2020). A comparison of low-income versus higher-income individuals seeking an online relationship intervention. *Family Process*, *59*(4), 1434–1446. doi: 10.1111/famp.12503

Zeleznikow, L. & Zeleznikow, J. (2015). Supporting blended families to remain intact: A case study. *Journal of Divorce & Remarriage*, *56*(4), 317–335. doi: 10.1080/10502556.2015.1025845

CHAPTER 11

UNINTENDED HIGHER-ORDER BIRTHS AND UNION STABILITY: VARIATION BY UNION CHARACTERISTICS

J. Bart Stykes and Karen Benjamin Guzzo

ABSTRACT

A robust body of scholarship has attached unintended childbearing, cohabitation, and stepfamily living arrangements to a greater risk of union instability in the United States. These aspects of family life, which often co-occur, are over-represented among disadvantaged populations, who also have an independently higher risk of union instability. Existing scholarship has modeled these family experiences as correlated events to better understand family and union instability, yet the authors assert a direct effort to test whether or how unintended childbearing differs across marital and stepfamily statuses makes important contributions to established research on relationship stability. Drawing on the 2006–2017 National Survey of Family Growth (NSFG), the authors test potential moderating effects to better understand the linkages between unintended childbearing and union dissolution among 7,864 recent, higher-order births to partnered mothers via discrete-time, event history logistic regression models. Findings confirm that unintended childbearing, cohabitation, and stepfamily status are all linked with a greater risk of dissolution. However, unintended childbearing is differentially linked to instability by marital status, with unintended childbearing being associated with a higher risk of dissolution for married couples relative to cohabiting couples. Unintended fertility does not seem to increase the risk of instability across stepfamily status. Findings provide

Conjugal Trajectories: Relationship Beginnings, Change, and Dissolutions
Contemporary Perspectives in Family Research, Volume 22, 213–231
ISSN: 1530-3535/doi:10.1108/S1530-353520230000022011

more evidence in support of selection, rather than causation, in explaining the association between unintended childbearing and union instability among higher-order births. Results suggest that among higher-order births, unintended childbearing may reflect underlying relationship issues.

Keywords: Childbearing; birth order; divorce; relationship dissolution; unintended birth; union stability

Despite recent declines, unintended childbearing remains a public health concern in the contemporary United States (Finer & Zolna, 2016). A robust body of scholarship consistently illustrates that unintended childbearing is associated with less healthy pregnancies (Gariepy et al., 2017; Hohmann-Marriott, 2009; Miller, Sable, & Beckmeyer, 2009), poorer mental health for mothers (Atzl, Narayan, Ballinger, Harris, & Liberman, 2021; Barber, Axinn, & Thornton, 1999; Stykes, 2019; Su, 2012) and fathers (Stykes, 2019; Su, 2012), less stable relationships (Lichter, Michelmore, Turner, & Sassler, 2016; Maddow-Zimet, Lindberg, Kost, & Lincoln, 2016; Stykes & Guzzo, 2020), less parental investment in children (Barber et al., 1999; Lindberg, Kost, & Maddow-Zimet, 2017), and worse outcomes for children (Lindberg, Maddow-Zimet, Kost, & Lincoln, 2015; Saleem & Surkan, 2014). Moreover, unintended childbearing is more common among younger, lower-income, non-white, less educated, and unmarried parents (Finer & Zolna, 2011, 2014; Musick, England, Edginton, & Kangas, 2009). Taken together, these findings show how unintended childbearing reflects and reproduces existing inequalities through its linkages with both structural disadvantage and a broad set of health and well-being indicators.

Much of the research linking unintended childbearing to health and well-being focuses on first births, or the transition to parenthood, as it is likely that the context in which a parent initially enters parenthood seems to "set the stage" for subsequent trajectories of family well-being. Yet, unintended childbearing is not limited to first births (Guzzo, 2021); unintended births at higher parities (particularly multiple unintended births) may compound the negative outcomes that are traditionally tied to unintended childbearing, as births to a particular mother are not wholly independent events (Guzzo & Hayford, 2012; Moore, Ryan, Manlove, Mincieli & Schelar, 2009; Wildsmith, Guzzo, & Hayford, 2010). We assert that consideration of a woman's most recent, higher-order birth is strategic in efforts to understand fertility intentions and relationship stability against a backdrop of family diversity and complexity. In short, the focus on first births overlooks family transitions that can occur later in women's reproductive careers and contribute to family complexity. In contrast, the examination of intendedness for a women's most recent, higher-order birth provides a snapshot that allows us to identify diversity and complexity in family relationships and is less susceptible to recall bias given its closer proximity to the interview. As such, our focus on higher-order births extends recent efforts to understand the nexus of fertility intentions and family characteristics in the United States context (Guzzo, 2017, 2018).

Unintended births are associated with an elevated risk of instability, as are family characteristics such as stepfamily status or marital status (Raley & Sweeney, 2020). Stepfamily status and marital status, in turn, are also linked to the risk of higher-parity unintended births (Guzzo, 2017). Thus, understanding how higher-parity births are associated with instability – with explicit consideration of both marital status and stepfamily status – will provide important insights into existing research and inform future program and policy efforts to promote family stability.

BACKGROUND

Births that are mistimed or unwanted remain a significant component of contemporary parenthood – approximately half (i.e., 45%) of mothers in the United States reported having at least one unintended birth (Guzzo, 2021). An established body of research on unintended childbearing consistently concludes that unwanted or mistimed births (the two components of unintended fertility) remain more common among less educated, younger, unmarried, and non-white parents (Finer & Zolna, 2011, 2016; Musick et al., 2009). Prior research has also uncovered a significant and negative association between unintended births and a range of well-being indicators for parents, children, and unions, though the extent to which the association is causal remains debated. Our aim in this chapter is to extend prior work that has demonstrated unintended childbearing goes hand in hand with a greater risk of union dissolution (Guzzo & Hayford, 2012; Lichter et al., 2016; Maddow-Zimet et al., 2016; Stykes & Guzzo, 2020) by considering its intersection with other key predictors of family formation and stability (i.e., relationship status and family structure). Unintended childbearing in recent years occurs against a backdrop of significant shifts in union formation and repartnering, which make it vital to consider whether unintended fertility is differentially linked to union stability across different family situations (i.e., marriage vs cohabitation; families with only shared children vs stepfamily family arrangements).

Cohabitation, which was previously more common among less-educated families (Brown, 2005), has emerged as a mainstay of union formation in the contemporary United States. Cohabitation is now the modal pathway into marriage, cutting across class and race boundaries, and attention to cohabitation must be part of any effort to understand family formation (Manning, 2020). Despite ongoing measurement issues in national survey data sets (Manning, Joyner, Hemez, & Cupka, 2019) and challenges in defining cohabitation, scholarship on cohabitation has continued to grow significantly, including work on fertility and cohabitation. Notably, the wide array of reasons couples choose to cohabit (from stepping stones to marriage to alternatives to marriage/singlehood) and considerable differences in cohabiting couples' economic resources (Manning & Smock, 2005; Smock, 2000) make it challenging to understand cohabitation's link with relationship stability. Indeed, prior research has shown that cohabiting unions among couples with plans to marry are, on average, more stable unions and concentrated among the better-educated (Brown, 2000; Willoughby, Carroll, & Busby, 2011). In contrast, serial cohabitation (where individuals have a series of cohabiting partners) appears to function as an economic survival strategy among the less-educated and has the loosest ties to marriage and greatest instability (Lichter & Qian, 2008). Although this research underscores a rather nuanced, complex portrait of cohabitation and relationship stability, recent evidence continues to suggest that cohabiting unions which do not transition to marriage at or closely following the birth of a child are typically less stable (Musick & Michelmore, 2015).

Prior research has illustrated three key findings from research on cohabitation, childbearing, and relationship instability that are significant in the development of our research questions and hypotheses. Research has (1) attributed the increase in nonmarital childbearing to births in cohabiting unions (Manning, Brown, & Stykes, 2015), (2) demonstrated that unintended childbearing remains more common in cohabiting relationships than in marriage (Finer & Zolna, 2011, 2016), and (3) indicated that cohabitations in which children are born are relatively unstable compared to marriages involving childbearing (Kamp Dush, 2011; Manning, Smock, & Majumdar, 2004; Wu & Musick, 2008), at least among cohabiting unions that do not transition to marriage after the birth (Musick & Michelmore, 2015).

Another factor that has garnered attention in recent decades concerns variation and complexity in biological ties within families. From a parent's perspective, recent work has sought to better understand the correlates and consequences of multiple-partner fertility, where parents have children with more than one partner (also known as MPF; Guzzo, 2014). Recent estimates suggest the prevalence of MPF for mothers ranges from 20% to 25% depending on operational definitions (Stykes & Guzzo, 2019). From a child's perspective, research has focused on stepfamilies and biological ties between both parents and siblings (Manning, Brown, & Stykes, 2014). Stepfamilies are a common experience for many adults and children (Stewart, 2007; Stykes, 2020). Although not all parents in stepfamilies have MPF, a considerable portion of MPF does occur within a stepfamily; by definition, parents who repartner and have a child in their new union have formed both a stepfamily and experienced MPF. As with unintended childbearing and nonmarital childbearing, stepfamily status (when contrasted with families with only shared children, referred to as "simple" families for brevity) is higher among marginalized groups (Cherlin, 1978; Raley & Sweeney, 2020; Stewart, 2007).

Disentangling Unintended Childbearing, Marital Ties, Family Complexity, and Instability

In the contemporary United States, marginalized and economically disadvantaged groups are more likely to experience (1) unintended childbearing, (2) childbearing within cohabiting unions, and (3) stepfamily living (see Finer & Zolna, 2011, 2016; Guzzo, 2017). These events often co-occur. Moreover, a robust body of literature has attached each of these factors to an increased risk of union dissolution. Next, we turn our attention to the intersection of unintended childbearing with both marital and stepfamily statuses to present theoretical frameworks for how and why the effect of unintended childbearing on union dissolution likely differs according to union and stepfamily statuses. Two leading explanations have been provided to understand why unintended childbearing is linked with a greater risk of dissolution. Causal frameworks have asserted that unintended childbearing introduces additional strain on a relationship and likely contributes to greater instability (Guzzo & Hayford, 2012; Kavanaugh, Kost, Frohwirth, Maddow-Zimet, & Gor, 2017; Stykes & Guzzo, 2020), whereas selection frameworks (see Lichter et al., 2016; Stykes & Guzzo, 2020) have suggested that both unintended childbearing and relationship instability are symptoms of "preexisting conditions" (e.g., strained relationships, economic hardship, etc.). Both explanations have been supported by recent empirical studies that link unintended childbearing to relationship stability (Guzzo & Hayford, 2012; Kavanaugh et al., 2017; Stykes & Guzzo, 2020).

When seeking to understand why unintended childbearing may operate differently across marital or cohabiting unions, it is helpful to frame competing hypotheses around these explanations. Nock (1995) applied Cherlin's incomplete institution framework to cohabiting relationships, asserting the lack of consensus on normative expectations for cohabiting unions, the absence of legal ties, and fewer social supports undermine the stability of cohabiting unions. Based on this assertion, if the link between higher-order unintended childbearing and stability reflections causation, then unintended childbearing should be more detrimental to cohabiting unions than marriages. Alternatively, if unintended childbearing coincides with greater instability in relation to a pre-existing stressor (e.g., relational, economic, etc.), then the association between unintended childbearing and dissolution is likely more pronounced for marriage (Guzzo & Hayford, 2012; Stykes & Guzzo, 2020). Put differently, cohabiting unions may have an elevated risk of instability compared to marriage, but selection into having a birth in a cohabiting union in terms of sociodemographic status may mean that unintended fertility may have little additional impact on cohabiting unions' instability. Conversely, given the normative expectation of childbearing within marriages and the more privileged sociodemographic profile of those who have children within marriage, marital births that are unintended may reflect underlying issues that increase the risk of dissolution.

The nexus of the intendedness of births, stepfamilies, and dissolution is best understood through the desire to have a shared, intended birth in higher-order unions. Scholarship in the European context reported that among stepfamilies, intended and shared births are a means to demonstrate one's commitment (and attachment) to the stepfamily fostering protective "effects" on relationship stability (Saint-Jacques et al., 2011; Thomson, 2004). This line of reasoning supports a causal mechanism to better understand the link between unintended childbearing and relationship stability. Alternatively, Guzzo's (2017) examination of stepfamily status and fertility outcomes in the United States found that that births within stepfamilies are more likely to be unintended than those in simple families, which is not consistent with the shared value attached to children approach. Instead, stepfamily fertility in the United States may be best explained by arguments used in the MPF literature, in that having children with different partners is more common among disadvantaged groups (Guzzo, 2014). In short, the European context has established evidence in support of casual frameworks where a higher-order birth with a new partner is deliberate and beneficial, but the limited research in the United States finds less evidence in support of this perspective. If shared, intended childbearing in stepfamilies is protective against relationship instability, the association between unintended childbearing and union dissolution should be stronger for stepfamilies (causation). If fertility in stepfamilies merely is more common among disadvantaged groups – reflecting a pattern of unintended child-bearing and MPF – then we have less reason to expect a different effect of unin-tended childbearing within stepfamilies compared to simple families (selection).

Prior work also indicates the importance of which partner (the female or male partner) is a stepparent (Guzzo, Hemez, Anderson, Manning, & Brown, 2019; MacDonald & DeMaris, 1996; Shapiro, 2014) and how many stepparents are pre-sent (Guzzo, 2018) for stepfamily dynamics and stability. Women face greater chal-lenges, barriers, and anxiety in navigating their roles as stepparents than men (see MacDonald & DeMaris, 1996; Shapiro, 2014), which suggests stepfamilies where the female respondent is a stepparent are less stable (see Stewart, 2005). Yet, in the Canadian context, stepfather families appear to be less stable than their coun-terparts in which the female partner is a stepparent (see Martin, LeBourdais, & Lapierre-Adamcyk, 2011). Additionally, there may be differences in stability among stepfamilies based on marital status. These findings suggest that consider-able variation exists among stepfamilies, and this heterogeneity needs to be mod-eled to ascertain ties between gender, stepfamily composition, and relationship stability.

CURRENT STUDY

Drawing on the pooled, 2006–2017 cycles of the NSFG, we revisit the association between the intendedness of a mother's most recent, higher-order birth and the stability of cohabiting and marital unions. The NSFG data are appropriate for this pursuit as they include a host of indicators concerning birth and union char-acteristics. In addition to sociodemographic controls, relationship histories, and fertility histories, our analyses explicitly consider coresidential union type (mar-riage vs. cohabitation) and family type (simple vs step) at the most recent birth and whether the link between unintended childbearing and stability varies across these two aspects of family structure. Then, we replicate these analyses with a sole focus on stepfamilies to include more nuanced indicators of stepfamily configura-tion (i.e., only stepfather, only stepmother, or both are stepparents).

Our aim is to better understand the interplay between key family character-istics (i.e., marital status and family type), family events (i.e., unintended birth), and union stability; this work moves beyond prior work that has focused on each of these aspects separately. This approach makes important contributions to existing research on unintended childbearing, family complexity, and relation-ship stability and embraces a more nuanced lens to understand how higher-order births are linked to stability across different family arrangements. Prior research informs two guiding questions and their associated hypotheses.

1. Does the association between a higher-order, unintended birth, and relationship stability differ according to marital status?
   * A causal framework suggests the association between unintended childbearing and union dissolution is stronger among cohabiting families.
   * A selection framework suggests the association between unintended childbearing and union dissolution is stronger for married families.
2. Does the association between a higher-order, unintended birth, and relationship stability differ according to family structure?
   * If intended, shared children in stepfamilies are linked with greater relationship stability, we expect unintended childbearing is more strongly linked to dissolution among stepfamilies.
   * A selection framework suggests the association between unintended childbearing and union dissolution does not differ according to stepfamily status.

Then as a robustness check, we revisit both questions in a subsample of stepfamilies to consider gender and stepfamily configuration. Moreover, given our focus on higher-order births, we acknowledge that separate births occurring to mothers cannot be treated as independent and isolated events. As such, our efforts to better understand the intersections between unintended childbearing, marital status, and stepfamily living must also take into consideration key factors that are linked to women's fertility careers (e.g., including prior histories) and union outcomes. Unintended fertility, union formation, and the chances of being in a stepfamily vary across race-ethnicity (Finer & Zolna, 2011, 2016; Smock, Manning, & Porter, 2005; Musick et al., 2009; Raley & Sweeney, 2020). Guzzo and Hayford (2011) demonstrate that analyses of higher-order, unintended childbearing should incorporate prior unintended births. In addition, the number of children has been linked to union stability (Thornton, 1977). As such these key correlates require attention as well in our efforts to isolate and extract the nexus of unintended childbearing, union type, and stepfamily status with dissolution.

DATA

We use the several cycles of the NSFG, a nationally representative dataset of men and women aged 15 to 45 (and births occurring to them); we focus only on women due to concerns about the accuracy of men's fertility data in nationally representative surveys (Joyner et al., 2012). After appending the continuous cycles of the data (originally in two-year groupings from 2006 to 2017), we identified 48,946 unique pregnancies. Following other work noting the under-reporting of pregnancies (Lindberg, Kost, Maddow-Zimet, Desai, & Zolna, 2020), we excluded 14,802 pregnancies that did not result in a live birth. Next, we employed two selection criteria to define our analytic sample. We restricted the data to (1) women's most recent higher-order birth[1], which yielded an analytic sample of 10,602 births, and (2) births that occurred to women who were in a coresidential union at the time of birth ($n = 8,506$). Final analyses are limited to 7,864 births that satisfied these criteria and provided non-missing data on the start and end dates of relevant marital and cohabiting unions and did not experience a dissolution within the same years as the birth (due to the inability to establish temporal ordering of events within a given calendar year). Additional descriptive analyses are limited to the most recent, higher-order, and partnered births occurring to women in a stepfamily configuration ($n = 3,003$); see details below for how stepfamilies are identified.

Using the year of pregnancy completion and year of either interview (if the union remained intact) or union dissolution, we transformed the data from 7,864 pregnancies to 39,103 person-years.[2] In short, we start tracking union stability beginning the year of the most recent, higher-order birth and continue to observe the birth unions until they are censored (by interview) or experience a dissolution.[3] First, we produce descriptive statistics for the sample according to intention, marital, and stepfamily configuration. Then, discrete-time event history analyses predict the risk of dissolution in a multivariate framework to formally test hypotheses via interaction terms. Given our focus on the intersection of three key aspects of a birth context (i.e., intentions, marital status, and family structure) and union stability, we employ a limited set of control variables that prioritizes key predictors of relationship instability.

Each set of multivariate analyses proceeds in three nested models. Model 1 includes all focal independent variables and covariates. Model 2 introduces the interaction between unintended childbearing and marital status to address our first guiding research question. Finally, Model 3 considers the interaction between unintended childbearing and stepfamily status to address our second research question. Finally, to consider potential variations among different stepfamily configurations, we employ event history analyses (with the same set of three models) to a sample limited to stepfamilies to better account for gender and the degree of complexity within stepfamilies.

Measures

Union dissolution (dependent variable). Data from the fertility and coresidential union histories attach the focal birth (i.e., most recent, higher-order birth occurring in a marital or cohabiting union) to its corresponding union. This differentiates between unions that experienced a divorce/separation "1" and those remaining intact up to the interview "0."

Unintended birth. The NSFG uses a series of questions to assess the intendedness of every pregnancy and birth; please recall our analyses focus on births. First, women were asked, "Right before you became pregnant, did you yourself want to have a(nother) baby any time in the future?" Those who reported "yes" were then asked questions to assess the timing of their pregnancy. Specifically, "So would you say you became pregnant too soon, at about the right time, or later than you wanted?" Based on information from these questions, we operationalize unintended births as a dichotomous variable that flags births identified either as unwanted or to soon as "1" and other births (those that were wanted or occurred later than intended) as "0."

Marital status at the time of birth. Using union histories, we operationalize married as a dichotomous indicator where marital births are coded as "1" and cohabiting births are "0."

Family structure. Using the detailed union histories we consider if the respondent's current partner had children from a prior relationship. This information is cross-referenced with the respondent's past fertility and union histories to operationalize family structure. Given limited statistical power (due to sample size) and our plan to consider interactions between unintended fertility and family structure, we employ a dichotomous indicator that simply differentiates between stepfamilies (1) and simple families (0) in multivariate, event-history analyses among the broader sample. Analyses limited to stepfamilies make use of more detailed stepfamily living arrangements based on detailed relationship and fertility histories. This information was used to identify complex stepfamilies in which both partners have children from past relationships (reference), only stepfather, and only stepmother stepfamilies.

Prior fertility experiences. We include three indicators to control for elements of fertility careers that may impact both the risk of having an unintended, higher-order birth and union dissolution. A dichotomous variable flags respondents who experienced prior unintended pregnancies as "1" from their counterparts who had not yet experienced an unintended pregnancy as "0." We also include a continuous indicator of age at first birth (in years). Finally, we include a continuous indicator of the respondent's number of live births total.

Sociodemographic characteristics.[4] Analyses also control for racial and ethnic status: White (reference), Black, Hispanic, and other; age at interview (in years); educational attainment (at time of interview): at least a bachelor's degree (reference), some college but no degree, high school diploma (incl. GED), and no degree. Lastly, analyses control for age differences in partners. Age "heterogamy" as a concept is extended to both marital and cohabiting unions and serves as a flag for couples where either the male partner is more than five years older than the mother or the female partner is more than two years older than the male partner as "1."

Duration variables. Analyses control for duration (in years) from the time of birth to either dissolution or censorship by interview (time-varying). Furthermore, analyses control for coresidential relationship duration prior to the focal birth (in years, time-invariant).

RESULTS

Table 1 presents the descriptive profile of our sample and according to the union outcome (i.e., intact at the time of survey versus dissolving). The majority (78%) of most recent unions in which a higher-order birth occurs remain intact at the interview. Among currently partnered mothers having a higher-parity birth, over one-fourth (29%) of the most recent births are unintended. Moreover, unintended births are overrepresented among unions that eventually dissolve

Table 1. Sample Descriptives for Recent, Higher-Order Births to Partnered Mothers, According to Union Outcome as of Survey Date.

	Total Sample		Intact Unions		Dissolving Unions	
	n or μ	p or σ	n or μ	p or σ	n or μ	p or σ
Unintended birth	2,608	0.29	1,625	0.25	983	0.42
Marital birth	5,898	0.81	4,458	0.82	1,440	0.75
Family Structure						
Not stepfamily	4,590	0.62	3,476	0.64	1,114	0.56
Only stepfather	1,644	0.21	1,294	0.23	350	0.17
Only stepmother	1,349	0.14	783	0.11	566	0.23
Complex stepfamily (both are step)	281	0.03	176	0.02	105	0.04
Fertility Histories						
Prior unintended pregnancy	3,608	0.43	2,363	0.40	1,245	0.56
Age at first birth	22.33	0.15	23.15	0.16	19.68	0.15
Number of live births	2.70	0.02	2.70	0.02	2.71	0.04
Sociodemographic Characteristics						
White	3,794	0.58	2,811	0.59	983	0.56
Black	1,134	0.09	632	0.08	502	0.16
Hispanic	2,316	0.24	1,809	0.24	507	0.21
Other	620	0.09	477	0.09	143	0.07
Age (at interview)	36.34	0.13	35.96	0.15	37.68	0.24
Educational Attainment						
At least a bachelor's degree	1,818	0.30	1,572	0.34	246	0.17
Some college, no degree	2,215	0.28	1,527	0.26	688	0.34
High school diploma (GED)	2,209	0.27	1,494	0.25	715	0.32
No degree	1,622	0.15	1,136	0.15	486	0.17
Age "heterogamy"	1,332	0.15	1,270	0.16	60	0.15
Years partnered prior to recent birth	4.94	0.08	5.33	0.09	3.67	0.14
Years observed in data	5.25	0.11	5.57	0.13	4.22	0.15
N	7, 864		5,729	0.78	2,135	0.22

(42% versus 25% that remain intact). The majority of higher-order, partnered recent births occur within marriage. Most births (62%) occur in simple family structures with only shared children, but a considerable share of most recent, partnered births occur to only stepfather (21%) and only stepmother (14%) families. Fewer than five percent of births occur to families where both partners are stepparents. Although patterns appear less stark, cohabiting and stepfamilies appear to be slightly overrepresented among unions that later dissolve.

Almost half (i.e., 43%) of currently partnered mothers having at least two children report a prior unintended pregnancy, and most unions that eventually dissolve involve mothers who reported prior unintended pregnancies. On average, mothers in our sample were 22 at the time of their first birth; delayed entry into parenthood appears to be somewhat protective as mothers whose most recent unions dissolve were, on average, four years younger at their first birth than their counterparts whose birth unions endure. Mothers in our sample report, on average, 2.7 children with minimal variation across union outcomes by parity. Our sample reflects the broader US population in terms of racial/ethnic status as 58% of mothers are White followed by Hispanic (24%), Black (9%), and other (9%). There are no stark differences in the racial and ethnic composition of unions that dissolve, though black mothers appear to be overrepresented (16%) among unions characterized by dissolution. On average, mothers having a partnered, higher-order birth are in their mid-30s with minimal age variation across union outcome. In terms of education, 30% report at least a bachelor's, 28% report some college experience but no degree, and 27% report a high school diploma, with fewer than one-in-five mothers reporting no degree. Those with a high school degree but no college degree are overrepresented (34% and 32%) among dissolving birth unions whereas the most highly educated are notably underrepresented (17%) in this outcome. A sizeable minority (15%) of mothers report either living with or being married to a partner with a noteworthy age difference, and age "heterogamy" does not appear to be more common among less stable relationships. On average, the birth unions we examine existed for five years before the most recent birth. Those unions remaining intact appear to have reported longer prior to the recent birth than their counterparts that go on to dissolve (i.e., 5.3 years vs 3.7). Lastly, unions were observed in our exposure period (i.e., from birth of most recent birth in a union to interview/dissolution) for approximately five years with approximately one year in variation according to union outcome.

Multivariate Findings

Table 2 presents coefficients from event history logistic regression analyses. Coefficients are more useful than odds ratios for interpreting interactions, but we sometimes refer to differences in the likelihood in the text for an easier understanding the of main effects.[5] Model 1 considers the associations between all focal predictors (i.e., intentions, marital status, and stepfamily status) and union stability net of fertility histories, sociodemographic characteristics, duration of coresidence before the birth, and time since the birth. Findings align with prior research and indicate that fertility intentions, marital ties, and stepfamily status are significant predictors of union stability. Net of covariates, unintended higher-order births are associated with a greater likelihood of dissolution ($b = 0.52$, $p < 0.001$) compared to intended births (i.e., a 56% increase in the chance of dissolving). Marital birth unions experience a lower likelihood of dissolution relative to those occurring in cohabiting unions (i.e., $b = -0.52$, $p < 0.001$; a 64% decrease in the probability of dissolution). Finally, stepfamily status was significantly linked to a greater likelihood ($b = 0.32$, $p < 0.001$) of dissolution compared to births occurring in simple families (i.e., 30% increase in the likelihood of dissolution).

Younger ages at first birth, lower levels of education, and older age at interview are associated with an increased likelihood of dissolution whereas union duration before the recent birth and the number of additional children are associated with a decreased likelihood of dissolution.

Models 2 and 3 introduce the interaction terms needed to assess support for hypotheses. Model 2 demonstrates that the effect of an unintended birth differs according to marital status, see the significant interaction term coefficient. To aid in the interpretation of this interaction, we factor out the effect of relationship status. Experiencing a most recent, higher-order unintended birth in a cohabiting birth union is not associated with union stability (see $b = 0.14$, $p > 0.05$ for

Table 2.   Event History Analyses Predicting Union Dissolution (Coefficients).

	Model 1	Model 2	Model 3
	b	*b*	*b*
Constant	−1.40***	−1.24**	−1.40**
Focal Independent Variables			
(Intended birth)			
Unintended birth	0.52***	0.14	0.53***
(Cohabiting at birth)			
Marital birth	−0.52***	−0.76***	−0.52***
(Not in a stepfamily)			
Stepfamily	0.32***	0.31***	0.33**
Fertility History			
(All prior births intended)			
Prior unintended pregnancy	−0.07	−0.06	−0.07
Age at first birth	−0.16***	−0.16***	−0.16***
Number of live births	−0.26***	−0.27***	−0.26***
Sociodemographic Characteristics			
Racial/ethnic status			
(White)			
Black	0.03	0.06	0.03
Hispanic	−0.09	−0.10	−0.09
Other	−0.15	−0.16	−0.15
Age at interview	0.14***	0.14***	0.14***
Educational Attainment			
(At least a bachelor's)			
Some college, no degree	0.41*	0.41*	0.41*
High school diploma (incl. GED)	0.46**	0.46**	0.46**
No degree	0.39*	0.39*	0.39*
Age "heterogamy"	0.05		0.04
Duration Indicators			
Years since most recent birth	−0.39***	−0.39***	−0.39***
Years partnered prior to recent birth	−0.08***	−0.08***	−0.08***
Interaction Terms			
Unintended × married		0.52**	
Unintended × stepfamily			−0.02
Model Fit Statistics			
F	91.10***	87.35***	87.56***
N		28,132	

*$p < 0.05$, **$p < 0.01$, ***$p < 0.001$.

unintended birth). Yet, unintended childbearing in marital unions is linked to a significant increase in the likelihood of dissolution ($b = 0.52$, $p < 0.01$). The total "effect" for unintended childbearing in marital unions (i.e., 0.14 + 0.52 = 0.66) demonstrates that unintended childbearing in marriage considerably reduces the "protective effect ($b = −0.76$, $p < 0.001$)" of marriage (i.e., −0.76 + 0.66 = −0.10). This finding aligns with the selection argument that unintended childbearing has more salient linkages with dissolution among married couples. In contrast, Model 3 presents evidence of a null finding; the association between unintended fertility and relationship stability does not differ according to stepfamily status. The nonsignificant interaction term in Model 3 provides further evidence in support of selection processes rather than causal mechanisms. Analyses that are limited to stepfamilies provide additional support for this substantive conclusion, while taking into consideration more nuanced indicators of stepfamily composition (Table 3). Among stepfamilies, only the mother being a stepparent is associated with a reduced likelihood of dissolution ($b = -0.81$,

Table 3. Event History Analyses Predicting Union Dissolution Among Stepfamilies (Coefficients).

	Model 1	Model 2	Model 3
	b	b	b
Constant	−1.02	−0.96	−0.97
Focal Independent Variables			
(Intended birth)			
Unintended birth	0.38**	0.21	0.09
(Cohabiting birth)			
Marital birth	−0.51***	−0.65***	−0.50***
(Complex stepfamily)			
Only stepfather	−0.19	−0.18	−0.37
Only stepmother	−0.81***	−0.81***	−0.90**
Fertility History			
(All prior births intended)			
Prior unintended pregnancy	0.15	0.16	0.15
Age at first birth	−0.17***	−0.17***	−0.17***
Number of live births	−0.21***	−0.22***	−0.21***
Sociodemographic Characteristics			
Racial/ethnic status			
(White)			
Black	0.03	0.03	0.04
Hispanic	−0.18	−0.18	−0.19
Other	−0.20	−0.21	−0.19
Age at interview	0.15***	0.15***	0.15***
Educational Attainment			
(At least a bachelor's)			
Some college, no degree	0.62**	0.61**	0.62**
High school diploma (incl. GED)	0.57**	0.56*	0.58**
No degree	0.36	0.36	0.37
Age "heterogamy"	−0.06	−0.05	−0.06
Duration Indicators			
Years since most recent birth	−0.38***	−0.38***	−0.38***
Years partnered prior to recent birth	−0.11***	−0.11***	−0.11***
Interaction Terms			
Unintended × married		0.29	
(Unintended × complex stepfamily)			
Unintended × only stepfather			0.42
Unintended × only stepmother			0.23
Model Fit Statistics			
F	28.13***	26.56***	25.64***
N		15,001	

$*p < 0.05, **p < 0.01, ***p < 0.001.$

$p < 0.001$) when contrasted with couples where both partners are stepparents. Once again, similar associations between fertility intentions and marital status are significantly linked to dissolution among stepparents. Unintended childbearing is associated with an increased likelihood of dissolution whereas being married at the time of birth appears protective in terms of relationship stability. Of note, among stepfamilies, analyses indicate that the association between intentions and dissolution does not differ according to marital status (see Model 2) or the configuration of stepparents by gender (see Model 3).

DISCUSSION

Contemporary families in the United States are marked by high levels of diversity and heterogeneity, which reflect patterns in structural inequality (Cherlin, 2010; McLanahan, 2004; Raley & Sweeney, 2020). Variation in family behaviors includes facets such as unintended childbearing, marital status, and the presence or absence of children from prior unions. In this chapter, we sought to contribute to an established body of research that links unintended childbearing (e.g., Guzzo & Hayford, 2012; Lichter et al., 2016; Maddow-Zimet et al., 2016), cohabitation (Manlove et al., 2012; Manning et al., 2004; Nock, 1995), and stepfamily living arrangements (Cherlin, 1978; Raley & Sweeney, 2020) with an elevated risk of dissolution. We asserted prior approaches have not yet adequately modeled how the association between unintended childbearing and dissolution might differ according to marital and stepfamily statuses, in part because much of the research focuses on first births. By focusing on a mother's most recent, higher-order birth occurring in a union, we investigated this intersection, and our analyses make significant contributions to existing scholarship by offering insight into the leading mechanisms (i.e., causal or selection) the field has employed to explain how unintended childbearing is linked to union dissolution.

Our findings provide greater evidence in support of selection over causal frameworks, among a sample of higher-order births occurring to partnered parents. Consistent with prior work, unintended childbearing and stepfamily status were positively associated with union dissolution whereas marriage had protective effects for stability. Nock's (1995) incomplete institution framework for cohabitation would suggest that unintended childbearing should exacerbate an already elevated risk of dissolution. However, on the contrary, analyses reported that unintended childbearing was only predictive of dissolution for married couples. At face value, this finding may seem surprising, but it aligns with prior evidence that unintended childbearing has uniquely strong associations with marital instability (see Guzzo & Hayford, 2012; Stykes & Guzzo, 2020). We interpret this finding as reinforcing the selection framework in efforts to explain the link between unintended childbearing and instability. Because childbearing within marriage is considered normative – perhaps even expected – marriages in which unintended childbearing occurs may have underlying challenges linked to both the unintended birth itself and marital stability. Alternatively, it may also be the case that the instability of cohabiting unions is already higher than in marital unions or that there are selection factors that go into having a birth within a cohabiting union, regardless of intention status, such that experiencing an unintended birth does not have an additional impact.

The intersection between unintended childbearing and stepfamily status appears to support a similar explanation through a different association between characteristics. In contrast to the previous interaction between unintended childbearing and marital status, the association between unintended childbearing and stability did not differ according to stepfamily status. Recall, we asserted that a causal link between unintended childbearing and stepfamily status should yield a significant association between unintended childbearing and stepfamily status whereas a nonsignificant interaction term would suggest other factors increased the risk of both unintended childbearing and instability. Notably, a significant body of research in the European context has demonstrated that stepfamilies bolster instances of shared, intended childbearing, which have protective effects on relationship stability (Saint-Jacques et al., 2011; Thomson, 2004). However, our findings align with Guzzo (2017) in that intended, most recent births in stepfamilies do not appear to be especially protective (nor unintended births especially disruptive) when contrasted to more simple family configurations.

Of course, research has increasingly articulated that diversity among stepfamilies is considerable and should be taken into consideration (Stewart, 2007; Stykes, 2020), with prior research illustrating that stepfamily configuration (considering whether the mother, father, or both parents is(are) a stepparent(s), along with whether stepfamilies are cohabiting vs. marital unions) has implications for stressors associated with parenting, relationship quality, and stability (Guzzo et al., 2019; MacDonald & DeMaris, 1996; Martin et al., 2011; Shapiro, 2014; Stewart, 2005). Given our simplistic indicator of stepfamily status in the primary models, we replicated event history analyses among a sample of stepfamilies to investigate the association between stepfamily configuration and union stability more precisely. This sensitivity analyses did not produce any evidence that stepfamily configuration moderated the link between unintended childbearing and instability with more nuanced indicators of stepfamily status, which we consider a robustness check in evaluating evidence in support of selection processes.

Despite the contributions that our study makes to existing research, noteworthy limitations need to be discussed. First, and perhaps foremost, our analyses were considerably limited by the NSFG's recent restriction of month data for births and union events. This shift had three significant implications for our analyses and findings. One, we are less precise in our ability to establish a temporal order for events occurring in the same year, and so we excluded cases where this occurred. Two, we lost significant statistical power, as our modeling strategy required the analyses of person-years rather than person-months. Three, our analyses cannot consider any cases where the union was either censored by interview or dissolved within one year of the most recent pregnancy. To this end, our analyses likely omit the least stable unions and provide downwardly biased estimates of instability. Our second major limitation is that, given our limited statistical power and a modeling strategy that relied on interaction models, we had to embrace fairly a fairly sparse set of covariates in our analyses and lacked adequate sample size to parse out more nuanced operational definitions of both unintended childbearing (i.e., differentiating unwanted and mistimed births) and stepfamily status. Although this is not ideal, significant model fit statistics indicate that our models remain reasonable. Finally, our reliance on a binary, retrospective indicator of intendedness certainly overlooks substantial ambivalence in birth intentions and is not immune to recall and social desirability biases, though our decision to focus attention on the most recent birth is an effort to minimize recall bias (e.g., Joyce et al., 2002). However, prior work finds that retrospective reports of unintended childbearing remain a reliable approach to operationalizing intentions (Santelli et al., 2009).

Findings show that higher-order, unintended births are indeed associated with union stability, suggesting that in the US context, selection processes appear to be more relevant than causal arguments in understanding the relationship between unintended births and instability. To that end, these findings have important implications for future research and programming. Certainly, more work is needed to identify the selection mechanisms at play. Does higher-order, unintended childbearing reflect the disadvantage of the populations most likely to experience such births, or is it indicative of an "already strained" relationship? Given steep economic pre-requisites for marriage (Edin & Kefalas, 2004; Gibson-Davis et al., 2005; Smock, Manning, & Porter, 2005) coupled with our finding that unintended childbearing is only linked with dissolution for married couples, we expect it may be the latter. To that end, a greater effort to include a more extensive array of indicators of relationship quality into this framework is needed. While the NSFG has many strengths, such an endeavor is better suited to different data. Second, the causal explanation concerning unintended childbearing among stepfamilies arguably assumed that intended childbearing was shared (that is, that both partners intended the birth). To that end, future research that is more readily able to employ a couple-level approach (incorporating both parents' assessment of intendedness) may be better suited to unearth a causal mechanism for unintended childbearing among stepfamilies, if it exists. Beyond simply informing future research, our findings provide unique insights into how programs should strive to promote stability among couples with children. In short, with regards to unintended childbearing, distinctions should be made between new parents and those with prior children. Among the former group, prior research indicates that programming efforts seeking to empower and equip parents to respond to the stressors associated with an unintended birth may indeed promote stability (Kavanaugh et al., 2017; Stykes & Guzzo 2020). Yet, for couples who have prior children, efforts that seek to respond to a recent unintended birth as a stressful life event may be less effective than broader strategies to promote healthy relationship dynamics more broadly.

NOTES

1. We define higher-order in the context of women's reproductive careers, not a specific relationship.
2. Given the recent changes to the NSFG public use data, we cannot attach months to events. This results in downwardly biased estimates of instability, as unions that do not endure the first year following the birth cannot be identified.

3. Please note, we do not count the transition from cohabiting union to marriage as a form of dissolution given our focus on relationship stability. Cohabiting unions which transition to marriages that eventually dissolve are coded for dissolution at the year the marriage ends in either divorce or separation.

4. Supplemental analyses (available on request) considered a more robust set of controls for the respondent's background. However, their inclusion did not substantively alter our conclusions.

5. To aid in the written interpretation of coefficients from our logistic regression, coefficients are exponentiated to produce an odds ratio. Odds ratios are then used to interpret associations in terms of a percent increase in the odds of dissolution by applying the following formula (1 – Odds Ratio) *100.

REFERENCES

Atzl, V. M., Narayan, A. J., Ballinger, A., Harris, W. M., & Liberman, A. F. (2021). Maternal pregnancy wantedness and perceptions of paternal pregnancy wantedness: Associations with perinatal mental health and relationship dynamics. *Maternal and Child Health Journal, 25*, 450–459.

Barber, J. S., Axinn, W. G., & Thornton, A. R. (1999). Unwanted childbearing, health, and mother-child relationships. *Journal of Health and Social Behavior, 40*(3), 231–257.

Brown, S. L. (2000). Union transitions among cohabitors: The significance of relationship assessments and expectations. *Journal of Marriage and Family, 62*(3), 833–846.

Brown, S. L. (2005). How cohabitation is reshaping American families. *Contexts, 4*(3), 33–37.

Cherlin, A. J. (1978). Remarriage and an incomplete institution. *American Journal of Sociology, 84*(3), 634–650.

Cherlin, A. J. (2010). Demographic trends in the United States: A review of research in the 2000s. *Journal of Marriage and Family, 72*(3), 403–419.

Edin, K., & Kefalas, M. (2005). *Promises I can keep: Why poor women put motherhood before marriage.* Berkeley: University of California Press.

Finer, L. B., & Zolna, M. R. (2011). Unintended pregnancy in the United States: Incidence and disparities, 2006. *Contraception, 84*(5), 478–485.

Finer, L. B., & Zolna, M. R. (2016). Declines in unintended fertility in the United States, 2008-2011. *The New England Journal of Medicine, 374*(9), 843–852.

Gariepy, A., Lundsberg, L. S., Vilardo, N., Stanwood, N., Yonkers, K., & Schwartz, E. B. (2017). Pregnancy context and women's health-related quality of life. *Contraception, 95*(5), 491–499.

Gibson, C. M., Edin, K., & McLanahan, S. (2005). High hopes but even higher expectations: The retreat from marriage among low-income couples. *Journal of Marriage and Family, 67*(5), 1301–1312.

Guzzo, K. B. (2017). Is stepfamily status associated with cohabiting and married women's fertility behaviors?*Demography, 54*, 45–70.

Guzzo, K. B. (2018). Marriage and dissolution among women's cohabitations: Variations by stepfamily status and shared childbearing. *Journal of Family Issues, 39*(4), 1108–1136.

Guzzo, K. B. (2021). *Unintended births: Variation across social and demographic characteristics* (Family Profiles, FP-21-02). Bowling Green, OH: National Center for Family & Marriage Research. https://doi.org/10.25035/ncfmr/fp-21-02

Guzzo, K. B. (2014). New partners, more kids: Multiple-partner fertility in the United States. *The Annals of the American Academy of Political and Social Science, 654*(1), 66–86.

Guzzo, K.B. & Hayford, S. (2011). Fertility following an unintended first birth. *Demography, 48*(4), 1493–1516.

Guzzo, K. B., & Hayford, S. R. (2012). Unintended fertility and the stability of coresidential relationships. *Social Science Research, 41*, 1138–1151.

Guzzo, K. B., Hemez, P., Anderson, L., Manning, W. D., & Brown, S. L. (2019). Is variation in biological and residential ties to children linked to mothers' parental stress and perceptions of coparenting?*Journal of Family Issues, 40*(4), 488–517.

Hohmann-Marriott, B. (2009). The couple context of pregnancy and its effects on prenatal care and birth outcomes. *Maternal and Child Health Journal, 13*(1), 745–754.

Joyce, T., Kaestner, R., & Korenman,S. (2002). On the validity of retrospective assessments of pregnancy intention. *Demography, 39*, 199–213.

Joyner, K., Peters, H. E., Hynes, K., Sikora, A., Taber, J. R., & Rendall, M. S. (2012). The quality of male fertility data in major U.S. surveys. *Demography, 49*(1), 101–124.

Kamp Dush, C. (2011). Relationship-specific investments, family chaos, and cohabitation dissolution following a non-marital birth. *Family Relations, 60*(5), 586–601.

Kavanaugh, M. L., Kost, K., Frohwirth, L., Maddow-Zimet, I., & Gor, V. (2017). Parents' experience of unintended childbearing: A qualitative study of factors that mitigate or exacerbate effects. *Social Science & Medicine, 174*, 133–141.

Lichter, D. L., Michelmore, K., Turner, R. N., & Sassler, S. (2016). Pathways to a stable union? Pregnancy and childbearing among cohabiting and married couples. *Population Research and Policy Review, 35*(1), 377–399.

Lichter, D. L., & Qian, Z. (2008). Serial cohabitation and the marital life course. *Journal of Marriage and Family, 70*(4), 861–878.

Lindberg, L. D., Kost, K., & Maddow-Zimet, I. (2017). The role of men's childbearing intentions in father involvement. *Journal of Marriage and Family, 79*(1), 44–59.

Lindberg, L. D., Kost, K., Maddow-Zimet, I., Desai, S., & Zolna, M. (2020). Abortion reporting in the United States: An assessment of three national fertility surveys. *Demography, 57*, 899–925.

Lindberg, L. D., Maddow-Zimet, I., Kost, K., & Lincoln, A. (2015). Pregnancy intentions and child health: An analysis of longitudinal data in Oklahoma. *Maternal and Child Health Journal, 19*, 1087–1096.

MacDonald, W. L., & DeMaris, A. (1996). Parenting stepchildren and biological children: The effects of stepparent's gender and new biological children. *Journal of Family Issues, 17*(1), 5–25.

Maddow-Zimet, I., Lindberg, L., Kost, K., & Lincoln, A. (2016). Are pregnancy intentions associated with transitions into and out of marriage? *Journal of Marriage and Family, 48*(1), 35–43.

Manning, W. D. (2020). Young adulthood relationships in an era of uncertainty: A case for cohabitation. *Demography, 57*, 799–819.

Manning, W. D., Brown, S. L., & Stykes, J. B. (2014). Family complexity among children in the United States. *The Annals of the American Academy of Political and Social Science, 654*(1), 48–65.

Manning, W. D., Brown, S. L., & Stykes, J. B. (2015). *Trends in births to single and cohabiting mothers: 1980-2013.* (FP-15-03). National Center for Marriage and Family Research. Retrieved from https://www.bgsu.edu/content/dam/BGSU/college-of-arts-and-sciences/NCFMR/documents/FP/FP-15-03-birth-trends-single-cohabiting-moms.pdf.

Manning, W. D., Joyner, K., Hemez, P., & Cupka, C. (2019). Measuring cohabitation in US national surveys. *Demography, 56*(4), 1195–1218.

Manning, W. D., & Smock, P. J. (2005). Measuring and modeling cohabitation: New perspectives from qualitative data. *Journal of Marriage and Family, 67*(4), 989–1002.

Manning, W. D., Smock, P. J., & Majumdar, D. (2004). The relative stability of cohabiting and marital unions for children. *Population Research and Policy Review, 23*, 135–159.

Martin, V., LeBourdais, C., & Lapierre-Adamcyk, E. (2011). Stepfamily instability in Canada – The impact of family composition and union type. *Journal of Family Research, 23*(2), 196–218.

Manlove, J., Wildsmith, E., Ikramullah, E., Ryan, S., Holcombe, E., Scott, M., & Peterson, K. (2012). Union transitions following the birth of a child to cohabiting parents. *Population Research and Policy Review, 31*, 361–386.

McLanahan, S. (2004). Diverging destinies: How children are faring under the second demographic transition. *Demography, 41*, 607–627.

Miller, W. B., Sable, M. R., & Beckmeyer, J. J. (2009). Preconception motivation and pregnancy wantedness: Pathways to toddler attachment security. *Journal of Marriage and Family, 71*(5), 1174–1192.

Moore, K. A., Ryan, S., Manlove, J., Mincieli, L., & Schelar, E. (2009). High-risk subsequent births among co-residential couples: The role of fathers, mothers, and couples. *Fathering: A Journal of Theory, Research, & Practice About Men as Fathers, 7*(1), 91–102.

Musick, K., England, P., Edginton, S., & Kangas, N. (2009). Education differences in intended and unintended fertility. *Social Forces, 88*(2), 543–572.

Musick, K., & Michelmore, K. (2015). Change in the stability of marital and cohabiting unions following a first birth. *Demography, 52*, 1463–1485.

Nock, S. L. (1995). A comparison of marriages and cohabiting relationships. *Journal of Family Issues, 16*(1), 53–76.

Raley, R. K., & Sweeney, M. M. (2020). Divorce, repartnering, and Stepfamilies: A decade in review. *Journal of Marriage and Family, 82*(1), 81–99.

Saint-Jacques, M. C., Robitaille, C., Godbout, E., Parent, C., Drapeau, S., & Gagne, M. H. (2011). The processes distinguishing stable from unstable stepfamily couple: A qualitative analyses. *Family Relations, 60*, 545–561.

Saleem, H. T., & P. J. Surkan. (2014). Parental pregnancy wantedness and child socio-emotional development. *Maternal and Child Health Journal, 18*, 930–938.

Santelli, J. S., Lindberg, L. D., Orr, M. G., Finer, L. B., & Speizer, I. (2009). Toward a multidimensional measure of pregnancy intentions: Evidence from the United States. *Studies in Family Planning, 40*(2), 87–100.

Shapiro, D. (2014). Stepparents and parenting stress: The roles of gender, marital quality, and views about gender roles. *Family Process, 53*(1), 97–108.

Smock, P. J. (2000). Cohabitation in the United States: An appraisal of research themes, findings, and implications. *Annual Review of Sociology, 26*, 1–20.

Smock, P. J., Manning, W. D., & Porter, M. (2005). Everything's there except money: How money shapes decisions to marry among cohabitors. *Journal of Marriage and Family, 67*(3), 680–696.

Stewart, S. D. (2005). Boundary ambiguity in stepfamilies. *Journal of Family Issues, 26*(7), 1002–1029.

Stewart, S. D. (2007). *Brave new stepfamilies: Diverse paths toward stepfamily living.* Thousand Oaks, CA: Sage Publications, Inc.

Stykes, J. B. (2019). Gender, couples' fertility intentions, and parents' depressive symptoms. *Society and Mental Health, 9*(3), 334–349.

Stykes, J. B. (2020). What we really know about stepfamilies: An elaboration on biases of White, middle class families in stepfamily research In S. D. Stewart's & G. Limb's (Eds.), *Stepfamilies: Multicultural perspectives.* San Diego: Cognella.

Stykes, J. B., & Guzzo, K. B. (2019). Multiple-partner fertility: Variation across measurement approaches. In R. Schoen (Ed.), *Analytical Family Demography,* Cham: Springer.

Stykes, J. B., & Guzzo, K. B. (2020). Unintended childbearing and marital instability: An emphasis on couples' intentions. *Journal of Divorce and Remarriage, 61*, 504–524.

Su, J. H. (2012). Pregnancy intentions and parents' psychological well-being. *Journal of Marriage and Family, 74*(5), 1182–1196.

Thomson, E. (2004). Step-families and childbearing desires in Europe. *Demographic Research, 3*(5), 117–134.

Thornton, A. (1977). Children and marital stability. *Journal of Marriage and Family, 39*(3), 531–540.

Wildsmith, E., Guzzo, K. B., & Hayford, S. R. (2010). Repeat unintended, unwanted, and seriously mistimed childbearing in the United States. *Perspectives on Sexual and Reproductive Health, 42*(1), 14–22.

Willoughby, B. J., Carroll, J. S., & Busby, D. M. (2011). The different effects of 'living together': Determining and comparing types of cohabiting couples. *Journal of Social and Personal Relationships, 29*(3), 397–419.

Wu, L. L., & Musick, K. (2008). Stability of marital and cohabiting unions following a first birth. *Population Research and Policy Review, 27*, 713–727.

CHAPTER 12

DYNAMISM AND CHANGES IN THE ABIA FAMILY STRUCTURE AND CONJUGAL RELATIONSHIP: THE INFLUENCE OF THE NIGERIAN CIVIL WAR

Chigozirim Ogubuike, Mofeyisara Oluwatoyin Omobowale and Olukemi K. Amodu

ABSTRACT

The family, as the most basic social institution, serves as the bedrock of any society. Family structures worldwide have undergone various changes in their forms, nature, and functioning, including Abia state, Nigeria. The Nigeria Civil war is one of the symbolic events attributable to changes in the Abia family structure. Changes in the family structure could influence conjugal relationships. The study explored the dynamism and changes in the family structure and conjugal relationships at different eras of the family life cycle in Abia society. A qualitative research method was used in this study. Twenty-two participants (4 life history and 18 in-depth interview participants) were recruited in this study with purposive sampling techniques. Using an archival checklist, life histories, and an in-depth guide, information was elicited on family structure and conjugal relationships. The study was subjected to thematic analysis. The findings revealed dynamism and changes in family structure, with polygyny being most prevalent prior to the civil war, the emergence of step-parent and single-parent families during the civil war, and monogamy being most prevalent,

Conjugal Trajectories: Relationship Beginnings, Change, and Dissolutions
Contemporary Perspectives in Family Research, Volume 22, 233–253
Copyright © 2023 by Emerald Publishing Limited
ISSN: 1530-3535/doi:10.1108/S1530-353520230000022012

with increasing single-parent and step-parent families contemporaneously. The conjugal relationship shifted from having concubines (acceptable and practised covertly) to having side chicks (been practised covertly). The Nigerian civil war had an impact on the observed dynamics in family structure during the civil war and immediate post-civil war. Other factors such as religion, education, civilization, and migration, among others, influenced the contemporary Abia family structure. Understanding family structure dynamics could be useful in solving issues regarding family and conjugal trajectories.

Keywords: Family structure; family dynamism; Abia family structure; conjugal relationship; Nigeria Civil war; intergenerational patterns

INTRODUCTION

The family is the most basic social institution and serves as the bedrock of any society (Cao, 2012; Labeodan, 2005). Different definitions of the family exist due to various manifestations, organizations, and structures in various societies (Jackson, 2015). A family is seen as a group of two or more people who are related by blood, marriage, adoption, or mutual commitment and who care for one another (Starbuck, 2010). Family life cannot sustain itself without marriage. Marriage is the means by which a family is established and is viewed as a necessary but not sufficient condition to create a family (Isidienu, 2015; Labeodan, 2005). Marriage and family are key structures in many societies (William & McGivern, 2012), and they play an important role. The family can be categorized based on the marriage types, which include nuclear families (monogamous or conjugal families) and polygamous families. One basic fact about the family is its dynamic nature and susceptibility to change (Nwanoro, 2013). Family structures worldwide have undergone various changes in their forms, nature, and functioning (Alabi, 2021). Family structure and family changes are not mutually exclusive, but they are conceptually distinct (Defo & Dimbuene, 2012). Contemporary families have undergone significant transformations in their structure and have experienced conjugal trajectories. Family changes are dynamic measures of family structure which measure the transitions from one family structure to another over the family life cycle (Defo & Dimbuene, 2012). This study focuses on intergenerational variations in conjugality, comparing family changes and conjugal relations from traditional times to contemporary times.

CASE STUDY

Igbo (Abia) Family Structure

The focus was on the Igbo family structure, particularly the Abia family dynamism. The family in Igbo society is referred to as *ezi na ụlọ*, literally translated to mean relations both within and outside the house (Ufearoh, 2010). *Ezi na ulo* means people united by a bond of kin network and interlocking functions and reciprocities, which portrays an extended family (Uchendu, 2007). There were many strengths in the traditional Igbo society, which had a high regard for the family as the pivot on which the wheel of regeneration rotates (Nwanoro, 2013). To begin with, polygyny was the most common form of marriage, consisting of a man, many wives, and children; Igbo people saw monogamy as a sure path to poverty; polygyny was widely practised due to the labor required for agricultural production. Having several women in a household enhanced not only a man's social status but also the prestige of the first wife, who presides over household deliberations. Junior wives enjoy the security and prosperity that large households provide (Achebe, 1958). Secondly, the extended family system was also one of the popular and important socio-cultural and ethical institutions of Igbo traditional society. The central features of the extended family were the kinship unit and structural extension (Uchendu, 2007). It played an important role in the development of the individual and in the maintenance of social-ethical order in Igbo land (Ekeopara, 2012). Strong attachment to lineage and distant family relatives were welcomed at any time as full members of the family (Agwaraonye, 2015). The extended family had the power and authority to exert influence on the attitudes, behaviors, and conduct of individual members of its unit and covered the areas of social relationships, interaction, and morality (Ekeopara, 2012).

Nigeria's Civil War as a Catalyst of Change in the Family

A major shift in the traditional Igbo family structure has been attributed to the Nigerian civil war. The civil war was the first modern war in sub-Saharan Africa after independence, which occurred between 1967 and 1970, causing great devastation among the Igbo people in South-Eastern Nigeria (Akresh, Bhalotra, Leone, & Osili, 2011, 2017). Ineffective attempts to reinstate Nigerian federalism were the root cause of the Nigerian Civil War, not ethnic rivalries. The Igbo had the strongest dedication to federalism before the conflict, and the two coups that occurred right before the Civil War were attempts to reaffirm federalist ideas amid escalating ethnic strife and a political crisis. The execution of the coups was allegedly biased to promote ethnic interests, which worsened rather than reduced ethnic tensions. As a result, ethnic pogroms in 1966–1967 against Igbo-originating Nigerians living in the northern part of the country were carried out by northern Nigerian civilians, who had previously carried out the coups, leading to the deaths of many Igbos (Owhorodu, 2020; Ukiwo, 2009).

The civil war also brought about significant social and demographic changes in the family structure. Studies have shown that the consequences of the civil war include the devastation of families, exchange of sex for survival, rape, early widowhood, and numerous deaths of men, amongst others (Akresh et al., 2017; Smith, 2005; Uchendu, 2007; Ukiwo, 2009). The civil war threatened Igbo traditional customs for marriage and family as a result of the increase in marriages among other ethnic groups. Most of the Igbo women married men from other ethnic groups from distant places, as the war brought in soldiers from different ethnic groups (Harneit-Sievers, Ahazuem, & Emezue, 1997; Smith, 2005). Other factors that are attributable to the change in the family structure post-war include urbanization, industrialization, education, globalization and technological development (Agwaraonye, 2015; Naila, 2012; Ohiagu, 2010; Ugwu, 2010). All these factors may, directly or indirectly, affect the contemporary family structure.

Observed Changes and Dynamism in Abia's Family Structure

The observed dynamism in the family structure is the upsurge of the nuclear family system with an emphasis on monogamy and individualism, diminishing the extended family system in Igbo society (Ekeopara, 2012). These changes have raised several questions and produced more complex relationship forms and dynamic family structures (Alabi & Olonade, 2022). Some of these changes include a decrease in polygyny, a decline in the size of the extended family household, lowered fertility rate, increase in divorce and introduction of stepfamilies, diminished parental control, change in discipline, inability to provide for the children, leading to loss of parental authority and less male dominance (Agwaraonye, 2015; Ekeopara, 2012; Mere, 1976; Ndem & Müürsepp, 2018; Obi, 2016). These changes in the traditional Igbo family structure may influence behavior and attitudes among children and society at large. Despite these notable changes, the family remains a vital part of contemporary society with significant influences (Alabi, 2021). The study was therefore conducted to explore the dynamism and changes in the family structure and conjugal relationships at different eras in the family life cycle.

THEORETICAL BACKGROUND

The theory of family development was explored in the study to explain the influences that impact the dynamism in family structure and conjugal relationships. Family development theory (FDT) was one of the earliest theories that had a specific focus on families because it was developed as part of efforts to solve family disarray in the years following World War II (Duvall, 1988). The origin of FDT precedes the theory itself because it is a combination of family sociology and human development within the context of a family (Duvall, 1988). Duvall's formulation of FDT (Duvall, 1957) placed a strong emphasis on the family life cycle and family developmental activities. The family life cycle is the belief that the family starts with marriage, grows as children are added and raised, and then contracts as the children leave home and start their own families of their own (Duvall, 1957). Family development is viewed by White (1991) as a dynamic process incorporating social context and events. The concept of transitional events in the family and conjugality is one modification that is crucial to the development described in this study. In family life, when a transitional event occurs it heralds the start of the end of a stage and causes a change in roles and responsibilities.

FDT places a lot of emphasis on the start and maintenance of marriage and acknowledges that, over time, families as a whole change. Thus, the nature and quality of relationships can change through time, not just from positive to negative but as a developmental process (Crapo, 2020). The FDT was used to illustrate the changes and dynamism of the family structure as a result of the influence of the Nigerian civil war. The Nigerian civil war influenced the family life cycle and caused a change over time. This brought about significant social and demographic changes in the family structure. These changes have raised several questions and produced more complex relationship forms and dynamic family structures (Alabi & Olonade, 2022). FDT also explored couple relationships and conjugality. Couple relationships in this context improve our understanding of the role of couple relationships in family development (Duvall, 1957). Marital relationships in FDT can be hypothesized as a trajectory within the couple dimension. Events and experiences within the couple dimension may shape that trajectory, and thereby implicitly change the nature of the relationship (Jensen & Rauer, 2014, 2015). Other aspects of development and cultural events are two more key variables that have an impact on the trajectory of marital relationships (Crapo, 2020). This invariably may exert an influence on couple conjugal bonds.

METHODOLOGY

Study Area

The study was conducted in Abia state, which is part of the Igbo region of Nigeria, originally in the East Central state. It was part of Imo state following the creation of more states in Nigeria in early 1976. Abia state was adversely affected by the Nigerian Civil War (1967–1970), which impacted so much on the economy and the family. Abia State, one of Nigeria's 36 states, was established in 1991. It is located in the South Eastern region of Nigeria with 17 local government areas. Farming is one of the major sources of livelihood; the elderly, in particular, are good at preserving culture as well as at retaining oral historical records on indigenous marriage institutions (Hoiberg, 2010).

Study Design, Population, and Technique

This study utilized a qualitative method to explore the dynamism in the family structure and conjugal relationships in the different eras. The research was conducted in four randomly selected local government areas in Abia state, namely Aba North, Aba South, Osisioma, and Obingwa. The participants included in the study were individuals with an age range (35 to 78 years), indigenes of these local governments who had pre-civil war, civil war-time, and post-civil war experience, and those who consented to participate in the study. Participants excluded in this study were individuals with memory loss and those who were ill at the time of the study. Twenty-two participants participated in this study (four participated in a life history interview while eighteen participated in an in-depth interview). A snowballing technique was used to recruit life history participants, while purposive sampling techniques were used in recruiting participants for an in-depth interview.

The Data Instrument and Procedure

Archival research, life histories, and in-depth interviews were conducted. For the archival research method, information on family structure and war experiences was elicited from intelligent reports, newspapers, books, bulletins, and all other relevant documents from the National Archives in Enugu and Ibadan using an archival checklist. Prior to the commencement of data collection, community entry was done in the local government area of study and permission was sought from the Community Development Chairman (CDC) and the council of chiefs. Before the onset of data collection, ethical approval to conduct the study was obtained from the UI/UCH Ethical Review Board and Abia State ethical review board. The participants who agreed to participate in the interviews were given a written consent form to sign after the study had been explained to them. The recorded interviews were kept private and made only available to the research team for transcription. The interviews were kept private and safe. Participation in the study was purely voluntary.

Data Management and Analysis

The recorded interviews were transcribed immediately following the interviewing process to ensure completeness that could be lost due to delay. The transcription was verbatim as this process protects the originality and reliability of the data collected. The interviews conducted in Igbo were translated and transcribed into English. The typed transcripts were read several times and cleaned; the transcripts were coded; and a code book was developed both inductively and deductively. Data was analyzed using the thematic analysis method with Atlas ti data qualitative software version 7.5.21. A clear, coherent, and integrated presentation of data was done in a sequential manner.

RESULT

Pre-Civil War (1901–1966) – Family Structure and Conjugal Relationship

Family Structure – Predominately Polygyny

Prior the Nigerian civil war, polygyny was part of the social life and sociological settings in the Igbo society including the Abia society. It was very common and widely practiced. It was well enjoyed by the head of house which is the "man." The native marriage and the government also promoted polygyny; this was vivid in an archival material by Basden:

> The head of the house dines alone in his private apartment, each wife in turn attending to his needs. Native marriage which is valid promoted polygamy, the Government recognized it as the custom of the country. In the native marriage there were no restrictions as to the wives a man may own. (Basden, 1921, A1/B2)

Apart from the man that enjoyed polygamous household wives enjoyed it equally. Polygyny was celebrated and encouraged due to the way new wives were treated in a polygamous family. They were relieved from house chores as summarized in the archival report below:

The first wife usually lives in the same house with the husband, but if there is already a wife, the husband usually sends her to live with the first wife. For a whole year a new wife does not work, her husband's mother or wife does the cooking, but if there is no mother and no other wife, she would probably do it herself; in any case she does not go to market or farm for a year. (Thomas 1913, A1/T74)

Polygyny was the most prevalent family structure in the traditional Abia society. Majority of the respondents were from polygamous family and their fathers had three wives and above. The quotes below illustrates the assertions'

Polygamy was more common, some of my brothers married two to three wives some married even ten wives. (AbaNorth_Male_78 years)

In corroboration, another participant averred:

My grandfather had 14 wives, had 14 sons and 30 daughters. He was the richest man then in our village. My father married just four wives. (Obingwa_Male_70 years)

Polygyny was widely practiced for so many reasons; it was seen as signs of affluence, prestigious and sound investment. This was shown in the report below:

Polygamy was favored and fostered especially by men and women; in some respects, the latter are the chief supporters of the system. The ambition of every Ibo man was to have a large family, and therefore marry so many wives as circumstances permit. It was an indication of social standing and, to some extent, signs of affluence; in any case, they are counted as sound investments. (Basden 1921, A1/B2)

Polygyny was practiced for subsistence livelihood, majorly for agricultural purposes, to have enough laborers in the farm and increase farm produce. Also, men married multiple wives for other economic reasons like helping in their business. One of the participants narrated that:

My father was a local preacher and still married four wives because he was a farmer then he needed many hands, the first and second wife delayed in childbirth before he married my mother even the same thing, it was only the fourth wife that had children immediately after marriage. (Osisioma_Female_72 years)

Another female participant shared her views:

Polygamous family was more prevalent, they were marrying many wives except the learned ones that married one. Businessmen, traders, farmers married more than one wives to help them in their business and farm work. (AbaNorth_Female_63years)

In addition, a desire to have a large family size, delay in childbirth and male child preference encouraged men into having multiple wives. Some of the women encouraged their husbands in such decision making. This was averred in an archival report that:

In the case of the women after a respectable period has elapsed since the marriage began, the man might take a second wife. Sometimes it was the first wife herself who took the initiative in procuring a second wife for the husband. (Ifemesia 1979, NHB/C/93)

Polygyny was also practiced for recuperation of women after childbirth, initiated and highly encouraged by women to relieve themselves from loneliness and from domestic burdens of the household. This was vivid in Talbot's report that:

> A child is suckled for several years until it had reached the age of four or five years. Some people forbid cohabitation between husband and wife. (Talbot 1969, NHB/C/4)

Polygyny protected girls from shame and dishonor that may result for not being married and the girl did not mind being a junior wife. An only wife perceived it as being put in a humiliating position and suffering because of domestic tasks. Basden averred thus:

> There is another aspect of the case for polygamy; a woman is not content to remain the sole wife of a man. An only wife considers herself placed in an unenviable and humiliating position. As the sole wife she has to bear, the whole of the domestic burdens of the household and that prospect does not appeal to her. Therefore, for the sake of companionship and to secure relief in her daily tasks, the first wife will willingly render assistance in bringing a second into the establishment. (Basden 1921, A1/B2)

Monogamy received vigorous oppositions from both sexes, both from the political and social standpoints. Igbo women never wanted to associate with a marriage relationship where monogamy was the rule. Monogamy was seen to be associated with disdain, persecutions, bitterness and shame. Igbo men perceived monogamy as a practice contrary to nature and deliberate attempts to frustrate the creation of women. This quote below summarizes the archival report:

> Hence where monogamy is the rule a large number of women must, necessarily, remain unmarried. No Ibo women would tolerate that condition. She would be exposed to every form of contempt and persecution, as well as obliged to suffer the bitter shame of her outraged feelings. The men, on their part, would declaim against the rule on the ground that is contrary to nature, and to the practice of their fathers. It would be a deliberate attempt to frustrate the very purpose for which women are created. (Basden, 1921, A1/B2)

Monogamy was seen as an act contrary to nature and being unfair to women who need sexual satisfaction from men. He averred thus:

> Monogamy left fifty women without husbands and since these fifty women cannot be denied sexual satisfaction; polygamy is the only natural and sincere solution to the problem. (Mbonu Ojike1948)

As reported by one of the respondents, marrying one wife was associated with being poor and impoverished. One of the male participants averred that:

> They look at those that marry one wife as poor people, very poor that why they can't marry more wives because he cannot see money to maintain them and their children not to talk of building house for them because you must build different houses for them. My father was very poor so he married one wife. (Osisioma_Male_65 years)

Conjugal Relationship Pre-Civil War (1901–1966)

Concubines. Apart from having multiple wives, most men had several concubines which were known by the wives. Having concubines was a paramour culture in the traditional Abia society. These women played a role of satisfying the man's sexual desires. Archival materials revealed that some of these concubines were slaves bought during slave trade. It was averred that:

[...] if she was merely a slave utilized as a concubine he could have sell her off at any time. (District office 1922, CSE 36/1/1)

To further buttress this view, it was reported that:

A man of substance would in olden days always have to be accompanied to the spirit world by one or more slaves. If possible one of these would be a concubine of the deceased. (District office 1922, CSE 36/1/3)

To corroborate this assertion, one of the female participants reported that:

My father's fourth wife was a slave who acted as a concubine but after the war he converted her to a wife because she was very helpful to my grandmother. (AbaNorth_Female_63years)

Having concubines was an accepted practice according to customs and tradition. It was viewed as protecting the lineage of family member who is deceased and avoiding the wife from venturing into promiscuous lifestyle and breeding "illegitimate" children. He averred that:

Some of these things were not practiced because of promiscuous life but because you want that lady not to misbehave and bring an illegitimate child to the family. We saw it as very ridiculous for a woman who is brought into the family to be taken by another person because of nobody to take care of her. No matter how ugly that person is she will find somebody to keep her busy within the kindred. (AbaNorth_Male_78years)

He further narrated who the concubines were:

The concubines are women whose husbands are dead, may be childhood friend of the man that married another person when the husband dies the man will still bring her back to be visiting. (AbaNorth_Male_78years)

He further narrated that no bride price is paid on behalf of the concubines, which is the reason the children born out of that union bears the first husband's name.

No, bride price is paid that is why the children will bear the name of the first husband. (AbaNorth_Male_78years)

On the contrary it was revealed in a particular situation, the children born by the concubines bore the later husband's name instead of the former, even though no bride price was paid. One of the female respondents reported that:

My father had many concubines, he did not marry any but two of the concubines had children for him... one of them had married earlier and the husband died early. She then befriended my father and had 3 children for him. She had 5 girls for the former husband. The children born by the concubines are still answering my father's name till tomorrow. (AbaSouth_Female_61years)

The concubines were reported to play a vital role on the family, they were perceived to act as a liaison between the husband and the legal wife to receive financial and material favor. It was narrated that:

The differences then were that our fathers behaved like David and women enjoyed it. They had concubines, when the concubines visit your husband that is when you will eat the most delicious meal ever. That fish that your husband won't buy, sometimes women then if they require anything if they have a newborn or if they have anything they want to buy they will go and call their concubines to ask and their husband he will give them. (AbaNorth_Male_78years)

On the contrary, apart from the positive roles described by the narrators, it was found that some of the concubines sowed a seed of discord, became selfish and diabolic. This was illustrated in the quote below:

Some of them came naturally to destroy fighting for their own selfish gain and dipped their hand in one evil thing or the other but God did not allow that, they will come in and demand for their own right. In fact at a point they didnot want my own siblings to exist, they wanted to bring them down. At a point the boys were too sick. My mother entered church to save her children. The last wife and the concubines were into diabolic things especially the concubine that had many children for him. (AbaSouth_Female_61years)

Another form of conjugal relationship was identified; a situation where an impotent man would allow his wife to have sexual interactions with another man and any issue born out of the intimacy would be considered children of the impotent man and to the family and posed no social or legal risks. An archival data averred thus:

A eunuch or impotent man would allow his wife to have connections with another man and any issue would be deemed children of the eunuch. (District office 1922. CSE 36/1/1)

The lexicon, concepts like "illegitimate," "bastards," "base-born," and others do not exist in the Igbo society. It is believed that no family should lack human beings, children were important in any marriage union. It was avowed that:

There are no such words as "illegitimate" "bastards" "base-born" and such like terms in the traditional Igbo vocabulary. (Ifemesia 1979, NHB/C/93)

Civil War-Time (1967–1970) Family Structure and Conjugal Relationship

Family Structure – Step-Parent and Single-Parent Family System. Prior to the civil war, polygyny was widely practiced. However a new dynamism in the family emerged featuring single-parent and step-parent families as a result of loss and displacement of spouses during the civil war. Stepfamily system was introduced into the Igbo family, a situation where a married man or woman with children ran in a different direction and started a new family with another married man or woman with children. One of the male participants has this to say:

Families that ran away during the war without their partners may go a new location and a form family, introducing step family into the Igbo family structure. (AbaSouth_male_71 years)

One of the female narrated how the war broke marriages and resulted in single-parent family:

Yes, during the war, the husband may run to a different direction and the wife to a different direction leading to broken marriages. One or both spouses died during the war, leaving one spouse to care for the children. (AbaNorth_Female_63years)

There was disorganization of marriages as some women both married and single started transactional sex, trading sex in exchange of relief of materials or protection. This was summarized in the quote below:

The war disrupted the family, many marriages were disorganized introducing stepfamily. Many married women started going to the soldiers to get relief materials for survival leading to unfaithfulness in marriages, and the young ladies conscripted by the soldiers started using their bodies for money afterwards. It affected all aspect of life; it was a total disaster. (AbaNorth_ Male_78years)

Conjugal Relationships Civil War-Time (1967–1970)

Cohabiting. During the civil war, cohabiting was introduced into the Igbo family structure due to displacement of spouses. One of the participants narrated how some members of the families especially spouses went in different directions and started living together with another as though married. This was illustrated in the quotes below:

> In my place we had refugees, some of them could not account for any good family set up, is either the man comes and sees a fellow refugee before you know it, they will be living together... the war broke down the family system. A situation where a married man ran away and didn't have the privilege of going with his wife; maybe the wife ran away to another direction, children ran away to another direction. That time there was no phone, no communication, you can't say am here o. Where the man ran to and saw another woman that also ran way before you know it the man and woman have started living together. It was just battle for survival. Whatever people did that time there was no control it was confusion. (Osisioma_Male_57years)

Surge of "Illegitimate" Children and Loss of True Identity
Prior to the civil war, vocabulary like "illegitimate," "bastards," "base-born," and others did not exist. The civil war brought "illegitimate" children into the family structure because some girls had children with Nigerian soldiers who abandoned them after the war. One of the female participants narrated that:

> Nigerian soldiers impregnated so many of the young girls and were abandoned afterwards. Some children grew up without knowing their father. (Osisioma_Male_65years)

Another female participant reported that parents lost their children which became members of another family. Some of these children lost their identity and the opportunity of growing up with members of their family. She averred that:

> Some parents threw away their children and ran for their lives, as some parents threw away their children and ran away, some people that needed children carried them and they became their children even after the war. Also, as we were running we saw some children on the road crying, some children died in the process. (AbaNorth_Female_63years)

Post-Civil War (1971–1980) Family Structure and Conjugal Relationship

Family Structure – Predominately Monogamy. Before the civil war, polygyny was widely practiced, however a new dynamism in the family emerged featuring single-parent and step-parent families as a result of loss and displacement of spouses during the civil war. Post-war due to the impact of the civil war on the family, most men resulted in marrying one wife. The war caused a break down in the family structure particularly the structure of the family. After the war, men had no need of marrying multiple wives; monogamy became widely practiced in the contemporary Igbo society. This was because of hunger, starvation and the quest for survival. The most prevalent family type in the Igbo family post-civil war is monogamy. One of the female participants narrated that:

We were at average level, as that time he was able to build a house that stood the test of time as at that time. We were actually very rich but polygamy ruined my father, if it was one man one wife we would have been at a higher level. He had to attend to everybody. After the war, my father regretted marrying so many wives because of the starvation at that time. (AbaSouth_Female_61years)

Also, after the war it was observed that farmlands were destroyed, thus there was a need to change occupation. Change in occupation was identified as reason for current prevalence of monogamy since farming was the major reason of polygamy. The quotes below collaborates that:

The second reason is change in occupation; people married many wives due to farming purposes, because the many wives you have, the more likely it is to give birth to many children but now people have gotten education and were working. Due to change in occupation people no longer need many wives. (AbaSouth_Male_71 years)

After the civil war, some men did not see any reason for polygyny once the wife gave the man a male child. Therefore, marrying multiple wives was not considered necessary as shown in the quote below:

What am I looking for in many wives? She gave me male children all I had to do is to work hard and train them. (Obingwa_Male_70 years)

Igbo men practiced monogamy to enjoy benefits that come with children at old age.

If that I married two wives when the time reaches for my children to feed me, they will not feed me, they will feel that if they give me money, I will give it to another person. (Osisioma_Male_65years)

Conjugal Relationships Post-Civil War (1971–1980)

Sugar Daddies and Sugar Mummies. During the civil war, cohabiting was introduced into the Igbo family structure due to displacement of spouses. Post-civil war, the concept of sugar mummies and sugar daddies emerged.

The participants narrated that sugar mummies and sugar daddies were economically motivated financial extramarital affairs. In the concept of sugar daddy, a wealthy man engages in a sexual relationship with a younger lady in exchange or financial gains. For the sugar mummy, a wealthy lady engages a younger man for sexual gratification in exchange for financial gain or connections. A male participant narrated that:

After the war, men that had money engaged in sexual relationship with young girls who they gave money in exchange for sex. Men will always look for a way to have sex outside their home, they are polygamous in nature. The called it sugar daddy or so. (AbaSouth_Male_71 years)

Another male participant narrated that:

Some women went after the rich men for help. In exchange they will keep them as mistresses and be providing for them secretly without their wives knowing. (Osisioma_Male_65years)

Another participant corroborated that:

I think is a change of name, then they called it concubines before the war, after the war is called sugar daddy. Sometimes it is to show financial power. I heard some wealthy women

looked for younger boys for the same purpose, that one is sugar mummy (laughs). (AbaNorth_
Male_78years)

Contemporary times (2000 – Till Date) Family
Structure and Conjugal Relationship

Monogamy, Single and Step-Parent Family. Prior to the civil war, polygyny was widely practiced, however a new dynamism in the family emerged featuring single-parent and step-parent families as a result of loss and displacement of spouses during the civil war. Post-war due to the impact of the civil war on the family, most men resulted in marrying one wife. Monogamy, single and step-parent families continued as a trend contemporaneously. One of the respondents professed that:

> Monogamy is the new trend in the family… single parenthood is now fashionable. Many young
> ladies are even proud to be a single mother. (AbaSouth_Male_44years)

In corroboration, another participant reported that:

> My dear, the way stepfamily and single parenthood is rising is alarming. One of my female
> neighours looked for a man that impregnated her and she relocated to a new city without even
> telling the man she was pregnant. She just wanted to have a child. Baby mama syndrome is
> trending now. (Osisioma_Female_40years)

Monogamy. Monogamy is predominately prevalent in recent times and polygamy is currently a rare practice in the Abia society with so many reasons. Some of the reasons include Christianity, livelihood dynamics, education, civilization, lived negative experience, disparities in the treatment of wives, conflict in the family and reduced life span prospects. Monogamy is perceived to give longevity, unity and contentment.

The practice of Christianity is considered by respondents as one of the reasons for monogamy in recent times. This was demonstrated in the quotes as shown below:

> Monogamy is more now because of our faith in Christianity that preaches. One man one wife,
> one trouble is a enough for a man and that trouble is a woman and if you want to die early
> marry two. I support that biblical injunction. (AbaNorth_Male_78years)

Another respondent narrated that:

> Christians don't marry two wives; also, if you want your family to be very organized doesn't
> marry two wives. Now, the Igbos don't marry two wives anymore because of Christianity.
> (Osisioma_Male_65years)

Livelihood dynamics was also identified as reason for current prevalence of monogamy. Farming was the major reason of polygamy and since there was a shift from large scale agricultural practices, marrying multiple wives is rarely practiced. The quotes below collaborates that

> Change in occupation; people married many wives due to farming purposes, because the
> many wives you have, the more likely it is to give birth to many children but now people have

gotten education and working, due to change in occupation people no longer need many wives. (AbaSouth_Male_71 years)

Education was also mentioned as a factor for the current practice of monogamy in contemporaneously. The increase in knowledge production was claimed to be one of the reasons of monogamy as shown in quotes below:

> With the level of education people have and want for their children people do not want to have many children they cannot cater for, they don't want children that would be hawkers of wood and fetchers of water so people now want small size family that can be educated. (AbaSouth_ Male_71 years)

Lived negative experience on polygamy fostered monogamy; many respondents gave reasons why monogamy is widely practiced in contemporary Abia society because of negative lived experiences. Some of the respondents shared negative lived experience associated with polygamy which includes ill treatment, neglect by the head of the household and suffering experienced by children. Some of the respondents narrated some of their negative lived experience in polygamous homes as shown in the quotes below:

> I did not like the fact that my father married two wives because they maltreated my mother badly. Since my father married the second wife we started suffering. I don't like polygamous family. (AbaSouth_Female_40years)

Another respondent affirmed thus:

> Ahhh! I will not pray for my children to marry a man that has another wife. It is not easy. That time my father neglected us and faced his new wife. My mother started taking care of us and forgot everything about my father. (Osisioma_Female_40years)

Polygamy was also associated with disparities in treatment of the wives by the man, and this brought about envy, jealousy, quarrel, strife, and fight. The respondents narrated stories that buttressed this, as shown in the quotes below:

> A family with two wives would normally have a problem a serious one ... The problem is that when you marry two wives, whatever the man does is a problem. My mother the first wife had luck and gave birth to children quicker than the second wife. The other wife became angry and jealous. In fact there were a lot of unnecessary competitions then. Moreover, such a man does not last for a long time because his life is in danger. (AbaSouth_Male_44years)

This assertion was corroborated by one of the female respondents:

> There was a lot of problem in a polygamous family I grew up in; each wife wanted their children to be best, to be on top than others. There was backbiting, quarrelling at times. You will see strife, quarrels, fighting, jealousy; you will see children quarrelling over nothing. The wives want to overshadow the other person, so the wives had to show their strength. (AbaNorth_ Female_63years)

Having multiple wives was associated with reduced life span of the man. It was noted that having a polygamous family was more of a death sentence, this was illustrated by the quotes by the respondents as seen below:

> Polygamy is not an easy journey ooo... Polygamous home is a real problem; the man has already dug his grave for somewhere. If it is a man that is supposed to last for 100 years, his years will be divided into two; my father died at a very young age. (AbaSouth_Male_44years)

Another participant reported that:

My stepmother was the one that sent my father to early grave. My father did an operation, she did not allow my father to heal and persuaded him to have sex with her so that she can bear him a child, after the sex the operation side busted and he later died. We tried everything to keep my father alive, sold lands and other properties yet he died. (Osisioma_Female_40years)

Monogamy was seen to give longevity, unity and contentment, marrying multiple wives was regarded as bringing damage to the family and burning house to ashes. Marrying one wife was associated with longevity and answered prayers from God. It was also associated with family unity, love and contentment; this was illustrated in the quote below:

If you watch the Igbo land now people don't marry two wives because they will bring damage, Igbo people are more educated and wiser now... If you marry two wives you will want to burn your house to ashes (laughs). (Osisioma_Male_65years)

Single and Step-Parent Family

Single and step-parent families emerged during the civil war, post-civil war and continued as a trend in contemporary times. One of the participant narrated that the occurrence of single parent families was as a result of loss of spouse and marital crisis. He averred that:

Now we have single parents, some as a result of loss of the man or woman. Some may be due to problems in the marriage; they may be separated or divorced. Now you will now see one parent raising the children alone. (AbaSouth_Male_44years)

Another added that:

Being a single mother is now trending. Some of these celebrities will intentionally look for a man to impregnate them without marriage. You will hear them say "baby mama." (AbaSouth_Female_60years)

Another female shared her view that:

Some of these single mothers with children will marry another single father with children. Marriage and family is becoming complex. (Osisioma_Female_40years)

Conjugal Relationships Contemporary Times (2000–Till Date).

Side Chicks (Mistresses). Preceding the war, apart from marrying multiple wives, men had other women know as concubines. During the civil war, cohabiting was introduced into the Igbo family structure due to displacement of spouses. Postwar, the concept of "sugar daddies and sugar mummies" emerged, now it has evolved to be called as "side chicks" in contemporary times.

The respondents further explained that monogamy were prevalent because of the concept called "side-chicks" also known as mistresses. It was noted that sidechicks was a function of social life and demand and supply. It was also a function of sexual satisfaction for the man in exchange for financial and material gain for the lady. One of the female participants explained the concept of side chicks in relation to monogamy. She averred that:

Yes is true men now marry only one wife because of side chicks, some women use their body for money and they men that have money will use them and give them money so is true. It is affecting the family except those that are living deeply rooted in Christianity. (AbaNorth_ Female_63years)

Another participant shared his view that side-chicks were a social trend:

Side chick is not a function of marrying more or less wives. Side chick is as a result of social trend, when you see others doing it you may want to follow. It is the celebrities who want to be slay-queen and need extra income now go and hunt for men that will satisfy their needs. (AbaSouth_Male_71 years)

He further elaborated that side-chicks was a function of demand and supply:

Side chick is a function of demand and supply, if the demand is there it will stimulate the supply and if the supply is there it will stimulate the demand, it takes two to tangle. But is mostly the change in social life. (AbaSouth_Male_71 years)

One of the respondents narrated the negative consequences associated with side-chicks which include contracting sexually transmitted infections, amongst others. This is what he has to say:

Side-chicks are the work of the devil... I have a brother who flirted and got gonorrhea. He bought medicine and told his wife this drug cures malaria, it gives blood and told the wife they would be taking it twice a day religiously, they did until they were whole, he later confessed to the wife what the drug was for, you see the danger in side chicks. (AbaNorth_Male_78years)

DISCUSSION

The current findings reveal dynamism and changes in the Abia family structure and conjugal relationships. Intergenerational variations in family dynamism and conjugality were compared from traditional times to contemporary times, featuring the possible contribution of the Nigerian Civil War to these observed changes.

The Archival evidence and life history interviews revealed that polygyny was the most prevalent family structure in Abia society. This finding was in line with reports by Achebe (1958) and Ekeopara (2012). Polygyny was perceived as part of the social life of the Igbos, which was common and widely practiced. There were gender variations in how polygyny was perceived. The head of the house, which is the man, perceived marrying multiple wives as a great achievement, and it was well enjoyed by him. Furthermore, native marriage, which was valid and recognized by the government, encouraged polygyny, with no limit on the number of wives a man could have. This corroborated findings by Mere (1976) that established that polygyny was seen as a status symbol. Polygyny was not only enjoyed by men but also by their wives. In terms of women, because of the way new wives were treated in a polygamous family, it was embraced and encouraged. A new bride was not allowed to work, go to the market, or farm for a year if there was already an old wife. This was similar to findings that revealed that junior wives enjoyed the security and prosperity that large households provided as a result of polygamy (Achebe, 1958).

From both sexes, vehement opposition to monogamy was experienced from both political and social standpoints. Gender differences existed in how monogamy was viewed. Igbo women never wanted to be associated with a marriage connection where monogamy was the rule. Monogamy was regarded as a source of scorn, persecution, bitterness, and disgrace by women. Igbo men viewed monogamy as a practice contrary to nature and a deliberate attempt to frustrate the creation of women. This was similar to a report by (Achebe, 1958). On the contrary, some people believe that in monogamous relationships, the wife has more influence in the family. She can, for instance, make her husband more dependent on her than a polygamous wife who can be abandoned for another wife (Mere, 1976).

The Nigerian civil war led to changes and dynamism in the traditional Abia family system. During the civil war, families were dispersed; some husbands fled without their wives, while others could not. In this new location, they created new families thus step-parent families emerged. Soldiers impregnated some of the young girls and abandoned them, and some young girls lost their husbands to the war, thereby creating single-parent families. This was in accordance with the finding by Smith (2005) and Akresh et al. (2017) that reported that many daughters had children with no fathers, introducing single parenting into the family structure. Immediately post-war, there was a return of the "army wives" to the community, which created tension in the community, as some came back with children without fathers, leading to single parenting (Chimee & Vitalis, 2016).

The war brought enormous misery and poverty to the Igbo family system because of the destruction of numerous farmlands and structures. Many families were overwhelmed by their struggle for life, and others relocated to other towns and states to survive the immediate post-civil war period. Dynamism in economic subsistence was observed. There was a progressive shift away from agricultural methods and toward other menial and white-collar jobs. In Abia state, monogamy became commonly practiced, which was a significant change in the Igbo society's predominately polygamous nature.

Contemporaneously, single-parent and step-parent families are increasing, with the concept of "baby mamas" (a version of paramour practices) becoming trendy and fashionable. Due to the avert of Christianity, marrying one wife became the most predominant family structure as the bible stresses no man to one woman. This was in line with research that indicated a transition in the Igbo family type, with monogamy being the present practice due to the shift from subsistence agriculture to an industrial economy as well as religiosity – Christianity (Mere, 1976; Smith, 2007).

The conjugal relationship or the paramour culture prior to the Nigerian civil war was having concubines. These concubines were slaves, women whose husbands had died, or former friends of the man who had married someone else and whose husband was late. A man could have multiple wives as well as various concubines who were known to the wives. The concubines were in a sexual relationship with the man, and no bride prize was conferred. The concubines played a major role in the family. When they visited, the man would direct the wife/wives to prepare a dinner that was rarely prepared in honor of the concubines, and sometimes a woman would negotiate with the concubine to help her get a particular request that had gone unfulfilled by their husbands. However, some of the concubines, particularly those who produced male children for the man, played a negative role; they became envious and dipped their hands into diabolic activities to ensure that their children received a share of the man's fortune. This was comparable to a study that demonstrated the Igbo society supported concubines; a man was allowed to bring his mistress into his home and sleep with her with the knowledge of his wife. In most cases, the wife is asked to go to the house of the mistress and invite her to her husband, cook for the mistress, and entertain her. His wife would retire to her hut while her husband entertained the mistress in his obi/hut (Urama, 2019).

Cohabiting was introduced into the family during the civil war because some spouses went to different locations without their partners, thereafter living together with a new partner as though married. As a result of the war, marriages were broken; there was also a decline in fertility and marriage rates. Additionally, children lost their identities throughout the war as parents lost their children while fleeing for safety. Some of these youngsters were taken in and adopted into new families. These children were stripped of their genuine identities and the opportunity to grow up with family members. Inter-ethnic marriage was introduced into the Igbo family as a result of the war. Nigerian soldiers became sexually involved with Igbo girls and women, resulting in the birth of "illegitimate children." Prior to the civil war, the lexicon of "illegitimate" children did not exist. Married women used their bodies in exchange for money and food, causing the dissolution of marriages. This was corroborated by a survey that reported that immediately after the war, some of the 'army wives' came back with children whose army fathers had abandoned them after the war, creating illegitimate children (Chimee & Vitalis, 2016).

In the post-Civil War era, the concept of "sugar mummies and sugar daddies" emerged. The participants narrated that sugar mummies and sugar daddies were economically motivated financial extramarital affairs. In the concept of "sugar daddy," a wealthy man engages in a sexual relationship with a younger lady in exchange for all sorts of financial materials. For the sugar mummy, a wealthy woman engages a younger man for sexual gratification in exchange for financial gain or connections. This was in line with a report that previously, economically motivated extramarital relationships were referred to as "sugar daddy" relationships, in which married men of resources engage in sexual relationships with much younger women in exchange for different sorts of financial support (Smith, 2007).

In contemporary times, the term "side chick" has emerged. This could also be referred to as "mistresses." Side chicks are girls who cling to married men for extramarital affairs in exchange for cash or other valuables. In corroboration, a study revealed that men still retain the desire and need for more than one woman, as stated in "Man no be wood," that it was only a piece of wood that lacked an outward-looking sexual appetite for women (Smith, 2007). Conjugal trajectories existed in sexual relationships from before the Civil War to the present. Unlike in the traditional Igbo society, where the concubines were fully known by their wives, these side chicks are kept hidden from their wives. Extramarital relationships were more easily hidden from wives, relatives, neighbors, and the local community in the context of economically motivated relocation, according to research (Smith, 2007). In a Life History interview, a man was discovered to have flirted with a side chick, had gonorrhoea, and infected the wife, and even when the wife knew, she did nothing. This was in accordance with a study that reported that men were exempted from adultery, but a man who catches his wife with another man in bed is permitted by culture to kill his wife's lover if he can. It is seen as a way of regaining that man's dignity from the shame brought to him by his wife (Urama, 2019). This buttresses the fact that flirting is acceptable when it is committed by a man but regarded as an abomination when it is committed by a woman. This shows gender discrimination as regards the marital relationships.

This conjugal relationship of side chicks was considered the work of the devil and a social trend. The men perceived it as a lack of contentment, ambition to be like others, a desire to be a celebrity, and a slay queen motivated this act. For the ladies, the main objective of side chicks' actions was found to be financial and material exchange for sexual gratification, and most of the time, the ladies look for these men who will meet their needs. This was similar to a study that found that extramarital relationships were frequently used by men to display their economic and manly status (Smith, 2007). The side chick was also thought to be a function of demand and supply, with the theory that if there is enough demand, it will stimulate supply, and if there is enough supply, it will stimulate demand, and it takes two to tangle. Most importantly, side-chicks were seen as a shift in social behavior. Most of the time, these shifts in the conjugal relationship negatively influence the marital relationship and family bonds.

CONCLUSION

The dynamism and changes in the Abia family structure were observed, and we can infer that the Nigerian Civil War was attributed to some of these changes in the family structure during wartime and immediate post-war. The observed dynamics in family structure were a shift from the predominant family structure, which was polygyny pre-civil war, to the emergence of step-parent and single-parent families in war-time, to predominant monogamy and an upsurge of single and step-parent families contemporaneously. Prior to the Civil War, marriage and fertility rates were increasing. However, due to the loss and displacement of spouses, both marriage and fertility rates fell sharply during the war. The conjugal relationship moved from having concubines' pre-civil war to cohabiting during the civil war to the emergence of "sugar mummies" and "sugar daddies" post-civil war to having side chicks contemporaneously. Understanding this dynamism and changes in the family structure and conjugal relationship would help further research in family and conjugal trajectory studies. It would also help interventions to minimize conjugal trajectories and strengthen the family system.

The study had its own limitations. First, the sample size was small and may not be generalizable to the general population. Secondly, the study may be prone to recall bias since they were asked questions as regards family structure and conjugal relationships pre and post-civil, war-time. To minimize this bias, archival sources were used, and the participants were informed ahead of time and a date was booked for the interview. Despite these limitations, this chapter makes several contributions to literature. It contributed to the literature on intergenerational variations in family dynamism and conjugality featuring the influences of the civil war. Considering the observed changes in the Abia family structure in the last 50 years, from predominantly polygyny to an increasing number of single and step-parent families, we predict further disarray in Abia's family structure and conjugal bond if prompt measures are not put in place to strengthen the family system. There is an urgent need for social intervention to curtail the futuristic negative impact of these changes on children.

REFERENCES

Achebe, C. (1958). *Things fall apart*. London: Heinemann.
Agwaraonye, C. (2015). *Influence of globalization on Igbo culture of South Eastern Nigeria*. Department of Religion and Cultural studies, University of Nigeria, Nsukka Enugu State. www.unn.edu. ng/17906.
Akresh, R., Bhalotra, S., Leone, M., & Osili, U. O. (2011). War and stature: Growing up during the Nigerian civil war. *American Economic Review, 102*(3), 273–277. doi:10.1257/aer.102.3.27340
Akresh, R., Bhalotra, S., Leone, M., & Osili, U. O. (2017). *First and Second Generation Impacts of the Biafran War*. http://www.nber.org/papers/w23721.pdf
Alabi, O. J. (2021). *Women's sexual agency and use of traditional in Ilorin, North Central Nigeria* Unpublished Ph.d. thesis, Johannesburg: University of Johannesburg.
Alabi, O. J., & Olonade, O. Y. (2022). Complexities, dynamism, and changes in the Nigerian contemporary family structure. In O. A. Fawole & S. L. Blair (Eds.), *Families in Nigeria: Understanding their diversity, adaptability, and strengths* (Vol. 18, pp. 99-112). Bingley: Emerald Publishing Limited.
Basden, G. T. (1921). *Among the Ibos of Nigeria: An account of the curious & interesting habits, customs, & beliefs of a little known African people by one who has for many years lived amongst them on close & intimate terms*. Philadelphia: JB Lippincott Company.
Cao, T. (2012). The impacts of modernity on family structure and function: A study among Beijing, Hong Kong and Yunnan families.
Chimee, I. N., & Vitalis, N. (2016). Sexuality and sex-related rituals among the Mgbowo women of Awgu local government area, Enugu State. *Nsukka Journal of the Humanities, 24*(2), 130–137.
Crapo, J. S. (2020). Family development and the marital relationship as a developmental process all graduate theses and dissertations. 7792. https://digitalcommons.usu.edu/etd/7792
Defo, B. K., & Dimbuene, Z. S. (2012). Influences of family structure dynamics on sexual debut in Africa: implications for research, practice and policies in reproductive health and social development. *African Journal of Reproductive Health, 16*(2), 147–172.
District office 1922, Southern Province, Tribal Customs and Crimes, with its former punishments Part 1, Chapter XIII 29/9/65 National Archives Enugu CSE 36/1/10.
District office 1922, Travel, Tribes with their languages and intercourse Part 1 Chapter VII Pg 1227 26/8/65 National Archives Enugu CSE 36/1/6.
Duvall, E. M. (1957). *Family development*. Philadelphia, PA: Lippincott.
Duvall, E. M. (1988). Family development's first forty years. *Family Relations, 37*, 127–134.
Ekeopara, C. A. (2012). The impact of the extended family system on socio-ethical order in Igboland. *American Journal of Social Issues & Humanities, 2*(4), 262–267.
Harneit-Sievers, A., Ahazuem, J. O., & Emezue, S. (1997). *A social history of the Nigerian Civil War: perspectives from below* (Vol. 17). Lit Verlag.
Hoiberg, D. H. (Ed.). (2010). *The new encyclopaedia Britannica*. Encyclopædia Britannica.
Ifemesia, C. (1979). *Traditional humane living among the Igbo: An historical perspective*. Enugu, Nigeria: Fourth Dimension. National Archives Enugu NHB/C/93.

Isidienu, I. C. (2015). The family as the bedrock of Igbo traditional society. *Journal of Modern European Languages and Literatures, 4,* 119–128.

Jackson, J. (2015). The institution of the family, marriage, kinship and decent. In A.-E. Edit (Ed.), *Selected topics in Nigeria people and culture.* Benin City: Dimaf Publishers.

Jensen, J. F., & Rauer, A. J. (2014). Turning inward versus outward: Relationship work in young adults and romantic functioning. *Personal Relationships, 21,* 451–467. doi:10.1111/pere.12042

Jensen, J. F., & Rauer, A. J. (2015). Marriage work in older couples: Disclosure of marital problems to spouses and friends over time. *Journal of Family Psychology, 29,* 732–743. doi:10.1037/fam0000099

Labeodan, M. O. (2005). *The family lifestyle in Nigeria, 1,* 1–25.

Mbonu, O. (1948). A review of surplus women, West African pilot September 11, 1948. Coiled from a pamphlet on prostitution titled "The surplus women" authored by Increase H. E. Coke, a West African Pilot Journalist and Editor.

Mere, A. A. (1976). Contemporary changes in Igbo family system. *International Journal of Sociology of the Family, 6,* 155–161.

Naila, K. (2012). Women's economic empowerment and inclusive growth: Labour markets and enterprise development. *International Development Research Centre, 44*(10), 1–70.

Ndem, S., & Müürsepp, P. I. (2018). *Influence of globalization on African cultures from the perspective of Igbo: What are the implications.* Thesis, School of Business and Governance Tallinn University of Technology (pp. 1–36).

Nwanoro, E. C. (2013). *Family violence in classical and Igbo literature.* Unpublished Ph.d. thesis, University of Ibadan.

Obi, M. N. (2016). *Nigerian literary artists and protection of African values in the present age of Urbanization: the Igbo example.* Awka: Department of Igbo, African and Asia Studies, Nnamdi Azikiwe University.

Ohiagu, O. P. (2010). Influence of information & communication technologies on the Nigerian society and culture. In N. Ekeanyanwu & C. Okeke (Eds.), *Indigenous societies and cultural globalization in the 21st century.* Riga: VDM Verlag Dr. Muller Aktiengesellschaft & Co.

Owhorodu, V. C. (2020). Fifty years after the Nigerian Civil war: Lessons from Chimamanda Adichie's half of a yellow sun. *Imbizo, 11*(2), 12.

Smith, D. J. (2005). Legacies of Biafra: Marriage, 'home people' and reproduction among the Igbo of Nigeria. *Africa, 75*(1), 30–45.

Smith, D. J. (2007). Modern marriage, men's extramarital sex, and HIV risk in South-eastern Nigeria. *American Journal of Public Health, 97*(6), 997–1005.

Starbuck, G. H. (2010). *Families in context* (2nd, rev. and updated ed.). Boulder, CO: Paradigm.

Talbot, P. A. (1926). *The peoples of Southern Nigeria: A sketch of their history, ethnology and languages, with an abstract of the 1921 census* (Vol. 3). National Archives Enugu NHB/C/4. London: H. Milford, Oxford University Press.

Thomas, N. W. (1913). *Anthropological report on the Ibo-speaking peoples of Nigeria: Law and custom of the Ibo of the Asaba district, S. Nigeria.* National Archives Ibadan A1/T74. London: Harrison and Sons.

Uchendu, E. (2007). Recollections of childhood experiences during the Nigerian Civil war. *Africa, 77*(3), 393–418.

Ufearoh, A. (2010). Ezi-na-Ulo and Umunna: In search of democratic ideals in traditional Igbo family. *OGIRISI: A New Journal of African Studies, 7*(1), 94–105.

Ugwu, C. I. (2010). Folklore in Igbo society: A panacea to the threat of home video. *African Journal of Local Societies Initiative, 5,* 45–51.

Ukiwo, U. (2009). Violence, identity mobilization and the reimagining of Biafra. *Africa Development, 34*(1), 9–30.

Urama, E. N. (2019). The values and usefulness of same-sex marriages among the females in Igbo culture in the continuity of lineage or posterity, *SAGE Open, 9.* doi:10.1177/2158244019850037

William, L., & McGivern, R. (2012). Chapter 14: Marriage and family. In *Introduction to sociology* (1st Canadian ed.). https://opentextbc.ca/introductiontosociology/chapter/chapter14-marriage-and-family

White, J. M. (1991). *Dynamics of family development: A theoretical perspective.* New York, NY: Guilford.

INDEX